THE
AUGUSTANA STORY

THE
AUGUSTANA STORY

Shaping Lutheran Identity in North America

MARIA ERLING *and* MARK GRANQUIST

Augsburg Fortress
Minneapolis

THE AUGUSTANA STORY
Shaping Lutheran Identity in North America

Cover photo: Augustana Synod, Minneapolis, Minnesota, June 1910. Photo provided courtesy of Maria Erling.
Cover design: Charles Brock, The DesignWorks Group
Interior design: Christy J. P. Barker

Library of Congress Cataloguing-in-Publication Data
The Augustana story : shaping Lutheran identity in North America / Maria
Erling and Mark Granquist.
        p. cm.
Includes bibliographical references.
ISBN 978-0-8066-8025-5 (alk. paper)
1. Augustana Evangelical Lutheran Church—History. 2. Lutheran Church—North
America—History. I. Erling, Maria Elizabeth, 1955- II. Granquist, Mark Alan, 1957-
BX8049.A94 2008
284.1'333—dc22   2007036819

Manufactured in the U.S.A.

12   11   10   09   08   1   2   3   4   5   6   7   8   9   10

This book is dedicated to our families,
for their wonderful love and support,
and to the heritage of Augustana,
from which we have drawn our inspiration.

CONTENTS

Acknowledgments   ix

Introduction: Shaping the Augustana Story   1

PART 1: THROUGH 1885: BEGINNINGS

chapter 1   Swedish Beginnings   7

chapter 2   Making Lutheran Connections in America   21

Doctrinal Controversy: Augustana and the Mission Friends   43

chapter 3   Mission Impulses   47

PART 2: THROUGH 1910: 50TH ANNIVERSARY

chapter 4   Creating a Swedish-American Lutheran Identity   61

chapter 5   Education for a New American Generation   75

Music for the Journey   91

chapter 6   Becoming an American Church   95

chapter 7   A New Century Brings Change   113

chapter 8   An American Church in a Changing America   125

chapter 9   Growth and Expansion of the Synod   145

PART 3: THROUGH 1935: 75TH ANNIVERSARY

chapter 10   Growing the Structures of Ministry   161

chapter 11   Go to Tanganyika   179

Assimilation: "Condensed in the last hours of a long day"   196

chapter 12   Reconnecting with the Church of Sweden   199

chapter 13   Meeting the Challenges of a New Century   217

chapter 14   Changes at the College and Seminary   235

PART 4: THROUGH 1962: MERGER

chapter 15   New Voices within the Synod   255

The Far Reaches of Art   270

chapter 16   Augustana's Youthful Edge   273

chapter 17   Augustana's Ecumenical Vision   291

chapter 18   The Social Purpose of Theology   301

chapter 19   The Road to Lutheran Merger   317

chapter 20   Augustana's Legacy   337

Notes   347

Appendix   379

Suggested Reading   383

Index   387

ACKNOWLEDGMENTS

IN ORDER TO MAKE THE RESEARCH AND WRITING OF THIS BOOK POSSIBLE, the authors were given either a sabbatical or research support from their respective institutions, the Lutheran Theological Seminary at Gettysburg, Pennsylvania, and Gustavus Adolphus College, St. Peter, Minnesota. Without that institutional support the project could not have been undertaken and completed. The authors and the members of the board of directors of the Augustana Heritage Association (AHA) express their thanks to those institutions and their officers.

Although those institutions provided time and accommodations for research and writing, financial support had to be obtained by the AHA to underwrite the costs of time away for the authors, as well as for travel grants and research materials. In order to make that possible, the following persons and institutions have made major contributions: Louis and Ardis Almén, G. Kenneth and Martha Andeen, J. Roger and Beverly Anderson, Louise and Floyd† Anderson, Marbury and Sylvia Anderson, Augustana College, Peter and Lydia Beckman, Bethany College, Mosaic (successor to Bethphage Mission), Glen and Elaine Brolander, Myron C. Carlson, Herbert and Corinne Chilstrom, Carl E. Christoffersen, Paul and Betty Cornell, Alpha Ekstrom, Barbara J. and G. Philip† Engdahl, S. Bernhard and Marilyn Erling, Hartland H. and Judy Gifford (in memory of Donovan J. Palmquist and in honor of Reuben T. and Darlene Swanson), James W. and Helen Hanson, Nils Hasselmo, Reynold E. Holmén, Arland J. and Carole R. Hultgren, David and Kathleen Hurty, Immanuel Health Systems, Theodore C. and Marietta Johns, Joanne E. Kendall (in memory of John Kendall and in honor of Maria Erling), John and Delores Kindschuh, Luther and Carol Lindstrom Luedtke, Richard and Kathy Magnus, Midland Lutheran College, Lyndon K. Murk†, George L. and Miriam L. Olson, Elsa and George† Orescan, Hilvie Benson Ostrow, Dorothy and Donovan J.† Palmquist, Roger W. and Elise R. Peterson,

Gladys Ekeberg Reed, Donn and Pauline Samuelson, Ruth E. Segerhammar†, Byron and Kathryn Swanson, J. Gordon and Anne Swanson, John O. (Jack) and Joanna Swanson, Reuben T. and Darlene Swanson, Dorothy Turner, Daniel C. and Linda Tsui, and L. Edwin and Astrid Wang.

Other persons who have contributed toward the production of the book include: Aina Abrahamson, Delbert and Betty Anderson, Herbert and Phyllis Anderson, Ernest A. and Martha M. Bergeson, Charles V. and Lois Bergstrom, Loran K. Bohman, Roger and Aina Boraas, Dale S. and Barbara V. Burke, Daniel and Faith Carlson, Robert A. and LaDonna M. Chalstrom, Donald and Janice Conrad, Kenneth and Eloise Dale, Albert and Lynne DeSimone, Elizabeth C. Elliott, Anita and Fredrick† Erson, Kenneth and Carolynn Granquist, Charles and Esther Gustafson, Raymond Hedberg, Charles Hendrickson, Richard L. Hillstrom, Louise A. Hoglund, John W. Johnson, Jr., Ben and Trudy Johnson, John D. Lind, Luther and Adele Lindberg, Marian and Wendell† Lund, Carl L. and Miriam H. Manfred, Norman A. and Joan† Nelson, Willard and Janice Nelson, Orville and June Nyblade, Ernest and Lois Ryden, Bertil and Lozetta Sandin, Donald and Trudy Sjoberg, Harold and Lois Skillrud, Doris L. Spong, Kenneth C. and Priscilla E. Stenman, Glenn C. and Meredith A. Stone, Irene M. Werner†, and Paul and Nancy Youngdahl.

Special thanks are extended by the authors for archival assistance by Joel Thoreson and Elisabeth Wittman at the archives of the Evangelical Lutheran Church in America and to staff members at the following institutions: the Swenson Immigration Research Center at Augustana College; the Swedish Emigrant Institute at Växjö, Sweden; and the archives of Augustana College, Bethany College, Gustavus Adolphus College, the Lutheran School of Theology at Chicago, and the University of Minnesota. Additional expressions of gratitude are extended to Karin Bohleke, Roberta Brent, Betsy Brodahl, Herbert Chilstrom, Ruth Ann Deppe, S. Bernhard Erling, Hartland Gifford, Susan Heng, Norman Hjelm, Arland J. Hultgren, Chester Johnson, David Lindberg, David Mattson, Karl Mattson, E. Earl Okerlund, A. John Pearson, Suzanne Posey, Donald Sjoberg, Byron Swanson, and Reuben T. Swanson.

The authors and the members of the board of directors of the Augustana Heritage Association express their thanks to all of these persons and institutions. Their generosity, support, and enthusiasm are deeply appreciated.

PAUL CORNELL,
President, Augustana Heritage Association
MARIA ERLING
MARK GRANQUIST

INTRODUCTION:
SHAPING THE AUGUSTANA STORY

THE OFFICIAL BEGINNING OF THE AUGUSTANA SYNOD—later the Augustana Evangelical Lutheran Church—occurred in 1860 when nineteen Swedish and Norwegian pastors gathered together with twenty laymen in the Norwegian church in Jefferson Prairie, Wisconsin, to formally constitute themselves as a church body. They named their church the Scandinavian Evangelical Augustana Lutheran Synod. The congregations represented at the June meeting had been working together for almost ten years as a Scandinavian subgroup in the Lutheran Synod of Northern Illinois, a synod in federation with the Lutheran General Synod. Because of theological disagreement and in order to advance the interests of Scandinavian Lutherans in America, they became a separate church body.

The nineteenth century in Scandinavia was a time of significant and broad-ranging religious change, and the Lutheran immigrants from that region brought with them to the city neighborhoods and pioneer settlements on the prairie the religious arguments and excitements of their homeland. In America they discovered new differences and possibilities, and the larger story of Lutheranism in America is a story of negotiation among many local and strongly held traditions from many other lands besides Sweden and Norway. Each of these many immigrant legacies were transformed also in America, defined by the circumstances of pioneer pastors and pious lay people who used the familiar language of home, with its particular feeling for long-cherished hymns and devotional practices, to understand the meaning of their migration from Europe to America. When they arrived in America, furthermore, they met immigrant Lutherans and other American Lutherans who had developed long traditions from colonial times. All of these groups claimed to be faithful Lutheran churches, though it became immediately clear that differences over liturgy, mission, devotional piety, the Lutheran Confessions, the role of the pastor, the role of laity, the integrity of the congregation, and the importance of the wider church in fact separated them.

At its founding in 1860, the small Augustana Synod had to explain why its theological professor, Lars Paul Esbjörn, had broken his contract with the seminary of the Northern Illinois Synod of the Lutheran General Synod. A doctrinal and personal conflict had emerged in the faculty, and Esbjörn felt he could not continue to satisfy the Scandinavian congregations if he stayed in the company of the American Lutherans. Lutheran history in the United States includes episode after episode of theological wrangling and confessional dispute. Often it is hard even for theological students to comprehend why Lutherans have fought so stridently. This history tells readers one aspect of the American Lutheran story by exploring how ethnic, linguistic, social, religious, and political aspects functioned to unite an immigrant Lutheran people, and further how the role of personality, of geography, and of memory worked to shape the community as a church. The authors of this history believe that the effort to understand the development of one church within the wider diversity of Lutheranism in America will contribute some depth to a wider appreciation of the strength of the Lutheran church in America today.

This study of Lutheranism is also a study of a denomination, fully mindful that, as institutions, denominations are at risk even among active church members. Historical understanding can assist church people in understanding themselves and can also help historians understand religious life in America. Historians of American religion have neglected denominational histories in the last fifty years, since they seemed almost self-explanatory, while they have treated formerly neglected topics with zeal. New light has been shed on the religious experience of women and young people and to the lives of religious visionaries, alternative communities, and social movements. Meanwhile denominations have lost influence in American culture while more local and independent religious groupings have drawn members and attention. The denominational schools, publishing houses, and programs no longer command the loyalty and attention of their own members. Denominations, however, still maintain an important role for many American Christians, through the institutions they have founded and the identity and stability they provide for millions of churchgoers. Contemporary disputes that threaten the unity of denominations are yet another witness to the continuing claim that they have in American life. People don't fight for something they think is unimportant.

Augustana Lutherans constitute only one small part of a much longer and diverse history of Lutherans in the United States. But the history that follows will make a claim for an Augustana distinctiveness that has made a significant contribution to the shape of American Lutheranism today. The Augustana

Evangelical Lutheran Church, as it finally was known, promoted in its members a strong sense of the broader church and used its church papers, youth programs, missionary outreach, and educational programs to instill in young people a sense of belonging to a wider fellowship of Christians around the world. Augustana's churchliness was a distinctive feature. Other Lutheran church bodies, while sharing theological, confessional, and programmatic emphases, rarely commanded the same level of spirited cooperation and trust as was evident among Augustana members. While Augustana certainly had dissenters and disaffected members and many moments of conflict, these did not result in schism or separation. Instead, Augustana leaders were able to resolve disputes, and the church moved forward.

The story of how Swedish Lutheran immigrants managed to stay together in one church body for more than one hundred years while other immigrant groups split into several factions is an interesting tale. Other Lutheran immigrant groups—German settlers in Pennsylvania, Ohio, Iowa, and Missouri; Norwegians in the upper Midwest; Danes on the plains and in Midwestern cities; Finns in the forests and steel mills; and Slovaks in the mining communities in the Northeast—all experienced serious theological conflict that resulted in rival Lutheran church bodies within their national group. The Augustana story is unique because its leaders managed to maintain personal ties of friendship and cooperation even while disagreeing and created arenas where many ambitions could be satisfied. These leaders formed institutions and instilled a common sense of purpose and commitment in Augustana's congregations that endured through several generations and successfully adapted to new challenges.

The Augustana Evangelical Lutheran Church, or Augustana Synod as it was commonly known, ended its separate institutional life in 1962 when it merged with the United Lutheran Church in America, the Suomi Synod, and Danish Lutherans (The Happy Danes) of the American Evangelical Lutheran Church, to form the Lutheran Church in America. For the next generation until the late 1980s, the Augustana Synod was a living memory in the work of pastors who had been trained at Augustana Seminary in Rock Island, Illinois. Augustana congregations maintained their strong convictions about stewardship and support for the wider church, and continued to support colleges and agencies they had founded. In the Evangelical Lutheran Church in America (ELCA), formed in 1988, memories of the Augustana Synod receded further from view, and the traditions and institutions fostered by the Augustana people depend now on more tenuous, informal, and residual memories of church members.

Augustana's legacy as an American Lutheran church also tells a story of how an ethnic religious tradition became an American Lutheran heritage.

The Augustana people were proud of their achievements in education, youth work, social programs, and missionary efforts. The church participated fully in the theological developments of twentieth-century Lutheranism and gave specific leadership in ecumenism. Augustana churches maintained a high level of commitment to what they call "the wider church," and generated enthusiastic commitment to efforts to attain unity among Lutherans for the sake of a broader witness to the world. The focus on strengthening the church for the sake of the world has much to offer for a meaningful encounter with a widening American and global pluralism that is usually premised on religious individualism. The Augustana Story is a story of how church leaders taught immigrants that they belonged not only to an ethnic group, but also to a church with a role in the world. The efforts of other immigrant church leaders also shaped their people as church people rather than simply ethnic religious participants.

In writing this modern history of one American Lutheran church, the writers recognize that contemporary Lutherans and other readers interested in Protestant denominational history will be drawn to the story of how a successful denomination came to the point of merger. Why was it enthusiastic about letting go if its own independent existence? The Lutheran identity fostered within the Augustana church was not closed in on itself, but open to a future beyond the limited scope of its own institutions. We hope that readers will grasp the enthusiasm that stirred within the Augustana people as they contemplated their united future with other American Lutherans. Their hopes for a dynamic and experimental, committed, and creative American Lutheranism are yet to be fully realized, but are entrusted to a new generation.

PART I

THROUGH 1885

BEGINNINGS

chapter 1
SWEDISH BEGINNINGS

THE AUGUSTANA STORY TAKES SHAPE IN A CONTEXT of dramatic social transformation that affected millions of people across Scandinavia and Europe. It begins in the villages and farms of a changing Swedish landscape in the middle of the nineteenth century, when industrialization broke apart settled communities and triggered mass migration, and the religious Awakening stimulated new associations in villages and railroad towns across the country. The causes of Swedish immigration—to North and South America as well as to Australia and Africa—included both classic "push" and "pull" factors. At first, a very few felt pushed to leave. Often a perceived religious persecution prompted them, or they sensed limited opportunities that could not be relieved at home. A search for adventure spurred some, like those who came to serve in the Union Army during the Civil War. After these few were settled, or returned home to tell their stories, others would follow, creating pull factors that multiplied through word of mouth. Family members, friends, and other acquaintances in the village or neighborhood relied on the advice of friends and on the money and tickets sent through the mail to pull them to America. As the cycle of push and pull emerged, large waves of people came. They now could rely on first-hand information from relatives and other countrymen and had clearer ideas about where to go and what established communities to join.

The story of Augustana and of the many other immigrant churches in American history is a story of ordinary people forced by circumstance to create churches in a new way in a new land. They had to be resourceful to be good, faithful people in their new home. They sorted through their religious experience and filtered out anything that was not useful to them in America. Influenced by progressive ideas about improving society, they left behind the magical world of trolls, forest gnomes, and farm *tomtes* and took along devotional literature, hymns, and prayer books.

Scholars who study immigrant religion often note the winnowing effect of migration on religious ideas and practice.[1] Established patterns of religious observance change in a new land. Some ideas about God and about the future are preserved, while migration contributes its own dynamics to religious thought and feeling, often intensifying it.[2] What immigrants experienced in coming to America was a huge change in their pattern of life as it had been lived out over centuries in the homeland. The simple act of migration went far beyond an economic decision. Immigrants who may not have been so religious at home found religious practice more appealing in a new settlement. Religious language and thought gave immigrants words to understand their choices and their lives and helped them make sense of a new future in America.

Patterns of Settlement and Connection in America

The first 19,000 Swedish immigrants came to western Illinois on the advice of two Swedish Methodist preachers, Olof Gustaf Hedström in New York and his brother Jonas Hedström in Illinois. Olof first came to America in 1825 as a twenty-two-year-old sailor. After losing all his money, he was forced to remain in New York where he converted to Methodism, married an American woman, and was ordained as a Methodist minister. In 1833 he returned to his homeland and convinced his brother Jonas to follow him back to America. Jonas took up farming and preaching Methodism in western Illinois. These two preachers served as guides to thousands of Swedish immigrants. In New York's harbor, Olof Hedström's Bethel Ship provided a chapel, a gathering place, and a source for practical information about America. Immigrants heading west looked for the second Hedström brother in Illinois.

About a decade after Jonas Hedström came to America, Erik Jansson, a religious prophet in Hälsingland, Sweden, ran afoul of the authorities when he and his followers claimed to be totally free from sin. Jansson was imprisoned several times, the last time in 1845. His followers (later called Janssonists) heard about religious freedom in America. One follower, a man named Olof Olsson (not to be confused with the founder of the Lindsborg, Kansas, community) traveled to New York, where he found Olof Hedström, learned about Methodism and western Illinois, and made preparations for Jansson to leave Sweden. Jansson escaped from prison and fled to Victoria in Knox County, Illinois. There he founded his perfectionist colony, Bishop Hill, in July 1846.[3]

Typical of what historians call the "push and pull" factors of migration, the first immigration wave from Sweden involved a limited number of people who felt forced to leave the country. The Janssonist migration from the province of Hälsingland followed several years of religious persecution. Erik Jansson's escape and settlement in America was widely publicized, and after several contingents of Janssonists joined him, there were more than 1,500 settlers in what soon became a tension-filled colony on the plains in Illinois. One of America's several "utopian" communities, the Bishop Hill colony had strict regulations separating the sexes and suffered under the autocratic leadership of its founder. Jansson himself was shot and killed by a follower in 1850, and the experimental community totally dissolved in 1862, but not before pulling many people from Sweden to western Illinois. These newer arrivals, less enamored of the colony's strict rules governing everyday life, tried to create a more traditional Swedish society within the broader American landscape of the rural frontier. With unfamiliar preaching from the Methodists and disillusioned exiles from the failed colony, they circled in an orbit of religious confusion, uncertainty, and social speculation.

Back home in Hälsingland, the idea of emigration began to spread beyond the early Janssonist circle. News about America also traveled into Sweden by word of mouth from neighboring Norway. At first the news traveled within specific circles of people along the pathways followed by merchants and suppliers, but more and more, news began to be shared among people who gathered to listen to traveling preachers and religious booksellers called colporteurs. Groups of "readers" or *läsare*, as the awakened Christians were called, joined the stream of people going to America. These religious pioneers also wanted to enjoy the broader possibilities of spiritual and economic freedom that America promised, but local church leaders watched them leave with some ambivalence, since their departure meant that the Swedish Awakening movement would lose important coworkers. The first groups left without pastoral leadership, however, and the ministers at home in Sweden sensed that America's religious freedom could also mean danger for a flock without a shepherd. But the established church position remained fixed: emigration was a sin because it put human motivations against the clear will of God.

These conflicting sentiments came to the fore when the Swedish Lutheran pastor Lars Paul Esbjörn let it be known that he planned to immigrate to America with a group of settlers in 1849. Writing to Jonas Hedström in Illinois, he received encouragement. Esbjörn's ministry would be welcome, especially to rescue the fanatical Janssonists. Even though Hedström was a Methodist preacher, Esbjörn wrote to him as a colleague because the famous Methodist preacher George Scott had impressed him on one of his tours of Sweden. But Esbjörn heard other words from his bishop, Conrad Fr. af Wingård, who admonished: "How can Esbjörn secure land, protect them from thievery, and provide continual pastoral care and worship? Do they now have to depend on a mortal, who leads them from their station where God's calling has placed them, and in which they ought to peacefully reside?"[4] The harsh words from the bishop were softened after some explanation. Esbjörn had not induced anyone to leave but was instead accompanying a group of emmigrants to provide care for them.

Pastor Lars Paul Esbjörn brought with him a strong missionary interest when he came to America in 1849. In 1843, he had founded a mission society in Sweden's Hille parish. The society sent contributions to Basel, Switzerland, where a mission institute trained missionaries for work in India and Africa. Hille's society was really a revival meeting under a different name; they provided an official way to encourage the private devotional meetings that were otherwise still forbidden by law.[5] Because of the service that mission societies provided for Esbjörn, it is hard for modern interpreters to gauge the actual scope of "foreign mission" interest of the time. It is apparent, however, that with ties to foreign societies, and enlivened by printed reports, songs, and traveling speakers, revivalists who called themselves "mission friends" joined an evangelical world of reform, lay activism, and international alliances. In 1846, at the London meeting that formed the Evangelical Alliance, local mission societies like the one in Hille now threatened to become conduits for what Lutheran churches on the continent and in Scandinavia called "Reformed tendencies" that would confuse, if not undermine, their clerical and theological authority.

Esbjörn's mission society efforts occurred in the context of this broader theological and ecclesiological debate. In fact, his organizing effort was an early sign of his ambition for a changed leadership in the church. When he encountered America's confusing religious diversity, however, Esbjörn adopted a more doctrinally Lutheran theological position. Still, his support of mission work remained intact. In the new congregations in America an interest in mission became the language of congregational expansion and outreach in new immigrant settlements. It was put to use also by women when they sewed, prayed, sang, cooked, and assembled items to raise money for mission. Like their counterparts in Sweden, Augustana's people sensed a personal spiritual responsibility for the spread of the gospel in the world.

Friends of mission or "mission friends" participated in mission society work not only to promote the gospel in foreign lands, but also to reform society. Mission enthusiasm focused on Lappland, China, India, and Africa, but the network of support circulated literature and founded training institutes for colporteurs (individuals who distributed pious literature) and preachers. Believers became more invested in the image of their own nation and people and debated where to send money. Should Swedish societies train and send their own missionaries, or continue to support institutes in Germany and England?[6]

These debates affect the Augustana story indirectly, for they played a role in Esbjörn's decision to emigrate. Every year his congregation's society in Hille had sent money on to the Stockholm mission society for use in mission work among the Lapplanders. In 1847, another pastor in his parish proposed that money should instead be divided, with half going to the Lappland mission and half to support the mission society in Lund, Sweden. Esbjörn seriously objected: "I and the other pious can not support sending money to Lund, where there is so much unspirituality, or so little spirituality that shows itself in the instruction at its Mission Institute."[7] But Esbjörn lost out. The influence of the other pastor had tilted the society toward the high-church-oriented Lund Mission Institute and effectively cut him off from mission work in the congregation. After this dispute Esbjörn bitterly withdrew and prepared to emigrate. We can deduce from this that mission society work was not something Esbjörn did on the side, but rather it was a cause that engaged his whole person and vocational identity. Similarly, views about mission were strongly related to the way that revival believers understood the nature and purpose of the church.

In spite of Esbjörn's bitter parting from Hille, his ties to the Swedish Mission Society continued. One of the new projects for the society was to support mission work among the Swedish immigrants in America, particularly Esbjörn's work with Swedish settlers in Illinois. As that work grew and new leaders joined Esbjörn, missionary ideals continued to shape the emerging sense of church among the immigrants.[8]

When he arrived in New York, Esbjörn realized that support from the Methodists was not available unless he himself would become a Methodist preacher. The non-dogmatic spirit that he brought with him from Sweden now met the new conditions of religious freedom and competition in America. As a result, Esbjörn became more Lutheran from the first day he arrived in the country. Still another form of competition for the religious loyalty of Swedish settlers existed in the form of a Swedish Episcopal priest, Gustaf Unonius, who came to America in 1841. Between 1841 and 1858, Unonius formed a colony in Wisconsin and then founded a Scandinavian congregation in Chicago—St. Ansgarius—that brought Norwegians and Swedes together under the banner of the formal liturgy and order of the Church of Sweden. The famed Swedish singer Jenny Lind gave the congregation a beautiful silver chalice forged by the Tiffany Company in New York.[9]

Esbjörn's arrival in the United States in 1849 took him through New York and on to Chicago. When he came to the young city he received support from other Swedes, from Norwegians, and from friendly ministers. But tragedy also struck Esbjörn in Chicago. His family and some in his party contracted cholera shortly upon arrival, resulting in the deaths of his wife and a small child. He already had buried a son at the port in Sweden. The party buried several more cholera victims on the way to western Illinois. When he arrived in Andover, Illinois, Esbjörn was sick, grief-stricken, broke, disillusioned, and responsible for those he had brought with him, in addition to many other Swedish immigrants already settled on the plains of the Midwest. Fortunately, he found that the Swedish settlers were not so disorganized and defenseless. They had already achieved some stability. But in the religious realm, Esbjörn was a true pioneer. He encountered former Janssonists, others converted to the Methodist preaching of Jonas Hedström, and some who, disillusioned, were fed up with religion all together. Other settlers had begun to take religious matters into their own hands. It was clear that he would have to reintroduce Swedish Lutheranism to the settlers.

Building on the Connections Immigrants Formed

Esbjörn's work in western Illinois had limited goals. He hoped to gather immigrants together, create proper congregations, and carry on the evangelical preaching to which he had dedicated himself in Sweden. Church life in America, however, provided additional social functions for the scattered immigrants that went far beyond strictly religious aims. Churches were the first enduring social groups that immigrants formed. In fact, the beginnings of an organized Swedish-American cultural life and the start of a Swedish ethnic consciousness began in small religious gatherings that at least partially reflected the mission-oriented revival movement in Sweden. Still, the variety of religious views and the varying intensity of religious feeling among immigrants made meetings in America contentious. Just because they wanted to gather and speak their native language did not mean that immigrants were interested in the strong dose of religion that revival proponents wanted.

By the 1850s, the Awakening movement in Sweden had become in many quarters an oppositional or separatist movement in relation to the authority of the established church. In rural villages, people traveled to hear revival preachers and read newspapers devoted to movements that sought to improve social conditions. Priests and lay preachers who advocated revival or gave temperance talks ran into opposition. In the paternalistic society of rural parishes, landowners did not want subordinates involved in the revival movement because awakened servants and workers too often spoke out against the social practices of their betters. Temperance preachers especially became suspect. In fact, those preachers who gained a reputation for stirring up piety seemed also to gain a reputation for stirring up trouble for their careers. Awakened ministers, lay preachers, song leaders, and pious wealthy women challenged the existing social order, and the targets of reform made trouble. Having a reputation of challenging bishops and others in authority did not diminish a man's clout within mission and revival circles and was in fact expected. When revival reformers gathered large audiences, bishops and other officials sought to rein in and circumscribe the pious activity. Like Esbjörn, two other early Swedish-American pastors, Erland Carlsson and Tufve Nilsson Hasselquist, decided to emigrate due to such opposition.[10]

Carlsson and Hasselquist, like the other Swedish ministers and pious people who gathered in small congregations in the early settlements in Iowa and Illinois, emerged from a revival-oriented mission movement that, especially in the first part of the nineteenth century, had been influenced by English movements—particularly Methodism—and also by Baptist ideas. Each of these evangelical movements challenged the Swedish Lutheran understanding of the individual's relationship to the church. Instead of ministering to a whole community, these evangelical preachers stressed the importance of personal, individual decision in shaping church life. In trying to reform the established religious culture, evangelical preachers joined hands with preachers in Norway, Denmark, Germany, England, and Scotland, sharing devotional literature, pious songs, and efforts to promote foreign mission and social reform. Lay people found new opportunities for leadership through these ventures, but predictably, traditional authorities in the churches resisted these broad, evangelical, impulses. They fought to protect the theology and leadership structures of the official church.

Swedish ministers Lars Paul Esbjörn (emigrated in 1849), Eric Norelius (1850), Tufve Nilsson Hasselquist (1852), Erland Carlsson (1853), and Jonas Swensson (1856), began their work in America as an extension of their previous careers as revival-oriented priests.[11] They operated in the circles of awakened believers and maintained their relationships with mentors and benefactors in the revival. They saw their work as pastors in America as a continuation of the revival in Sweden. So they were not content to build up scattered congregations in isolated settlements, but envisioned their own work as a part of a larger process of building up God's kingdom among the Swedes. Soon, however, the immense needs of the mass of Swedish immigrants forced these ministers to rethink their goals. Instead of focusing on recreating a pure, revived circle of believers, they developed a broader sense of the church. As early as the 1850s, because they were located in western Illinois at the center of a hub of relationships, the ministers received letters from all over the region further up the river in western Illinois, Wisconsin, and southern Minnesota, and further west in Iowa. Surprisingly, they also received requests for ministerial service from Swedes in New York, New

Jersey, and Pennsylvania. These seemingly scattered settlements of Swedes knew of each other and wanted ministerial care. The calls from so many settlements impressed upon them the understanding that they would have to create a broader institution to minister to the needs of the larger constituency. This constituency was a national one, from the start, because it was created out of a far-flung network of immigrants who kept in touch with each other through their letters.

How They Knew of Each Other

Immigrant pioneer Peter Cassell's migration to New Sweden, Iowa, in 1845, was a fixture in the early histories of the Augustana Synod. Cassell came from a relatively prosperous farm outside of Kisa, in Östergötland. He owned land and operated a mill. His decision to organize an immigration party initiated a new phase of Swedish emigration because the group did not leave for religious reasons or because of any persecution. In Peter Cassell's home village the idea of emigration was an idea talked about often in the town, particularly at the local pharmacy. The proprietor's son had spent some time living in Pine Lake, Wisconsin. The migration out of Kisa and the settlement process in America were not one-time events, but rather they were part of a longer process involving many stages and developments. His departure and subsequent settlement in New Sweden, Iowa, set in motion the movement of many other people from his hometown. The ripple effect of his decision to migrate with a company of farmers affected the geography of migration from Sweden to America in the nineteenth century. The congregation begun in New Sweden in 1848 became the oldest congregation in the Augustana Synod.

The company of people who traveled in the group led by Peter Cassell arrived in Iowa in 1845, and settled in Jefferson County on the Skunk River. The settlers eventually improved the name and called the settlement New Sweden.[12] Once they had settled there, a second party from their home village Kisa decided to attempt the voyage and join them in Iowa. This second group highlights the importance of focusing on the connections made by correspondence. Certainly the decision of the second group to follow Cassell was probably made after the people at home heard that the first voyage had been successful. We can infer that letters must have been exchanged between members of the first emigrating party and friends and family members back in Kisa.

The second party set out in springtime. Some of the members, however, did not make it all the way to Iowa. They were robbed in Albany, New York, survived by eating plums along the route of the Erie Canal, and were forced to stop in Buffalo, New York, because they had no means to continue. One couple in the party, Germund Johnsson and his wife, were forced to place their minor daughters in the keeping of two women who were farming in Chandlers Valley, Pennsylvania. The parents apparently worked somewhere in Western Pennsylvania, regained financial stability, and returned two years later to rejoin their children. They stayed and worked on the farm in Pennsylvania and established a Swedish settlement that also grew. Again in 1847, a third group set out from Kisa, but changed course for Andover, Illinois, after following the advice of Methodist preacher Olof Hedström in New York.

Immigrant letters maintained relationships with people at home through changing experiences and new contexts, and they also helped keep immigrants in touch with each other in their new land. The ongoing communication with family and friends maintained a network of relationships and association that expanded when Swedish immigrants discovered each other in America and began to create a transplanted Swedish-American national culture. Even when circumstances, job opportunities, accidents, and adventure separated close friends and family members, through letter writing they kept in touch and often were able to reunite.

Even though significant distances separated the migrating groups from Kisa, they kept in touch. Andover settlers sent word to those in Sugar Grove, Pennsylvania, advising them to continue on to Illinois. Some came while others stayed in Pennsylvania. Unlike other Lutheran immigrant churches, the Augustana Synod was formed out of a network of geographically dispersed individuals who maintained a loose network with each other.[13] Several geographically disconnected settlements had formed by the end of the 1840s, but they knew about each other. Eric Norelius's 1890 history lists in chronological order twelve early migrant groups spanning the first decade of settlement, from 1844 to 1854. With the exception of the Janssonists, the first three groups intended to settle near Pine Lake, Wisconsin, relying on information they had from the published reports of Episcopalian priest Gustaf Unonius. Secondary migrations noted in Norelius's account, based on stories passed on to him in Minnesota, indicate that several family groups changed course after getting information in New York from the Methodist pastor Olof Hedström or from other contacts. These course changes resulted in early Swedish settlements in Andover, Illinois; Brockton, Massachusetts; Jamestown, New York; and Sugar Grove, Pennsylvania, in addition to the pioneer settlements in Wisconsin and Iowa. Germund Johnsson, the first settler in Sugar Grove, later settled in Vasa, Minnesota, where he could give Norelius all his first-hand information about the early connections he had relied on in coming to America. Because of this active correspondence network, immigrants unhappy with their first choice of settlement knew where fellow Swedes were living and where they could find community. It is probably from this man, a rather fervent Methodist, that Norelius got the information that separated families "exchanged letters once they found out where they had landed, and advised friends to come to Andover, which some of them did."[14] The Sugar Grove, Pennsylvania; Andover, Illinois; and Vasa, Minnesota connection was made, and the congregations that later formed the Augustana Synod had a beginning as a national network.

How Lutheran Would They Be?

Immigrants who came to North America experienced radical change, but they also sought to preserve a way of life. According to historian Robert Ostergren, Swedish immigrants came to America in order to farm, making it possible for younger sons who would have become landless in Sweden to continue longstanding family patterns of inheritance.[15] In the wide-open fields of the Midwest parents could obtain land also for sons and daughters. They could recreate a village culture much like the one they left behind. Even without a preacher, they had sermons to read and holidays to remember. When the occasional preacher visited a settlement, baptized the children, and convinced them to build a church, they recreated much of the social and cultural structure of Swedish rural life.

The people who settled in these scattered communities were not devoid of religious ideas or attitudes. They brought with them the full range of religious experience, and when they contacted a Swedish minister in America and tried to form a congregation, they encountered all of the complexity of Sweden's long religious history, as well as the freedom that America offered. One of the freedoms that America offered was the ability to opt out of a religious life altogether. Scholars have debated how important religion really was for Swedish immigrants, since only about half of them were affiliated with one of several Swedish-American churches. The first histories of Swedish immigration highlighted the immigrant churches as preservers of culture. Non-religious dimensions of immigration remained under reported. Later interpreters compensated by focusing on economic or political factors as primary. A combination of these two approaches is most likely closer to the truth. Religious dynamics were a part of a process of settlement and social formation.[16]

It is not surprising to find that religious concepts and quoted hymns surface often in the letters sent to loved ones back home in Sweden, for the Swedish immigrant had a common education based on the catechism and included memorization of a select number of hymns. In Sweden, the ideal educational environment revolved around fathers who led the household in devotions and instructed children and servants in Lutheran doctrine. This was not always held up in the homes of the parish, however. To make sure that some efforts at least were made in the right direction, the local minister was expected to visit the farms and households and hold examinations. The minister's reports of these official visitations, called *förhör*, give modern researchers detailed knowledge about social conditions in Sweden between 1686 and throughout the period of mass migration. From these records, and also from the ample religious references in private correspondence, we know that religious concepts and phrases provided a familiar way for Swedes to express themselves.

Church records kept track of literacy and Christian knowledge, residential changes, and even health and vaccination records. Religious officials could wield power in this system in ways that fueled resentment, too. Immigrant stories about repression and a cold, spiritually stale formalism in the State Church signal a growing independence on the part of ordinary parishioners. Priests like Esbjörn, Hasselquist, and Carlsson, who gained a reputation for their warm religious piety and their interest in the moral and spiritual welfare of parishioners, became associated in the popular mind with new ideas of religious freedom.

The responsibility Swedish priests traditionally felt for their congregants extended also to the new reality of emigration. In 1854, Swedish priest Anders Stenwall wrote to immigrant pastor Erland Carlsson in the hub city of Chicago. Stenwall and Carlsson were not strangers to each other; they had developed a collegial relationship through their own participation in fostering the Awakening. Now that Carlsson was in Chicago, Stenwall could get reliable information about the religious conditions for immigrants. "Most of them write that you have a better brand of Christianity over there than here, that there is no swearing, no drinking, and so on," wrote Stenwall. Given what he knew about the role of a priest, he inquired, "How is it possible to control and hold together such a motley mass of people in the long run?" Carlsson knew the whole spectrum of religious and other enthusiasms among the Swedish settlers, and his congregation provided a model for a new way to meet the religious needs of ordinary people. Stenwall sought Carlsson's advice because he had suffered a few blows: "What do we accomplish by our much preaching, after all?" he asked. "Most people remember nothing at the close of the sermon—possibly the fault is ours."[17] The sense of failure multiplied for priests when the people they cared for assumed control of their own religious lives and left their villages.

Some areas of Sweden had revival-friendly bishops and priests, while other areas had leaders who staunchly opposed challenges to their authority, religious or otherwise. Authorities who tried to squelch pious efforts toward education and renewal became the foils for oft-repeated stories that buttressed the revivalists' sense of martyrdom. Stories were familiar to Swedish Americans because so many of their early religious leaders had themselves experienced this kind of persecution. They had begun their careers as ministers in Sweden, only to run afoul of church leadership when they began to advance the cause of temperance or had spoken to workers in private devotional meetings. While in Kalmar, a coastal town in southern Sweden, well-known revival leader Paul Peter Waldenström began to visit the poorhouse and conduct devotional meetings to counter the weekly visit of the "drunk school teacher" and the monthly visit of the priest. When the "door was closed to him," Waldenström defiantly confronted the official: "If a person gets food six days a week, they can probably survive a fast on the seventh, but to only get food one day a week—that cannot be borne."[18]

Swedish Piety

Predominantly negative images of the Swedish priest and of the Church of Sweden survive among immigrant descendants in America, even though there were many priests who were well regarded. Early images tended to be simplified as they were passed on, and American notions of egalitarian freedom were often contrasted with old country formality and class hierarchy, with priests as foils. A subtlety that has been erased in passing is that the reputation of the Church of Sweden varied considerably from region to region and even from parish to parish. A Swedish immigrant knew only his or her very local provincial story and had little exposure to the culture of other areas of the homeland before coming to America. Only in America did the ordinary immigrant become a "Swede." The immigrant congregations in America contained people who might hail from several regions of Sweden, and the expectations of these worshipers could vary significantly. Swedes from the southern portion of Sweden had experienced a pietistic movement[19] of extraordinary emotional intensity, countered by a high church reaction within the official structure.[20] Other areas of Sweden had experienced dramatic episodes of ecstatic religious behavior by individuals who cried out, or preached while asleep. In other places religious enthusiasms stimulated reactions dedicated to order. Legalistic forms of pietism frowned on heart religion and advocated a rigid process of sanctification.[21] Given the variety of backgrounds among immigrants it was not easy to create consensus even in small settlements. Thus, immigrant societies and churches had to create an ethnic, national Swedish identity, transcending local loyalties, in order to survive.

In all areas of Sweden, religious behavior had been one of the few avenues of dissent and expression available to ordinary people. Revival of piety in Sweden and in America meant an increased level of religious bick-ering and contention. As more people became religiously active, they also developed critical views. Pious networks of people met to pray, but also to complain.

While pietist movements in Sweden provided some religious vari-ety outside of the official church, there were also developments within the established church as they reacted to external influences and sought to adapt to changing conditions. Two Swedish universities, Lund and Uppsala, had theological faculties to train ministers. Lund's theological faculty, in southern Sweden, was known for its "high church" emphasis on ministerial authority and leadership, while Uppsala's theological faculty, north of Stockholm, had imbibed some of the energy of the revival preachers and taught that min-istry derived its authority from the active piety of the congregation.[22] For avid revival proponents, neither university supplied pastors who truly could sustain a lively spiritual life in the congregation. Alongside the more formal, university-based system for training pastors, mission-oriented schools pre-pared men for missionary service or home mission work. The most famous of these for the purposes of understanding Augustana's story were Peter Fjell-stedt's Missionary Training Institute and P. A. Ahlberg's Mission School.[23]

Many other dimensions of Sweden's long religious history are also rel-evant to the story of Swedish Lutheranism in America, but this brief survey is enough to make the point that the religious scene in Sweden was conten-tious, and this would cause problems for immigrants in America. The fervent participation in religious life by some and the avoidance by others provides a context for understanding the many disputes that emerged in American congregations, where immigrants from several regions encountered not only varying dialects but also distinct differences in piety.

The confusion generated by these debates provides an important con-text for understanding how a heightened Lutheran consciousness emerged among immigrants just as it had in the Church of Sweden during these important years of change. Impulses from the missionary and revival circles that had become so popular with lay people trickled up into the ranks of the official clergy and mission societies and devotional emphases were incor-porated into the official structure of the Church of Sweden. While changes occurred in Sweden that loosened the strict formalism of the establishment, a need for theological clarity became more pronounced especially among Swedish immigrants. They recognized the need for some kind of unifying force to help them form stable religious communities. For many, traditional Lutheran teaching provided this foundation. The first Swedish-American pastors, though they had valued the free evangelical openness of the revival, in their adjustment to America realized that they also needed to define themselves more strictly as Lutherans. In the letters exchanged between the separated fellowships across America, in Illinois, western Pennsylvania, Minnesota, and New York, the revival spirit that united believers now had to be defined in the context of America's religious "free for all," a place where the simple unity among believers needed to be articulated and defended in relationship to the task of creating a church. The letter network that initially had connected Peter Cassell's separated emigration chain and begun to seek religious guidance from the trio of Carlsson, Hasselquist, and Esbjörn in Illinois, gradually became more self-consciously a church fellowship.

chapter 2

MAKING LUTHERAN CONNECTIONS IN AMERICA

SWEDISH LUTHERAN IMMIGRANTS BROUGHT WITH THEM the full range of religious fervor that had enlivened the revival movement in Sweden. But in this new land their Swedish spiritual vitality became complicated by the experience of migration and a newfound longing for tradition, once immigrants discovered how "new" the new world really was. Additionally, America's religious freedom gave lay people many options but made it difficult for ministers. Immigrant pastors Lars Paul Esbjörn, Erland Carlsson, and Tufve Nilsson Hasselquist all held ministerial credentials from the Church of Sweden and a kind of street credibility from their revival preaching, but even this compounded legitimacy did not foster trust. In America trust had to be earned. Within the smallest settlement, arguments over worship, church discipline, and clerical garments emerged right away. In response to revival sensitivities, Hasselquist and Esbjörn did not wear the traditional priestly garb of the Church of Sweden when they began their ministry. But since they read from the official church handbook when conducting some of the services, they were still labeled as formalists.

Esbjörn and Hasselquist, and the few Swedish-trained priests that followed them in the 1850s, created an alliance with other ministers and preachers and, in turn, they created a network of congregations that later evolved into a denomination. The character of the Swedish Lutheran immigrant church body they founded differs in significant ways from the other immigrant Lutheran churches emerging at the same time. For instance, the Augustana Synod stands out in the annals of American Lutheran history as the only ethnic Lutheran church body that suffered no schisms or divisions during its entire history. This is very unusual, given that warring synods were the norm. Norwegian Lutherans had created three synods by the time Swedish Lutherans arrived in the Midwest.[1] The reason that Norwegian Lutherans fought so strenuously with each other stemmed from their early contact with conservative Missouri Synod Lutherans in St. Louis. C. F. W. Walther had lain down the gauntlet and challenged the orthodoxy of other Lutherans through the pages of *Der Lutheraner*, published in St. Louis, Missouri, beginning in 1844. Even the small Danish community created two rival synods, colloquially known as the happy and the holy Danes.[2] All these Lutheran efforts to found church bodies were extremely conscious of each other, and their leaders were not sparing in their judgment of other Lutherans. In this combative environment, Swedish unity was remarkable and needs to be explained.

Those who followed Lars Paul Esbjörn, Tufve Nilsson Hasselquist, Eric Norelius, and Erland Carlsson did not disagree on whether or how to make their Lutheran heritage conversant with American ways. Early on the pastors agreed on common practices and leadership, and they were able to make their leadership visible. They aimed their message at Swedish immigrants who had formed a loosely spun network of communities through the writing of letters and personal visits. In their ongoing communication with the scattered settlements—through letters, visits, and newspaper reports—these pastors and their followers were able to answer religious challenges and convince enough members of congregations to stay with them. Even though there were painful splits in congregations, most of the departing groups did not insist on retaining the Lutheran confessional subscription that Lutherans insisted upon, so that congregational disagreement generated Swedish Methodist, Episcopal, Baptist, and Mission churches, instead of rival Lutheran synods.

Becoming Visible as Religious Leaders

In order to carry out a ministry on the frontier, Lars Paul Esbjörn needed outside funding. The little that came in from pious friends in Sweden did not last long. Hearing about the funding available from the Congregational American Home Missionary Society for Protestant Preachers in the West, Esbjörn applied and received a stipend.[3] In an environment where every Lutheran preacher had to prove his orthodoxy, however, this non-Lutheran support caused problems. The accusations thrown at them by other ministers forced the Swedish pastors to explain themselves publicly to the growing Swedish immigrant community. Gustaf Unonius, the Swedish Episcopal priest in Chicago, bristled at charges that he had left the true Swedish church, and he accused the so-called Lutherans of hypocrisy for accepting Congregationalist help. Who were they to denounce him for turning to the Episcopalians? Esbjörn and Hasselquist waged a public debate to defend their Lutheranism. Esbjörn truthfully admitted the connection but argued that he was not obligated in any way to conform to Congregationalist teaching. Unonius had, by contrast, accepted ordination from an Episcopal bishop. In the heightened atmosphere of America's religious competition, and especially among immigrant preachers vying for positions, the public debate became an educational process in the varieties of American religion.

Methodists supported Olof Hedström, who met immigrants in New York harbor's Bethel Ship. In western Illinois, his brother Gustaf took hand of them and guided them into an inland Methodist harbor. Preacher C. A. Palmquist connected his warm-hearted revival piety to the Baptist movement, while Swedish Seventh Day Adventists challenged the ordering of the week. Mormon preachers drew a surprisingly large number of Scandinavians to Deseret, their promised land that later became the state of Utah. American Protestant denominations saw immigrants in the Western territories as fair game for their civilizing and evangelizing work. The variety of Lutheran views spouted by preachers caused confusion, especially among the majority of settlers who, though properly churched in their homeland, had not been party to any of the religious movements in their homeland. American support, given through "home mission" societies in several denominations, provided funding for frontier preachers as part of a design to assimilate, or at least influence unchurched immigrants on the western frontier.[4] Well-meaning and well-heeled American society members in Eastern states knew little about the internal doctrinal disputes within immigrant communities, and immigrant preachers did not inform them about their internal politics. The societies instead learned about numbers of converts and the successful methods used by preachers.[5] The system of reporting on organizational aspects of their religious activity that American home mission societies demanded also had an indirect influence on all Swedish groups. It taught preachers and congregations the American methods of church development.

Lutheran churches in the Eastern states were also interested in home mission work, because many of their own members had joined the westward migration into Ohio, Indiana, and Illinois. The Rev. William A. Passavant in Pittsburgh, Pennsylvania, a promoter of home mission among Eastern Lutherans, knew of the presence of large numbers of Scandinavians and Germans in the West. In his monthly magazine, *The Missionary*, he announced that Eastern Lutherans also wanted to help fund Lutheran ministry among the immigrants. Even though no society existed for this purpose, the mention of this vague intent was enough to inspire hope in Lars Paul Esbjörn, who somehow saw a copy of this issue. It reached him, he said, "like an arrow in the dark."[6] He began to take heart when he realized that Lutheran ministry could find funding. The result was a speaking tour to the Eastern states in the summer of 1851. Esbjörn collected almost $3,000, and began to write to friends within the American Lutheran General Synod, who followed his ministry among immigrants with interest.

In 1852, the Rev. Tufve Nilsson Hasselquist came to the United States. Like Esbjörn, Hasselquist also received funding from the American Home Missionary Society. The two ministers now entered into a complicated time of negotiated image making. On the one hand, they needed to maintain ties with American Lutherans, but on the other, they continued to receive funding from the Congregationalists. In a letter to Hasselquist dated April 2,1853, Esbjörn wrote: "I am sending you the change from the $100. . . . Write directly to Rev. John C. Baker, D.D. Philadelphia, Pa, and thank him, and at the same time say that in order to avoid any collision between two mission societies, you are obligated to refuse the commission offered by the Lutheran society." Esbjörn apparently had made the contact with the Lutherans, and now Hasselquist would have to turn back the money. He continued, "Do not forget to say that your refusal of the commission by no means implies an indifference to the Lutheran church or teachings, which you are from the heart devoted to, etc." Esbjörn could count on Hasselquist's ability to supply the proper, and probably formulaic, wording. He also gave another rationale for their decision to continue receiving funding from the American Congregationalists: Baker should learn that the Swedish immigrant congregation knew the Lutheran society had limited funds while the American Home Mission Society, with its bigger treasury, generously supported missions in several denominations. Again Esbjörn mentioned orthodoxy, encouraging Hasselquist to say, "both you and the congregation are fully Lutheran, subscribing to the Book of Concord, and so on. Say also that you hope that the other priest who is coming can receive the support that you are returning."[7]

This letter gives some indication of Esbjörn's stance toward traditional Lutheranism in the first years of his ministry in America. While in Sweden he had participated in a broadly evangelical, mission-oriented reform movement. Now in America he combined the language of devotion with the standard formulas used to subscribe to Lutheran teachings. These statements did not need to be carefully elaborated in his letter to Hasselquist, since both men were familiar with what needed to be said to other Lutherans in order to establish one's orthodoxy. In 1853, in nearby Wisconsin, Herman Amberg Preus had recently arrived from Christiania University in Norway, complete with the full agenda for transforming the immigrant congregations of the Norwegian Synod into fully confessional and compliant church people.[8] Within the immediate circles around Esbjörn and Hasselquist, and especially in Chicago, this hyper-confessional emphasis affected the self-understanding of the Swedish pastors as well.

The settlements of Swedish immigrants, however, were not limited to the upper Midwest, and the Swedish pastors had more to worry about than whether their own congregations in Illinois had the proper language about the Lutheran Confessions. Early in 1853, Swedish settlers in Sugar Grove, Pennsylvania, wrote and requested pastoral services. The Pennsylvania Swedish settlement that had begun with the single family left behind in 1847 had grown and maintained contact with their friends in Illinois even after six years had passed. Now a Swedish preacher had found them and offered his pastoral services. The Sugar Grove Swedes knew enough to be wary. They wrote to the Swedish pastors in Illinois for advice. Should they go ahead and hire him? This remarkable letter reveals that Swedish immigrants sought out religious authority and relied on the testimony of their contacts in Illinois to be certain that their decision was not made in isolation. As much as the revival had made inroads among Swedish immigrants, the heightened religious competition in America made orthodoxy and clerical authority more appealing than it had been at home.

After hearing from the people in Sugar Grove, Esbjörn and Hasselquist exchanged correspondence because they recognized that by taking care of this request, they were establishing a kind of superintendency, that is, a relationship of oversight with this far away congregation. In effect they were jointly taking on the traditional role of the bishop. Hasselquist made the trip out to Pennsylvania, examined the candidate Bergenlund, and gave his approval. But barely a year later, nineteen men from Sugar Grove sent back a long list of grievances against the new preacher. The credibility of Hasselquist and Esbjörn now depended on whether they could intervene in this disappointing dispute and supply a worthy candidate.

After the experience with Bergenlund, Hasselquist stepped up his correspondence with revival stalwarts in Sweden, P. A. Ahlberg and Peter Fjellstedt, in order to press upon them the need for pastors to the immigrant community. They were writing to the leaders of the Swedish Evangelical National Foundation (*Evangeliska Fosterlandsstiftelse*), which had trained preachers and evangelists for two decades. Fjellstedt, who was well known for his promotion of missionary work, recruited ministers for immigrants in America from the students at his missionary school. Personal contacts were also important: Hasselquist's wife was Fjellstedt's younger sister.[9] The personal connections that Hasselquist maintained with Fjellstedt and Ahlberg worked to bring candidates to America who shared a similar revival-oriented piety and who also revered the same spiritual leaders. Writing to Sweden for ministerial candidates, however, was not a quick way to supply the needs of congregations. Even when a few men were willing to come, the American-based pastors had to supply additional training in order to help these new arrivals understand the American situation. The real impact of Hasselquist's fervent pleas for help did not make itself felt until the decade of the 1870s when this training had been satisfactorily completed. Several students in every ordination class appeared to have studied first with Ahlberg before studying for a time in America. Fewer came from Fjellstedt's school.[10]

While Esbjörn and Hasselquist waited for reinforcements, they continued traveling from settlement to settlement, preaching, baptizing, convening meetings, and teaching young people. Then they went home and wrote many letters. Conveying information for immigrant communities, soliciting support from Americans, and pleading with Swedish friends for funds and personnel soon became overwhelming. The ministers shared letters and met together frequently. Soon their letters to each other became more important, since the situation in America among the settlers began to present unique problems that friends in Sweden, no matter how sympathetic, could rarely understand.

Serendipity

Erland Carlsson, a young priest in a working class parish, came to America in 1853 after Peter Fjellstedt recommended him. Fjellstedt had himself been called by the newly founded congregation in Chicago, but he could not accept. Anticipating this, the congregation had left a blank space on their letter of call and had also indicated that they would accept another name. Apparently, while praying about this, Fjellstedt received a letter from Carlsson and put two and two together. He wrote Carlsson's name in the space, sent the form to the young pastor, and indicated his warm approval of the call. Since Carlsson had recently been reprimanded by his superiors for having conducted too many mission meetings and drawing too large a crowd, he was open to a new opportunity. It was clear that his career prospects were limited in his Swedish diocese. He came to Chicago in June.[1]

1. This story appears in Carlsson's autobiography, included in Eric Norelius, *De Svenska Lutherska Forsamlingarnas och Svenskarnes Historia i Amerika* (Rock Island, Ill.: Augustana Book Concern, 1890), 416–418.

Finally Esbjörn and Hasselquist received the help they so badly needed. After arriving in Chicago, Erland Carlsson had broad sympathies for the range of religious impulses that stirred within the Swedish community there. The other Swedish priest in the city, Gustaf Unonius, was Episcopal and was not connected with the Swedish ministers in Illinois. A member of the upper class in Sweden, Unonius held rather romantic notions about creating a Swedish community in America. Carlsson's more practical bent found more to emulate from the Norwegian pastor Paul Anderson, who had been in America long enough to have developed a broader social vision. He belonged to the Lutheran abolitionist Franckean Synod, and he provided hospitality for the growing numbers of Swedish immigrants in his Chicago congregation. Carlsson's association with Anderson not only provided the Swedish immigrants with a place to worship, but also introduced the Swedish pastors to a small group of Norwegian preachers who had very strained relations with other Norwegian pastors, especially Herman Amberg Preus in Wisconsin. Inter-Lutheran disputes over doctrine and Americanization dominated the encounters that Swedish ministers had with Norwegian, American, and German Lutherans, so it is no wonder that Esbjörn, Carlsson, and Hasselquist preferred working with their own more cohesive group of Swedish people, even though there were plenty of reasons for Swedes also to argue about religion.[11]

Carlsson's warm piety impressed the immigrants in Chicago and his pastoral practice reassured them. His reporting on the first confirmation class at Swedish Immanuel Church in 1854 reveals how the formal practice of the Church of Sweden gave him a sense that finally, in Chicago, he could feel at home. He wrote that "a heavy sense of strangeness has followed me ever since I arrived in America, even in the temple, but when I held confirmation here yesterday I completely forgot that I was in America. . . .[It] was also the first confirmation in the congregation, and became a real feast day for them."[12]

Carlsson took other steps that distanced him from his earlier embrace of the simple revival style by restoring some traditional signs of ministerial authority. He used the recently adopted handbook of the Church of Sweden for conducting the service and donned the official outer coat, the *prästrock*, as he made pastoral visits, a move that caused enough comment that he had to explain himself to Hasselquist and Esbjörn who had been challenged on that account. In the first years of Swedish-Lutheran pastoral ministry in America, ordinary decisions like these made in response to a pastor's local situation resulted in an increased volume of correspondence and consultation with the other ministers. Carlsson's decisions, especially, affected the others, since everyone went through Chicago to get to points further west or north.

The Swedish Immanuel Church that Carlsson founded in Chicago witnessed firsthand the surging immigration into the Midwest. Carlsson met immigrants at the port in Chicago, at the railway stations, and on the streets. He helped separated parties find each other, and he rescued stranded families. He even published an immigrant guide that directed settlers through the complicated process of entry and resettlement. Carlsson knew virtually every Swede who came to the city. When the 1854 cholera epidemic raged, he arranged help and assisted with the many burials. Gruesome stories of the epidemic were passed on through letters, so that Carlsson learned of the fate of those he had helped. One group from Elmboda in Sweden on their way to Chisago Lake, Minnesota, had some in their party who succumbed to cholera on the steamship voyage up the Mississippi. The captain put them ashore, so as to avoid bringing the sickness any further. Those who were stranded had no implements with which to bury their dead companions, so they made rough graves in the sand. Prairie wolves consumed these bodies, and soon only a few widows and small children were finally rescued. The hospitality that Carlsson's family and the congregation extended came at great cost to them as well. One tenth of the adult members of the Immanuel congregation died in that year, and many more children.[13]

Going National through the Newspaper

In order to keep immigrants informed about the expansion of settlements and to help them keep track of family and friends, the Swedish ministers shared their letters and reported to their congregations. The ministers met as often as they could physically manage to share information, but a more formal system of communication became necessary in order to make new immigrants fully aware of the expanding Swedish-American community. To keep a consistent order in their church practices, the ministers were motivated to write letters informing far-flung congregations of the joint decisions they made over worship, pastoral leadership, and church discipline. But this kind of reporting was unwieldy. Esbjörn pressed for a Swedish newspaper. Hasselquist, Carlsson, and Norelius agreed in principle, but one more time-consuming venture, and an expensive one at that, made them hesitant. In the fall of 1854 Hasselquist heard a more insistent tone from Esbjörn: "You must push Carlsson to get a proof done of *Svenska Posten*. We can't delay any longer." Rather than try to push Carlsson to further overwork, however, Hasselquist took this task on himself. Then Esbjörn, learning that a paper might come from Galesburg instead of Chicago, wrote to Carlsson, prodding him harder. "Hasselquist is in the process of creating a trial issue. Certainly you must avoid competition and confusion. If you have the ability, I believe Chicago is the better place for a paper." In the end the persistent pressure of letters from Esbjörn did the trick, and a Swedish newspaper started up in Galesburg, Illinois.[14]

The newspaper became the means used by ministers to strengthen their religious authority within the immigrant community, but their efforts to get a newspaper off the ground involved them in a venture that would extend their expertise far beyond its normal range. The first Swedish newspaper needed to appeal to a general readership, since enough subscriptions couldn't be sold by focusing solely on theological questions. A wider readership meant a bigger pulpit, too, and the envisioned paper would ultimately give the ministers a place to preach more widely. Esbjörn promised to write on a wide range of topics: "I can furnish temperance talks, farming and household advice, but I wouldn't want to be limited to these topics."[15]

Finally, on January 3, 1855, Hasselquist in Galesburg, Illinois, succeeded in issuing *Hemlandet*, a paper devoted to general and religious topics. The newspaper announced it would provide proper churchly guidance for Swedish Americans, but Hasselquist also aimed to serve the whole immigrant community. Using the familiar image of a letter writer, he promised that he would be a trustworthy uncle who relayed news from home to keep everyone in touch. The newspaper in fact read very much like a familiar letter from home. "For a long time and from many corners the wish for a Swedish newspaper in America has been noted. Many of us have left parents, dependents, and friends in our native land, whose well being depends on the general conditions in the country, and we in this land feel an urgent need to hear news from home."[16]

Hasselquist used the paper to create a national unity among Swedish Americans. His well-known emphasis on a centralized Augustana Synod emerged also in his early work as a newspaper editor. He believed that immigrants needed to learn about their new country and hear what other settlers were doing. Readers heard about "fellow Swedes" spread throughout "this America, or better said, this United States of America." Hasselquist's herding instinct included the recognition that there were large Swedish-American settlements with established congregations and leadership that should be corralled into the fold. Well-informed Swedish Americans should know about these places. "There are not just individuals here and there, or clusters of families, but in fact large settlements consisting of several hundred people in each place."[17] Hasselquist had been invited to several of them, visiting congregations and solving disputes. In the first issue he listed New York City, Jamestown, New York; Hessel Valley in Northwest Pennsylvania; New Sweden, Iowa; Attica, Indiana; Galesburg and Andover, Illinois; and Chisago City, Minnesota. The geography of Swedish America had been explored by the pastors, who could attest to the need for information in these far-flung settlements. Through letters these few ministers had kept up contact with people in these settlements. Now the newspaper would pick up the work and provide a way for new readers to enter this wider circle of information and friendship. And the paper was popular. *Hemlandet* began with a subscription list of 400, and within three years there were 1000 households receiving the paper.[18]

Hasselquist encouraged the scattered Swedes to think of themselves as a united people: "as countrymen we must be interested in one another, and be glad to hear about the news from one another."[19] The importance of sharing information from the scattered communities gave Swedish immigrants a sense of their place on the vast American landscape. Through the paper they learned the names and places where they had a connection with fellow countrymen. Using the information from the newspaper allowed immigrants to move from settlement to settlement and to find one another.[20] Hasselquist made the word-of-mouth network established through correspondence visible in the newspaper.

Once he had gotten the paper off the ground, Hasselquist did more than post information. "We are becoming citizens," he wrote, "and we need to know what our new country is made of, and our part in it." The Swedish immigrants, addressed collectively, could be thought of as a "people." This beginning of a Swedish-American ethnic or national consciousness was framed religiously: "Sin is something that destroys a people," admonished Hasselquist, "and the progress of God's kingdom will be the best way to create well being, so we are ultimately interested in the victory of the King of Kings among us." Later publishers and newspaper editors from New York to San Francisco promoted an ethnic consciousness based on secular interests and activities, but insofar as they hoped to gain a national readership, they built on the network initially created by the Swedish ministers. Hasselquist's vision for a newspaper continued to attract a broad readership because he kept an even balance between religion and politics. Religious matters filled one half of the paper, while the other half combined news of war and politics from Sweden with information and instruction about forms of government, political topics, and cultural issues in the United States.

The newspaper gave Hasselquist and the Swedish ministers a platform to shape immigrant opinion. Hasselquist broadcast his opposition to slavery and gave support to the new Republican Party. Swedish Americans followed his advice and voted for Republicans well into the twentieth century. The reason that Hasselquist was successful in guiding the views of newly arrived immigrants surely included his method of conveying these positions to readers. The conventions of letter writing were extended in the newspaper format, and this informal and familiar way of communicating what was presumed to be a common viewpoint helped shape the developing Swedish-American community. Already in the second issue, for instance, Hasselquist addressed the evil of slavery by using excerpts from a letter written to him by Swedish travelers in Kansas. The travelers had written about the various parties they had encountered on their journey: "We saw no workers except some ragged Negroes, some who looked so poorly handled and beaten by their masters that there were deep scars on their bodies. One day there were two alongside us as we walked." The letter writer then related how it had felt to be near these slaves. He conveyed the fear that marked them as they spoke of their masters and described the dread that hovered over the traveling party when slave handlers came near. The Negroes suddenly made ready to separate from their companions: "'We have to leave right now. If they see us talking to you they'll think you are trying to take us away.' So they left us quickly, but not before giving us a blessing."[21] Hasselquist's use of intimate personal accounts like this provided readers with trustworthy information about the strange system of slavery in the United States. Providing readers with extracts from letters extended further the mechanism of personal testimony that had brought about the process of emigration and settlement in the first place.

Hemlandet's person-to-person accounts established the paper as an open forum for immigrants in every part of the United States. Stories invited readers to consider moral questions. Hasselquist used reports from Småland settlers in Minnesota to provide a counter narrative to tales in the popular press that magnified the threat of hostile Indians. A kind of ethnic pride is evident as these stories suggest that Swedish settlers had good relations with Indians where other Americans had failed. Simple accounts of sharing food gave readers lessons in cultural interactions that probably helped Swedish settlers avoid violence. "Some Indians camped near us during their hunting rounds, and they came into our house for warmth," wrote one Swedish settler. "They would take our food, but then they left us meat in return, and if we continued to give them food we got more meat next time."[22] In characteristic Småland fashion these writers also noted that Indian supplies of meat represented quite a savings, for they noted that this kind of barter saved a lot of money.

After the violent Sioux Indian uprising, the positive, upbeat tone of the early years changed.[23] The immigrant newspaper now reported on the development of the congregations and pushed to create a sense of kinship and mutual regard within the expanding and more internally focused settler community. While other immigrant newspapers folded, even those who relied on a similar network of correspondents and newsy reports from friends, *Hemlandet* did not, attesting to its importance within this growing Swedish-American community. Hasselquist's use of the newspaper as a public letter was part of a broader effort to create a church by reconnecting and deepening relationships among a network of immigrants who had preexisting, personal ties. The separated branches of the immigrant stream that had followed pioneer Peter Cassell from Östergötland were only one of several scattered Swedish fellowships in America. The immigrant newspaper created a mechanism that helped this scattered community to coalesce; it fostered the national network and conversation that provided the framework in which a denomination could be created. But more than a newspaper was necessary to form a church body. In order to bring some institutional coherence to the work they were doing, the Swedish pastors needed to associate with an established Lutheran church body. And there were several choices they could make among the American, German, and Norwegian groups that had begun to organize as official church bodies.

Lutheran Associations

The Swedish ministers viewed their options in Northern Illinois. They could join one of the Norwegian synods, but they would not receive much financial help this way, even though Norwegians had been in the Midwest for several years and had established farms and settlements. Norwegian churches had also developed independently of each other in an environment of mutual suspicion that they quickly directed toward newcomers. Norwegians in Wisconsin and Illinois were not united. One of the region's first pastors, J. W. C. Dietrichsen, held the views of the Danish theologian Nicolai Frederick Severin Grundtvig, and he had drafted the first constitution of the Norwegian Synod along those lines. When Herman Amberg Preus arrived in America in 1853, he forcefully removed all Grundtvigianism from the constitution and publicly admonished the pastors responsible, creating a hostile feeling among the older veterans in Wisconsin. Lay preacher Elling Eielsen, a follower of Hans Nielsen Hauge, led another Norwegian synod. "Eielsen's Synod" was a strictly revival-oriented synod and at the opposite end of the spectrum from Preus's Norwegian Synod. A few Norwegian pastors, and presumably many settlers, were caught in the middle.[24] These pastors were also seeking some kind of Lutheran affiliation apart from the strongly clerical Preus, and a few of them had already joined the American Lutheran General Synod through membership in the loosely structured Franckean Synod. Norwegian pastor Paul Anderson, with whom Carlsson had contact in Chicago, was one of these pastors. Esbjörn also had contacts with William A. Passavant, the Lutheran pastor and newspaper editor in Pittsburgh, who was for the time being a member of the General Synod.

Esbjörn had earlier joined with Norwegian pastors Ole Andrewsen, O. P. T. Hatlestad, and Paul Anderson as a member when the Synod of Northern Illinois formed on September 18, 1851. This new synod was more American than traditionally Lutheran and drew nothing but scorn from the conservative Norwegian Synod. The General Synod's constitution allowed that the Lutheran confessional teachings were "mainly correct." Lars P. Esbjörn and his delegate arrived at the founding convention a day late, and thus couldn't have influenced the constitutional formula, but did go ahead and apply for membership. Along with the Norwegian pastors, the newly named "Scandinavian pastors" added the words "the symbolical books of the Lutheran Church contain a correct summary and exposition of the divine Word, wherefore we declare and adopt them as the foundation for our faith and doctrine, next to the Holy Scriptures"[25] to their application, to make it clear that they subscribed more closely to the traditional Lutheran confessions. With their signing statement this small group of Swedish and Norwegian pastors were thus on the ground floor of the creation of the Northern Illinois Synod of the Lutheran General Synod.

As Swedish Lutheran pastors arrived on the scene during the 1850s they joined this American Lutheran General Synod. Hasselquist favored assimilation into American society, and association with American Lutherans provided a good way for that to happen. The Synod of Northern Illinois was not immune to the doctrinal disputes typical of Lutheran groups. There were parties within the General Synod who advocated the promotion of personal religion and the methods of frontier Methodism. Samuel Simon Schmucker, the founder at Gettysburg Seminary, endorsed "new measures" and believed that evangelical principles might bring about unity among Protestants in America to help them fight off Roman Catholic advances. He blurred differences in doctrine to achieve unity, however, creating enemies of others in the General Synod who were staunch "symbolists" promoting a stronger confessional adherence. Since the General Synod allowed for a diversity of opinion on essential matters of faith, the Swedish and Norwegian pastors constantly warded off criticism from other Lutheran Synod leaders who chided them for their unholy associations. Of the Swedish pastors, L. P. Esbjörn and Eric Norelius grew more confessionally minded, but the Swedish ministers kept their association, hoping they could steer the General Synod in a more conservative direction.[26]

As Esbjörn became more conservative, he worried about the collective reputation of Scandinavian preachers and how the ever-increasing number of congregations made consistent teaching more difficult. Methodists and Baptists traveled widely in western Illinois and Iowa and disrupted newly founded and fragile congregations that were surprisingly hard to manage, especially in spiritual matters. While pious individuals had been encouraged to go out to hear evangelical preachers in Sweden, now in America, Swedish preachers argued and drew fine distinctions. Hasselquist and Esbjörn had only a precarious hold on leadership among the congregations, and they needed to project a united Lutheran stance. The four ministers—Esbjörn, Hasselquist, Norelius, and Carlsson—engaged in a collective effort to portray their church development work favorably on two fronts: toward the confused situation within the immigrant community and toward the observing American Lutheran church leaders. In April of 1854 they were in crisis management mode. Reports about a Swedish Lutheran preacher who had been rebaptized circulated even among English-speaking Lutherans. Hasselquist wrote to Esbjörn that American Lutherans wondered who was in charge of religious affairs among the immigrants.

When settlement stretched further north into Minnesota, the association with the Synod of Northern Illinois created the need for some reorganization purely on geographical grounds. The synod had two conferences—one in Chicago and another along the Mississippi. The majority of Scandinavians belonged to the Mississippi Conference, and gradually the Swedish and Norwegian pastors in the Chicago Conference also began attending the meetings in the western part of the state, eventually creating a de facto division along linguistic lines that enabled the Swedish and Norwegian pastors to have meetings on their own. When the Northern Illinois Synod's theological seminary was founded in 1856 under the grand name of The Illinois State University, the united Scandinavian congregations meeting as the Mississippi Conference agreed to support a Scandinavian professor at the school. The selection of a candidate, however, revealed tension between Hasselquist and Esbjörn. Hasselquist pushed for Peter Fjellstedt as the professor and wrote to him in Sweden with an invitation. When the pastors and delegates met in 1857 at their conference meeting, they voted for Esbjörn, leaving Hasselquist visibly disappointed. Esbjörn wrote to Norelius in Ohio and reported that the debate was quite clumsy. First, he said that Hasselquist suggested they choose the professor by lot, then argued for a man who was more spiritual. Esbjörn commented, "I played dumb," so as not to draw attention to the slight.[27]

Students began training at the school, where their study put them under the direction of American professors for part of their theological education and with Esbjörn for subjects especially suited for work with Swedish and Norwegian congregations. For the first year it went well enough, but Esbjörn complained about his course load, which included several non-theological subjects like botany. He found life difficult in Springfield, where there was no Scandinavian congregation. By the end of 1859, reservations about the confessional standpoint of the Synod of Northern Illinois began to affect his view of colleagues. He developed an aversion to the Americanization of the Swedish students who seemed to grow more and more like their fellow Americans with each passing month.

The dissolution of the relationship between the Scandinavians and American Lutherans in the Synod of Northern Illinois occurred abruptly at the end of March 1860, when Esbjörn resigned in the middle of the spring term. Official reasons for his resignation included the charge that administrators had interfered with his teaching and had used the money he raised for general purposes rather than direct support of the Scandinavian students. Esbjörn argued with the school's president, William Reynolds, accusing him of false teaching, and a general "looseness" of conviction.[28] The school had severe financial problems. Students left because of a lack of food. Esbjörn's departure brought more defections, and only a few Scandinavians stayed at the now shaky institution.[29] Esbjörn had gone to Chicago, and most of the Scandinavian students followed him there.

Leaders who had been present at the founding of the synod in 1860 gathered for a picture in 1890. **Top, from left:** *John Erlander, Peter Beckman, Rev. John Pherson, Rev. Hakon Olson, Dr. G. Peters.* **Bottom:** *Rev. P. A. Cederstam, Rev. Peter Carlson, Dr. Erland Carlsson, Dr. Tufve Nilsson Hasselquist, Rev. M. F. Håkanson, Dr. Eric Norelius.* Photo courtesy of Evangelical Lutheran Church in America Archives.

The congregations and pastors of the Synod of Northern Illinois quickly convened a meeting to find out what had happened. The Scandinavians felt obligated to support Esbjörn, but his decision to leave the school forced them to declare independence from the Synod of Northern Illinois. They did not have to fumble around for theological reasons, since they had long been critical of other American Lutheran pastors in the association.

A further reason for separation was regionalism. Minnesota had become a favored destination for new immigrants and several pastors, including Peter Carlson, Peter Beckman, and Per Cederstam now served congregations there. These three had aspirations to found their own school and little interest in draining further resources on an experiment in Illinois. On June 7, 1860, the Scandinavian pastors and some laymen assembled in Jefferson Prairie, Wisconsin, to form the Scandinavian Evangelical Augustana Lutheran Synod. The name *Augustana* in the title was important, recalling the Latin name for the *Augsburg Confession—Confessio Augustana—*and indicating the doctrinal standard for the new church, something on which both the Swedes and Norwegians could agree.[30]

The rest of the summer was filled with recriminations as American Lutherans complained that the Scandinavian congregations had not offered them an opportunity to tell their side of the story. They indulged in a vigorous public campaign to protest Esbjörn's actions.[31] For the Scandinavians it was an awkward way to start a church.

After the episode with the seminary, Esbjörn also lost the confidence of other Norwegian and Swedish pastors and congregations. He advocated locating the seminary permanently in Chicago, and for three years the seminary managed to eke out a program in the basement of the Norwegian Lutheran Church there, but these were hard years for Esbjörn and the students. The Civil War had begun to darken hopes for steady progress in developing the school. During the years Esbjörn lived in Chicago, his oldest son died in the war and another son served with the Second Illinois Artillery. This was a most difficult time for Esbjörn, and he suffered from depression and homesickness. His letters to Eric Norelius during this period complain of a lack of support from the churches. He becomes more averse to Americanization, spotting an "American streak" in the fundraising plans of the other Swedish ministers.[32] He meant Hasselquist's innovative schemes to support the school.

Establishing a Seminary

Hasselquist, supported by Erland Carlsson in Chicago, proposed that the theological seminary would better be able to support itself in a country setting. Several of the railroad companies would sell land at a good price to organizers of colonies. Similar colony ventures had been advertised and attempted in Kansas and Iowa, and the idea was familiar to enough people in the synod that Hasselquist could argue that this might provide a way to raise the needed start up funds and create a supportive local community for the school. Esbjörn and Hasselquist locked horns on this proposal. During the agitation for the plan, Esbjörn made an extended trip to Sweden, ostensibly to raise money for the school, but he also set plans in motion to return to Sweden permanently. While in Sweden he followed the developments and wrote to Norelius, hoping that he would be able to stop the momentum for a settlement scheme: "I become completely agitated when I think about this and realize that everything we have done and all the money we have gathered will be wasted and will go up in smoke through miserable land speculation." He pleaded with Norelius: "You in Minnesota have burned your fingers on the purchasing and selling of land. Stand up as one man and say *no*, and eternally *no* to all speculating when you are at the synod meeting."[33]

Leaders pulled in different directions. Esbjörn sought to shield the synod from American influences, dreaming of returning to Sweden. While still hopeful of swaying the synod, he sensed futility in arguing against Hasselquist, who with Carlsson had begun investigating properties in Iowa and Paxton, Illinois. Each of these locations disappointed the churches and pastors in Minnesota and farther west. Peter Carlson, Esbjörn, and other unhappy leaders wrote to Norelius, who led a unanimous Minnesota opposition to Hasselquist's plan. They were livid when a contract was signed that placed the theological school in the most distant location, in far away Paxton, Illinois.[34]

Esbjörn's trip to Sweden in 1862 kept him from directly participating in this debate, but it did accomplish several things. He visited mission-friendly colleagues, preached in several churches, and collected support for the seminary. An important errand was to attempt to contact Paul Peter Waldenström, the sought-after revival preacher and school director from Gävle, and hand deliver a call from the synod to become the next theological professor at the seminary. In a letter to the Rev. P. Wieselgren in Göteborg, a long-time mission supporter and friend of the immigrant church, Esbjörn sought help in contacting Waldenström. Esbjörn knew that the popular leader had received a competing offer to head a possible Göteborg mission society, but he hoped that Wieselgren's regard for Augustana's needs would outweigh his loyalties to the potential mission society: "If you run into Waldenström before I do, plead with him to avoid saying *yes* to the Göteborgians before I have seen him *personally*," wrote Esbjörn. "I have with me a whole list of things and pieces of information that I have to give him *orally* before he makes up his mind."[35] It is possible that, given Esbjörn's own frustrations with the spiritual dangers of Americanization and with his fellow ministers, a personal visit with Waldenström may have actually discouraged him from accepting the call. In any case, Waldenström chose not to come to America.

While in Sweden, Esbjörn also visited the offices of the archbishop in Uppsala to inquire about formal procedures for returning to the Church of Sweden. In November 1863, he began work in Östra Våhla parish, north of Uppsala. In explaining his departure from the United States, Esbjörn reported in 1865 that one factor in his leaving was that he no longer wished to stand in the way of other leaders. He no doubt meant Hasselquist.

Back in America at the synod meeting in 1863, it was apparent that Esbjörn's departure was imminent and the need for a new professor acute. Waldenström's refusal was joined by bad news from O. C. T. Andrén, a pastor from Sweden who had served near Moline, Illinois, between 1856 and 1860. After returning to Sweden to gather a library for the seminary, Andrén had decided to send the books but stay in Sweden. He also refused to return to become a professor. The Norwegians in the synod also reported that their efforts to secure a teacher had come to naught. They hoped to "at least give the Norwegian students some instruction in the Norwegian language, and to that end they could only suggest one option, and that was to use the free time between terms when the students could travel to Chicago and receive what instruction the Norwegian pastor there was able to give."[36]

The call to Hasselquist as theological professor at the seminary thus became a less than robust tribute to his theological competence. He was really the only person who they could think of who could do an adequate job and who was willing to go and live in Paxton. Hasselquist also had reason to leave the congregation in Galesburg, where a conflict over lay leadership had been brewing, when he finally came to Paxton in 1863. There he had to mind the newspaper venture, serve a congregation, and be the sole professor of the school.[37] Any free moments away from teaching were occupied with synod concerns and parish work. He managed his farm. His wife took in students, providing board by adding to the family circle. Hasselquist did get assistance in Paxton when the Norwegian theologian and educator August Weenas was added as the Norwegian Professor, but soon after he arrived in 1868, he reacted strongly against what he perceived as an "Americanization" spirit among the Swedes. He became the leader of the movement to separate the Norwegian congregations from the joint Augustana Synod, since Weenas' desired unity within the broader Norwegian religious community would never come via churches in such close association with a predominantly Swedish synod.

The Paxton experiment to create a jointly run Swedish and Norwegian school supported by a farming colony proved ill-fated. Launched right in the middle of the Civil War, when immigration had been virtually cut off, very few families bought land, even after several extensions of the deadline. Probably more important, once the war was over, was the fact that the distance from Swedes in Minnesota and most of the Norwegian settlements made the Illinois school much less central to the westward expanding geography of the synod. Hasselquist sought to hold things together among the Swedes after the Norwegian section of the synod left in 1870. Even within the remaining Swedish fellowship, however, growing distances from Paxton challenged Hasselquist's efforts to concentrate efforts of the synod.

The twelve years in Paxton, Illinois, represented a short interlude in the overall development of the synod, but the time spent there established Hasselquist's influence, especially on new pastors. From 1863 to 1875, Hasselquist provided the main theological instruction for 129 pastors and developed a program of study adapted to the theological and spiritual needs of Swedish immigrants in America. In 1875, the seminary left Paxton and moved to Rock Island, Illinois, near the established settlements in Andover and Galesburg.

Theological Battles

Alongside the economic and physical difficulties that eventually forced the synod to move out of Paxton, a theological battle had been brewing that would compel Augustana leaders to articulate more clearly their doctrinal and ecclesiological understanding for the immigrant community. The conflict had also been stirring within the revival movement in Sweden, and developments there had an impact on American congregations as the pace of immigration increased after the Civil War. The problem was that as believers found their way to Swedish settlements, they often did not recognize immigrant churches as equivalent either to their familiar revival gatherings or to the parish church of the homeland.

Augustana congregations had developed in response to the immigrant setting and had become more open to the broad needs of the immigrant community. In effect, Augustana churches had become less focused on the Swedish revival and had failed to or refused to keep up with newer developments. While revival leaders had become more critical of the established Church of Sweden and enjoyed a kind of theological freedom from enforcing correct understanding of doctrine, in America challenges from other Lutherans forced Augustana pastors to articulate and defend their Lutheranism. Erland Carlsson in Chicago experienced this first hand when an immigrant, Martin Sundin, asked in 1864, "Are there no believers in this church?" Carlsson indicated a revival in 1857, but Sundin was not impressed. He could only locate a couple of people in Chicago who shared his fresh Swedish sentiments.[38]

Hasselquist and Carlsson responded to these challenges by maintaining a robust visiting schedule to congregations. At the same time, the synod proceeded at a good pace in 1868 to educate members about organizational dimensions of an American church body. Delegates spent long hours drafting and revising constitutional language in order to create uniform practices throughout the expanding territory of the church, and church leaders proposed new responsibilities for conferences, dispersing leadership but also creating an additional layer of institutional structure.

The new constitution proposals for accepting and transferring members from Sweden and between congregations spelled out an approach to church membership that was a direct affront to revivalists, who advocated a more personal and rigorous approach to church membership. They advocated that each individual be known to the congregation and his or her spiritual life be subject to correction, so that a congregation would consist only of true believers who lived above reproach. They called this type of congregation a "pure congregation," as opposed to the lax folk church of the homeland. Augustana's reception of immigrants as members of their congregations without demanding proof of religious conviction seemed to set the stage for the same social problems that plagued the Church of Sweden.

If Augustana seemed loose in relation to accepting of ordinary members, revival believers found the synod to be inexplicitly rigid in relation to accepting the credentials of preachers. Hasselquist and other synod ministers stipulated that they had to study for at least a year at the synod's seminary in Paxton. A preacher named John Anjou who had recently arrived from Sweden came to the annual meeting of the Augustana Synod in Carver, Minnesota, in 1868. He sought affiliation with the synod. Hasselquist wrote: "A young farm boy apparently just arrived from Sweden, presented himself as a minister. . . . He made an unpleasant impression on me because of his conceit." Per Sjöblom, a fierce defender of orthodoxy and rules, explained the confusion to a friend in Sweden: "In a country as full of sects as this one, it is absolutely necessary for a Synod to make use of only those men who have the needed credentials. Brother Anjou seemed to interpret the reluctance to use him, before he was known, as rejection of him and withdrew from us, which bred new suspicions."[39]

A theological dispute finally severed ties between revivalists and more traditional defenders of Lutheranism. The issue at stake was the doctrine of the atonement. On a local level the dispute had deep personal ramifications. Anna Olsson, the wife of immigrant pastor Olof Olsson, who emigrated to Kansas in 1869 with a tightly woven religious fellowship, kept up a correspondence with friends in Värmland. In describing her husband's travel, however, she gave a glimpse of the moment when the simple, pious community she and her husband had set out to create became more complicated: "Olle has already been to a pastor's meeting in a city called Molin [sic], seven hours train ride from here. And he has preached here a few times."[40] Olof Olsson had not just gone to a meeting of revival-oriented pastors and preachers but had linked up with the Swedish-American pastors of the Augustana Synod.

He would, through this association, later become a theological professor, president, writer, and inspirational leader. First, however, he would experience many trials.

Immigrating via Chicago connected Olsson with the Swedish-American pastors, as they were familiar with each other from work they had done together in the Swedish missionary societies. Would an association with Hasselquist, Norelius, Carlsson, and Swensson help the Lindsborg colony? For fervent members of Olsson's company the practices of the Augustana Synod caused suspicion. They worried that belonging to a synod could itself bring the contamination of formalism, and association with strangers might dilute their ideal of an intimate, whole-hearted spiritual fellowship. Anna's writings gave a bird's-eye view of the development of church conflict among the settlers. After reporting in several letters dated 1870 to 1874 that a kind of harmony reigned within the settlement of dugouts and rough log homes, she reported that by 1875, a split had developed in the small congregation. "There are many conflicts now in the congregation," wrote Anna. "Olle does not always have calm days. No, there has been now a long period of strife. His old friends [but just some] have turned from his teaching and gone over to Waldenström's, which is a false teaching. Those who have separated call Olle spiritually dead, and they invent lies and stories."[41]

A violent rage seemed to have erupted on the other side: "Enemies became so rough in their ways that the upright in spirit saw clearly that it was pure anger and temptation." The raging conflict came to a head at an official church meeting. Anna wrote that "the enemies rejoiced that they would now have the chance to vote out the Pastor, and take over the church; but at the meeting the Lord God was there . . . 80 were for the Pastor, and only one vote for the enemy." Everything seemed to confirm for her words from David's Psalm 64: "Their own tongues shall make them fall." It was an emotional time for a pastor who was known for his sensitive and heartfelt way of preaching.[42] The conflict exacted its toll: Olsson left for Sweden shortly afterward on a trip to restore his mental and spiritual health. He did not return to his post in Lindsborg. Instead, when he returned in 1876, he became professor of theology at the new location for Augustana Seminary in Rock Island, Illinois.

The Augustana Synod in its first decade created a theological school to educate pastors and a newspaper to spread information. In 1860, at its founding synod meeting, thirty-six congregations and 3,748 communicants belonged to the Augustana Synod. There were seventeen pastors. In 1870, when the Norwegian group departed, the synod had forty-five pastors, ninety-nine congregations, and 16,376 communicants. The baptized membership added another 10,000. These 26,322 people represented only a small portion of the Swedish population. Other religious movements and American religious freedom offered stiff competition.

The Herculean effort to get a theological seminary up and running was accompanied by equally strenuous efforts to establish other schools and institutions in other regions. These began to provide a visible structure for the immigrant community. As the towns and cities developed and agricultural production expanded, former immigrants became settled citizens. Newly arriving immigrants now had recognizable Swedish–American communities to move into not only in Chicago, but also in Rockford and Moline in Illinois, Minneapolis in Minnesota, and farther west in Iowa and Nebraska. Older settlements in western New York, Pennsylvania, Indiana, and Wisconsin also continued to grow. In this as in other respects, the immigrant community in America was no stranger to the sweeping changes in society both at home in Sweden and in America. In the next generation impulses for change were closer to home: among their children, in America.

DOCTRINAL CONTROVERSY:
AUGUSTANA AND THE MISSION FRIENDS

Olof Olsson came to Lindsborg, Kansas, in 1869 with hopes to conduct missionary work among freed slaves or Native Americans, but also to found what revival believers called a "pure congregation." The ideal of a pure congregation of believers was dear to the revival in Sweden, where the awakened were frustrated with the dormant spirituality of the established church. A pure congregation meant a fellowship of believers actively engaged in pursuing a life in Christ. In a pure congregation, the sacrament of Holy Communion would be celebrated by a congregation of believers, not by a mixed company of indifferent, habitual, churchgoers. In the context of the Swedish established church, the severe application of church discipline this would demand would have brought on civil challenges. In America, the separation of church and state made the ideal a real possibility, or so thought Olsson. But in Kansas, he soon became a pragmatist. He learned that excluding all but those who could testify to a saving encounter with Jesus would not serve all the settlers. Immigrant congregations would have to include a mix of people.

In Lindsborg the median piety seemed quite high, but this did not prevent the eruption of serious theological disputes. Believers in America followed developments in the revival in Sweden, and arguments found their way across the ocean. The most damaging disagreement among Swedish settlers occurred when Paul Petter Waldenström, revival leader in the mid-1870s in Sweden, challenged the church's understanding of atonement and rejected an aspect of traditional Lutheran teaching. Waldenström took a stance against the Lutheran Confessions at a time when he was also estranged and bitter over difficulties in getting an appointment as a rector, a post assigned by the Church of Sweden. Church authorities were wary of Waldenström's advocacy of lay preaching and questioned his theological views.

Traditional teaching on the atonement followed the medieval theologian Anselm's view that Jesus' death on the cross was a once and for all, completed atonement that satisfied a wrathful God. Waldenström instead claimed that God's mind had not been "changed" by Jesus' sacrifice and demanded that scholastics show him "where it is written" that God had been changed. Instead of a once and for all atonement through the cross, Waldenström put the focus on the believers' acceptance of Christ's suffering, which changed the sinner. The effect of Jesus' death on the cross was to draw sinners to recognize God's love, and the suffering was effective when it confronted the individual. Salvation became a subjective, rather than objective process.

Needless to say, the subtleties of theological reflection rendered believers suspicious of each other. They did not know whom to trust, now that the charismatic Waldenström charted a new path. Throughout the controversy in Lindsborg and in his book on the dispute, *Reformationen och Socinianismen* (*The Reformation and Socinianism*), Olsson argued that the church must remain Lutheran.[1] The debate was technical, bitter, and personally grueling for the spiritually sensitive Olsson. The rancorous atmosphere sent him into depression. He lost longstanding friendships, and fellow believers decided to leave and establish a congregation that could be free in spirit and unfettered by Lutheran dogmatic disputes.

Doctrinal controversies surfaced in practically every Swedish community during the 1870s and into the 1880s. The Augustana Synod constitution demanded a strong confessional subscription. Olsson wrote long arguments for the synod's newspaper. Moving to Rock Island, Illinois, in 1879, he prepared students at Augustana for pastoral controversies they would face. The growing college also became a place where Olsson could communicate something of his own free spirit, which had been dampened during the disputes. He started societies for young people, introducing them to literature, music, and art.

Olsson was a strange protagonist for orthodoxy, and perhaps because of this, its most effective advocate. Having attended a performance of Handel's *Messiah* in London he came back to Illinois so enamored of the event that he introduced it to the college. The *Messiah* is still performed each December at Augustana College and during Holy Week at Bethany College in Lindsborg, where it was introduced by Carl and Alma Swensson. Olsson's popularity in the synod was based on his creative and contagious spirit, not on his defense of orthodoxy. When

someone with his generous and free spirit would insist on staying with the dry and unmoving Lutheran Confessions, then perhaps even revival believers could stay moored to Lutheranism.

The dispute in America resulted in a separate Swedish denomination, the Mission Covenant founded in 1885. This Swedish denomination survived at first with support from the American Congregationalists, who made inroads into Swedish revival circles especially in New England, where Mission Friend preachers became their home mission agents.

It was almost an inevitable part of the Americanization process for Lutherans also to define themselves vigorously on theological terms. To modern readers doctrinal debates seem quite overwhelming. The subtle, precise points of doctrine to be defended kept theological professors in seminary faculties on their toes. They were frequently called upon to defend the position of their church. In Norwegian and Midwestern German communities, debates over predestination divided seminaries and church bodies. Danish Lutherans fought over Grundtvig's idea of the living word and the pietist devotion to the Bible as God's Word.[2]

In 1887, Olof's wife Anna died. In his bereavement and the depression that followed, he found solace in writing. He published his musings in *Det Kristna Hoppet* (*The Christian Hope*), a book about what the Christian could expect after death. At the synod meeting in 1888, two guardians of orthodoxy, S. P. A. Lindahl and Peter Sjöblom, brought charges against Olsson. Lindahl had a reputation for guarding the old piety while

Sjöblom often got into disagreeable arguments on the synod floor over fine points of the constitution and had a reputation for attacking people. An inquisition of sorts transpired.[3] Olsson resigned his professor role and also pulled back from fundraising and newspaper writing in order to recover his emotional balance. Olsson's friend Carl Swensson offered him a kind of respite in the form of a solicitor job for Bethany College, which was then in serious financial trouble. So Olsson moved far away from Rock Island and back to Kansas to avoid scrutiny. But with his new position he needed to travel, write funding appeals, and raise money. Unfortunately, he was not up to the rigors of promotion, and he buckled under the load. Carl Swensson did what he could to recover the situation. At the next synod meeting in 1889 a collection was taken to help Olsson restore his health in Europe.

Olsson retained bitterness toward the men who controlled the synod and conference meetings and who had turned them into places of posturing and scrutiny. When he got to Germany in August 1889, he put his thoughts down on paper in a letter to Swensson. The synod's newspaper and especially its editor S. P. A. Lindahl grieved him:

> If you only knew how hideous *Augustana* appears to me now. But I should not say anything because I was myself a mighty and vigorous warrior. . . . So for twenty years I have helped to build a church body where I am now wholly in the dog house, a denomination whose honored and leading men burn with unquenchable fanaticism.

> I just now sat and read "The year of horror in Lindheim" a true story from a witch burning time. These words "you cannot afford any sympathy with witches; those who persecute them do God a service," apply to Augustana in relation to me, who through God's word cherishes the hope of mercy for poor unfortunate persons.[4]

During the next year, Olsson thanked Swensson for advancing his name in the synod but thought that a call to a small congregation would be the only thing that he could possibly accept. When a congregation near Rock Island extended him a call, he expected that the watchdogs would come out from the seminary to spy on him.

The synod's younger leaders who had defended Olsson through his ordeal gained some wisdom after seeing what kind of mean-spirited atmosphere had been created through charging someone with heresy. Swensson traveled to Sweden in the summer of 1889 after the synod meeting, and circulated in the old orbit of his father's friends among the Mission Friends. There he heard Paul Petter Waldenström and later gave a report of it in his book, *I Sverige*: "Waldenström disappointed some of the American Mission Friends—they'd expected a brilliant speaker—but instead heard a simple Bible message. Augustana and the Mission Covenant share the same spirit, and in Sweden the atonement theory of Rosenius is also held by Mission Covenant people in preference to Waldenström's." In effect, he told his American audience, that except for some pockets the hard fighting was over.

In 1891, T. N. Hasselquist died, and the controversy over Olsson's orthodoxy withered. Another professor, Revere Weidner, the solid confessionalist of the General Council, also took his leave from teaching at the Rock Island seminary and moved to Chicago. The synod elected Olsson to take the professorship and the presidency of the school. The amazing turn around in his fortunes showed that a dogmatic spirit, even when it seemed fiercely present, could not in the end become the defining characteristic of the seminary or the synod. Carl A. Swensson wrote privately to Olsson to signal his support when his name would come before the synod: "God bless us with a large measure of his spirit of love and little, nothing, of Sjöblom's and Lindahl's cardinalesque—and popish—diplomacy."[5]

chapter 3
MISSION IMPULSES

ANYONE IN THE ORBIT OF A SWEDISH-AMERICAN CONGREGATION was exposed to missionary ideas. *Augustana* and *The Missionary*, two names and two themes that wove in and out of the synod's newspaper venture, represented the Swedish-American version of the enthusiastic missionary movement in Europe and in America. During the latter half of the nineteenth century, a transatlantic mission interest kept Swedish and American believers connected for more than two decades, since a large number of students studying for missionary careers at Swedish institutes became pastors in immigrant congregations in America instead. They carried their adventuresome vision for ministry to their work in America and were important voices for keeping missionary ideals alive among Swedish Americans.

Carl Frederick Johansson came to Boston in 1874 after an abbreviated tour as a missionary in the Sudan. His story illustrates how a missionary career represented a way out of the traditional life for a young man in rural Sweden. The personal account of his early boyhood and education in Sweden is a "call" narrative that relates how he came to become a missionary first and then a Lutheran pastor. Written for his children in 1902, Johansson's autobiography provides insight into the important role the local priest played in recognizing talent in young boys. Having learned the alphabet from his father, the young Johansson earned a small coin and was sent off to a neighbor woman who taught village children. His lessons focused on learning to "respect God and recite the catechism."[1] Reading and recitation were public exercises and boisterous. Readers spoke the texts—hymns, Bible verses, devotional messages, and parts of the catechism—aloud with gusto. When the priest came to "hear" the family (*husförhör*)—an official visit to examine the religious status of households—Carl Frederick pressed forward and recited as if on a march. Bits of Luther's explanation of the First Article of the Creed were mixed with portions of the Seventh Petition of the Lord's

Prayer. The story must have circulated in the family for many years. Amused but also impressed, the priest spoke to the boy's father.

Carl Frederick's hopes for an education soared upon overhearing the exchange between the priest and his father. He hoped to follow the traditional path into the profession, for he knew that bright farm boys noticed by the local priest could hope to go to university and enter the ministry. His father, however, had no trust in promises by upper class folk. Years passed and Johansson felt that a future life away from the farm would slip away. So he sought a way out of farming by joining a sharp shooter's club. He dreamed of a military career until, as he related, "God's word, like a sword, changed my heart in a total conversion from darkness to light."[2] His friends wondered about his mental state, for he became intensely interested in religious literature. As a "reader" (*läsare*) he sought knowledge about the world and God's mission. The Swedish newspaper *Mission Tidings* contained helpful reports from the Hermannsberg mission society.[3] As Johansson awakened to the great need of the heathen, he became a mission friend and decided to train for missionary service when the first Swedish-run school was opened, in 1867.[4]

In 1868, Johansson was one of eight missionaries from the *Evangeliska Fosterlands Stiftelse* who went to the Kunama people in East Africa, in the western part of Eritrea. In his autobiography, Johansson recalled how he "couldn't silence the inner voice and command."[5] After a long journey down the Nile and across the desert to the Kunama region, the missionaries encountered Arab slavers, hostile tribes, and the extreme physical challenges of a broad, treeless, and pathless plateau. They fell ill with tropical fever, but Johansson and one other missionary survived the journey to the mission post, Kulloko, on the banks of a branch of the White Nile. The tribal language seemed to the missionaries to lack religious concepts, making evangelical work difficult, but the people appreciated Johansson's hunting prowess, no doubt gained from his training as a sharp shooter. But Arab slavers came on a raid, and the missionaries failed to protect the villagers. The Kunama people turned hostile, believing that instead of protecting them the missionaries had created a target. After being warned, the missionaries escaped from hiding places under their beds. Tropical fever set in again on the voyage home.

Serendipity Revisited

Missionary Johansson's health remained precarious for some time. He spent the summer of 1873 at a health spa in Carlsbad, Germany, hoping to return to missionary service. That same summer, Chicago pastor Erland Carlsson traveled to Sweden to retrieve his daughters from school there. Carlsson was raising money to rebuild after the 1871 Chicago fire and recruiting pastoral candidates through Peter Fjellstedt, missionary promoter and old friend, with whom his own story had intersected twenty years before. Just as Carlsson had been the right man at the right time for the call to Chicago, twenty years later, Carl F. Johansson returned to Sweden just in time to become the right man at the right time for Boston. Carlsson convinced Fjellstedt to recommend Johansson for the seafarers mission in Boston, a mission supported by Swedish dollars. Johansson's ministry there broadened when he was ordained a pastor in the Augustana Synod.

Carl's remarkable journey was written in 1902 on a rainy day in Brattle-boro, Vermont, as a testimony to his family. The family shared portions of his story in the synod's devotional annual, *Korsbaneret* ("The Banner of the Cross"). The dramatic experience of immigration, in its many personal manifestations, was extended to a new generation through this journal. Reading these deeply revealing personal portraits helped the Augustana people gradually to gain a deep sense of shared kinship. No one could really hide in the synod. Ordinary lives were important models, for in the simple language of scripture, they too could be hailed as one of the "quiet in the land."

Mission as a Life-Shaping Outlook

Carl Johansson's journey out of a farming career is typical of the first generation of pastors in the Augustana Synod. Many ambitious young men missed out on a classical, university-oriented education in Sweden. The revival circles that Johansson frequented also provided important opportunities to develop skills at speaking and preaching to a supportive circle of listeners. Many of these young men first heard about opportunities for further education in these small, local, mission meetings. When they came to America, these men received a second chance at an education and a future.

This mission-oriented network brought many leaders to the Augustana Synod. Olof Olsson wrote to Hasselquist in 1868 inquiring whether it would be possible for him to come to America, and for at least a part of the year be a missionary to the Negroes. His real desire was to do mission work with them, and he inquired about a congregation that would be satisfied with a "teacher" who would not be with them all the time. "Could Swedish Lutheran mission work among the African American freed slaves be started in a state at not too great a distance from Swedish settlements?" he inquired.[6] Hasselquist heard also from P. A. Ahlberg, the rector of the missionary training institute. "It is heavy on my heart that my school might provide a service in love for the American Negroes," wrote Ahlberg. "I have made this possible mission a theme in my newspaper, and have even received money towards this. Three well prepared students have begun to learn English."[7] Ahlberg planned a trip for them in 1869 and wanted to know if Hasselquist's school in Paxton could help in training.

Ahlberg's letter was more like a brainstorming session than a list of concrete proposals, but the very loose nature of his questions suggested that Hasselquist would know his mind. He finally proposed that if it were not feasible to go to the Negroes and there start a Lutheran mission work, perhaps his students could do mission work with Native Americans or be trained in America to serve in another part of the heathen world. Ahlberg was scouring the world to find a way to get his students into missionary service because he had far more candidates and money than real missionary stations. America seemed like a real possibility because new settlements could conceivably be places of missionary work. We have seen already how early reports in the synod's paper, *Hemlandet*, included stories from Minnesota about contact with Native Americans. Similar stories circulated out of Kansas. The freeing of the slaves created a large, needy population. Swedish imagination about America was woefully deficient when it came to geographical understanding, but missionary leaders like Ahlberg gradually came to understand that the needs of Swedish immigrants also constituted a mission field.

Mission Societies and an American Spirit

Augustana's early orientation to the missionary movement showed up in institutional ways, too. A missions committee was the first working committee formed by the synod. Minutes were not kept until the eighth year, when an official minute book appeared. In its opening pages, the Augustana attention to history was evident. The secretary left space for the early history to be recorded and suggested that, "Pastor Carlsson in Chicago should best be able to provide this." This note in the margins testified to the role that the Chicago pastor played in shaping the missionary orientation of the synod.

The first meeting recorded for the committee occurred in Berlin, Illinois, on the July 30, 1868. Already the committee was almost exclusively focused on what later became known as "home mission," as opposed to "foreign mission." Home mission efforts brought tracts, preachers, and funding for church planting to frontier communities. Augustana's people had themselves been beneficiaries of the home mission efforts of Eastern Lutherans. The American term became Augustana's *hemmission*, and referred to work on Augustana's own frontier in western Iowa and Nebraska and further south into Kansas. At the September 1868 meeting, the committee passed a resolution: "Resolved: that in the Lord's name call Pastor S. G. Larsson in Knoxville as *missionary* at the next synod meeting to work specifically in Omaha, Nebraska; and *if the Lord gives there an open door* to erect a Swedish Evangelical Lutheran congregation in connection with the Augustana Synod."[8] A new step had been taken with this simple action, for the committee for missions, and not a congregation, "called" a pastor to this work of planting congregations.

The need for pastors to start congregations—to do mission work—changed the synod into a mission-oriented, future-leaning church body. America's landscape made all of its churches focus on their future ministry and not on their limited, local terrain. When the synod's missions committee called pastors for congregations yet to be formed, it took on functions that Lutherans traditionally had reserved for a settled church.

The language of the missions committee reflected the rhetoric of mission and revival popular with nineteenth-century Protestants. The great mission field Augustana encountered was with its own people. For the most part mission work was conducted by neighboring pastors who took on extra responsibilities and went on repeated trips to preach, baptize, and prepare young people for confirmation. The shortage of pastors meant that almost every congregation in the synod shared their pastor with neighboring settlements. The missions committee brought order to new incoming requests. Members of the committee consisted of the president of the synod and leaders who lived near at hand and were able to come to meetings in the president's home congregation. From July 1868 to the summer of 1870, when Jonas Swensson was president, meetings were held in Berlin, Illinois.

The mission committee's members all hailed from Illinois and Iowa, and they knew first-hand of the needs in their conference, so naturally their focus at first was on Kansas, Nebraska, and Iowa. The synod was growing, however, and pastors from several areas of the country pushed the synod to draft a new constitution, in large part to regulate mission work and put each region on an equal footing. Informal methods of letter writing, personal requests, and meetings of the whole, would no longer suffice to manage the task of a church body that was becoming an American denomination.

In 1870, the synod adopted a new constitution and directed mission work through conferences.[9] The Minnesota, "Central" (including neighboring states around Illinois), and New York Conferences created mission committees that would report to the central mission committee of the synod. The Augustana Synod in this way began to develop a structure that dispersed leadership but increased the need for overt efforts to centralize decision making at the synod level, so as to keep all the conferences and their ambitious leaders pulling with each instead of in opposite directions.

In the fall of 1870, the first item of business for the central mission committee was "a general discussion of the great spiritual need." A request from the Minnesota Conference for a mission pastor came next on the agenda. The committee referred them to the just adopted constitution, Article II, paragraph 4, where the role of the central board was clearly outlined: "The missions committee in each conference shall find and recommend to the central board capable and proven men, and if approved, determine the work and area of service, and provide oversight. At least four times a year the conference president shall report on the progress and funds appropriated for mission work."[10]

The constitution also stipulated how mission support should be generated in each congregation: "Every conference shall not only work for the awakening of Christian spirit and true mission zeal in their congregations, but also seek to introduce an ordered system for the gathering of means for mission and for other charitable institutions." Further, the constitution stipulated that every congregation should have mission prayer meetings every month, and establish a systematic way to gather mission gifts.

By reorganizing mission outreach, the synod could prepare for more expansion. The synod had clearly changed in character along with its growth during the 1860s. Through planning for mission and systematizing the work of conferences and congregations, a more "Americanized" spirit had entered the church. Norwegian members of the Augustana Synod responded negatively to the systemization and organizational structures. The synod had become dominated by Swedes, since the growing congregations and new settlements were almost exclusively Swedish. Norwegian members began to articulate reasons for separating from their Swedish companions; this largely had to do with their mission orientation, to become a more influential force in uniting Norwegian Lutherans. August Weenaas, the Norwegian professor at Paxton since 1868, became the leader for those who advocated separation. Weenaas perceived that the separated Norwegian immigrants also needed a church body to unite them. As long as the Norwegian moderates (his view of where the Augustana Norwegians fell on the spectrum of Norwegian Lutheran piety) were tied to the Swedes, this would never happen. Swedes had become too Americanized. "Business matters have come to the fore in the meetings, which have lost their original edifying character," wrote Weenaas. This had affected also the

baptisms. Augustana's mission pastors, even if they were straight out of seminary, had to do as Lindberg had and don a role as a true defender of Augustana's theological positions. Lindberg so imbibed this regimented theological spirit that he later become professor of dogmatics at the seminary. Mission areas throughout the synod, and especially in cities like New York, Boston, Worcester, Chicago, and Minneapolis demanded a kind of "company loyalty," or at least a cultivated deference to synodical decision making, as Swedish Lutheranism debated its way to a uniform understanding of doctrine and church order. C. F. Johansson, having come from the mission field in Africa to carry out evangelical work among sailors in Boston, now also found himself defending a Lutheran understanding of church order. Swedish Lutherans in the Campbello neighborhood of Brockton, Massachusetts, needed him to help them back into a churchly formation after Princell's railing against "Augustana popes" subsided.

As seminary professor, it was clear to Hasselquist that all the students, especially those sent out into the mission areas, needed careful instruction in ecclesiology. An inquisition of sorts commenced within the Augustana ranks, and young candidates were grilled on sensitive doctrines and were required to preach an orthodox sermon before the ministerium on the doctrine of the atonement before they were approved for ordination.[12]

The move to enforce doctrinal clarity alienated some of those who became church members because of a spiritual experience. They did not want to belong to an exclusive organization. They believed that these debates in effect showed that the mission impulse seemed to have run its course. The architects of organization, however, were building new foundations for the further development of the synod. At the end of the 1870s two significant contingents of people left the synod, choosing not to follow a program they deemed to be too tightly ordered ("churchly") and businesslike. When the Norwegian pastors left the synod meeting, they were able to conduct their business in the nearby Jenny Lind chapel, where barely fifty people could be comfortably seated. The more important alienation occurred between the "churchly" Lutherans and "Mission Friends," for they both claimed the Swedish revival as their lodestone. Instead of drawing people together, however, the revival had sparked dissension.

As Augustana leaders pushed for stability within the immigrant religious community, they claimed the name and theological tradition of Lutheranism. This label eventually drew them into association with the contested field of American Lutheranism. The "Mission Friends" sought to avoid further doctrinal controversy by leaving the Augsburg Confession to the Lutherans and relying instead on what seemed to them a more simple biblical authority for defining their beliefs. They no longer claimed to be Lutheran. Swedish immigrants thus became unique among American Lutheran groups since they had only one Lutheran church within their ethnic community. Germans, Eastern State Americans, Norwegians, Danes, Finns, and Slovaks all fought over the content of their Lutheranism and together made every one of the several groups self conscious of their own confessional standing. This happened especially in the Midwest, where the staunch Missouri Synod Lutherans challenged the legitimacy of every interpretation of scripture and confession that they did not themselves produce.[13] Augustana's leaders became self conscious of their Lutheranism partly because of the inter-Lutheran fighting around them, but they were lucky in their own development that the simple believers who cared more for spiritual talk than for definition, decided to let the Lutheran combatants have the name.[14]

Mission impulses were not paramount, but remained as an important dimension of this new Lutheran self-understanding in the Augustana Synod. It was the job of the mission committee of the synod not just to start a congregation, but to start a properly ordered, Lutheran Augustana congregation, one that would quickly adopt an official constitution, send their delegates to the annual meeting, and support the seminary and fledgling college. In a remarkable way, the lives of believers in ordinary congregations continued uninterrupted. Mission meetings continued in local congregations, and the mission committee of the synod provided a place to discuss ongoing disputes and disruptions in congregations. What had changed was the business of mission. The synod mission committee related to a growing institutional structure of boards, commissions, and official reports. These aspects of denominational development were in one sense a continuation of the mission societies and mission impulses that had inspired pastors like C. F. Johansson to go out as a missionary, but the structures that formed in America became the foundations for the functioning of a denomination, a church body. Though they retained the title of mission, they fostered a devotional spirit within congregations, according to a schedule.

Harnessing the Mission Spirit

Pastor Olof Olsson, who in 1868 had written to Hasselquist about the possibility of a ministry to freed slaves or Indians, was called to a congregation in Kansas in 1875. His hope was that this location would somehow allow him to pursue his missionary ambitions. He got his wish upon leaving his congregation in Kansas for a trip south into Indian territory, where he investigated possibilities and determined that missionary work with the Pawnee tribe would be a good possibility for the synod. Olsson's enthusiasm for the venture sparked an interest throughout the synod, and soon the large sum of

$15,000 had been collected, generating hope that a substantive mission was really possible. Olsson's ability as a fundraiser was also duly noted by other synod men.

With this support the missions committee sent Johannes Teleen, who was then a pastor in the western region of Des Moines, Iowa, to visit more extensively in Indian territory and send in a report. Teleen's initial contact was with a chief and pastor to the Delaware Indians, a Rev. Journeycake. The Delaware Tribe was made up of the historic people who had lived in the Swedish Delaware Colony and who had been forced to relocate in the West as part of the larger American process of Indian removal. Members of the Augustana Synod, therefore, felt that perhaps they might claim some kind of proprietary responsibility for this tribe. While rain poured down outside his tent, Teleen wrote to express his disappointment upon learning that the Delaware Indian tribe had already been assigned to the Methodists. Swedish Lutherans would have to look further for an "open" station.[15] Teleen preached at several of these, which had apparently been subjected to several previous visitations. One Indian told him that Teleen's preaching finally explained something about Christianity. That tribe had Quaker missionaries assigned to them, who apparently mostly kept pretty quiet and hadn't explained to the tribe much of their teaching about the inner light. This exploratory visit encouraged him to make a formal request that the Augustana Synod should also be assigned to a station in Indian territory.

The missions committee named Johannes Teleen to join Eric Norelius and Erland Carlsson in a delegation to Washington, D.C., to seek official permission to form a mission agency. Carlsson anticipated the bureaucratic delays ahead and told Teleen, "I think you should just go and be the missionary right away, and if we get an agency, fine, but if not, we'll still start the work." Teleen felt instead that the official permission would really make a difference. If they started work that was later given to another official agency, they would have to leave. The three men had contacts in Washington that seemed to give them access, but in the end, the effort was all for naught and fraught with the disastrous corruption of Indian Bureau politics. The agent they paid to get them access to an official disappeared, and the synod delegation had been out maneuvered by the rampant fraud in the system.[16]

Johannes Teleen then took a separate tour to investigate Indian territory once again. He discovered this time that white settlers around the Indian agencies were hostile to ministers, and Indian tribes did not know whom to trust. When Teleen first entered Indian territory, he wore his Swedish *prästrock*—priest garb—with tabs, and was instantly recognized at one town's borders, where they asked him, "Don't you know that we kill priests?"[17] Teleen also had shaved off his beard, knowing that Indians trusted those who had clean faces, but negotiating a peaceful place for work on the border between such hostile encampments made him fearful of taking such a call himself.

The missions committee tried again to interest him in taking any call to Indian territory, and then approached others, issuing calls three times, with no takers. They approached Teleen yet again, but he had a wife and two small children. The synod finally enlisted a student named Matthias Wahlstrom, who had indicated an interest in missionary work during his seminary studies. He agreed to take a call as a missionary to the Indian territory in Colorado, where there were also some beginning Swedish-immigrant communities near enough at hand that a mission effort could conceivably also include work among them. Wahlstrom accompanied Teleen on an exploratory visit to south Colorado and New Mexico. This venture also failed to result in more permanent work. According to contemporary accounts, Wahlstrom's health suffered, but the cultural shock of work in such a setting no doubt contributed to some kind of collapse, from which he needed several months to recover. During his recovery period he received and accepted a call instead to become president of Gustavus Adolphus College in St. Peter, Minnesota.

After Matthias Wahlstrom decided to leave Indian territory in Colorado to become a college president, the missions committee continued to lobby the government for permission to open a permanent station, but these efforts also failed. In the end the Augustana Synod realized that, in this case, due both to their lack of access to the right government agency and because they did not have the resources or wherewithal to provide for missionary work with the Indians near at hand, the door was closed. The needs of their own younger generation and the newly arriving young immigrants instead became their designated mission field.

PART 2
THROUGH 1910
50TH ANNIVERSARY

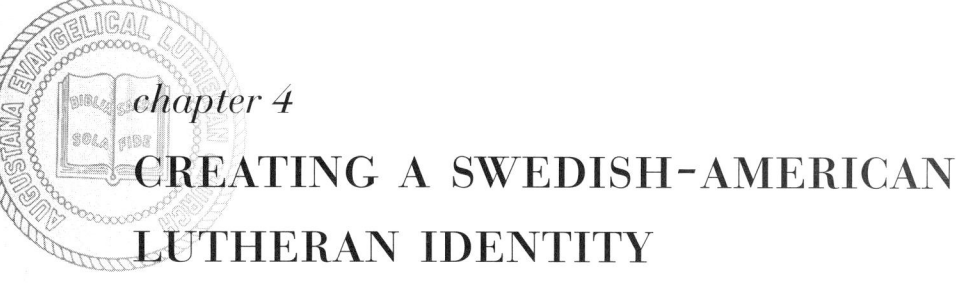

chapter 4

CREATING A SWEDISH-AMERICAN LUTHERAN IDENTITY

AUGUSTANA'S FIRST FAMILIES—the Hasselquists, Esbjörns, Carlssons, Swenssons, and Noreliuses—all arrived in the United States in the 1850s. Their pioneering work established a viable church connecting Swedish immigrants in widely scattered settlements, and they also advanced the hope that their religious work would shape the Swedish immigrant community in America in accordance with God's purposes. As true pietists, they focused on creating congregations and training pastors, but the needs of immigrants soon pressed them to expand their vision. Close to home, this meant training and educating their own children and the next generation of youth to be faithful Swedes, Americans, and Lutherans.

In the 1870s a new generation of young people filled the immigrant community. The years after the Civil War brought a wave of new immigration to the Midwest—to Iowa and Nebraska, north along the Mississippi and Missouri Rivers into Minnesota and the Dakotas, and south to Kansas and Missouri. The pioneer leaders had families with sons going into the ministry. Students from Swedish missionary schools, both Ahlborg and Fjellstedt, had completed their education under Hasselquist and swelled the ranks of leaders. The efforts to educate pastors had paid off as well. By 1875, there were more than a hundred pastors in the synod, even after twenty-three of them transferred into the Norwegian Augustana Synod in 1870.[1] With more congregations, a greatly expanded network of connected settlements, a corps of students studying not only in Illinois but also in Minnesota, and pastor/editors sending out newspapers from Chicago, Galesburg, Minneapolis, and Red Wing, the synod had multiple ways to communicate its program, even if the editors sometimes became competitive. Some of the changes spelled a loss for the spontaneity and friendship that had characterized early gatherings, but the common education pastors received at the seminary, the regular discipline of attending meetings, and the long deliberations that had been resolved over congregational membership practices had resulted in a ministerium and people who understood and shared a Lutheran confessional orientation and who genuinely knew and prayed for each other. The members of Augustana's congregations still felt like a family who kept in touch. The correspondence that had shaped them as a network of caring friends still functioned.

The Congregational Model for Learning

The revival spirit that had suffused the friendship circles of the first generation proved hard to replicate in the American geography of the growing synod. While a religious awakening within the Church of Sweden had to focus only on religious formation, Swedish-American Lutherans needed also to attend to a broader education for their children. American public schools did not include religious instruction at all, and young men who were needed for ministry could not get the classical preparation in one-room schoolhouses. Pastor Jonas Swensson, who came to the United States to serve the congregation in Sugar Grove, Pennsylvania, in 1856, resorted to hiring a Swedish tutor for his sons. Their instruction in Swedish history, the classical languages, literature, and hymnody replicated the kind of education aspiring clergy might receive in the homeland. Carl A. Swensson grew up hearing the stories of famous Swedish soldier kings and thrilled to the heroism of Gustavus Adolphus and Carl XII. Most parents were less choosy, but even ordinary farmers thought young people needed to be confirmed and probably needed language instruction in order to get much out of Swedish worship. Members of congregations realized that their church needed support to provide a religious and cultural education for their children.

Creating congregational schools and teaching children how to read in Swedish solved one problem, but youth arriving directly from Sweden demanded a different kind of effort. They didn't need a basic religious education as much as they needed orientation to the religious environment of Swedish America. What pioneer pastors saw in the youth coming into their congregations in the 1870s began to alarm them. According to Pastor Adolph Hult, born in 1869 in Moline, Illinois, the new arrivals were loose and wild, too much in love with freedom, and worst of all, a dangerous influence on the children of the pioneers.[2] The piety that had shaped the first generation would need to be taught.

Expanded immigration also brought more "worldly minded" settlers, forcing an adjustment of congregational programming. A church life that provided recreational and educational opportunities replaced devotionally focused meetings. This kind of program was implemented in Chicago's

Immanuel Lutheran congregation and became a model followed throughout the synod. Pastor Erland Carlsson's early ministry at Immanuel maintained a close connection to the seasons of revival that were occurring in Sweden, but by the time he wrote a history of the congregation in 1881, he detected a change in the source of new spiritual impulses. After noting that a spiritual outpouring occurred in Chicago directly upon the arrival of Swedish believers in 1857–1858, he observed that the second emerged in 1870 in the confirmation class. "It was a special time of seeking. A pentecostal wind blew through the garden."[3] Instruction focused on Christian experience and living. Carlsson felt this was only the beginning, for he extended his contact with the young people after they were confirmed. At Immanuel, each class moved automatically into a Bible class after confirmation, and each year the numbers of young people were so large that more than one class had to be started. During the twenty-two years he was at Immanuel, 558 young people were confirmed. In the first five years of his successor's ministry, another 307 young people were added. In the 1870s Immanuel established a successful pattern of ministry to youth, instructing them thoroughly in the catechism, and then creating ongoing social and religious experiences for them.

In the fall of 1871, the congregation built a new sanctuary, but within a few weeks, the great Chicago fire destroyed it. The devastated congregation dug in and rebuilt. By this time there were choirs, women's groups, and young people's societies to house. Even though 90 percent of the members had also lost their homes, they renewed their financial pledges. They shouldered not only the debts on the destroyed building but also committed more money to build a new building. Carlsson traveled back East to raise money among sympathetic Americans. Then he went to Sweden in 1873 and returned with a big collection as well as a gift from King Oscar. The disaster of the fire made Immanuel even more visible than it had been before, establishing it as a cultural and religious center for Swedish Americans. With musical and mission societies, a hospital in the works, a young people's society, book discussion group, and Sunday school Bible classes, the people in the congregation were busy every day of the week. The revival in the confirmation class of 1870 generated a spirit of commitment and support that spread far beyond the congregation's young people to include people throughout the synod.

As pastor of Chicago's largest Swedish congregation, Carlsson's influence in the synod was second to Hasselquist, but his example in emphasizing a youth-oriented educational ministry was the dominant model for the next generation of the Augustana Synod. Carlsson knew how to mobilize and inspire the large youth contingent in the immigrant congregation. His wisdom in focusing on youth made Immanuel a vibrant place, and many young

Augustana ministers in training hoped that they would also have a chance to come to Chicago and work as an assistant to Carlsson. Dozens of future leaders in the church, like Sven Peter August Lindahl, later publisher of the synod's newspaper *Augustana*, spent a couple of years at Immanuel, assisting with educational and pastoral work. The work was indeed daunting for one minister, and the extra strain of erecting two buildings in short order must have taken an enormous toll on Carlsson's physical and spiritual energies. In addition to congregational work, however, there were other initiatives that demanded Carlsson's attention. The congregation founded a school for its younger children in the facility that the seminary had occupied for a time before moving to Paxton. There were efforts underway to start a hospital in the city, and even a center for the training of deaconesses. Immanuel in Chicago had become a flagship congregation.

In 1873, while things were going well in Chicago, Carlsson's very good friend, Jonas Swensson, died suddenly of a heart attack, leaving behind his family, the presidency of the synod, and his congregational work in Andover, Illinois. Carlsson decided to leave Chicago and move his family to take up the work in Swensson's place. He returned from fundraising and assumed responsibility for the large mother church of the synod, which was by contrast a solidly country congregation. Carlsson moved to Andover just when the Augustana Seminary finally gave up work in Paxton, intending to relocate in Rock Island, a city on the Mississippi River about twenty miles north of Andover. Carlsson's old congregation in Chicago did not have to wait long for a successor, however, since Carl Evald, who had trained for awhile in Paxton after being recruited by Hasselquist in Sweden, was willing to move from Minneapolis to Chicago right away. He married Carlsson's older daughter Anna two years later, so the transition in leadership happened within the family.

Training New Leaders

The informal networks of trust and spiritual friendship that eased Carl Evald's path into leadership in Chicago still functioned as the next generation of Augustana leaders emerged. Augustana's network continued to grow, especially as the synod's schools expanded, creating the possibility for more and more young men to meet each other. Focusing on the education of future pastors, however, limited the possibilities for developing the leadership of the large numbers of other young men and women in congregations. Small steps were taken when the seminary in Rock Island added a college division and graduated its first class of young men in 1877. Colleges in Minnesota and Kansas were more innovative. Gustavus Adolphus, an inheritor of several educational ventures in Minnesota, was founded as early as 1862 and admitted women right away. Bethany College, in Lindsborg, Kansas, had a college division by 1887. The numbers of students in all the colleges stayed small throughout the 1880s, however, so the synod's wide-scale work with young people relied primarily on pastors in congregations.

In 1877, Augustana's church in Moline, Illinois, where students from the new campus in Rock Island worshiped, founded an association dedicated to the spiritual welfare of young men in the congregation. Peter Colseth, a prominent contractor and lay leader, served as the first chairman. Students at the college signed on as members. Carl A. Swensson, son of the pioneer pastor Jonas Swensson, served as secretary. Olof Olsson, a new theology professor at the seminary, who had his hand in many of the synod's creative ventures, wrote the constitution. The society meetings consisted of devotional readings, song, and prayer. The church in Moline served as the congregational home for future pastors of the synod, and the association provided a model for many other congregations. Meetings of the society also generated new ideas among the young people present. They knew they had a place and the opportunity to influence youth throughout the Swedish America.

The first college graduates of Augustana College in Rock Island and members of the Moline's young people's society began to think much bigger thoughts. It was as if they had been tapped for leadership.[4] At the end of the year, four faculty members and the six members of Augustana's senior class founded a publication society called *Ungdoms Vänner*, or "Friends of Youth," to spread throughout the synod devotional tracts and printed resources to prompt a revival in piety and a deeper spiritual life among young people.[5]

Other publishing ventures during the 1880s showed that Swedish-American Lutherans had a growing interest in a wide range of materials. The newspaper *Ungdomsvännen* provided an alternative news and features magazine targeted at the youth in the church. The Augustana Tract society responded by publishing more material to shape a new Swedish-American generation as loyal and enthusiastic church members. Recitations and literary exercises at society meetings created a market for short, dramatic poems and stories. These were performed on a weekly basis by the youth of Swedish America, so churches needed a pretty extensive library of resources. Into the breach stepped Olof Olsson and C. A. Swensson, who provided pages of inspirational stories and thematic articles not only on devotional topics but also on the history of Sweden and the literature of the homeland.

The magazine intended to promote a "true fear of God" as well as the spread of practical knowledge. In June, right after many young people were confirmed, an article focused on what it was like to live "among other confessions and unbelievers" and gave advice about holding onto confirmation promises. Other articles in the June 1 issue included a profile of several martyrs of the Reformation period, a portrait of the cathedral in Strasbourg, and a historical sketch of the book-printing trade in the city during the time of the Reformation and afterward. A characterization of "the worldly man" was number eleven in a series of such portraits. The magazine provided basic information to young people about a church-centered, Lutheran view of the Christian faith. The illustrated magazine had articles by several Augustana pastors and leaders giving perspective on practical Christian life in America's pluralistic religious environment, and it was written in vivid Swedish-American Swedish.

Swedish immigrants had begun to assimilate into the surrounding American life and had absorbed some of the progressive idealism of the late nineteenth century, too. They had been taught in school that America was a land of promise, and they believed they had a part to play in their nation's development. American-born Swedes also wanted to join almost anything, but for a start this meant congregational youth leagues, Sunday schools, and women's missionary societies. Graduates of the seminary were ambitious, too, and wanted to make their own mark on the church as executives, newspaper editors, and writers. The challenge facing the next generation of leaders was how to keep a distinctive Swedish-American ethos in the context of rapid Americanization. The new generation created a new kind of ethnic consciousness, neither immigrant, nor American, but both—Swedish American.

To foster a Swedish-American identity involved a dual process of providing instruction in the Swedish language that was particularly suited to the American context. The literary effort needed to teach youth first about the Lutheran faith and about the Lutheran church. Using Swedish materials helped in part, but soon it was apparent that immigrant children needed basic language instruction as well in order to understand the lessons. Bible history, church history, and the basic catechism were all well and good for dutiful confirmation students, but something lighter and more interesting for young people had to be provided as well. So the leaders of this literary venture emphasized Swedish arts, culture, literature, and history. Swedish-American Lutheran youth needed to hear about the heroes and high points of their Swedish heritage.

Challenging the Old Arrangements

The publishing work begun by the Friends of Youth (*Ungdoms Vänner*) society and the flowering of young people's societies here and there in the synod did not have the whole-hearted support of the old guard. The society promoted the establishment of societies in all the congregations of the synod and published Olsson's original constitution for young people's societies in the fifth edition of *Ungdomsvännen* in 1881. T. N. Hasselquist, still writing regularly for the synod's newspaper, *Augustana*, responded by issuing a warning. Far from building up the church, Hasselquist believed that instituting separate organizations for young people placed them in thrall to the whims of yet another institution. This posed a threat to the one society that had been founded by God: the congregation.[6] Hasselquist sensed that the new initiative among young people signaled a wider change in the synod, and his natural instincts for control of this new impulse emerged.

The old father of the synod, Tufve Nilsson Hasselquist, resisted this new effort not only because he felt that new societies challenged the preeminence of congregations and pastors, but also because the modest publishing ventures by the society challenged an earlier 1874 contract he had made when the synod sold its publishing house to the Chicago book firm, Engberg and Holmberg. The firm, whose owners belonged to the Immanuel congregation in Chicago, purchased the exclusive right to print the synod's newspaper and its books and devotional materials. Hasselquist's tenure as editor continued, but all decisions about publishing belonged to the firm. They had the understanding that no other publishing firm would produce materials for synod uses. The decision to sell the printing enterprise had been controversial, but proceeds from the sale had kept the seminary solvent. Almost as soon as the sale was official, there were regrets. Eric Norelius commented on the sale in his biography of Hasselquist:

> Since I have been blamed for being the one who had perhaps pushed the most for the separation of the synod from the old printing firm and sold out Hemlandet, the book concern, and the print house, which has since then been called the greatest idiocy, if not something worse, I shall here take the liberty to do a little explanation. Any action has to be judged according to its time and not according to a later context, if you want to judge it correctly.

Norelius recognized that leaders in the synod did in fact feel that they had to challenge this situation, if only to provide a way to communicate with the younger generation.[7] Norelius might also have noted that when the situation improves, you try to pick up the pieces. The charge of "idiocy" came from later recognition of the crucial role that newspapers, magazines, books, and printed reports played in the work of the synod. When church control over publishing was restored finally in 1889, it was too late for a centralized approach to young people's work. In the intervening years, ventures by new leaders to establish newspapers violated the gentleman's agreement that Norelius and Hasselquist had made. In spite of this, the new generation of leaders forged ahead with new publishing alliances.

After two years, the *Ungdoms Vänner* literary society incorporated as the Augustana Tract Society and directly challenged the Chicago firm. The stakes were high: books, magazines, and devotional tracts communicated with a broad and growing market, and arrangements that met the modest needs of the pioneer period could not satisfy a church that, in addition to expanding into Iowa and Minnesota, was developing new readers and new constituencies. The magazine was only one of several ventures by the team of Swensson and Olsson. They tried many publishing formats, large and small. The work that became the longest running of any serial for Swedish-American church people, *Korsbaneret* ("The Banner of the Cross"), came out in 1880. A small, pocket-sized, hardcover book of 157 pages, written in Swedish, was printed in Chicago by Enander and Bohman, another rival of the synod's ordinary publishing firm of Engberg and Holmberg.[8] It contained a Bible calendar with verses for every day in the coming year, along with poems and sermons that were typical fare for devotionally minded church people. Unlike other devotionals, *Korsbaneret* also contained historical sketches of the early years of pioneer settlement and detailed portraits of early congregational activities. Several Christmas meditations made it an attractive purchase as a year-end gift.

Korsbaneret called Swedish Lutherans to fall in line behind the advancing banner of the Augustana Synod. The series started out as a very church-centered production and stayed that way. In the first volume elements of the focus on pastoral leadership and congregational vitality appeared in the life sketch of the pioneer pastor and educator L. P. Esbjörn, in the drawing of the new parsonage for the congregation in Andover, Illinois, and in the extensive history of that congregation. Carl A. Swensson edited the volume and chose to present his father Jonas Swensson's story not only to pay tribute to his memory, but also to fashion stronger ties between the generations. He believed that the Augustana people also had their own history, and that telling that history was the way to foster pride and commitment.

Through the story of Jonas Swensson and the historic church in Andover, C. A. Swensson could also inform young readers about all the synod pioneers. Esbjörn had been the first pastor of that congregation, but the longer tenure of Jonas Swensson gave the writer the material he needed to develop the edifying message that might make the Andover congregation serve as the flagship model for other Augustana churches. Veterans of the synod's early years knew that when Esbjörn left the congregation in 1856, his successor, who remained unnamed in the story, failed utterly as an organizer and teacher. The congregation stood on the brink of a major split.

According to the history recounted in 1881, Methodist wolves were at the door. Jonas Swensson's arrival in 1858 rescued the situation. The new regime involved educating the young people in the fundamentals of the faith to clear up the confusion that afflicted so many believers.

The historical account went into great detail. It included an almost word-for-word version of the sermons delivered at Jonas Swensson's funeral, including the address by Olof Olsson based on Hebrews 13:7, the verse carved into the memorial stone erected by the congregation. A drawing of the monument provided one of the rare illustrations in the volume: "Think of your teachers who have delivered God's word to you, and consider the outcome of their way of life." Olsson then preached: "Such stones become living preachers for us missionaries and teachers, but the Holy Spirit works also in the hearts of the congregation, making them the teacher's epistle; their hearts are fleshly tablets that bear the mark of the words they have heard."[9]

Olsson and Swensson emphasized the personal dimension of history not only to tell the story of what happened in a congregation but also to give a moral lesson. Pious living and faithful struggle would win victories for the individual and for the church far greater than any worldly success. The aim to instill pride and loyalty among pious young people created a kind of churchly patriotism. Beginning in 1881 the *Korsbaneret* volumes sported a cover that emphasized humble victory—a lamb holding a cross banner, similar to those popularly used in nineteenth-century Sunday school processions, seated on an image of the Bible. The printing was in gold, on a cloth binding. The little books were handsome keepsakes. The publishers of *Korsbaneret* developed a devoted reading public, and in turn, well known leaders for Augustana's coming generation.[10]

The ties uniting Olof Olsson, C. A. Swensson, and Erland Carlsson circled around the congregation in Andover, Illinois, where the Augustana Synod had begun its organized work, and also in Lindsborg, Kansas, where so many creative efforts on behalf of youth were inaugurated by C. A. Swensson after he moved there to become president of the fledgling Bethany College. Swensson's vision of the grand legacy and immense promise of the Swedish-American people could be put directly to work when he became the president of a striving college on the Kansas plains.

The society at Augustana College also shaped a cadre of leaders for the synod who replicated the program in their various places of service. By 1881, the colleges of the synod had leaders or presidents who had all belonged to the *Ungdoms Vänner* literary society that Olsson had started. Olsson was the theological professor at Augustana in Illinois, Carl A. Swensson was pastor of the Bethany congregation and later founder of Bethany College in Kansas, and Matthias Wahlstrom agreed to serve as president of Gustavus Adolphus in St. Peter, Minnesota, after his failed attempt at missionary work in Colorado. Swensson and Wahlstrom had graduated in the first college class at Augustana in 1877.[11] The three schools did not enjoy stable financial support for the programs they envisioned, but they did have a reservoir of goodwill sustaining the ambitions of leaders. It was a pretty closed circle of influence, however. Bethany's president, Carl A. Swensson, received his job upon the recommendation of Olof Olsson who promised the congregation he would find a successor.

Swensson's almost meteoric rise to leadership in Lindsborg as well as in the synod came in large part from his prolific writing and publishing for an eager Swedish-American readership. Kansas was for him the land of opportunity. A promoter through and through, he had a lot at stake as he made a name for himself and the college. His fervent efforts to build the reputation of the school and recruit students created a national reputation for the educational institution and naturally triggered resentment.

The publication ventures that had been launched by the *Ungdoms Vänner* society had gone so well that a new college-based culture did in fact become the dominant feature of the young people's experience in the Augustana Synod. Rivalries among the colleges emerged, with students working hard to convince their sisters, brothers, and friends to join them at their college. Peter Froeberg, a student at Augustana Seminary at the turn of the century, tried to dissuade his brother, Sven, from attending Bethany. Eventually, however, Sven did fall for the allurements of the school in Kansas. Peter had so often derided the school founded by C. A. Swensson that he could not resist one more opportunity to ridicule the school in Lindsborg. When Augustana's football team was invited to a match up with Bethany he explained why the Augustana boys stayed home.

> As to the talk of the game between Bethany and Augustana, I believe that our team could easily have beaten yours because this year we have the best team we've ever had. But our faculty would not let our boys go to Bethany for several reasons. Our boys do not have the means to be away for a whole week during the time of exams. Further there is not much trust in the honesty of Bethany. Swensson could do what it is said he did before at a similar occasion, hire professional players who may or may not be associated with the school, and so on. On my part I've lost all respect for Swensson on the basis of his latest stupidities, intrigues, and hate filled newspaper articles. I will say that our president, Andreen stands, in relationship to character and honesty, so high over Swensson as the sun passes the moon.[12]

The competitive spirit among the colleges had by the turn of the century become quite intense, shaping strong regional loyalties and pulling at the older centralized pattern of Hasselquist. Another aspect of the shift can also be seen in the fact that in later years students boasted more typically of their football teams than of their presidents. The educational program of the synod generated a cadre of leaders and eager young people who could thank the church for newfound friendships and opportunities.

The funeral procession for Olof Olsson in January 1901 passes by the seminary and college in Rock Island, Illinois. The seminary building is in the foreground, with the main college building next to it. Although the road by the campus is not yet paved, there are trolley lines and electrical lines that indicate that the avenue is a main corridor in the city. Photo courtesy of Special Collections, Tredway Library, Augustana College.

As important as the colleges and seminary were for the formation of Swedish-American youth, these institutions still served only a small number of students, and very few women. The larger task of educating and training the next generation of Augustana youth would initially belong to the congregations, and especially to the church's young people's societies. One of the early societies in Andover, Illinois was formed in 1880. Its charismatic leader was Emmy Carlsson, another child of Augustana pioneer pastor

Erland Carlsson. The society's purpose was, according to its constitution, "To give the young people an opportunity to develop a useful and Christian personality; to procure a lending library of popular Christian books in Swedish and English; and to provide opportunity for expression by talks, declamation, discussion, song and music."[13] This model, pioneered in congregations throughout the synod, trained up a generation of young men, and even women, to become persuasive speakers and leaders.

Inviting Youth into the Wider Society of the Church

While newspapers and devotional books provided reading material for young people in their homes and congregations, young people at the colleges had themselves developed their own social programs—college football, singing clubs, and debating societies. These social programs, coupled with the official curriculum, shaped a growing number of ambitious Swedish-American youth. Just as the gilded volumes of *Korsbaneret* and the amply illustrated issues of *Ungdomsvännen* drew students to the schools, graduates influenced congregations to provide cultural programs to draw young people into their orbit. The college experience, and especially the literary societies on the campuses, became models for libraries, society rooms, and social outings for youth in congregations. Seminary and college students spent their summers running Swedish schools for children, where they also met young people and enlivened the meetings of the local societies. At the colleges, literary societies helped train teachers for these schools so that they would be adept in speaking and preaching a language that was otherwise uncultivated, and would become a remnant of childhood.

The energetic response of youth, both men and women, to these organizational efforts had a ripple effect throughout the synod. Congregation after congregation began to organize societies to promote Swedish culture and the Lutheran faith. Augustana congregations in places as far away as western New York or Orange, Massachusetts, developed small libraries to support the activities of congregational literary societies. The reading material came largely from the program inaugurated by *Ungdoms Vänner* to instill Swedish Lutheran pride in young people. The success of the program can be seen in the names chosen for local societies—such as "Idun"—indicating that a steady emphasis on Nordic imagery and ideals made a mark on Augustana's young people.

Ideally, congregations would begin the process of preparing young children and youth for an ever-deeper immersion into Swedish culture and faith, and in turn, these young people would come to the colleges ready for more strenuous work learning the classical languages and refining their use of the Swedish language. In actuality, the effort to promote a "high" Swedish culture in the colleges was a fragile enterprise, possible only for a couple of decades. Already in 1899, S. P. A. Lindahl, editor of the synod's largest Swedish-language newspaper, *Augustana*, addressed a growing difficulty faced by educators at the synod's schools—the Swedish language requirement. At the synod convention coming up in June of that year, the curricular focus of the schools would again be a matter for discussion, and the synod had to face some changes. Lindahl mapped out the debate over the instruction of Swedish, which had by 1899 become a factor in the attractiveness of the Swedish-American colleges to modern young people. "If obligatory Swedish drives a great deal of our Swedish-American youth to other schools, this should tell us something,"[14] Lindahl argued. He was by no means a progressive voice in the synod, but even he could sense the need for a more open policy, if only to promote what he believed was the ultimate aim of the church: to keep young people under the sway of its own leaders, at its own schools. "The question then becomes whether our schools have a greater and more important influence for Swedish culture and Lutheran faith through . . . making the study of Swedish a free choice." He allowed that there were differences of opinion on the matter, but that the experience of the educators should determine the outcome of the debate.

Lindahl argued against coercion and argued on pietist terms in the debate over the school's curriculum. Just as pioneers of the Augustana Synod realized that a free church environment in America had ultimately created a church life more lively than in the formal Church of Sweden, so also did love for Swedish have to be "awakened" rather than expected. Lindahl used old revival phrases to establish his point: "The Swedish language is certainly not preserved among us through coercive laws but through awakening love for it. If the aim for our schools is to show the beauty of our mother tongue and foster love for its rich literature they will best do this through keeping youth under their influence and not through driving them away." That this task of awakening love for Swedish was difficult is shown by the many turnovers in professors in Augustana College's Swedish department. Constantine M. Esbjörn, whom Olof Olsson dubbed "the most Swedish man in America," brought the study of Swedish to a high plane in 1883 but left in 1890. Johan Enander held the position for three years after that and then was dismissed. Ernst A. Zetterstrand occupied the post during the debate over compulsory study. He left in 1901 to take a parish call in Naugatuck, Connecticut, where more recent Swedish immigration made Swedish a more natural part of parish ministry.

Pastors speaking for young people, whether by providing literature or arguing for their inclusion in all aspects of synod life, became highly visible leaders. Their collective efforts to write, educate, and inspire young people would reshape Augustana as a modern denomination, but would also retain an important element from the tightly connected network of the founders. These leaders introduced young people in congregations both to expanded horizons and opportunities for their individual lives and to a wider conception of the purpose of the church. The relational networks that the pastors and young people created and renewed through these modern publishing ventures further maintained Augustana's strong feelings of unity and common purpose.

chapter 5

EDUCATION FOR A NEW
AMERICAN GENERATION

EARLY RECORDS OF THE AUGUSTANA SYNOD focus almost exclusively on the difficulties of maintaining a seminary. Congregations needed pastors, so providing an education for young men dominated the correspondence, newspaper appeals, and reports at conference and synod meetings. But speeches at synod meetings and even the articles in the official church paper tell only part of the story of how the synod created its common religious culture. Young men *and* young women needed to understand their religious heritage in order for them to participate in common endeavors. Swedish Americans had daughters too, and parents desired an education also for them. When young women began to sense that the church's vision and a program also included them, the synod became more than a ministerium, more than a board of directors for a small, struggling seminary, and the loose ties connecting congregations were deepened and strengthened.

Pioneer pastor Erland Carlsson and his wife Eva had four children. Immanuel, Carlsson's congregation in Chicago, operated a school where boys and girls received a Swedish education, learning to read, figure, and understand their faith in the Swedish language. This elementary school competed with the American public schools, so as young people began to speak English exclusively at home, the school's future was threatened, and so also was a church-sponsored education for young women. While the Carlsson boys, Eben and Samuel, could attend Augustana College in Rock Island, the Carlsson's daughters, Annie and Emmy, had no options for a church-based Swedish education once they finished primary school. When they exhausted the opportunities at home, they went to Sweden where they attended Cecilia Fryxell's school in Kalmar. "Mamsell" Fryxell was a pioneering educator, having devoted her career to designing an appropriate religious and cultural education for young women. Erland and Eva Carlsson knew her personally, and even though she was now at the end of her career, they persuaded her to postpone retirement in order to teach their daughters.[1] In 1870, fourteen-year-old Annie and thirteen-year-old Emmy became boarding students to receive an education they could not get in the United States.

The Carlsson girls received an education aimed toward women's needs, including devotional exercises, instruction in household management, and lessons in speaking, writing, natural history, and mathematics. Educating women, both in America and Sweden, created the possibility for significant change in society. Societal improvement had been part of the pietistic ethos of the revival, and in Sweden, Cecilia Fryxell's educational efforts drew heavily from these revival sensibilities, and attracted the daughters of the more prosperous among the pious. Eva and Erland Carlsson had attained a level of financial security through shrewd real estate investment in the rapidly growing city of Chicago. They were certainly not wealthy, but the Carlsson girls were not going to marry farmers. Their parents provided them with an education to prepare them for leadership in a refined, Swedish religious society.

The model of wealthy sponsorship of a pious school may have worked in Sweden, but it was not an option in America. Swedish immigrants had to start schools on their own, and support them also, while building churches, parsonages, and funding the struggling seminary, which for many cash-strapped and imagination-taxed delegates to the regular synod meetings was the only educational priority. Educating women was not the first, second, or even third priority of the male delegates. The daughters of immigrants lived in an American context, however, where a primary school education equipped them to think about continuing their learning. They pushed their parents and congregations to enlarge their vision not only of what women were capable of doing, but also of what a congregation should do. These young women changed the synod. In Minnesota, young women were admitted to Gustavus Adolphus College and Academy in the founding year of 1862. The academy may well have depended on their tuition dollars from the start, but the presence of women also forced teachers at the school to adapt. Business, music, and general courses in the sciences and humanities had to be added.

While educational opportunities for women seemed to depend on economic factors—the need for more students or the increased willingness of families to spend money on their daughter's education—there also were religious reasons for the promotion of women's education in the nineteenth century. America's young Protestant women had become involved in the missionary movement, and they realized the responsibility they had for evangelizing the women of Africa, India, and China in closed communities that could not be reached by male missionaries. Women needed to be educated in order to extend a helping hand to their sisters around the world.[2] In Sweden a similar enthusiasm sparked the founding of sewing circles and societies for mission, and Swedish-American women who had become familiar with American Protestant movements and with similar efforts in Sweden did not need much prompting to start missionary societies and sewing societies in their congregations, and in turn, in the synod's schools.

The Ambition of Ordinary Girls

In an autobiography prepared for her children, Augusta Stenholm explained how her lifelong commitment to women's missionary work began in the late 1870s, when as a young western Iowa farm girl, she had read her *Augustana and Missionären* newspaper avidly. Through the paper she learned about the Rev. A. B. Carlson, the first Augustana Missionary to India. "The reading intrigued me and when visitors to my home would say, 'Well Gusty, what are you going to do when you get big?' I'd answer 'I'm going to be a missionary to India.'"[3] Augusta gathered other young women and formed a missionary society in Gowrie, Iowa. She learned how to run a meeting as the society's president. Her friends Hilma Blomgren and Selma Callerstrom were the other officers.

Creativity for a Cause

The Gowrie congregation was a trendsetter for the Iowa Conference and in the first ranks of those who organized a society for its young women. Augusta remembered: "We met in the homes once a month and made things to sell at auction. Much of the handwork consisted of embroidering perforated cardboard, which was the style then. We made wall mottos, "God Bless Our Home" in colored yarns, book-marks, picture frames, etc." The girls attended a Swedish-speaking congregation, but Sunday school material and religious tracts were often only available in English. Swedish girls sold their items to a wider English-speaking market, too. "The large piece," Augusta recalled, "was an "aircastle" ornament in three tiers, which when hung from the ceiling or in a high doorway would swing around and glisten and jingle for at the bottom of each three cornered ball we hung beads." These strange decorative items did not appeal to the more practically minded adults, who clearly retained a more Swedish aesthetic. "Mr. Blomgren, Hilma's dad, used to tease us for our 'paper products.' Then we sewed aprons and collars." The girls must have known what would sell. "When we had the auction sale in the fall the huge sum of $30 was realized for missions."

Augusta kept reading the synod's paper and learned that the Augustana's Iowa Conference planned to open a girls' school in Madrid, Iowa, though this plan met resistance from the college in Rock Island. When wind of the Iowa plans for Madrid first reached Rock Island, Hasselquist relented on his opposition to opening the college to women and the board of the school reluctantly changed its policy. This maneuver scuttled the Madrid plan but really didn't result in any kind of enhanced opportunity for women like Augusta, who had more modest goals. Rock Island was too far away for Augusta, so she and no doubt several other girls had to change their plans. Even three years later, only seven women had enrolled in Rock Island's college program. The Iowa Conference plan for a women's academy in Madrid was an alternative proposal for women's education aimed at a much younger student. That Hasselquist and the board of the college and seminary in Rock Island saw these modest proposals as a threat pointed to the precarious nature of the synod's common educational endeavors.

Indeed, throughout the 1880s the college and seminary in Rock Island limped along on very precarious financial footing. Hasselquist experienced and resisted the increasing competition for funding that resulted when conferences sought to expand and improve the educational offerings of their schools, no matter how modest. Competing visions for the educational program of the synod would have to wait until at least one of the schools could be counted on to survive. Meanwhile, several conferences had forged ahead. In 1883, the Nebraska Conference advertised in *Augustana* the plans to open a new college and academy that would admit women. Augusta drummed up her nerve. "I took the paper to mother one day as she sat on a bench under the trees in her 'lofsala' [hall of prayer] and begged her that I might go. She approved but said it was useless to ask papa for money. He just didn't have any." If, however, Augusta could raise some money, she would help her.

Augusta knew a girl who had gotten a certificate to teach children in the public schools so she studied and went to Fort Dodge to get a teaching license. Augusta made progress, taught for a short while, and saved her money. In 1885, the Swedish Lutheran Academy and College in Wahoo, Nebraska, was ready for its first students. "Papa took me to the station in Gowrie in the spring wagon, and though a man of few words, he did say he didn't think it was of much use for a girl to go in for an education as 'you will most likely be getting married pretty soon anyway.'" Augusta had worked out what to say: "I told him I thought a little education would be good for me whatever I did and that I loved books and school and wouldn't be happy if I couldn't go." She promised him that, "if I succeeded in earning some money by teaching, I would pay him back what he spent on me." But the exchange between father and daughter at this moment also showed that the rough calculations of a farmer were not the only factor for her father. Augusta left home with a blessing: "With a tear in his eye and a quiver in his voice he bade me goodbye on the station platform and said 'God Bless you, Augusta.'" Her father's feelings helped her recognize the seriousness of this venture.[4]

Conference Initiatives and Counterproposals

Educational efforts in several of Augustana's conferences had long placed the leaders in Illinois in a defensive posture. Eric Norelius, the pioneer pastor, newspaperman, and educator of the Minnesota Conference, became president of the synod during the last two decades of the nineteenth century, supported by votes coming from the growing conferences in Nebraska, Iowa, Kansas, and Minnesota, who pushed for their own regional interests. They competed with the Central Conference in Illinois, Wisconsin, and Indiana in offering educational opportunities for young people, and increasingly for women students. The conference schools that began to spring up participated in a widespread "college mania" affecting towns and settlements west of the Mississippi.

Support for limiting the synod's educational effort to the one college and seminary in Rock Island, Illinois, began to wither as young Swedish Americans multiplied in the several regions of the country. Colleges and academies cropped up across the rural landscape, where students like Augusta seized the chance for an education. While expanded courses enabled women and young men who were not called to be preachers to attend, this change unsettled the first generation of pastors, who wished to protect theological students from the distractions of women nearby on the campus. Later critics, like University of Minnesota historian George Stephenson, had no patience with the pious arguments for the superiority of the older, theologically focused program: "Most students were young men with a smattering of education who worked on farms, as unskilled laborers, until the call to 'preach Christ' brought them to the preparatory department where they were taught the rudiments of English and other common branches."[5] But Stephenson failed to notice the significance of church colleges as unique resources for shaping the future of the church. He disparaged new, and female students as "business boys" and "music students," and measured Augustana's fledgling schools by a university yardstick.

Far from the rarified air circling Augustana's hill in Rock Island, practically minded school promoters in the conferences had long been working to advance a broader conception of a church-based education in an environment where women students had been welcome from the start. When the synod delegates in 1862 located the seminary south of Chicago, in Paxton, the Minnesotans decided to go their own way, with a different kind of school for young people in their own congregations. Eric Norelius in Vasa and Carl Hedengran, pastor of the congregations around Chisago Lake, Minnesota, began fashioning alternative plans on the train ride home from the synod meeting in 1862.[6] The result was the founding of a school in the East Union, Carver congregation that very same year.

The school the Minnesota pastors envisioned was not a seminary, but something else. Andrew Jackson, who after immigrating to the U.S. had attended the seminary when it was briefly in Chicago, began his ministry in Minnesota in 1861. He escaped from the Sioux Indian uprising in 1862, and then took charge of starting a school for immigrant youth.[7] He wrote to Norelius about his vision for a proper Swedish-American college:"We are in a moral and religious sense high over the people of this country but are considerably under them in worldly education."[8] He proposed to start a "Folk School," designed to educate the common people. The Folk School movement was popular in Denmark, where it was promoted by cultural leader and bishop Nicolai Frederick Severin Grundtvig. In Minnesota, plans for such a school had to be hurried along, since the Sioux Indian uprising that summer had forced the conference to move its meeting away from Scandian Grove to a safer location, and leading pastors had fled from the region. But the rump of a conference, all eleven of them, agreed to support a school so long as the goal was to train teachers for the congregational schools they were all attempting to establish. They could call it a Folk School, or whatever they wished, but many of them had also come through Chicago and had experienced the work at Immanuel Church, with its school and educational program, and they also used this as a model.[9]

The Minnesota Conference accepted women in the first class at the school, training them to be teachers in congregational schools, preparing them for work as pastor's wives, and even as deaconesses, a new religious role for women. Bethany College in Lindsborg, Kansas, began its work in 1881 and also admitted women from the start. The school in Wahoo, Nebraska, followed the lead of these other innovators. Conference schools had the freedom of making decisions about curriculum and faculty at a conference level, and they did not have to design their programs around the special needs—imagined or real—of aspiring pastors.[10]

The fast growth of Bethany and the almost simultaneous founding of Luther Academy in Wahoo, Nebraska almost overwhelmed the congregations of the Kansas Conference, who were expected to support both schools. Kansas Conference delegates resolved to ask for more support from the whole synod, thus challenging the system of shared obligation for the synod's main school, Augustana College and Theological Seminary in Rock Island, Illinois. Conferences wanted a portion of the common fund for education, or they wished to be released from an obligation to support Augustana College.[11] This debate was not resolved until 1948, a full fifty years later, when the college and seminary separated. But many, many attempts were made in the intervening decades to relieve the financial burden felt by the conferences, even while ambitious pastors convinced their conferences to found schools in new regions.

Swedish-American church bodies outside of the Augustana Synod also founded schools. The Swedish Evangelical Mission Covenant started a school in North Park outside Chicago and in Minneapolis. Swedish Baptists began a school in Minneapolis, and the Swedish Methodists joined with American Methodists in Evanston, Illinois. Danish and Norwegian churches also founded colleges and academies throughout the same immigrant settlements. All of these church groups appealed to the same cohort of Americanizing immigrants. Swedish Americans had many options for gaining an education under church auspices, and no congregation was exempt from appeals from increasingly desperate college promoters. Competition among the schools for students steadily increased.

Whenever the synod convened, inter-school and inter-conference tensions were evident. Throughout his career as president of Augustana College and Theological Seminary, T. N. Hasselquist advanced the view that the synod could not afford to support more than one college and seminary if it really wanted to compete well with the public universities. Hasselquist meanwhile discouraged efforts to turn Augustana College into a university, based on his realistic appraisal of the level of support in the constituency. Hasselquist usually managed to win these battles. In the final years of his life, however, the "old man's" position on a range of issues was so well known, and so fixed, that younger leaders began to figure out how to create a sphere of influence all their own in their several conferences. These men became college presidents and conference leaders with ambitions for a much grander and challenging role for the Augustana Synod and for Lutheranism in the United States.

The Colossus in Kansas

Back in Kansas, Carl A. Swensson gained a reputation in many quarters of the synod for inflating the reputation of his school in Lindsborg, but he defended his grand schemes with the excuse that, without the efforts made by the Swedish Lutherans to found schools to elevate and mold the character of students, many talents and skills would remain hidden and undeveloped, while the worship of the almighty dollar and materialism would win the day.[12] Early on Swensson had received warnings from Hasselquist, who wrote to him that starting a college was easy, while it was "intolerably difficult to continue."[13] This intolerable difficulty increased, and Swensson had soon tapped dry the resources in and around Lindsborg, Kansas. He made constant trips out of town to raise money but still barely managed to stay ahead of creditors. His vision for the school had captured the imagination of many friends, but not enough financial support.

The Carl A. Swensson family gathers with friends from Moline, Illinois, at a picnic in Lindsborg, Kansas, September 29, 1894. **Front, from left:** *Bertha Swensson (on bicycle), Christine Lindberg Chester, Alma Lind Swensson (Carl's wife), Alice Chester (seated on the ground), Alvina Chester Johnson, and Erland Chester and Annie Swensson (on bicycle).* **Back, from left:** *Carl A. Swensson, Jenny Lind, and Agatha Chester Sodergren.* Photo courtesy of Chester Johnson, St. Peter, Minnesota.

Swensson, the leader, publisher, and pastor who pushed, scrambled, and founded Bethany College, made the 1880s a decade of transition for the synod's educational vision. Bethany College represented a model for Swedish-American education and an example of the independent striving of immigrant communities that wished to take matters into their own hands when it came to educating their young people. Swensson wrote a short sketch in 1893 about Bethany College for the readers of the *Jubelalbum*, a book he published in the anniversary year of the Swedish adoption of the Augsburg Confession. The celebration provided a festive way for several factions of the synod to come together to lift up the many initiatives and successes of its schools, hospitals, and orphanages. Bethany College, like the other schools profiled, had grown quickly, and Swensson credited this to a natural inclination on the part of immigrants to support institutions that would lead to the improvement of the image and circumstances of Swedish Americans. "A place of higher learning for the [Kansas] conference that could compete with the American schools, became a pure necessity,"[14] he wrote.

Swensson's educational vision for Swedish-American youth was voiced whenever he had the chance to speak. He wrote books, columns, and letters to newspapers. The rising Swedish-American generation and its possibilities were never far from his mind. He even made his first trip to Sweden in 1889 because of the new generation of young people in the Augustana synod.

> Here in America a generation is growing up which is only in the second or third degree Swedish. Many of them speak their fathers' tongue well, and go to the "Swedish church" but a portion of them have begun to be considerably indifferent, in comparison to other Swedish Americans, toward everything Swedish. This situation disturbs me, I can truthfully say. But I have also had this experience: it doesn't take a great effort, if you handle it correctly, before these young people can be awakened to what they really are: first Swedish, and then American.[15]

Swensson had been hobbled in successfully promoting his educational vision by the fact that he himself had never gone to Sweden. The trip gave him added authority to speak. "I was drawn to the possibility of being able to say to these youth: Now I have been there, it is so, hear what I have seen with my own eyes! In this way the young can be awakened to more interest and enthusiasm for our history, our memories and the possibility of a Swedish nationality."[16] The Swedish culture and heritage that Swensson promoted also had strong patriotic tones with consequence for American society as well. The Augustana people were not to be a separate people, piously grouped in congregations, but were to be a people who added something to the American society that was in an emergent form.

Through the synod's *Jubelalbum* and at college events Swensson repeated his conviction that the American people needed immigrant people to be true to themselves. He did not hold a view that Swedish culture needed to be cultivated because it was better than any other, but because it had something to add to the whole:

> If the American people would become what they ought and can become, so must every portion of it, representatives from each and every one of Europe's nations where immigrants have come from, zealously, yes almost guardedly preserve the good qualities of their national character and let be only the defects. For this practical reason, if nothing else, every Swede in America and even the Americans occasionally point to this and are earnest that true Swedishness does not die out in Svea's sons in the new world.[17]

Carl A. Swensson's ambitious vision inspired a corresponding building program at Bethany that needed extraordinary support from struggling farmers and Lindsborg merchants in order to succeed. While his vision may have resonated beyond the borders of Kansas, it had a hard time mustering a harvest in the soil of the hard-baked Kansas farmer. The debt mounted. He promoted his college within a wider circle than any of the other conference school leaders dared imagine. And he became a noted writer, politician, and leader to people in and out of the church and far beyond the plains of Kansas. Even Worcester, Massachusetts's general Swedish newspaper, *Skandinavia*, ran a large front page spread on Bethany College in 1889, in a series comparing the three Augustana Synod schools—Augustana, Gustavus Adolphus, and Bethany. Swensson impressed New England readers. Bethany College's lithograph boasted a large main building and striking allée laid out along the newly surveyed road leading up to its main gate. Lindsborg, Kansas, looked like a destination.

The college in Kansas, like the charismatic personality at its head, aimed to expand and even exalt the Swedish name and people. Swensson's big ideas, however, were matched by a struggling reality. Bethany College's first professor for all subjects was J. A. Udden. Udden's training had been in geology, under Joshua Lindahl at Augustana, and his time in Kansas, especially during the summers, was devoted to field explorations in the area around the school. He had an arrangement with Swensson to share any windfall that might come with a lucky discovery, and he also used the summer months to assemble artifacts that would go into a natural history museum. Udden left Bethany in 1889 to teach at Augustana College, where he could devote himself more explicitly to his field of geology, filling the position vacated by his teacher, Joshua Lindahl, who left in 1889 to become curator of the Illinois State Natural History Museum.

Synodical Growing Pains

Augustana College and Seminary also faced serious financial difficulties in the 1880s, as did Gustavus Adolphus in St. Peter, Minnesota, and Luther in Wahoo, Nebraska. In trying to rescue Bethany from creditors in 1888, Carl A. Swensson traveled 25,000 miles on railroad trips to solicit funds, attend meetings, and promote the school. He gained celebrity status through his constant presence on the lecture platform and, in the words of University of Minnesota professor George Stephenson, he "jolted the synod out of its complacency and conservatism."[18] The jolt hit the synod in the pocketbook, however, since the optimistic scenarios outlined in Swensson's florid descriptions did not include instructions on how to pay for them. The debt on the new, very large, campus building in Lindsborg was $39,000. Bethany College added buildings and programs at a faster rate than Augustana, Luther, and Gustavus, but all of the schools had to compete for students and prestige, so the example set by Swensson nearly bankrupted the whole educational enterprise of the synod.[19] The founding of so many schools and the efforts of all of them to maintain attractive standards placed each school in a situation of fierce competition, with each conference taxed to the utmost to support their local enterprises.

With conferences, pastors, college presidents, and newspaper editors weighing in and pressing for their own causes, an elusive unity suffered. In 1888, synod president Erland Carlsson reported that sectional interests presented a spiritual challenge to the next generation of leaders. He used an argument familiar to an increasingly American audience:

> In the political realm we are all good Republicans and wish for a strong general government; but in the churchly relationships we have become unconsciously Democrats with weakened general government, while "the state right" plays the master. . . . See how it goes: each one wants mission for themselves, schools for themselves and their own newspapers etc. One must be blind to not see where all this leads. Soon every department will be pulling for its own direction and the strength and blessing that is in churchly unity, in common work and purpose will be lost.[20]

Carlsson, like Hasselquist, was closing out his career. The waning ability of these two men to keep track of and regulate all the initiatives of ambitious younger leaders became more and more apparent. They defined new initiatives from conference leaders and college loyalists as threats that weakened a cherished unity. In actuality, decentralization was a symptom of growth, and in fact, the transition that the Augustana Synod was about to make involved a reassertion of a centralizing vision for the synod, but it would be a tumultuous passage. Hasselquist's death in 1891 was hastened by his exertion in traveling to a synod convention in far away Jamestown, New York, to intervene in yet another dispute over the centralizing control from Rock Island that was so resented by younger men in the far-flung conferences. A contingent of Minnesota delegates and younger leaders proposed to separate Augustana College and Seminary and change the constitution to put more power in the hands of conference and regional leaders.[21] The machinations Hasselquist feared were stalled that time, but his exertions also exacted a personal toll: Hasselquist's end came later that summer.

The efforts to give more autonomy to the conferences had a direct relationship to the problem or opportunity of providing an education for women. In his report to the 1890 synod meeting, President S. P. A. Lindahl spoke of the joint seminary and college and praised its remarkable growth. "Through the congregations' freewill offering and God's clear blessings it has won stability and recognition." Then he addressed the key issue on the minds of conservatives: "From the beginning, the school's goal had been to give the necessary classic education for future pastors in the congregations, and as long as this goal has been kept the results have been positive and encouraging." Times had changed, however, due to the competition of the conference schools. "The new arrangements—coeducation, musical conservator and the business department—have in a large part moved the institution from its given goals and made it like the other conference schools, and the result has already appeared."[22] Lindahl's last remark was a veiled reference to the worldly focus of the conference schools, where women students apparently had diverted the stream of God's blessings.

Lindahl believed that providing an education for women and for young people interested in commercial courses was really not the purpose of the synod as a whole. "As a church body we need one school, one can call it what one will, whose goal is not to give a generally useful, but a foundational education, where Christly oriented young men, under proven and capable teachers, can be fostered for the tasks of being pastors in God's congregation."[23] The primary concern of the centralization party now became conservative, and the older, pastor-focused education became their rallying cry. They argued that the synod as a whole ought to maintain a theological school to train pastors, and it should let conferences create colleges to provide for the education of women elsewhere. The synod's pastors should be educated in a male only environment. Lindahl's design would lead to a separation of the college in Rock Island from the seminary. C. A. Swensson in Kansas and Matthias Wahlstrom in Minnesota were also in support of this, because it would mean that less of their conference's money would be diverted to Rock Island.

Science ahead of Its Time

The teaching of geology at schools of the Augustana Synod came off without a hitch at several schools. Biologist Joshua Edquist taught additional courses in geology at Gustavus, where he introduced students to modern theories about evolution. Throughout the synod's schools, an openness to science had been a part of the curriculum since Esbjörn began to teach natural science to seminarians as Swedish professor in Springfield in 1857. Later, in the 1920s and 1930s when the Scopes Trial made evolutionary theories a battleground between Fundamentalists and Modernists, Augustana schools already had established departments and highly regarded professors in the field of geology. The nationally known Fritiof Fryxell, who taught geology at Augustana and made the evolutionary character of the earth's development clear to his students, did not go unchallenged, but for every detractor several supporters spoke out in the church press. The Augustana Synod schools provided an early contrast with other Lutheran colleges in the country that did not have geologists on their faculties or offer courses in the field to their students.

Progressive ideas about the education of women seemed not to factor in at all in the deliberations of male delegates to synod meetings. Meanwhile, women students seemed to be something of an attraction for the male students. At Luther Academy in Wahoo, Nebraska, Augusta Stenholm recalled, "The girls living in the dormitory were carefully guarded. We had to ask for permission to leave the campus to go downtown to shop, etc., and were not allowed to be out at night at all."[24] They could go to church, but it had to be in a group, and they had to be escorted. On the way to church the girls followed the "lady principal" but "sometimes the girls would be escorted home by some young fellow." It seems that the fellows then decided to come up with approved excursions, and they scoured the churches for opportunities. Augusta wrote that she attended a lecture on the "creation" in the Presbyterian church. "Some of the boys went to Dr. Hill and asked for permission to take the girls. That night the young men called at the dorm for us and brought us safely back, too." One wonders what kind of dangers lurked in Wahoo, Nebraska, but at least there was something to do at the Presbyterian Church. The lecture impressed Augusta, revealing that students in a very small Nebraska town were not sheltered from one of the most controversial issues of the day. "It was a very interesting illustrated lecture on the six days of Creation. The speaker showed that the Bible account is not contrary to the evolution theory. But that in the case of man, a special act, a soul was created."[25]

Augusta did not recognize in this event any challenge to her piety. The concept of evolution was clearly something she could simply absorb. What she further mentioned was, for the time being, more significant: "My partner that night was Alfred Larson." Typical for a young woman, the friendships she established at school registered at least as much as the subjects taught, lectures attended, and courses completed. The synod's young women and men found lasting attachments through their college experience, and these networks of friendship amplified the strong ties that had been formed by the previous generation of pastors at the seminary. Augustana's strong network had expanded to include a new and larger generation.

The development of programs that appealed to students interested in music, the arts, and the sciences gave some schools a recruiting advantage. Luther Academy and College in Wahoo, Nebraska, suffered by comparison with the more expansive program offered at Bethany. Resentment toward encroachments made by Bethany's president C. A. Swensson on the Nebraska territory—an area that Luther's president Samuel Hill felt belonged to Wahoo—boiled over in the newspaper *Svenska Journalen*, on Nov. 5, 1896. Hill's letter set out the accumulated frustration of several years of competition:

> At last it has happened! For 12 years Dr. CA Swensson has been work-ing for the death of Luther Academy so as to reunite the Nebraska Conference with Kansas. He has always feigned friendship. . . . we have not repaid her with the same currency. The ingathering determined upon for 1892 was not carried out because we let the Kansas Con-ference come into Nebraska to save its school. When they had gone over the field, then came the hard times so that Luther could not wipe out its debt. Two other schools went under—Hope in Minnesota and Martin Luther in Chicago.[26]

Luther Academy and College had to focus on a program quite different than Bethany's if it was going to survive. Instead of art, music, and teacher training, Luther generated pious students interested in missionary service. This laudable effort did not create the kind of campus culture that drew students to Bethany, Augustana, and Gustavus.

Swensson responded to Samuel Hill's charges by pitying him. On Dec. 31, 1896, he wrote: "Luther has only a handful of students. Last year the catalogue showed only 68 in all departments. Such a situation for a school! What could be more depressing? With my whole heart I sympathize with

Professor Hill and his helpers."[27] Swensson also faced financial ruin but his way forward was to create an impression. The rest would follow. Inevitably he would be criticized for posturing and stagecraft, and he tried to counter these charges:

> Hill thinks that Bethany lays too much stress upon neatness, politeness, good customs, and gentlemanly bearing—all on the outside. We lay stress on both inward and outward culture, and since Hill has never been to Lindsborg, how can he know? At Bethany we do not believe that a person, young or old, is a Christian because he has a dirty collar or no collar, a handkerchief around his neck, unbrushed shoes, uncut hair and beard.[28]

This exchange in the newspaper referred to dress and style, matters signaling a departure from the older and simpler days of the pioneers. Instead of cultivating a spirit of renunciation and sacrifice, Swensson defined education in new terms:

> We believe that everything good and beautiful in this world belongs to Jesus Christ. This coincides with our educational program. Our music conservatory and art school have pleasant classrooms. One of Dr. Hill's favorite topics is "Wahoo is something so poetical and God fearing and Bethany is just the opposite." I have heard this for years and I'm tired of the whole thing. The people of Nebraska asked me to break this soap bubble. . . . Come, Professor Hill, and be with us next year. Become inspired, glad and friendly.[29]

Swensson's invitation probably did nothing to smooth relationships between these two men, but women in the several colleges did visit each other. Bethany's closing ceremonies drew Augusta Stenholm, a faculty member at Luther Academy in Wahoo, to the college in the spring of 1892. "I stayed in Hilda Blomberg's room [her old friend from Gowrie] in the dormitory for nearly two weeks, and I got to be present when the Augustana Women's Missionary Society was organized at the home of Rev. C. A. Swensson by Mrs. Emmy Evald. This event has had lasting results in my life."[30] The next year she went to the Augustana College campus, but she had a much less enjoyable experience there: "The alumni banquet was held in a hotel in Rock Island. Frank Sard was my partner. Flodman asked to take me too late. One thing that surprised me at the banquet: Two or three glasses of wine were placed at each plate. I did *not* drink mine. I can't say that I really enjoyed that stay in Rock Island. There were too many disturbing factors."[31] Augusta had a long career teaching English at Luther College in Wahoo, Nebraska. Her education not only had brought her into the sphere of a Swedish–American college where she had influence on young people, but it also brought her into the orbit of other Augustana women who knew how to tap the energies of the rising corps of educated women in the synod. The synod's half-hearted and experimental efforts in women's education had taken her there.

MUSIC FOR THE JOURNEY

The hymn tradition of the Church of Sweden, contained in the *Psalmbok*, shaped the literary world of the ordinary person. Rife as we are with words, texts, and books, with advertisements, billboards, screaming radios, and televisions, it takes an enormous leap of the imagination to realize the impact of a culture where families may have owned two or three books: the Bible, a *Psalmbok*, and a devotional guide, especially Johan Arndt's *True Christianity*. The *Psalmbok* contained material for corporate worship, a treasury of personal prayer and a language of praise and reflection that fundamentally shaped the self-understanding and imagination of millions of people. An examination of any of the old *Psalmboks* surviving in family collections will show signs of wear that tell devotion and careful, daily use.

In 1819, the Swedish *Psalmbok* was revised. For many, the new hymnal did not reflect their understanding of the faith. At the same time, settled habits of well-established parishes were being challenged by much more than a new hymnal collection. The time of migration was a time of industrialization and urbanization, of dislocation and reorientation, and words and melodies from the revival songs articulated longings for intimacy and homecoming, for safety and reunion better than any the newer *Psalmbok* might offer.

Songs and hymns that immigrants brought with them then reflected a range of pieties, from old and new *Psalmboks* and from popular revival songs. The hymn, "I'm a Pilgrim and a Stranger," expresses clearly the spiritual hope that sustained people on their journey through life, and still more the hopes of immigrants:

> *I'm a pilgrim, and I'm a stranger,*
> *I can tarry, I can tarry but a night;*
> *Do not detain me, for I am going*
> *To where the fountains are ever flowing;*
> *I'm a pilgrim, and I'm a stranger,*
> *I can tarry, I can tarry but a night.*[1]

Some of these revival songs became so well known that they have survived multiple translations and have entered the spiritual memory bank of Lutheranism at large, such as, "With God as Our Friend," (*Lutheran Book of Worship*, 371), or the even more popular, "Children of the Heavenly Father" (*Evangelical Lutheran Worship*, 781). The Swedish revival movement created a strong network of like-minded believers able to recognize their "friends" and fellow believers wherever they found them. Idioms and ideas from the revival were so pervasive in immigrant communities that all church groups, from the bishop-friendly Episcopal mission of Gustaf Unonius to the ultra congregational Swedish Free Church, had to contend with ideas and words from the religious Awakening.

The common spiritual language of the revival served to articulate the meaning of the transitions immigrants faced. Hymns that focused on pilgrim wandering, pious friendship, and heaven as an ultimate homecoming linked immigrants with family and revival networks back home, reassuring them that, even though they had left so much behind, they finally would be reunited. Phrases from songs quoted in letters from the immigrants to the "folks back home" pointed to a longed for heavenly reunion.

Augustana congregations used the hymnal, *Psalmbok*, for morning services. For evening services and for home devotions they used collections of songs from *Pilgrimssånger* ("Pilgrim's Songs") or *Lammetsvisor* ("The Songs of the Lamb"), or one of several other collections. In 1891, a synod committee began work on *Hemlandssånger* (Songs of the Homeland), a collection for congregations to use on their own or alongside the official Swedish *Psalmbok*. It included hymns and songs from the revival tradition, translations into Swedish of American hymns, and favorites from the Swedish hymn tradition. The work done on this compilation was also important as a preliminary stage in the production of the first English language hymnal, which came out ten years later. Many of the struggles over how to balance Swedish and American influences appeared in the work of this group.

Olof Olsson, sensitive lover of all things musical and spiritual, was by 1891 the president and theological professor at Augustana College and Seminary in Rock Island, Illinois. He was on the hymnal committee and pushed for retention of spiritual songs that moved the hearts of the immigrant generation, songs he felt would unite the faithful. In personal letters to C. A. Swensson, who shared his devotional orientation, he gave reports on the meetings of the committee. His first letter about the subject, written after the committee met in August

1891, enjoined Swensson to come up and help in the struggle ahead:

> Through desperate efforts I was able to get in 4 verses of 481 as a "picnic" song with 2 verses just like in *New Pilgrim's songs*. The psalm sung to the melody Integer vitae excels as "picnic." That's all. We have in all our wretchedness done the best we could. . . . Holmes promised me that he would defend the anti-psalm[bok] program. They are dear churchly brothers, you understand, not sloppy like you and me.[2]

Psalm 481 in the *Psalmbok* was an eight-verse text by J. O. Wallin. The first line read: "Where is the friend for whom I'm ever yearning?" The four verses that were in *Hemlandssånger* began with the second stanza: "I know God's there in every force and power" and the verses enumerated flowers, fields, and wind. As a hymn to creation's beauty it worked outdoors.

Olsson's letter in January 1892 commented more directly on the varying streams of piety that would come out in the published version:

> O, Brother, we have done the best we could with the melodies and the same with the texts. New and old, sanctification and atonement in all nooks and crannies, Småland—and Yankee melodies high—low—broad—old—and new churchliness, orthodoxy, pietism and Moodyism—everything that is good, a wonderful unionism. Sandell and Rydholm chose and chose

again the Melodies, and the rest of us have tested, practiced, and judged. The whole thing is now a manuscript. We are still waiting for the *Nya Pilgrimstoner* from you for final comparison. . . . "Jesus lover of my soul"— yes several wanted this in a real translation.[3]

The list of influences included the regional pieties in Sweden blended with the revival songs of America, all superimposed on several English, German, and Swedish hymn traditions. The decisions made in 1891 determined a broad path forward. Number 481 from *Psalmbok* appeared in *Hemlandssånger* in four verses as hymn 413. In 1901, the remaining four verses were restored in the first English hymnal as hymn 325, "Where Is the Friend?" The hymn survived the transition to the more widely used 1925 *Hymnal* where it became hymn 517, out of the picnic mode and included under "Hope and Aspiration." Olsson's words about the committee's work record the values preserved in the spiritual memory bank of the people and deposited in a hymnal.

chapter 6

BECOMING AN AMERICAN CHURCH

In 1890, the Augustana Synod was overwhelmingly a denomination of first-generation immigrants, led by pastors and lay people who had emigrated from Sweden and who used Swedish almost exclusively in their worship and organizational life. By 1930, some forty year later, Augustana was predominantly composed of second- and third-generation Swedish Americans, whose leaders were born and educated in North America, and who relied almost exclusively on the English language in their work together. This period of transition is referred to generally as the time of Americanization or acculturation, a time during which this immigrant religious group took on the attitudes, ideals, methods, and commitments of its adopted country. Although hardly an unexpected development, it was filled with both tension and creativity as the immigrants and their children sought to sift through the two cultures available to them—Swedish and American—to find what sort of an identity they could create for themselves. Some wished the synod to remain Swedish for as long as possible, to be a bastion for the carriage of Swedish culture in North America, especially for new immigrants who were expected from Sweden. Others impatiently pushed the synod to become "English" (that is, American) as quickly as possible, so as not to lose the Swedish-American young people of the second and third generations for whom Swedishness was no longer a primary identity. The tensions inherent in these conflicting visions were sharp, painful, and real, but they were signs of inevitable change, one that had been affecting immigrants to North America from the beginning, and that in some form continues to work in contemporary immigrant communities.

Augustana and the Process of Acculturation

To explore fully the topic of acculturation or Americanization among Swedish immigrants to North America would take much more space than is available here. The process of acculturation is both tremendously complicated and controversial, and immigration scholars debate its varied points with much zeal. But in general it is clear that there is a definite process by which immigrants encounter and manage the culture of their new country, neither rejecting it totally nor embracing it fully, but managing to pull together disparate elements of cultures old and new in such a way that they create a new identity for their group. This is a moving target, for the identity continues to shift in ways that are most helpful for the immigrant community as it makes its transition through time. Often referred to as the construction of identity, the process develops a useful group identity—an ethnic or sometimes hyphenated identity—that serves to delimit the boundaries of a particular group of people. The identity will remain as long as its usefulness in maintaining the group outweighs the disadvantages of being a community in some tensions with the larger cultures around it, and then it will be modified again to fit whatever new realities a particular group finds to be most useful. As the largest organized community within the Swedish-American immigrant tradition, the Augustana Synod was a primary vehicle by which the immigrants developed their own useful identity in North America. By tracing the development of changes within the synod itself, we can have a sense of how these Swedish immigrants acculturated and Americanized over time.

One element in the process of constructing identity involves developing boundaries to define who is in the group and who is not, and what sort of identity one would have to adopt if one were to be considered a member of the group. One group of immigrants might associate with another based on a variety of present or past commonalities, including religious backgrounds, nationality or race, political views, occupations, or other shared experiences. Depending on the group, boundaries are established to identify who belongs and who does not.[1] This element of acculturation may, in fact, appear to be counterproductive, as its essential element seems to be the declination of a particular ethnic group from the larger society around it. This can certainly be seen in aspects of Augustana's own history, including the departure of the Norwegians from the synod in 1870, the battle over Waldenström's theology in the 1870s and 1880s, and the refusal of the synod to join with the General Council in the 1918 merger that created the United Lutheran Church in America (ULCA). Yet it is often vital for a group to know and define exactly what it stands for, and boundaries do the work of definition in a clear and productive manner.

The building of boundaries is not nearly enough, however, to explain the full development of ethnic identity through organizations such as the Augustana Synod, for boundaries work only if there is a cultural content to an ethnic identity. There must be a particular cultural content to the group that the boundaries enclose, defend, and strengthen. The pastors and leaders within the Augustana Synod sought constantly to define the cultural and theological content of the synod and often fought over the elements that would constitute this definition. There were quite a few elements in these disputes, including local and regional differences, competing theological visions and institutional loyalties, and differing stances on moral, social, and political issues. But synod leaders sought to make a way for all the various elements of the synod to be combined under a single identity, that of *our* synod, *our* church, *our* Augustana. This constructed loyalty or identity was intended as a broad culture that would transcend particularities and bring together all of the immigrants and their children. In the tremendous literary outpouring that came from every side of the synod itself, one can see this attempt to define a common theological and cultural identity for the synod, and to control the means by which this identity was created. The regional struggles within the synod over the role of the conferences and the long-running conflicts over the control of central institutions (especially Augustana College and Theological Seminary) were just two of the elements in this struggle for definition.

The third defining element here was the fact that the definitions of boundaries and culture needed to be adjusted constantly in light of changes within the immigrant community and in the larger American culture that seemed to accelerate through the end of the nineteenth and into the twentieth century. In his detailed study of the Swedish immigrant community in Isanti County, Minnesota, during this time period, historian Robert Ostergren calls this process redefinition:

> This was a time of growing cultural confusion, but certainly not a time of dissolution. Leadership was passing from one generation to another, with all the adjustments that such a process normally entails. Economic change was bringing the outside world within a society that had been closed to many external influences. . . . These were ethnic communities rapidly acculturating, becoming more outwardly American with each passing decade. . . . Yet inwardly they remained island communities.[2]

This process of redefinition, seen so plainly in the rural enclaves of Swedish America, was even more pronounced in urban Swedish America, where the outside forces on the immigrant community were so much closer and stronger than they were in the rural areas. It is seen in the famous formulation of Hansen's law of immigration: that one generation seeks to recover elements of the ethnic identity that a previous generation had sought to discard as being an impediment to its own useful identity.[3]

One of the key points in this process of definition and redefinition was balancing two different sets of needs within the Augustana Synod: the need to be as open as possible with the culture, especially the religious culture around it, and the need for a useful theological identity that would provide the synod with its unique "center." This balancing act is defined by Hugo Söderström as being between two disparate forces: the need to maintain and vitalize the confessional Lutheran identity on which the synod was founded and the need to be open to cooperation with other religious groups—Lutheran and other adSoderstrom book Protestants—with which the new religious organization had to contend. The construction of identity was complicated not only by the constantly changing nature of the outside world but also by the competing internal dynamics of confession and cooperation, both of which had their own methods of dealing with these changes.

The Augustana Synod was, then, part of a larger construct—the world of Swedish America—that was itself a constantly changing entity throughout the nineteenth and twentieth centuries. It was in this period from 1890 to 1930 that the most dramatic changes and conflicts occurred, as this growing immigrant denomination struggled to develop internally, while at the same time confronting a rapidly changing world outside its own boundaries. According to Augustana leader and historian Conrad Bergendoff, "The role of Augustana was that of a midwife, easing the travail of an older generation in a strange world, in giving birth to a new generation, in a fateful century."[4]

The Language Transition

One of the ways to measure the acculturation of the Augustana Synod over time is to track the adoption of the English language in the life and work of the denomination. This was a huge issue within the synod from 1890 to 1930, as much a clash of generational power as anything else, and it consumed a great deal of time and energy. It is characteristic in immigrant communities that the last two places where the immigrant language is spoken is in homes and religious organizations, so typically Augustana lagged in the language transition in comparison with other aspects of the Swedish-American community.

Yet change was inevitable, and the question was really the degree to which the older generation would fight the change, and the degree to which the synod would suffer in its mission to Swedish Americans because of these disputes. The younger generation, already reasonably fluent in English from school and community and whose knowledge of Swedish was often limited, pressed hard for the use of their natural language in worship and in the synod. How many of the younger generation were lost to the synod because of the intransigence of their elders is impossible to know, but doubtless the number was considerable.

Although the earliest leaders of Augustana, such as Esbjörn, Hasselquist, and Carlsson, sought to promote the use of English within the synod, the mass immigration of the period from 1865 to 1914 overwhelmed the immigrant denomination and the Swedish language and culture were seemingly fixed as a permanent aspect of its existence. It was a Swedish church that ministered to Swedish immigrants in Swedish, and as long as the immigrants continued to swarm to North American shores, they saw no reason to change this core mission. If one wanted to worship in English, there were "English" churches for that purpose. Furthermore, the massing of Swedish ethnic and cultural institutions and the creation of a thriving Swedish literary culture in North America meant that those who wished could live their lives almost completely in Swedish, even in this new world. In 1914, a proponent of Swedish could confidently proclaim, "There are many indications that the Swedish language will never die out completely in Swedish America. . . . [I]t ought to be able to maintain itself for centuries, if not forever."[5]

But there was a tidal wave of change in the offing, as second and third generation Swedish Americans began to agitate for the use of English in local congregations, a movement that was intensified by the sudden end of mass immigration in the 1920s and the nativist pressures of World War I, which sought to force out everything "foreign" from American life. The increasing rate of change in the 1920s and 1930s obliterated the Swedish language from daily use within the synod. By 1931, a separate association of English-speaking congregations within the synod was dissolved as being no longer necessary, while at the same time a few resistant pastors were forming a Swedish Lutheran society to bring together the few remaining congregations where Swedish was used in worship and instruction.[6] The linguistic collapse of Swedish in Swedish America was as dramatic and sudden as it was inevitable.

Second- and third-generation Swedish Americans naturally gravitated toward the use of English, especially through their education, first in the American public schools (firmly embraced by Swedish-American families) and then through the academies and colleges of the Augustana Synod, where English very quickly became the dominant language of instruction. By 1884 more than half of the classes at Augustana College, for example, were taught in English, and by the beginning of the twentieth century Swedish ceased to be a language of instruction and instead became a subject for study as a separate language, albeit a popular choice. Even the courses in Christianity were shifted to English.[7] It was among such young graduates of Augustana

College that the first English-language synodical publication, the *Augustana Journal*, was launched in 1892.[8] This publication became a strong voice for the adoption of English within the synod, even as the religious language of preaching and liturgy. To those who argued that the Lutheran heritage of the synod could be communicated only in Swedish, A. W. Williamson replied in 1895, "To thousands of the children of Swedes born here the Swedish language is at best a sort of sacred tongue giving a solemn impression by its associations, but giving no definite religious and Christian instruction."[9]

College and Seminary president Olaf Olsson posed the question this way: was Augustana to be a "temporary *Swedish* organization" or a "*Synod*, a spiritual home?"[10] But for a new generation of young people moving into synodical congregations, Swedish was becoming a language of religious nostalgia and not the primary means by which they encountered God.

For local congregations, especially for the education of the young, there was a growing demand for English-language hymnals and educational materials. Already in 1885 the Engberg-Holmberg Company, a secular firm that published a large number of books for the Augustana market, brought out a bilingual Sunday school hymnal, *Barnsvannens lyra no. 2: svensk och engelsk*, with facing Swedish and English pages.[11] The Augustana Book Concern followed suit with a similar publication in 1903, the *Söndagsskolbok/Sunday School Book*, which had been preceded in 1901 by the first English-language hymnal for any of the Swedish ethnic denominations in North America, the *Hymnal and Order of Service*. Increasingly after the beginning of the twentieth century, the greatest demand was for children's literature and Sunday school materials in English, though this trend was slow to emerge.[12] It is unclear how many congregations turned to English publishers instead of the Augustana Book Concern for the English-language materials that the synodical publisher did not supply, but the anecdotal evidence is that they did, much to the displeasure of synodical officials. There was a rapidly growing demand for Sunday school textbooks and juvenile literature in English, along with materials for youth and adults. World War I was the beginning of the end for Swedish-language books and publications, although the Swedish-language newspaper *Augustana* was continued (at a financial loss) until 1956. According to the historian of the Augustana Book Concern, demand for Swedish books slumped suddenly after the war and the publisher was forced to dispose of stock on hand at a loss.[13]

During the 1920s, English-language publications eclipsed their Swedish-language partners. Early in the 1920s the Book Concern began publishing more English titles than Swedish, and Swedish book publishing ceased in 1929. By 1921, the circulation of the children's English periodical *The Olive Leaf* overtook that of its Swedish-language counterpart, *Barnens Tidning*, and by 1927, the English-language *Lutheran Companion* had more readers than *Augustana*.[14]

In the congregations of the Augustana Synod, transition to the use of English was slow to occur, mainly because of the resistance to change from synodical leaders, clergy, and the older generation. In 1900, only thirty of the 469 pastors within the synod had been born in North America, and among them "the language of home and church was Swedish." It was not until 1933 that the American-born segment of the ministerium exceeded that of the Swedish-born.[15]

Although there was an element within the synod with an ideological opposition to the use of English in worship and preaching, the main reason for the reluctance to change was that most pastors simply were not very proficient in the new language and congregations generally did not demand it. It is estimated that as late as 1921, fully 85 percent of the sermons preached in the synod were preached in Swedish. Even though bilingual pastors were becoming more desirable by the 1920s, few congregations used English exclusively.[16] Some pastors pushed for the transition to the new language, such as the pioneering English home missionary, John Telleen, who established a number of new congregations on the West Coast, but leaders like Telleen were scarce.

The first two English congregations in the synod were located in close proximity to synodical colleges: Grace at Rock Island, Illinois (1888), and Trinity at St. Peter, Minnesota (1891), were formed by college people who wanted the use of English, but they faced stiff opposition from many in the synod. The pastor of the Swedish-speaking First Lutheran in St. Peter, for example, attempted to place the new competitive English congregation under severe restrictions, insisting that Trinity would have little or no contact with any Swedish-speaking individual in town; in reply, Trinity's pastor simply stated that no one would be turned away from his congregation.[17] Other early English-language congregations were Emmanuel in Rockford, Illinois (1895), Messiah English in Chicago (1896), Grace in Minneapolis (1903) and Gloria Dei in St. Paul (1908), which were organized by English-speaking Augustana members who were frustrated by the slow transition to English within their home congregations.[18] Sixty members of the Augustana congregation in Cambridge, Minnesota, presented their pastor and church council with a petition in 1897, in which they called for English-language worship, preaching, and instruction. The demands eventually were granted.[19]

Scenes like these were being repeated throughout the synod, and local pastors and congregations struggled to add English worship, preaching, and teaching to that of the Swedish, creating a bilingual ministry. This posed a terrible difficulty for the older pastors, especially those with only a rudimentary knowledge of English. The demands on congregational pastors and leaders were vocal and intense, and many lacked the language skills to bridge the gaps. "I had such confidence when I came to this country," Alfred Bergin, a leader in the Augustana Synod and pastor in Lindsborg, Kansas, one day cried out to his daughter. "Now I stand there and teach the children in a language that they don't actually learn. And they will never know about God in Swedish, and I can't teach them about him in English."[20]

The bilingual compromise satisfied neither the Swedish nor the English partisans. Those who sought to defend Swedish as the language of the church were appalled by the use of English, finding it to be totally unsuited for divine purposes. Swedish partisans, such as J. A. Enander, professor at Augustana College and long-time editor of *Augustana*, charged that "English was good enough for business and all ordinary affairs, but not for religion and literature," where only Swedish would suffice.[21] They believed that the central purpose of the synod was to proclaim the gospel in Swedish in America, and that the use of English would destroy this distinctive mission. The partisans of English responded that refusal to use English would drive away the younger generation and eventually destroy the synod. Many partisans of English viewed bilingualism as merely a stopgap measure. John Telleen expressed this clearly in 1904, stating, "It is self-evident that the Augustana Synod can only continue as an English body. . . . Only by becoming English can our Synod retain its younger element, continue to grow, retain those of mixed marriages, and save its portion of the unchurched."[22] And the editor of the *Lutheran Companion* noted in 1911, that "[t]o have English services only once a month, or even every other Sunday evening, is almost worse than nothing. It hurts the Swedish, and is of no conserving value to the English element. It is merely a poor excuse.[23]

As Karl Olsson, historian of the Swedish Covenant Church in America, observed about the parallel language transition in his own Swedish-American denomination, by about 1915 Swedish had become a "liturgical language, like old Greek or old Slavonic . . . the only way of talking about God, singing about him, and perhaps even of communing with him."[24] Even though Swedish was rapidly losing out in everyday speech, the inherent conservatism of the synod, the inertia of local congregations, and the resistance to change among many people cannot be under-estimated.

If the synod and its congregations were generally slow to adopt the use of English, there were always plenty of other denominations, Lutheran or not, who were glad to provide English services to those immigrants who wanted them. As the Augustana Synod was a part of the General Council, synodical leaders tended to look toward these Eastern Lutherans (many of whom had gone through this language transition decades earlier) for help with English-language resources and assistance. Augustana's first English hymnal was, for example, heavily indebted to the *Church Book*, the English hymnal of the General Council, and the synod borrowed many other materials as well. Augustana was somewhat of an anomaly in the General Council; it was a large, national, ethnic synod, while the rest of the synods in the Council were local or regional groupings of German and English-speaking Lutherans. Since Augustana really saw the Upper Midwest as its prime and exclusive territory and all Swedish Americans (even English-speaking ones) as its constituency, trouble began in the 1880s and 1890s when the General Council began English-language home missions work in the Upper Midwest.

In the 1880s, the General Council Home Missions organization sent two pastors, George Trabert and A. D. J. Haupt, to begin English home missions work in Minnesota. Since Augustana considered this its territory, Trabert and Haupt and the congregations they developed joined the Augustana Synod initially, even though they did not use Swedish and many of their members were not Swedish Americans.[25] Though Trabert and his colleagues displayed a good amount of patience and tact toward the Augustana Synod, it soon became clear to them that a long-term affiliation with the synod was unworkable. In 1888, a proposal in the Minnesota Conference to create an English Conference was postponed amid strong opposition and strong words. In 1891, the English congregations withdrew from the Augustana Synod to form the Synod of the Northwest, which was accepted as a part of the General Council. This was, of course, much to the displeasure of the Augustana Synod, which had no English-language ministries and which stood to lose many of its younger, Americanized members to these English congregations. In 1894, Eric Norelius challenged the Minnesota Conference convention to do something about it. "Shall we permit English Lutheran Synods to take over the English work among us," asked Norelius, "or shall we do this ourselves, and try to retain the generation now growing up in our conference and Synod?"[26]

But it would take another fourteen years to establish an organized English-language presence in the synod, and this was accomplished only in the face of heavy opposition. Through the early twentieth century, the Augustana Synod struggled against the Synod of the Northwest over territorial claims stretching from Wisconsin to Washington. In 1923, synodical president G. A. Brandelle wrote to the president of the Synod of the Northwest about a disputed territory, stressing "that the field in question is overwhelmingly Swedish, that our men were first on the field, that our people have bought a church, and that there is room for but one English Lutheran church."[27] Despite the close personal ties that Brandelle had with many of of the United Lutheran Church in America, which contained the Synod of the Northwest, there are many similar letters in his file, as well as similar letters to leaders of other Lutheran denominations.

The problem of the encroachment of other denominations on the synod's Swedish-American field was, however, much larger than just a rivalry with other American Lutheran groups. Augustana also competed with other Swedish-American denominations, such as the Covenant and Free churches, the Methodists, and the Baptists. But beyond this, many other American Protestant groups saw the Swedish-American community as an attractive field for their own recruiting efforts. Swedes were seen as the "best foreigners who come to American shores" and "more nearly like Americans than are other foreign peoples," said the American Congregationalist leader M.W. Montgomery, who himself headed up Scandinavian work for the American Home Missionary Society.[28] Many immigrants were themselves eager to join an American church, whether for language or status or simply because they were now Americans. In 1914, Pastor Trabert wrote about one such Swedish family:

> Neither he or his wife are very proficient in English, but they have a daughter and want to form more prominent social connections than the leading Swedish congregation. . . . On the plea that their daughter does not understand Swedish . . . they land in the leading Presbyterian church.

Trabert also complained that some Augustana pastors "would sooner see the children of their people go to the Sunday Schools of the sects than to an English Lutheran mission."[29] Indeed, there was a long list of denominations eager to work among the Swedish Americans, in Swedish and in English, including Congregationalists, Episcopalians, Presbyterians, Methodists, Northern Baptists, Seventh Day Adventists, Salvation Army, and Unitarians.[30]

Eventually, in 1908, the Augustana Synod approved the formation of an Association of English Congregations as an official part of the synod. Though some of its founders would have wished for this to be a separate conference of its own, non-geographical in nature, such an idea was politically unfeasible at the time, although the association did ultimately receive official representation on synodical boards and institutions. The Association of English Congregations pushed the synod to call an English home missionary, which they did in 1912, after various territorial issues were settled. The association grew fairly rapidly, from eleven congregations in 1908 to 124 in 1931, the last year of its existence.[31] By the early 1930s the need for such an organization seemed to be past—almost all of the synod's congregations reported at least some English work among them, and the language transition was occurring with increasing rapidity. Even the synod itself was "going English" in the 1920s; the minutes of the Illinois and Minnesota Conferences were printed in English, and the synodical minutes followed in 1924. The rapid switch to English was dramatically seen in the periodicals and publications of the synod at this time, and in 1928, the constitution of the Augustana Synod was translated into English; A. D. Mattson asserts "that the English Language was made official" by this event.[32]

Although the degree to which the language transition signaled the level of Americanization is complex and controversial,[33] it is very clear that the transition from Swedish to English was one of the most important developments in synodical history. As long as the synod continued to see itself as primarily a "Swedish" organization within North American society, it would voluntarily limit itself to a smaller realm of public life and discourse. Its mission was to the Swedish immigrants, present and future, and English had to be resisted to maintain the necessary linguistic resources to minister to these immigrants. But the younger generations would be served, and their demand for English-language ministry among them brought the synod, eventually, to a new self-definition as an American denomination.

Changes and American Influences in Worship and Hymnody

The rate of acculturation within the Augustana Synod would seem to be fairly slow if measured solely by the transition to the use of English, for as we have seen, the synod was overwhelmingly Swedish up to World War I. Yet there are other ways in which American influence can be seen in the synod at a much earlier date, and that is in the adoption of English and American religious forms and materials, especially hymns and worship materials. Though in general the synod retained the Swedish language as the principle medium of its worship life for quite awhile, the content of its worship life was often strongly affected by Anglo-American religious culture. This is somewhat true about the choice of worship materials, but is much more evident in the hymnody of the Augustana Synod.[34]

Many of the leaders and immigrant members of the Augustana Synod were deeply influenced by the nineteenth-century pietistic Awakening in Sweden. Where eighteenth-century Swedish revival movements were shaped by pietistic and Moravian influences from Germany, the nineteenth-century Awakening was strongly influenced by Anglo-American religious traditions, especially the evangelical revivals. Some of these influences led to the formation

of non-Lutheran denominations in Sweden and in Swedish America, including the Mission Covenant, Methodist, and Baptist denominations, among
others. Within that larger part of the Awakening that remained Lutheran,
the main influence from England and North America was in worship and
communal piety. The warm, personal, subjective piety of English-language
hymnody was quickly adopted in Sweden, as well as freer liturgical forms for
small group meetings. As many as 650 English and American gospels hymns
were translated for use in Sweden in the nineteenth century,[35] and they also
deeply influenced Swedish pietistic hymn writers such as Lina Sandell and
Oscar Ahnfelt.[36]

The Augustana Synod was strongly influenced by the Awakening movement in nineteenth-century Sweden; although its leaders chose to remain
theologically Lutheran confessionalists, there was strong strain of this pietism
in the worship life of the synod. For public worship Augustana congregations initially used the Swedish *Psalmbok*, although they generally used an
1849 pietistic revision of the *Psalmbok* by Thomander and Wieselgren rather
than the official 1819 version. However, Augustana pastors quickly moved
to supplement the *Psalmbok* with collections of pietistic hymns, a number of
which were published by pioneer Augustana leaders, such as Hasselquist and
Norelius. The most important of these, however, was the immensely popular *Hemandssånger*, first published by Jonas Engberg in 1860. The Augustana
Synod officially adopted a later edition in 1892. The influence of English
and American hymnody on this volume was strong; most of the 500 hymns
were by Swedish pietist authors, although it did contain fifty-three Swedish
translations of English and American gospels hymns.

Both the *Psalmbok* and *Hemlandssånger* were used in the Swedish-
language worship of synodical congregations, though the mixture between
the two varied widely. In theory, the *Psalmbok* was to be used for the
formal, Sunday morning worship, and *Hemlandssånger* was intended for
evening services and other informal worship opportunities. But there is
clear evidence that this theoretical pattern was often breached. "We need
to discuss the questions of what difference there is between a psalmbook
and a songbook," complained synod president Hasselquist in 1874. "I think
there is a difference, and that they should not be combined."[37] But they
were combined on a regular basis, and the protests of Augustana leaders
and historians against the practice suggest that it was widespread within
the synod.[38] The fusion of these two traditions is further suggested by the
example of the synod's first English-language hymnal, the 1901 *Hymnal
and Order of Service*. The basic outline of the formal worship service was
from the Swedish liturgy, though the music was generally taken from the
General Council's *Church Book with Music*.[39] Of 355 hymns in the 1901

American sources, and 160 from Scandinavian and German sources; of the Swedish hymns, seventy-two were from the *Psalmbok* and sixty-seven were from *Hemlandssånger*, suggesting that a fusion of the two worship traditions had already taken place.[40]

The influence of English and American hymns on hymnals for Sunday schools and youth meetings is even more dramatic and clearly represents the future direction of the synod. In 1903, the Augustana Synod published both a Swedish and an English-language Sunday school hymnal, bound together in one volume. This work had 235 Swedish hymns, of which 42 were translations of English or American hymns into Swedish, and 160 English-language hymns, 105 of which were of English or American origin. Most of these English and American hymns came out of the nineteenth-century evangelical or gospel song traditions, from authors such as Ira Sankey, P. P. Bliss, Lewis Hartsough, Catherine Hankey, and above all, Fanny Crosby, who in a number of Swedish-American hymnals had more hymns than did Lina Sandell. One historian has noted that these hymnals "were bringing an American religious cultural influence into the very heart and soul of Swedish immigrants to America."[41]

The influence of these early English-language Sunday school hymnals on twentieth-century synodical worship cannot be overestimated, as several generations of youth in Augustana grew up singing American gospel hymns in Sunday school, church camps, and Luther League meetings. Even today, when Augustana alumni get together for reunions and meetings, their hymn sings are dominated by this style of hymnody, especially the hymn, "Living for Jesus."

The Americanization of the Augustana Synod can also be seen in the two successive English-language hymnals published by Augustana, in 1901 and in 1925. In the 1890s, many in the synod sought the production of a revised version of the Swedish *Psalmbok*, which would be an American produced, Swedish-language version of the 1819 Swedish book. But synodical leaders realized that the more crucial need was for an English language hymnal, and work on this began in 1895, leading to the 1901 hymnal. Though this was a pioneering English-language hymnal (a generation before those of the other Swedish ethnic denominations), it was generally considered to be provisional and very much ahead of its time.[42] The hymnal of 1925 was a complete and polished work that intentionally drew from many different English and American sources, most notably the *Common Service Book and Hymnal* of the United Lutheran Church in America, and the *Book of Common Prayer* of the Protestant Episcopal Church. The liturgical forms of this hymnal drew their music generally from German and Scandinavian Lutheran sources, but the wording of prayers and liturgical texts was drawn heavily from these two American hymnals. The synod was rapidly moving to the use of English for its worship life and was seeking to borrow as many good examples of English-language worship as it could.

Americanization and Generational Transition in Leadership

Another way in which the transition to American life can be measured is in the generational transition of leadership within the synod. Although this is in itself very hard to quantify with any great accuracy, a number of observers have suggested that there was a definite shift in leadership within the Augustana Synod in the first decade of the twentieth century. A number of the pioneer leaders of the synod had retired or died right around the turn of the century, including synodical presidents Erland Carlsson (d. 1893) and T. N. Hasselquist (d. 1891), and Augustana College and Seminary president Olof Olsson (d. 1900); President Eric Norelius served a second term from 1899 to 1911 but died in 1916. The change in leadership was most pronounced leading up to the Fifty-Year Jubilee of the Synod in 1910. According to G. Everett Arden, "In the years immediately preceding the Jubilee a dramatic change in leadership had taken place, as one by one the pioneers had stepped out of the line of march." Besides those previously mentioned, Arden noted the retirement of college presidents Matthias Wahlstrom (Gustavus Adolphus) and L. H. Beck (Upsala) and the death of college presidents Olof Olsson (Augustana College and Seminary) and Carl A. Swensson (Bethany), though the latter was still a relatively young man (forty-seven years old).[43] The old guard who had founded and built the synod was turning it over to a younger, American-born, and educated generation.

This transition was slow to occur because the overwhelming majority of the pastoral leadership within the synod were still first generation immigrants. In 1910, the Jubilee year, only 115 of the 625 pastors in the Augustana Synod had been born in America, and the second- and third-generation pastors would not be a majority within the synod until 1933.[44] Among the synodical leadership, a number of transitional figures would hold power during the early twentieth century, including president Lawrence A. Johnston, who served from 1911 to 1918. But the younger generation of leaders would soon take power in the synod. There was a generation of leaders born around the 1860s that gained positions of leadership and prominence beginning in the early twentieth century. These included G. A. Brandelle, synod president from 1918 to 1935; C. J. Bengston, editor of *Augustana* and then the *Lutheran Companion*; Adolf Hult, Augustana Seminary professor; Emmy Evald, founder and long-time president of the Woman's Missionary Society; and C. A. Wendell, prominent Minneapolis pastor and proponent of liberalism.[45] They were joined eventually by a generation born in the 1890s, such as P. O. Bersell, synodical president from 1935 to 1951; Conrad Bergendoff, seminary professor and president of Augustana College; Samuel Miller, founder and dean of Lutheran Bible Institute; and E. E. Ryden, editor of the *Lutheran Companion* after Bengston.[46] The generational change came in waves, and each generation brought its own unique ways of leadership styles to the synod.

This changing of the guard also slowly worked its way through the pastoral ministerium of the Augustana Synod, though this change was less noticeable than that of the top leadership.

Characteristics of the Newly Ordained, 1890–1930[47]					
Year	Ordained	Swedish-born	Arrived in US after age 18	Augustana Synod College graduate	US-born
1890	21	20	16	11	1
1895	16	15	12	11	1
1900	17	11	7	17	6
1905	32	17	9	30	15
1910	24	19	10	16	5
1915	33	11	8	29	22
1920	11	7	5	10	4
1925	26	9	5	21	17
1930	33	3	1	32	30

The ministerium of the synod was still largely foreign-born until the 1920s, and the predominance of the second and third generation was slow to appear. Up to the Jubilee year of 1910, the majority of those being ordained had been born in Sweden and a substantial number had not come to America until they were at least eighteen years old, though most were graduates of synodical colleges. This meant that these pastors were Swedes first and became Americans only after their early life in Sweden, a fact that must have had a significant impact on their worldview. By the 1920s and 1930s, the vast majority of candidates for ordination were American-born and American-educated; almost certainly they knew enough Swedish to function in this still immigrant denomination, but most likely their primary point of reference was as English-speaking North Americans.

The simple fact that the leadership of the synod was changing over to an American-born generation, however, does not imply that these new leaders shared a common understanding or ideology; rather, they often drew from different parts of the American religious experience for their inspiration and ideas. Some of the new leaders, including seminary professor Adolf Hult and Lutheran Bible Institute dean Samuel Miller, adopted elements of conservative American Lutheran confessionalism and American evangelicalism. Other leaders, such as University of Minnesota professor C. A. Wendell, Augustana historian George Stephenson, and Vergilius Ferm, professor at the College of Wooster, gravitated toward the liberal Protestantism of the leading American denominations. Both Stephenson and Ferm pressed hard for synodical change and became rather disillusioned with Augustana when change did not come soon enough.[48] A number of these leaders, and those who followed them, worked on the margins of the synod, and were critical of its changes, or lack thereof.

The majority of these new leaders, however, remained committed to the basic direction that the synod had charted during its first fifty years, although they often sought to modernize synod structure and theology. Synod presidents G. A. Brandelle and P. O. Bersell modernized the structure of the synod and moved the sometimes insular Swedish-American denomination toward a much greater engagement with the religious denominations around them. Editors C. J. Bengston and E. E. Ryden sought to educate the rank and file of the synod with the changes going on around them and provided leadership for Augustana during a very turbulent period of change. Conrad Bergendoff presided over a revolution in seminary and collegiate education and was the leading theological voice of the synod. Emmy Evald pioneered the role of women in the Augustana church and built a strongly effective women's missionary organization that for many years dwarfed the mission efforts of the synod itself. By the 1920s and 1930s, with these new leaders firmly in charge, Augustana had definitely made the transition to being an American denomination.

The period from 1890 to 1930 saw the relentless, if not always painless, transition of the Augustana Synod from an immigrant religious group to a decisively American denomination. The transition to a Swedish-American identity was the key, as the synod and its members began to build their own useful religious culture from both Swedish and American elements, gaining in strength and confidence as they went. Though the synod was often glacially slow in moving toward the adoption of changes, such as the use of English in worship and preaching and in the utilization of some American religious forms, the movement was, in the end, the inevitable outcome of Americanization and acculturation. If the older clergy and leaders of the synod resisted these moves, the newer generation of pastors and leaders eventually prevailed. One story, told in the church press in 1913, embodies the full drama of how the synod was changing:

> At a meeting of the Illinois Conference in the Augustana College chapel on Friday evening, Dr. Andreen announced hymn 124 in the Psalmboken and 193 in the Hymnal. The older men on the platform began to sing the old familiar words in Swedish, but the younger people in the audience took up the strain in English . . . and before long the latter sang with such emphasis that the Swedish tongue was drowned in the flood of English, and the Swedish singers began to grow silent.[49]

chapter 7
A NEW CENTURY BRINGS CHANGE

SHORTLY AFTER THE TURN OF THE CENTURY, in 1902, the Augustana Synod marked the passing of two of its pioneering pastors. Pastor Per Anders Cederstam, a survivor of the Sioux Indian uprising, died that year in Minnesota. Upon his death, Cederstam's long-time Minnesota colleague, Eric Norelius, wrote a biographical sketch for *Korsbaneret*.[1] He recalled Cederstam's childhood, attendance at the Ahlsborg mission school in Sweden, struggles with dangerous religious teachings, and then his Lutheran certainty gained through Hasselquist's fatherly guidance. Norelius related that the Indian uprising had broken Cederstam's mental stability and that he had tried to recover in Illinois. His wife had suffered spiritually, often alienated from congregational life. Quietly, Cederstam had focused on care of souls for the remainder of his ministry. These details alert modern readers to the fact that the circles of friendship within the Augustana Synod did not spare Cederstam from scrutiny. Norelius wrote sympathetically, but with a frankness that startles. "My intention was to briefly describe his character as a Christian, a priest and a person." This ordinary rural preacher became one of the "quiet" in the land, a man who, through personal trial, gained the sensitivity to nurse fragile souls to religious certainty. Though Cederstam "was naturally sensitive, sympathetic, careful, modest, sacrificing, and humble, he had very little self confidence for he held back near overly confident people." His preaching was "intelligent but not original, and certainly not speculative."

In the same volume of *Korsbaneret*, a profile of Carl Peter Rydholm traced a similar pattern. He also had attended the Ahlsborg School, entertained theological speculation, and became a disciple of the Finnish pastor Hedberg before finding theological stability under Hasselquist's tutelage. Rydholm worked on the first hymnal compiled in the synod, where he advanced his pietistic love of spiritual songs.[2] Like Cederstam, Rydholm also concentrated his energies on saving individuals. Personal piety marked these pastors, and their lives were measured according to the way that their spiritual character had developed, rather than by an assessment of their tasks and accomplishments in the world. As these pastors passed from the scene, however, the interests of the Augustana Synod became much more pragmatic. Stories were still told about pastors, but these accounts focused much more on the buildings, programs, and societies they had organized and constructed.

The beginning of the twentieth century brought a wave of change for the Augustana Synod. Older models of piety did not stretch to fit the profile of the up and coming church member who typically was a young person attending a growing, often urban congregation, and whose attention was directed not at his or her inward state but instead to the church as a progressive force in society. The pages of *Korsbaneret* and the church paper *Augustana* were still written in Swedish, but the introspective piety of the pioneers was fading fast. Organizational genius became the new model of success. Each volume contained the biographical sketches of departed church members, but these were now followed by faces of the future. The new seminary graduates and the upbeat tone of the new century came into view with pictures of new parsonages and churches, hospitals, and orphanages.

The Successful Congregation

Korsbaneret provided space to record the individual lives of pastors, but a broader historical effort at commemoration occurred across the synod as flagship congregations began celebrating their anniversaries. C. A. Swensson and L. G. Abrahamson, who had ignited a spark of historical interest among the college students and young people, knew that celebrating history was a good way to promote a future-oriented agenda for a congregation and for the synod. New printing technologies allowed congregations to produce commemorative albums filled with tributes, speeches, portraits, and memories of church elders. The albums also included many photographs of lavishly decorated podiums, floats, Sunday school parades, and youth assemblies. The books were sold to members of congregations, conferences, and the synod, raising money for new initiatives.

The Immanuel congregation in Chicago marked its fiftieth anniversary in 1903 with the publication of one such memorial album. Full of congratulatory epistles, nostalgic anecdotes, pictures, and a wealth of detail, the volume celebrated this influential congregation's history in the synod. L. G. Abrahamson, pastor at the neighboring Salem congregation in Chicago, composed the biographical sketch of Immanuel's first pastor, Erland Carlsson, and several well-known leaders in the Augustana Synod who at one time had served as assistants in the congregation shared their recollections, bringing to life the years that had passed. So many wrote of their memories of revival in the Sunday school, the recovery from the Chicago fire, and the subsequent growth and influence of the congregation, that it was clear to the reader that Immanuel's story and perhaps its sphere of influence included the whole Augustana Synod.

The anniversary volume gave extensive credit to Carlsson and celebrated his vision and charismatic ministry, but it also gave credence to the intelligence and dedication of many women and men who followed in his footsteps. Pastoral assistants went on to pattern their ministry after Immanuel's model. As these pastors copied the Sunday school work, Bible classes, prayer meetings, young people's societies, women's societies, hospital societies, and literature clubs in their churches, they showcased a ministry far more public than the ministries of the late Pastors Cederstam and Rydholm and their contemporaries. Instead of focusing on cultivating the inner lives of parishioners, they organized societies and trained young people to be public speakers. The anniversary album reflected this change, too, for after profiling its founding pastor, the rest of the volume focused on the growth of the societies, schools, and works of mercy. The book even included charts and tables documenting the congregation's modern and progressive image.[3]

One of the many societies showcased in the album was a sewing society to support the missionary movement. Formed on the model of the sewing societies in Sweden, it had begun as a devotional group in the church under the guidance of Eva Carlsson, Pastor Carlsson's wife. The devotional group turned into a social ministry as the items the women sewed made their way into poor homes, and later to students, hospital patients, and mission posts. The work of the women also added beauty to the worship space. Handmade altar cloths and drapes for communion vessels and the altar rail were fashioned at meetings dedicated to devotional exercises and social engagement. By the anniversary, however, it had become a fully modern society, a unit of Augustana's Women's Missionary Society, patterned on the national societies of the Congregationalist, Baptist, Presbyterian, and Methodist denominations.

A Place for Women

Emmy Evald, younger daughter of Pastor Erland Carlsson and wife of his successor, Carl (Urbanus) Evald, was responsible for most of the statistics in Immanuel's fiftieth anniversary album, including the charts, tables, and lists of organized societies. Married to Pastor Evald after his first wife—Emmy's sister Anna—died, she lived and worked out of the church in Chicago for most of her very active life. Emmy Carlsson Evald was not a typical Augustana woman, but the methods and style that she perfected in Chicago modeled a new program for men and women in the congregations of the synod. At Immanuel she led a large English language Bible class that grew to 500 members and gained typical Chicago acclaim as the largest in the world.[4] Her activities did not stop there, however. She was a strong proponent for women's programs in the church and worked hard to organize women in the congregation into societies that benefited both the church and the women themselves. The Sunday school at Immanuel had once enjoyed the talents of the young D. W. Moody, so Emmy was no doubt familiar with his famous school and also with the struggles of women teachers there, who had to be satisfied with secondary status. Emmy's work with Immanuel's young people and its women's societies evolved into a public career. In 1895, she achieved national attention when she addressed Congress on the issue of suffrage.[5]

Emmy's genius for leadership was founded on her ability to tap deeply into the wellspring of the older piety. In this respect she shared her husband's passion for a quiet inner-directed world, but she knew also how to harness that powerful spirit and use it for mission. Her success in organizing women in the congregation was broadcast to a wider public when Emmy "realized" that the synod's women "did not have enough to do."[6] At the annual synod meeting in Center City, Minnesota in 1891, Emmy and her friend Alma Swensson, wife of Bethany College president Carl A. Swensson, introduced the idea of a national Women's Missionary Society for the Augustana Synod. They and the women who accompanied their husbands to the official synod meeting had ambitions themselves for pushing the church ahead; they wanted to do more than provide meals and sing along during public worship services. To get synodical recognition, the women asked their husbands to present at the next year's synod meeting in Lindsborg, Kansas in 1892 a resolution establishing a women's auxiliary. The women had waited a year when they gathered in the parsonage in Lindsborg, Kansas, to wait in suspense over the outcome. After quite a debate, permission came and Augustana's women had a national society and a leader.

The launching of this new organization did not make the headlines of the official publications of the church, however, for 1893 was the anniversary year celebrating Sweden's official adoption of the Augsburg Confession. This event warranted a jubilee year and the publishing of a large volume containing the history of every conference, school, orphanage, hospital, and deaconess institution. The publication pictured every pastor, including his biography. It also described the synod's missionary work in home mission and foreign mission, concluding with a ringing call to clasp onto hope, to let "Swedish blood ignite the fires of resolve, initiative, and victory in each Swedish Lutheran man so that he can hold fast to the confession." Not a word was mentioned about any women's organization or activity in the church. This oversight was telling, especially since the editor of the volume was married to the Women's Missionary Society secretary, Alma Swensson, and the society was organized in his home. Augustana's women could organize, virtually undetected by their husbands and pastors.[7]

"The ideal pious woman"

The synod's newspapers and Sunday school materials provided not only instruction in the Swedish language but also instruction in gender roles. The format for young children was a little book, or literary journal, containing moralistic stories, poems, puzzles, craft projects, and fairy tales. Every year a special Christmas book was available. A letter sent November 26, 1904, from Peter Froeberg to his brother Sven, showed how a pastor used these items in his ministry. Sven was an agent for the Augustana Book Concern, selling books and subscriptions in New England. Peter wrote at the end of November, advising his brother on when to visit the congregations. "If you visit around Boston first . . . I have asked them to wait as long as possible with their orders, until you come . . . then visit Fitchburg, Gardner, and Brattleboro at least 8 days before Christmas. . . . I will be ready with my order a couple of weeks before Christmas. . . . Kron and Holmgren always buy a few books." At the Christmas party for the Sunday school in Orange, Massachusetts, Froeberg and the Sunday school superintendent presented each child with a book.

In one story, Maja, an eleven-year-old girl stayed home while her older brothers attended school. She liked to play and seemed very uninterested in chores, but she was troubled because she needed the right present for her mother. Her mother suggested that Maja should help with household work, and Maja thought this would be the perfect gift. On Christmas she dressed herself, helped her younger brother, cleaned her room, set the table, and dried the dishes before going out to play. The message for young girls was obvious.

Church publishers also seemed to feel that edifying material of the same sort belonged in the devotional annual *Korsbaneret*. So, in 1902, an article extolled the foundational work of the home, where "the mother of the house is the ruler. Home feeling and home peace are for the most part her work; it is she, who, often silently, lays the foundations for future homes, for the coming generation, for the church and state." J. A. Dahlberg, the pastor of the Augustana congregation in Rock Island, wrote the article also to warn against threats to the home—the dance hall, the theater, bad books and magazines—that should be avoided. "These all cost more than it costs to belong to the church."

The Protestant Women's Missionary movement provided the largest arena for women's activity and leadership in America. Far more women participated in congregational and denominational missionary societies than in temperance and suffrage movements. Augustana's women were part of a large national movement through their own congregations.[8] Missionary work was popular because it gave women a world-shaping, Christian task: "women's work with women." Women went to meetings and learned that sisters in "heathen" lands were often secluded. Male doctors could not treat them, and in their closed worlds, neither could Christian missionaries, because they were male. In order for true Christianization to take place, women had to reach these women.

The need for women missionaries created a support structure in congregations across the land, including Augustana. We have already seen how young Augustana women began attending the synod and conference schools. Larger enrollment of women in the colleges led to higher education levels also for women in congregations. These women were capable of greater leadership tasks. Since women did not think they were doing this organizing for their own benefit, the enthusiasm for this work can't really be understood as women asserting their rights. Instead they were recognizing their responsibility. Women responded to the movement because it appeared to them to be, as historian Patricia Hill described it, an extension of their household duties.[9] Organizing to support missionary work appealed to the domestic and motherly qualities that Protestant women were encouraged to cultivate. The Christian home, both in America and in missionary lands, was something that women in the church valued and wanted to share.

The creation of the Augustana Women's Missionary Society provided women in the synod with their own vehicle for expressing themselves; they would not have to read material provided solely by well-meaning pastors. The society determined that the board would consist of women who lived in Illinois, or near enough to Chicago to enable them to attend board meetings. This meant that Augustana's women had centralized leadership from the beginning that developed from a strong base of support in the large Immanuel Church in Chicago. Emmy Evald's local organization included a congregational women's missionary society, a women's aid society, a young woman's society, and her very large Bible class. The work of all these societies contributed to the advancement of the congregation's social ministry. Now these women would be enlisted in the missionary cause.

Lutheran women in the Eastern Lutheran General Synod and General Council had long been at the work of raising money and interest in missionary work, and they provided valuable sisterly advice in how to put together a newspaper for women. *Lutheran Women's Work* came out in 1901, providing an easy way for organizers to communicate with their base. The newspaper was based on *Women's Work*, a Congregationalist publication with a similar focus. By 1906, Emmy Evald had started a newspaper for Augustana's women, and for readers of two languages, Swedish and English. The little paper was named *Missions-Tidning* ("Mission Tidings"), after a similar publication in Sweden, and was published out of Immanuel Church in Chicago. After only two years it became a monthly magazine, and by January 1909, there were 1,800 subscribers.[10]

Pioneering a New Language for Action

In addition to her administrative ability, Emmy Evald was an effective speaker. In 1908, organizers of the fiftieth anniversary celebration of the Minnesota Conference included a session sponsored by the women's organization in the conference, featuring a talk by Evald. Most Swedish-American festival occasions featured inspirational speeches about the glory of the Swedish past and how well-suited the Swedish character was for the battleground of faith. Viking heroes and mead hall speeches were not far from the rafters of the imagination when C. A. Swensson spoke or wrote his columns. The contrast between these images and the work of women was not lost on Emmy Evald. She suggested that women's work was so invisible to historians because they were always looking on the battlefield. She referred to the deeds of heroes, and the battle cries and victory language that was otherwise so popular in Swedish-American festival orations, but turned the language into a woman's discourse by introducing Miriam and the song of victory that women in the Old Testament sang after the battle. "My friend," she reminded her listener, "you cannot participate with these victorious women if you have not been to the women's meeting that is held under Jesus' cross. . . . If you have stood there, you have been prepared to be a messenger of good news."[11]

Her development of this theme continued on to the women's meeting at the empty tomb, where Jesus, always woman's friend, gave her the task to "go and tell." This had been the work of the Women's Missionary Society in Minnesota, and Evald listed its many accomplishments so far. "Our society's goal is to gather funds to send messengers of victory, and in these days we are sending Dr. Betty Nilsson as our goodwill messenger to the poor Hindu woman, who is sacrificed to the worst religion on earth."[12] She gave statistics on female infanticide, young ten-year-old girls who were forcibly married, stolen, or enslaved. Augustana's women were just about to begin building a hospital. But how would it be supported? Evald used her talk to ask for a commitment from all the women gathered there. In two years the synod would celebrate their fiftieth anniversary. That was the year to aim for in their next campaign. "Let us also be along with the women celebrating victory!" Evald urged.

Evald's rhetorical ability gave her an edge as an organizer. Simple memorable statements—"Go and Tell," "See, we go up to Jerusalem," and "Work while it is day"—show her deft handling of biblical phrases to inspire her women listeners. Through her monthly column, "Among Ourselves," in *Missions-Tidning*, she demonstrated how womanly bonds of friendship could be enlisted in a kind of marketing advance, and she employed modern business methods to launch her many campaigns to increase participation in the society. With reminders in bold print—"No Conference can afford to be a slacker in our Drives"—written across the foot of every page of the May issue, she demonstrated a gift for promotion and revealed a hint of her formidable personality. Evald was also well acquainted with the role that Women's Missionary Society organizations played in the larger American society. Another banner phrase from the January 1920 issue pointed to her familiarity with the women's movement: "A Godless feminism would be a fatal blow to Christian civilization."[13]

Women's Missionary Society Board, 1916. Emmy Evald, president of the society, is seated at the table, on the left. Photo courtesy of Evangelical Lutheran Church in America Archives.

Evidence that Evald's leadership was noticed came from outside the synod as well. No doubt taking stock of the success of Augustana's women in raising money for mission, the United Norwegian Lutheran Church, facing a deficit in 1903, realized that lack of funds prevented their sending missionaries on the field. They resolved to organize their work at home, and part of that effort involved asking their women to create a national organization out of their local societies. Resistance to centralization was stronger among Norwegian than Swedish Lutherans, but finally in 1911 the United Norwegian Lutherans formed a Women's Missionary Federation to help increase donations to mission from $18,000 to $153,000.[14] By this date, presidents of the national Lutheran Women Missionary groups had begun to meet. Women leaders from the Lutheran General Synod, General Council, General Synod of the South, Augustana Synod, and United Norwegian Church met in Philadelphia and coordinated their support of mission work in India and China.

Emmy Evald's superb organizing efforts among the women in the Augustana Synod were also a large factor in the positive development of the church. In 1910, the women surpassed by $2000 their goal of raising $10,000 to retire the synod's Home Mission debt. In the same year they completed and dedicated a hospital in Rajahmundry, India. The large gift "inspired" the male leaders of regional conferences in the synod to go home and "do something" in their respective conferences. For these second generation Swedish-American Lutherans, "It was an awakening and realization of the power in organization."[15] Missionary Society women learned what it was like to serve on a board of directors and to draft and amend a constitution and its bylaws; they produced and published newspapers; and they mastered the ins and outs of financing for construction and maintenance of hospitals, schools, and residence halls. The women who led these efforts were college-educated, and they shared their organizational talents with women in congregations. The effect was a broadly educated and tightly managed corps of women.

What Were the Men Doing?

The 1903 anniversary album from Immanuel Lutheran Church in Chicago not only featured the modernist developments pioneered by the pastor's wife, but it also served as a scrapbook of the Augustana elite. Many of the synod's leaders had spent some time in apprenticeship at the congregation. Emmy Evald had steered Immanuel's women in a progressive direction, while her husband, Carl Evald, conducted a quieter ministry in the city. According to the tributes in the 1903 volume, he never held a political office in the synod, but through a regular column in *Augustana* his views were advanced beyond his home base in Chicago. His code name, Urbanus, signaled his intention to speak for a cosmopolitan, modern view, but during the anniversary year, his column contained one very public complaint. In the spring of 1903 he complained in his column that, "the younger pastors lacked the piety of the older generation." Their reaction proved that he was right.

In the competitive field of Augustana's ambitious pastors, Urbanus's remarks created sore feelings, especially among the younger pastors. Carl Evald really was an old timer. Hasselquist had recruited him, and Carl retained in Chicago a focus on pastoral work familiar to the earlier, revival-oriented generation. The remarkable organization and programming that had begun to emerge at Immanuel during early 1900s had more to do with his wife's initiatives than with his own. The process of getting through Immanuel's fiftieth anniversary seemed to have made Carl nostalgic for the piety of the old days.

A neighbor and one of the supposedly deficient younger pastors, J. N. Brandelle, wrote a snide letter to a Carl J. Bengston, the youngish assistant editor at *Augustana* to express his impatience. "I don't think that the younger pastors suffer in comparison with the Doctors and Knights [of the North Star] in conducting their office." In fact, he felt the opposite was true. "The more humble consciences are to be found not among the doctors but among the younger [pastors]." Brandelle's derisive references to Knights and Doctors was intended to skewer those senior ministers like Evald, who talked about piety and humility but hardly ventured forth without their ribbons and medals or a series of letters after their name. He had a proposal for one of the paper's editors. "Couldn't S. P. A. Lindahl [a nit-picking champion of the older piety] write a series under the title 'pious, piouser, and piouest to catalogue us all?'"[16] Brandelle registered a shift in Augustana's culture. Younger pastors did not defer to their elders. Piety for Evald meant deference; Brandelle thought that at least the older pastors should look more humble.

Bengston's perch as managing editor of *Augustana* gave him an inside view of the political scene in Rock Island, too, where the seminary buildings were next door to the book concern where the newspaper was published. His friend Jules Mauritzson was the college's professor of Swedish who was then studying in Lund. Bengston kept him up to date on developments. Mauritzson shared impatience with posturing, but he targeted another colossal figure who shared a lot with Carl Evald, even his wide girth. "Is there no way to hinder our wannabe Brazilian mine agent, land speculator, and Knight of the North Star C. A. Swensson from filling, week after week, one and a half columns in *Fosterlandet* with drivel?"[17]

Members of Augustana's ministry were not of the same stamp any longer. More had been born in America, and their orientation was toward a future, English-speaking, American church. They faced an uphill struggle. The majority of newly ordained pastors were still Swedish-born.[18] But the younger pastors and the lay members increasingly turned to American-born peers for leadership. Positions such as editors, college presidents, and elected positions at the conference and synod levels went to men born in America or who emigrated while still young enough to learn English without an accent. Leaders who spoke and thought in the American idiom gained influence.

Young Leaders and Their Politics

During the first decade of the twentieth century, celebrations marking historical milestones gave synod leaders the opportunity to define the church and its purpose. Most of the voices heard at these gatherings, however, were from established leaders who celebrated what they had accomplished, and this made it next to impossible for younger leaders to really articulate their own, more modern views. J. A. Krantz, in a presidential sermon to the fiftieth anniversary gathering of the synod, declared that Minnesota had the reputation for being the most conservative of all the Augustana conferences. The label was a badge of honor, and in 1908 well earned, because Minnesota had passed a resolution against the new constitution for congregations that had been approved by the synod in 1907. The new constitution eliminated wording about gender and opened the way for congregations to allow any member in good standing to vote in congregation meetings. It was the first, minor step toward full participation of women. But Minnesota balked. "We cannot recommend the proposal to our congregations, but we desire that the synod convene a new committee to prepare a new constitution that will promote unity in our church."[19] The resolution provoked a long discussion and dissension. Norelius was president at the time and he argued in his presidential report that since states were more and more giving the vote to women, it would make for too many difficulties and challenges for the church to forbid what the states allow, but he did not prevail, and the issue continued to cause frustration.[20]

Norelius's ability to keep conservative and progressive factions within the synod in some kind of balance depended on his deep historical knowledge of the churches—he had prepared the first history of the synod in the mid 1890s—and his position of leading the more pietistic and rural spirit of the synod into the new century. Newer leaders, like C. J. Bengston, who pushed against the restraints put on them by elder ministers, would have to wait. The politics within the synod began to heat up after 1910, when Norelius announced he would not run for reelection. In February 1911, Jules Mauritzson wrote to Bengston who was then serving a parish in Montana after having a falling out at the newspaper in Rock Island. Mauritzson gave Bengston the latest news about editor L. G. Abrahamson, who had ambitions to be elected as the next synod president: Abrahamson "bit himself in the thumb regarding the upcoming vote for president. He won't get the Kansas conference vote, because Gustaf Alfred Brandelle has now got a medal."[21] Back in Rock Island, Mauritzson heard all the stories circulating around the synod's big egos. "I don't think that New York will blindly follow Fritz [Jacobson]—even if he talks ever so many languages." Mauritzson had scathing things to say about practically everyone. Sven Gustaf Youngert, who edited *Ungdomsvännen*, for young people, did not impress him. "Of S. G. Youngert we shall not speak. Is it because he greeted the 'bishop' with a speech in Greek in front of the gaping Hartfordites? He feels it rather deeply. On top of that he hasn't gotten a call from a congregation for the last two weeks!!!"

At the June 1911 synod meeting in Duluth, Minnesota, Norelius handed over the gavel to Lawrence Albert Johnston. L. G. Abrahamson hailed Norelius on *Augustana's* editorial page and mourned the change of guard: "None of the pioneer fathers are longer with us and the sons of the pioneers are being challenged to prove their mettle."[22] The new president was so much an underdog that Mauritzson didn't even mention him. Johnston had been a vice president of the Iowa and Minnesota Conferences and was pastor in nearby Moline, Illinois, but even the generous account of G. Everett Arden dismissed him as a president who lacked administrative or leadership ability. Perhaps synod members voted for him because they thought since he spoke English fluently and had been born in America he would have hidden talents in administration.[23]

Johnston's tenure as president covered the time when, independent from the official meetings of the synod's men, the women had begun to organize and direct their own future, dramatically changing the synod by demonstrating new ways of organizing and communicating a message and program. Mauritzson's letter to Bengston gives an inside view of the political scene in Rock Island, but just as he missed the name of L. A. Johnston, he also did not recognize the rising influence of the pastor's wife in Chicago.

chapter 8

AN AMERICAN CHURCH
IN A CHANGING AMERICA

As the Augustana Synod struggled to become an American denomination, its efforts were complicated by the fact that American society was, itself, undergoing rapid change. A tremendous social, cultural, and intellectual revolution occurred in America between 1910 and 1960. The task of acculturation and Americanization for immigrant denominations like Augustana was akin to trying to jump onto a moving vehicle—just when it seemed reasonable to jump, the target shifted. Religious groups generally are cautious, even resistant to social change. In the early twentieth century, Augustana's common bonds of ethnicity, religious heritage, and denominational loyalty diminished the impact of social change somewhat, but as with any religious group the size of the Augustana Synod, factions and divisions developed. At times this was all too evident in their reaction to social change; yet the synod held together through it all.

Augustana and Code Morality

The synod traditionally took a strongly negative stance toward engagement with American popular culture, a stance that has been called "code morality." The code was generally expressed in terms of prohibitions against all sorts of personal conduct that the synod found objectionable. The list, as described by synod president G. A. Brandelle in 1923, seems to be as sweeping as it is complete:

> The church is still in the world and for this reason is surrounded by all kinds of enemies. . . . [G]reat numbers . . . are drawn these days to indifference, materialism, greed, worldliness, pleasures of all kinds, gossip, slander, the dance, card playing, profaning Sunday, especially at harvest time, the inroads of secret societies, motion pictures, socialism, and the misuse of automobiles.[1]

This code morality had its roots in the Lutheran pietism of the eighteenth- and nineteenth-century Awakening in Sweden, which prohibited its followers from participating in all types of worldliness. In the United States, this pietistic morality was reinforced by the influence of conservative Protestantism coming out of the Reformed tradition (Puritanism), though this was an additional factor and the synod's moral stance would likely have been the same without it. The Swedish pietistic movement viewed the world in a dualistic way: whatever was not of the awakened community of Jesus Christ was certainly of the devil, and certainly the devilish amusements of the world had a strong attraction, even for those in the Church of Sweden. The Augustana Synod was mainly composed of those who shared this awakened pietism, and the strict moral code that accompanied it.

This is not to say that all members of the synod were pietists or held such a strong stance on issues of personal morality. While Augustana sought to pull as many Swedish Americans as possible into its ranks, many in the community were certainly more relaxed about issues of personal morality than the synod itself. One old Augustana pastor related that he was almost afraid to light the altar candles for the Christmas Eve service because the fumes of alcohol from the congregants were so strong that he feared an explosion! The constant drumbeat from synod leaders to maintain the code's standards may have been due, in large part, to the fact that it was not being universally observed, even within Augustana institutions. But synodical leadership was strongly committed to this morality, even if it cost them members and influence.

In America, where church membership was voluntary, Augustana's strong stance on a strict personal morality was costly. At the fiftieth anniversary of the synod in 1910, Brandelle admitted this strict attitude had taken a toll on Augustana's fortunes. "The Synod has never minced words about these evils," he remarked. "This is the main reason why in certain circles of the present day the Synod is more or less unpopular. 'The Synod is all right, if only it were not quite so strict in these and kindred problems.' Such expressions are frequently heard in the quarters of those . . . whose moral code is more or less elastic."[2]

Many other Swedish-American denominations were equally influenced by pietism, and so there were relatively few religious options for those with an elastic moral code. Some switched to more "open" denominations (such as the Swedish Episcopalians or other American groups).[3] Others opted out of church membership, choosing only to employ the services of the Augustana congregations when they so desired. This is perhaps one of the factors that explains why the Swedish ethnic denominations in the United States only gathered into their collective membership about 20 percent of the Swedish-American community. But synodical leaders persisted in defending the strong personal moral code until pressure from the synod's own members made them grudgingly seek a limited modification of some of its elements.

Code Morality's Contents and Boundaries

The long list of taboo worldly pleasures was frequently distilled into a tight collection of prohibitions against the use of alcohol and tobacco, dancing and card playing, listening to popular music and the radio, and watching theatrical plays and movies. Synod publications regularly extolled the need for sexual and personal morality, but the prohibition against alcohol garnered the greatest and most impassioned attention. Church periodicals regularly ran stories about individuals whose lives had been ruined by alcohol. One editor wondered, "Shall we continue to be unconcerned while Bacchus claims new sacrifices every day for his unholy altars?"[4]

The abuse of alcohol was nearly epidemic in nineteenth-century Sweden, and the pietist movement, borrowing from English and American sources, was fervently attached to the cause of temperance from the beginning. As early as 1880, in response to a query from the Women's Christian Temperance Union, the synod responded that it was "the duty of the Christian Church to see that all her members lead strictly sober lives and to discipline them for intemperance arising from the use of intoxicating liquors."[5] At synodical conventions from 1875 to 1961, Augustana passed more than fifty resolutions opposed to the use of alcohol or extolling the virtues of temperance and prohibition.[6] Typical was this resolution from 1938, that passed by a wide margin: "The Augustana Synod has always recognized the liquor traffic as a destroyer of souls and therefore, as an enemy of the church. . . . [T]he liquor traffic challenges the church with grave social problems in its heartless waste of human resources and human life."[7] "Demon rum" was a moral trap into which legions of individuals were ensnared, but more than that, it was a theological issue tied to human sinfulness.

The synod was a strong proponent of all forms of temperance and laws against alcohol, and wholeheartedly supported the constitutional amendment banning the manufacture and sale of alcohol. Following the repeal of the Eighteenth Amendment ending Prohibition, the synod redirected its focus toward those who profited from the manufacture and sale of alcohol, the "liquor traffic." The synod increasingly cast the issue as one of a vast industry conspiring to turn Americans into alcoholics. Attacking the industry's plans to push alcohol sales at Christmas, one writer declared, "It might be suggested to distillers that they cease their efforts to corrupt the day of our Lord's incarnation, and that they set aside instead a day of drunken revelry to their own god Bacchus. But perhaps such a 'holiday' would not prove popular enough to serve their mercenary purposes."[8] Advertising aimed at women and youth was especially excoriated, and those in the liquor traffic were seen to be in league with the devil. Augustana writers rarely ever reached such rhetorical heights as when they were attacking alcohol and the liquor industry.

Synodical members were assumed to be of one mind on this issue: devoted to temperance and opposed to alcohol. In 1954, synodical president Oscar Benson wrote that he had no doubt "that the vast majority of the people of the Augustana Lutheran Church and certainly the pastors are completely out of sympathy with the habit of drinking."[9] An earlier president, responding to a pastor's inquiry about how to deal with a congregational member who held a liquor license, suggested that the erring brother be brought before the deacons of the congregation to prevail upon him to quit selling liquor or be excommunicated from the church.[10] However, church discipline was rarely carried out in such cases, although much social pressure was often brought to bear.

The synod spoke out loudly against other forms of worldly amusements too. Traditionally, theatrical performances were rejected because of the "frivolity" and "immorality" of their subject matter and because of the reputed low morality of actors and actresses. With the development of the motion picture, the theatrical menace was multiplied exponentially, as movies took hold in almost all sections of the culture. As early as 1913, one writer referred to the movies as "a curse," while another, in 1933, complained that movies were taking up the time and interest of children who should otherwise be engaged in Christian education. Still another called the whole enterprise "moral filth . . . presented as 'art' and defended by some as a 'mirror of life.'"[11] Some saw a more diabolical hand in the movie industry, a conspiracy against Protestantism itself. An article in the *Bible Banner* suggested that "the whole proposition is a well-laid propaganda backed up by Jewish money and Jesuit intrigue. They are largely the promoters of all the big corporations."[12] A 1927 editorial in the *Lutheran Companion* even attacked Cecil B. DeMille's *King of Kings*, a film depicting the life of Christ. The editorial argued that the exploitation of Jesus' story by "the promoters of an industry that is wholly in the hands of members of a race that crucified Him, seems little short of blasphemy."[13]

Eventually the synod did warm to the possible positive uses of motion pictures as an evangelistic device, and in 1947 formed an audiovisual service to develop such uses. The commercial movie industry, however, remained suspect, and as one writer put it, "The occasional good film . . . is almost completely submerged by the welter of sordid pictures that depict life at its worst."[14]

If going to the theater or movies was to be shown life at its worst, then dancing was to be a participant in that type of degraded existence, a forum for excited passions and surrounded by a culture that promoted liquor and easy virtue. Social dancing "sacrifices health, it tends toward wasteful expenditure, it lacks true purpose socially, it interferes with intellectual improvement, and most serious, it is immodest and immoral,"[15] admonished one writer in an address to a Luther League convention in 1911.

Certainly the sexual element of dancing was at least on the minds of the dance critics, even if they were shy about broadcasting this in a public forum. One writer asked rhetorically, "Where are the young people [who can] . . . dance and not have the finest moral powers toyed with, the richest physical inheritance corrupted, the purest ideals and purposes left intact?. . . [I]t cannot be done by an ordinary human."[16] Others argued that though one might avoid the traumas and temptations surrounding social dancing, this might be seen as an invitation for others younger and weaker to be drawn into a world they could not readily withstand. As one fictional "College Girl" put it, "There may be nothing wrong with dancing . . . [but] I cannot say that I see no harm in it."[17] Dancing was the doorway to other, more serious temptations.

A similar sort of attack was often launched against all sorts of popular amusements, from card playing and gambling to popular jazz music and the instrument of its transmission—the radio. One writer imagined a meeting in hell where the devils were planning a campaign of ruin for American society by the gradual introduction of "popular amusements," such as drinking, dancing, and Sunday entertainments in place of going to church. One devil applauded the "broadening of ideas [that] has removed many obstacles to our [demonic] work."[18] Although music itself could not easily be condemned in total, many railed against "popular" music, such as jazz, which they saw as a virtual invitation to wickedness. One writer asked, rhetorically, "But what can be said of the abominable jazz music that is so prevalent today? Can such music be a source of enjoyment and an aid to efficiency to any one?"[19] The obvious answer, in his mind, was no.

Card games and gambling were also derided frequently as corrupt and immoral gateways to great evils. Theological professor Adolf Hult saw card playing as an unnecessary diversion from the Christian task, taking away from the mission of the church. Christians, he contended, did not need such diversions unless they had "degenerated" to the point that when meeting with fellow Christians they could come up with nothing else but "sit up till the midnight hours at the card table."[20] Other critics saw social card playing as an initial opening to the evils of gambling, leading to moral, economic, and social degradation. The *Lutheran Companion* editorialized in 1937: "The spread of the gambling mania can not be denied. Like other evils that follow in the train of legalized liquor, it has become a baneful influence in American life."[21] With that attitude, in 1938 and in 1943, the synod passed several resolutions against gambling.

Changes in the Synodical Moral Code

All the admonitions and rhetoric, however, could not mask the reality that although the leaders of the synod denounced these activities as moral and social failings, they were, nevertheless, invading the homes and congregations of the synod and the lives of its members. In a Swedish settlement in rural Minnesota, Pastor Alfred Bergin complained in 1904, "We have been troubled by irrelevant and foreign elements. The worldly life of the large cities has invaded our community. It seems like one is not able to differentiate between good and evil . . . because we are not prepared to meet the dangers and temptations."[22] One conference president reported in 1931 that there were "severe deviations from our moral standards . . . such as partaking in the nasty dances, card parties and other worldly amusements." He further bemoaned, "What right has a church member . . . to enter in the nasty dance hall?"[23] In an article on the pernicious effects of the movies, the *Lutheran Companion* grudgingly admitted that "many church members will attend the movies," but refused the suggestion that it begin to assist its members in distinguishing good movies from bad.[24] It seemed the vices were everywhere. One letter writer complained in 1957 that there were such a large number of people smoking at a church convention that "they were hardly able to refrain long enough to attend services and other programs."[25]

Though it finally would not yield on the question of alcohol, there was, beginning in the late 1930s, a distinct relaxation of the absolute prohibitions on card-playing, dancing, and other popular amusements, with the attempt to assist members to make moral judgments of their own. As one historian of Augustana described it, "The Church, for a number of reasons, had to face and finally yield to mounting opposition to certain aspects of its moral code."[26] One of the first areas in which the synod had to compromise was in the matter of radio programming. The Gustavus Adolphus college catalogue during the 1920s and 1930s, for example, stated that while students were permitted to have radios on campus, their general use was discouraged.[27] However, since elements of the synod were broadcasting worship services locally and regionally over church radio stations like WCAL, and even the conservative Lutheran Bible Institute of Minneapolis was broadcasting Bible studies on commercial stations such as WCCO, they could hardly condemn radio wholesale. Rather, the attack was more on the commercialization of the medium and on programming that lacked morality and refinement. LBI's *Bible Banner* editorialized in 1935 that "one of the most marvelous secrets of God's creation, has been subsidized by Mammon. A stupendous miracle has been diverted by hucksters for the sake of revenue."[28]

The synod's strategy shifted from outright prohibitions of popular amusements to moral advice on how to avoid the immoral elements of a particular activity. An article in a 1947 issue of the *Lutheran Companion* cautioned, "[W]hether or not the radio continues to *invade* the home or whether it will be used to *aid* home life depends ultimately upon parents themselves."[29] Augustana members were being asked to help develop standards and strategies for discernment, rather than being urged to forbid the medium all together. The same shift occurred with regard to movies and theatrical performances; how could Augustana prohibit movies and plays, for example, when the synod itself used movies as an evangelistic medium, and church colleges staged plays and entertainments?

One of the key areas of debate during this period was over the question of dancing. Despite prohibition against dancing, Augustana people danced, and there were rumors that pastors even turned a blind eye to dances being sponsored by local congregational organizations. The issue was most acute at the church's colleges, where, despite emphatic prohibitions, dancing was becoming a regular event for some college organizations, although always unofficially and off campus. A historian of Gustavus Adolphus stated, "In the '20s there was an occasional dance sponsored by a fraternity or sorority after a banquet but by the end of the '30s this was a standard though officially forbidden practice"[30] One mother even wrote to the college's president, O. J. Johnson, during the 1930s to defend her daughter from being disciplined for dancing. "She is a good, pure, girl, and dancing is music in motion," argued the mother. "Anyone who sins in dancing, sins when not dancing."[31]

At Augustana College, the enforcement of bans against dancing and smoking were still in place, but increasingly, both bans were ignored.[32] After World War II, Augustana College students petitioned for the right to have dances on campus; this led the Superior Conference to ask the synod to restate the prohibition on dancing. The matter was referred to the commission on morals and social problems, which returned a report to the convention in 1950. Instead of the expected restatement of the ban on dancing, however, the commission broke new ground. Dancing was not to be absolutely forbidden, but the "decision to take part or not take part in dancing must remain the responsibility of the individual." The report went on to restate the traditional moral advice about the dangers of dancing, and its attendant activities, and prohibited dances in congregational buildings or under the sponsorship of congregational organizations. College officials were permitted to allow dancing on campus, however, in recognition that dancing off campus was a widespread reality, though they were asked to supervise these activities so that they did not "reflect adversely . . . on the church and school."[33]

This action was much more significant than previous unofficial advice about radio, movies, and plays; it represented an official change in the traditional moral code of the synod, brought about by the invasion of the synod by the world. Though attitudes against alcohol and some other moral evils, such as lodges and other secret societies, would remain in effect, there were significant changes in other areas of moral prohibitions toward the middle of the twentieth century.

Augustana and the Progressive Era

The influences of American popular culture, seen in the gradual acceptance of social and popular amusements during the first half of the twentieth century was mirrored by Augustana's increased interest in serious social, economic, and political developments of the day. Augustana leaders and laypeople were taking to heart the need to be engaged citizens and were taking public positions, albeit cautiously at first, on the issues affecting the country and the world. Although the synod was, in general, composed of people who tended to be by nature rather socially and politically conservative, it also often exhibited a strong streak of American populism and interest in individual liberties, especially in reaction to the increasingly complex political and economic world of the day.

During the Progressive Era, from about 1900 to 1915, the younger generation of the synod began to show their intense interest in the larger, social world of America, and especially in the corporate dimension of individual and societal problems.[34] It would be too much to say that they were influenced by the Social Gospel movement of the day, though some did take a positive notice of this school of thought. Rather, as middle-class workers and citizens, they analyzed the world around them in light of their Lutheran faith and saw that the rise of large governmental and business units was having a negative impact on the country's workers and small businesses. Since many of the synod's members were located in the rural Midwest, where populism was the strongest, it is not strange to see that there are overtones of this movement within Augustana, including concerns about the rights of workers and child labor, an opposition to business trusts and a tight monetary policy, concerns about conservation and militarism, and a wariness about socialism and women's suffrage.

One of the major concerns of the day was the overwhelming influence of large corporations and industrial trusts on the workers and the consumers of the period. The rise of large and impersonal economic forces, against which many had little defense, was a source of continual alarm. As one writer editorialized in 1910, "A growing number of people . . . are growing dissatisfied with the present industrial conditions, the economic situation, and the social [dis-]order."[35] The writer went on to catalog a long list of abuses inflicted on the general population by large industrial and economic organizations and the collusion of the government in this situation. In applauding a judicial decision in 1907 to attack the Standard Oil Trust, another writer concluded, "God's plain commandment, Thou shalt not steal, is being qualified by so many nice distinctions that many men, who ought to be in the penitentiary, are now looked upon as some of our most distinguished citizens."[36] Along these lines, yet another writer suggested that "monopoly of industry and the means of subsistence [are] the great danger of the age," and generally praised a government initiative to go after trusts and monopolies.[37] Other similar articles praised the establishment of child labor laws, a minimum wage, and the conservation of natural resources—all common populist themes of the period.[38]

In distinction to older views that strictly delineated and separated theological inquiry from governmental or social legislation, some voices were beginning to suggest that the synod had a religious obligation to take a stand on the economic issues of the day. The writer of an article on the minimum wage, for example, suggested that "there should be . . . honest legislation to make such adjustments in the wage scale as shall put an end to these inequalities. . . . This is a religious question, and it is the Christian duty of the Church to declare itself."[39] Another supporter of child labor legislation listed the abuses of children in the workplace and then mocked those who would ignore these practices: "And still there are men who say: 'Hands off! Everything that is, is right! . . . We are enjoying "prosperity" and ought to leave well enough alone.'"[40]

Although there is no way in which the synod could be considered as being opened to the socialist movement of the day—it even had bitter feuds with a number of editors of Swedish-American socialist periodicals—some in the synod were in sympathy with the various aims of the movement. "[W]hile we are not socialists," stated one writer, "we also believe in truth and fair play." Suggesting that socialism was not necessarily anti-religion, the writer continued that he was against both "unchristian Socialists and unsocial Christians."[41]

Another pressing social issue of the day was the question of greater rights for women, especially the right to vote. In this area, the synod took a rather traditional outlook, although Augustana women were quietly press-ing for their place in the church, whether as deaconesses or missionaries, or through the efforts of the powerful Woman's Missionary Society. One measure of this was the resolution that passed in 1907 allowing women to vote in their local congregations, though it is unclear how many congrega-tions actually did allow for this. In response to the "new women" of his day, The *Lutheran Companion* editor C. J. Södergren, suggested that God had cre-ated the sexes "as distinct forms of our human life," with very different and separate roles. Yet another writer worried about the single young women working in the cities, asking, "How shall they resist the temptations in their path? This is one of the 'social problems.'" One Augustana writer opposed the suffrage amendment, seeing behind it a "deeper motive . . . to emancipate women out of the sphere she has been so well adapted by God and nature," but another argued that since the synod tentatively allowed for women's suf-frage in the congregation in its 1907 decision, how "much less does it violate Divine Law for her to vote for the election of an alderman, or a mayor?"[42] Certainly the changing role of women in society was an issue of the day, though the synod was slow to address it. Even the conservative Lutheran Bible Institute movement had to face the women's issue, for a majority of its own graduates were women, and they were going out to teach the Bible in congregations. Dean Samuel Miller walked a tightrope here, finally suggest-ing that while women could teach under the direction of male pastors, they should avoid leading public lectures and teaching mixed classes.[43]

Capitalism, Labor, and the Great Depression

With the rise of the major industrial corporation, the economic affects of a rapidly industrializing country, and the development of the labor movement during the early twentieth century, the United States was racked by conflict over economic issues. The Augustana Synod was generally removed from these disputes, though at times it did have to sit up and take notice. How-ever, the synod could not escape the direct effects of the Great Depression of 1929–1941, and the larger economic and social issues that it raised. Although Augustana leaders were generally conservative in their attitudes toward both organized labor and large-scale capitalism, they could be critical of both sides of the issue, suggesting that Christian love and social concern were far better than the antagonistic attitudes shown by labor and management. As one Augustana writer suggested in 1894, "Love your neighbor as yourself is about as good a principle as any and a faithful application of this certainty cannot fail to bring about its salutary effects alike to both employee and employer."[44] Though this may have been good advice, if applied consistently, the love commandment seemed not to be effective in these disputes, and Augustana had to face a rapidly changing economic world.

At the beginning of the twentieth century, the economic profile of Augustana members tended to keep them away from those areas of the economy where industrial agitation was the strongest. In the rural areas Swedish Americans were usually farmers, laborers, and small business owners, while in the cities they were domestic servants, trade and craft workers, along with a small but growing professional class.[45] When Swedes were employed in large industries, such as in some of the settlements in New England, they tended to be skilled workers rather than laborers, and would generally move up the economic scale fairly quickly. Although there were some Swedish immigrants who were active in professional guilds and trade associations, there were generally few of them involved in the new, large-scale labor unions.

Attitudes in Augustana toward these new labor organizations tended to be rather negative. To many in the synod, unions represented a form of tyranny and coercion of the workers, a conspiracy to remove from them their right to work, and from the employers, their right to choose and discipline their employees. The labor movement and many of its strongest proponents were disaffected from traditional organized religion, and the movement, in many eyes, tended toward atheism and socialism. The violence of some of the labor actions, and the trend toward socialism and atheism turned many away from support of organized labor. To many in the synod, labor unions took on the appearance of being secret societies and organizations that would supplant the church in the lives of industrial workers. In 1903, one Augustana writer observed:

> Large portions of the labor unions have committed themselves to the Socialist party. Thereby they propose to take the reins of government into their own hands by degrees. . . . [T]hey can ill afford to espouse the cause for which the red flag stands. The fundamental laws of the Word of God must be respected and lived up to.[46]

On the other hand, synodical voices could be equally opposed to aspects of capitalism and to the actions of industrial management. It was assumed that the leaders of industry were just as guilty, and disaffected from the tenets of the Christian gospel, as were the labor leaders. In 1902, G. A. Brandelle wrote, "Time and again what is called business becomes but a sort of a system of legalized robbery. . . . The moral sense of the individual is blunted and even in many cases destroyed. The only law that is acknowledged is this: might is right."[47] Business leaders were blasted for their oppression of the working people and for creating a hopeless situation for their families. Violence on both sides was generally condemned, and the *Lutheran Companion* applauded President Woodrow Wilson when he sent troops to break up a violent labor-management dispute in the Colorado coal industry in 1914.[48]

Through the economic prosperity of the 1920s there was little notice of industrial issues, but this changed with the depression of the 1930s. With an upsurge in labor unrest and the rise in industrial violence, the synod was again focused on labor rights and tactics. Voices were heard from both sides. One editorial, focusing on sit-down strikes, opposed them: "The spirit of lawlessness . . . grows the more ominous when court orders are defied and law enforcement officers and large groups of workers come to actual grips. When law and order are flaunted, then the dissolution of organized society is near at hand."[49] A later editorial claimed that "Americans are getting somewhat tired of the present warfare," though one reader wrote in to defend labor, stating, "The 'sit down' thus far has proved its worth. Really the violence is minimal and results are maximal. . . . Remember, not all strikers unionize. Unionization is begotten in the inflexibility of corporation wage scales."[50]

In 1939, the synod adopted a resolution recognizing the rights of both labor and management to collective bargaining and called on employers to provide safe and reasonable working conditions, urging both sides to "work for the public good and not to abuse their power by trampling on the rights of others," and to build on a "spiritual rather than a materialistic basis."[51] The synod would also repeat this general line of thought in resolutions adopted in 1953 and 1958.

One proponent of unions and labor activities was A. D. Mattson, professor at Augustana Seminary, who attempted to open up synodical attitudes toward the subject through his influence on seminary students, and through his advocacy within Augustana.[52] When the *Lutheran Companion* carried an editorial implying that the rising cost of living during the 1950s could be attributed, in part, to the wage demands of labor unions, Mattson responded, "Those who criticize high wages for labor perhaps ought to be willing to trade economic status with the laboring man. Generally speaking, labor has not been getting too much of the economic plum."[53]

When Mattson put his ideals into action, however, and as a professor at the seminary lent his support in a letter to striking workers at the John Deere factory in Rock Island in 1960, the church's president, Malvin Lundeen, wrote him a strong letter of rebuke, stating that he had received "a number of complaints about this letter." Lundeen allowed that Mattson might have his own private opinions, but when he spoke as a seminary official it took on the character of an official statement. "It is at this point that I register my strong disapproval of what you said and did," wrote Lundeen.[54] Even as late as 1960 the synod could be very wary of even the appearance of social pronouncements on labor issues, and the reaction to Mattson's actions are indicative of this.

The Great Depression of the 1930s presented more than just a theoretical issue of labor-management relations; it was a direct threat to the welfare of the members of the synod, and because of this, to the institutions and ministries of Augustana.[55] The decline in national prosperity touched directly on the synod itself: on average, per capita giving to the national organization dipped from $22.13 in 1930 to $13.82 in 1935, and giving to the educational and social service institutions and to missions fell accordingly. A number of these institutions, especially the colleges, collapsed entirely during the depression, and those that remained did so only through the most stringent economies and cutbacks.

The economic collapse began at the congregational level, where members were unable to pay their pastors. One such minister wrote to President Brandelle in 1933: "I am not getting my salary. . . . My two congregations are now in arrears on my salary to the amount of $1315.00. . . . I have not managed to lay up anything to live on and am totally dependent on my salary, myself, my wife, and, three children in minor ages."[56] In 1932, only 20 percent of the seminary students had any prospect of calls, and home missionaries were informed that the Board of Missions was deeply in debt and unable to provide for their salaries; they were asked to directly solicit their congregations for support.[57] Synod leaders attempted to rally their members for additional funds to support synodical ministries. Conferences sent out urgent appeals; typical was this one from the Minnesota Conference:

> [W]e are now compelled to retrench . . . decrease our aid to our home
> mission, and to defer payment on the salaries of our workers in the
> field. . . . Our Emergency Committee cannot make bricks without
> straw. We have no other recourse than to lay the matter before our
> membership.[58]

The president of the Iowa Conference, P. O. Bersell, urged his readers that this was "no time to quit," but suggesting that it was not the fault of the membership, he derided what he saw as a lack of leadership from synodical officials. "Oh, for the voice of a prophet, in the Augustana Synod, a voice vibrant with divine authority," he scolded. "This time calls for such leadership."[59]

President Brandelle, seventy-two years old in the crisis year of 1933, came under attack from other leaders in the synod for not doing enough to meet the challenges, and the synodical committee on church extension and home missions, which included Bersell, publicly criticized Brandelle in reports to the synod convention in 1934 and 1935.[60] Even an anonymous "sincere friend" took Brandelle to task for the perceived lack of "economies" at Augustana College, suggesting that he himself should "control and adjust matters which seem very unfair."[61] The worst year for the synod seems to have been 1933. The church slowly adjusted to reduced spending and began to climb out of its financial predicament after 1934.

The larger, national debate over the Great Depression, and how to get out of it, was also reflected within the synod. Traditionally the Swedish Americans had been largely Republicans, and distrustful of government programs for social relief, but the crises of 1929–1933 seem to have softened these attitudes. Early in 1933, Augustana pastor Theodore Matson wrote: "The leadership of our nation is pretty much of an old-time tug-of-war . . . and no peer in statesmanship, leadership, and unselfishness appears on the horizon with a worthwhile solution to offer."[62] Yet, at the end of the year, after the introduction of President Roosevelt's New Deal measures, the *Lutheran Companion* was cautiously supportive: "Like most emergency solutions, the present project is far from ideal. Its prime movers admit their and its fallibility [but because] . . . many of the causes in it are just, it should not altogether fail."[63]

In another editorial four years later, a new editor, E. E. Ryden showed his support for Roosevelt's economic initiatives but also suggested that the president needed to pay attention to the "moral" recovery of the nation as well: "The economic standards of a whole nation may be lifted . . . and yet the nation may not be right with God. The present moral trend in America is sufficient proof of this. Flood gates of iniquity have been opened. . . . The conscienceless liquor traffic is one that might be mentioned."[64] During this time Ryden was also particularly critical of Roosevelt's push toward rearmament and support for the British and French military, which might have tempered his support for the president.

Social Conflicts and Issues

Besides issues of personal morality and economic troubles, the leaders and members of the Augustana Synod also took positions on a range of other social and political issues during the first part of the twentieth century, including attitudes toward race, inter-faith relations with Roman Catholics and Jews, and the changing nature of American society, to name a few. Much of this notice was wrapped in traditional Lutheran attitudes, but at times the synod could be quite forward in its thinking.

With the exception of a few northern cities, the Augustana Synod was not generally located in areas with large African-American populations, so the synod did not have a long history of dealing with racial issues. It was consistently for Christian love in all social relationships, and thus decried violence against African Americans, with comments in the synodical press against lynching in 1901 and 1927, condemning this as a travesty of justice and a "contempt for the orderly process of law."[65] C. J. Bengston called the lynching of Leo Frank in 1915 an act of premeditated murder and as much of a crime as the one for which Frank was originally sentenced.[66] Synodical attitudes on race relations, however, were still generally along the lines of "separate but equal," although they would have insisted on the equal part of the equation. In the early 1930s, a young African American named Jesse Routte was allowed to enter Augustana Seminary, but when he graduated in 1932, the synod placed him in a home mission of the United Lutheran Church in America because Augustana did not have a "Negro mission" of its own and had no prospects of beginning one.[67] In 1943, E. E. Ryden reflected on the racial division inherent in the country: "What is really involved here is not the indiscriminate mixing of the races, but rather an attitude of heart and mind to do what is right. White people must come to realize that even the darker races were created in the image of God."[68] The synod, however, did not have to face this issue in its own congregations, so its support for race relations remained more of a theoretical issue than a practical one.

In a similar way, Augustana had more than a passing interest in Judaism, but generally only as a mission field for conversion. Augustana members had a long history of support for an inter-Lutheran organization called the Zion Society for Israel, half of whose support came from Augustana sources and whose reports and appeals for funds appeared regularly in synodical sources; annually, the synod approved a denomination-wide offering for the work of this organization.[69] The concern for Jews was often a self-interested one; they were the target of conversion. One writer stated in 1912: "Remember that 'salvation is of the Jews' and that they gave us our Christ and our Bible . . . according to the scripture that people has a glorious future. When the fullness of the Gentiles shall come in, Israel shall be saved."[70]

As Jews began to return to Israel after World War I, the religious implications of this return were not lost on some within the synod, who saw this return as a work of God. "[The] rapidly approaching restoration of the Jew to his homeland," commented Charles W. Erickson in the *Lutheran Companion*, was an event suggesting "the hope and promise of his turning from unbelief to faith in Christ."[71] There was, however, some equal support in the synod for the plight of the Arab Palestinians, and the predictable anti-British, anti-imperialistic attitude.

The self-interested goodwill that was exhibited in some quarters of the synod toward the Jews was not replicated in Augustana's attitudes toward Roman Catholics. Rather consistently the synod displayed a general and uniform hostility toward Roman Catholicism, one that mirrored the attitudes of American Protestants in general. Synodical writers expressed resentment toward Roman proselytism, feared the parochial schools as an agent of church control over education, and saw the Vatican as in a constant conspiracy against Protestant Americans in general. In 1892, and again in 1893, the synod convention approved resolutions aimed to maintain the non-sectarian nature of American public schools, in the face of what one commentator called the "Jesuits' . . . double war . . . against the Protestant private schools, higher as well as lower, and . . . against the neutral, or non-religious, state schools." Further, he claimed, "After they have crippled the former, they can more easily control or crush the latter."[72]

Suspicions were widespread that Roman Catholics were trying to usurp or control the public school system in America. The Roman church was also charged with attempting to undermine American democracy by attempting to implement a theocracy in America, which, claimed one writer, was "the ideal" of the Roman Catholic Church. "What misery this greed of power has brought to the world every student of church-history knows."[73] Protestantism, and more specifically, Lutheran Protestantism, was seen as the champion of the separation of church and state, while Catholicism had "vigorously opposed the separation of church and state, and . . . its present day policy is consistent with the past."[74]

The question of public and private schools died out as the twentieth century progressed, but not negative attitudes toward Roman Catholicism. Much criticism was directed at the Vatican, for example, for its strong opposition to Protestant mission work abroad, especially in Latin America and other countries where the Catholic Church was dominant. One editorial in 1937 criticized the Italian government for restricting mission work in Ethiopia to Catholic groups, and attacked Roman "hypocrisy":

> The Church of Rome has a strange idea of religious liberty and toleration. It wants neither one in countries where it occupies the supreme position; but when its own prerogatives are restricted in any way by government action, it becomes exceedingly vocal in its protests.[75]

Although rank-and-file American Roman Catholics were by and large seen as decent and respectable people, the Roman hierarchy was generally viewed as advocates of despotism, indoctrination, and drink, and completely hostile to Protestantism, public liberties, and the traditions of America.

The increase in numbers and prominence of the Jewish and Roman Catholic populations in the United States gave rise in the early twentieth century to a nativist backlash and calls for strict immigration reforms and limitations, a movement that culminated in sharply curtailed immigration after 1924. The Augustana Synod was itself a denomination full of immigrants, and there was a strong anticipation within the synod that mass immigration of Swedes to America would resume after World War I. The synod thus wanted to avoid restrictive immigration, if it would keep out Swedish immigrants. On the other hand, a general attitude of suspicion toward non-Protestant immigrants was widespread and mirrored that of the rest of Protestant America. In one editorial from 1914, C. J. Södergren commented: "Drastic measures are uncalled for. They are the desperate measures of blind prejudice against foreigners—a remnant of the old Know-Nothingism. But it is left to you to judge . . . and it is confidently hoped . . . you will lend your whole strength in opposing all further restriction of immigration."[76] Yet just the next year, the new editor of the *Lutheran Companion*, Carl J. Bengston, wrote of his general approval of restricting immigration "so as to exclude as far as possible the undesirable and admit the desirable." He suggested that a literacy test, while not perfect, would be welcome.

In 1922, the Swedish-language *Augustana* favored restrictions only on immigrants from Southern and Eastern Europe, who "had totally different conceptions of morality than those which gave the people of Northern Europe their pre-eminent position." A 1929 article in the *Lutheran Companion* opposed new immigration restrictions as an unfair conspiracy against Northern European immigrants and wondered how the country would benefit "by the immigration of more Italians, Poles, and Irish."[77] Largely on the basis of this perceived unfairness to immigrants from Sweden and Northern Europe, in 1926 the synod convention passed a strong resolution against the immigration reforms of 1924, as adopted by Congress.[78]

A Change in Social Outlook, 1937–1962

Often lifted up as a dramatic change in the synod, the 1937 formation of the Commission on Morals and Social Problems (later, Commission on Social Action) by convention action was probably not as drastic a development as it might appear.[79] Augustana conventions and publications had long taken stands on social and cultural issues, as we have seen, and the formation of a commission was as much of a sign of the organizational maturity of the synod as anything else. But it is true that this commission centralized the task of developing social policies and certainly did give a "more official status to the growing concerns for social questions," and many more social pronouncements were made by the synod during this period than in previous times.[80]

In 1937, theological professor A. D. Mattson urged Augustana to take a wider role in social affairs than it had previously. He wrote that theories of church and society that considered only individual salvation or only social transformation were inadequate. Understanding that much of the synod would be traditionally with the former, he affirmed the church "need not fear that an insistence on the social application of Christianity will tend to minimize the importance of individual salvation. Both processes work harmoniously together."[81] However, another writer, Pastor Paul Andreen, looked around at the troubled American society of 1937 and saw that the battle had shifted in many of the parishes "from faith in the Christ-given tenets of the Church, in its objective relation to God, to an attempt to evolve a new social ideal of man's relation to government, neighbor, and property."[82] This battle was seen in modern movements such as atheism, communism, and Nazism, but also in social trends that denigrated church and home. It was not necessarily in conflict with Mattson's idea, though Andreen clearly saw the modern world in a darker light than did Mattson. Both elements of piety were evident in Augustana's engagement with the larger social world around it.

As early as 1927, the editor of the *Lutheran Companion* had worried aloud about the beginnings of the social changes that would transform American life: "The drift is toward the suburbs, leaving the 'downtown' churches either abandoned or with an inner mission problem on their hands." And the change was not limited to cities, for those from the rural churches ". . . drift away and are lost in the surging stream of city life."[83] This trend only accelerated after 1945, when the rise of automobile transportation and affordable suburban homes became a reality for masses of Americans. In 1947, a home missions official wrote that because of changing demographics and settlement patterns, many of the urban congregations in his conferences were seeking to relocate. He suggested that the synod needed to re-envision the role of the local congregation; it was no longer enough to serve just a scattered "Scandinavian" population, but "our responsibility is to serve a [geographic] community as well as an [ethnic] constituency." He added that congregations needed to consider the "will of God" and not just their own "fond desires and sentimental attachments." Another writer in 1943 argued that Augustana had the duty to gather in all unchurched Americans, regardless of race or background; "they too are children of our God—that they too have been bought with a price."[84]

The movement to metropolitan and suburban areas, along with the baby boom, created a challenge for the church. As there had been little in the way of church construction from the Great Depression through World War II, there was a tremendous need to build new churches and to add on to older structures. The *Lutheran Companion* reported almost weekly of new congregations founded and new church buildings and parsonages erected. A new suburban congregation, Emanuel Lutheran in Modesto, California, reported: "During the past year [1952] 94 adults and 41 children became members of the church. The growth of the Sunday School is taxing the facilities that were expanded two years ago."[85] The California and Columbia Conferences more than doubled their membership from 1950 to 1960, during a time in which the synod's entire membership increased by nearly one-third. In 1953, the rapidly growing Florida district of the New York Conference was incorporated, virtually becoming a separate conference of its own.

As Augustana members and congregations spread out across the American landscape and began to think about opening their doors to those beyond their traditional ethnic borders, the social problems of the 1950s became a topic of comment for many in the synod. The civil rights movement was cautiously supported by the synod in six different resolutions from 1948 to 1958, and the synod sought during this time to minister to African-American populations, either on its own or with other Lutheran partners. When, in 1947, the American Lutheran Conference, of which the Augustana Synod was a part, failed to pass a resolution calling for the inclusion of African Americans in white congregations, one Augustana member called it "the most outrageously un-Christian act committed by any Lutheran church body since the days of the infamous German Christians, whose basic philosophies seem not to be unknown within our own Synod." But another member suggested that "God has made the marked difference which exists between white and colored people, and we are not disobeying when we respect the law of race which He has made."[86] The larger events and conflicts caused by the civil rights movement occasioned much comment within the synodical press during the 1950s. The firebombing in Alabama of the home of a white Lutheran pastor who supported integration was soundly condemned, while the violence surrounding the 1957 integration of schools in Little Rock, Arkansas, was called "a disgrace to the nation."[87]

Traditional attitudes toward Roman Catholicism and Judaism seem to have remained largely unchanged by Augustana's move toward ecumenism. During the middle of 1943, E. E. Ryden wrote about "strange maneuvers" by Cardinal Spellman of New York, who was visiting European capitals. Ryden was very suspicious of these visits, because of "the sinister designs of the political-spiritual hierarchy of the Church of Rome which is ever scheming to bring all of Christendom back into the 'true fold.'" The *Lutheran*

Companion continued to worry about Catholic attempts to take over public schools in the United States, a "deliberate plan" to divert money from public education into the parochial school system. When television station WGN in Chicago proposed to show a movie about Martin Luther, and Roman Catholic pressure was brought on the station not to air the film, Augustana voices raised cries of censorship. According to the newspaper, "Rome has tried once more to silence the voice of Martin Luther, and apparently has failed." In 1960, when some leading Augustana theologians endorsed John F. Kennedy for president, there was quite a public outcry, though it was hard to tell if the reaction was due to the fact that Kennedy was a Democrat or because he was Roman Catholic.[88]

Traditional synodical support for Judaism was modified because of the formation of the state of Israel in 1948. On the occasion of the United Nations vote for partition, an Augustana editor noted Arab outrage at the idea, but then reminded his readers that this might be a part of God's plan for the world: "Certain it is that God has an unfulfilled destiny for His chosen people, and it may be that the events we are witnessing today is the opening chapter of that divine plan." On the other hand, E. R. Danielson, an Augustana missionary en route to East Africa, wrote of the destructive power of Arab anger at these events, and wished that "the American public might get the Arab side of the political question—and not just the Jewish." After running an article in 1953, showing the plight of the Palestinian Arabs in a very sympathetic light, the *Lutheran Companion* editorialized that the "principle sin of the United States, of course, has been its policy of expediency in supporting Britain's position, not only in the Holy Land, but also in relation to Iran and Egypt." The *Lutheran Companion* seemed often to make the distinction between religious Judaism (whose members it still sought to convert) and political Zionism, which it opposed.[89]

On its way to becoming an "American" church, the Augustana Synod cautiously began to interact with the elements of modern life in the United States, sorting out its own positions on the issues involved. At times, the synod would remain quite conservative and resolute in its pronouncements, and at other times, it would take fairly courageous stances, always trying to be faithful to its Lutheran Christian roots and its understanding of what the gospel might mean for a new and often bewildering world.

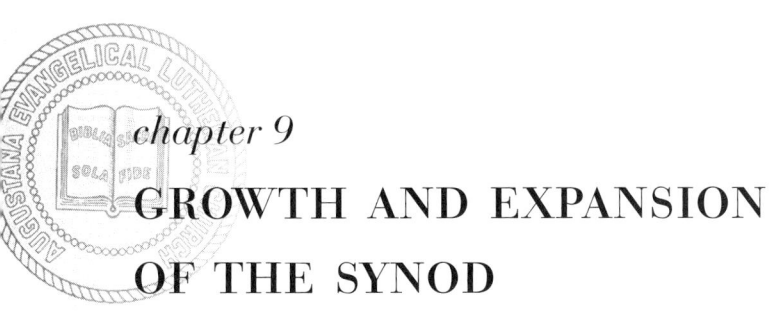

chapter 9

GROWTH AND EXPANSION
OF THE SYNOD

For most of its existence, Augustana was an immigrant denomination, and the flow of people from Sweden to North America determined much about the development of the synod. After the cessation of mass immigration at the beginning of World War I and immigration restrictions of the 1920s, the wanderings of the Swedes did not end, as the second and third generations of Swedish Americans spread out through North America. Some moved away from older ethnic settlements in the Midwest to the East and West Coasts of America and up into Canada, while newer immigrants headed there directly. As the twentieth century progressed, they joined the great migration of North Americans from farms and villages to developing metropolitan areas. And they moved constantly, looking for new land, new jobs, and new opportunities in this New World, looking, as was everyone else, for the American dream. As Swedish Americans went, so went the Augustana Synod, building new congregations and all the attendant social, educational, and administrative structures necessary for a modern American denomination. While it grew, the synod worked to find ways to reach beyond borders of land and ethnicity to spread the gospel.

Contours of Swedish Immigration to North America

The major immigration of Swedes to North America from 1820 to 1930 was part of a much larger migration of peoples from Europe to North America, a migration that totaled more than 30 million individuals, perhaps one of the largest mass movements of human beings in recorded history. A total of 1.2 million Swedes immigrated to North America during this period of time, representing 20 percent of the total population of Sweden, a percentage that was exceeded by immigrants from only a few other European countries.[1] The Swedish immigrants settled in North America, and with their children and grandchildren, they formed an immigrant world often referred to as "Swedish America," a world that combined elements of both Swedish and American cultures. Although Swedish America was in part at least an ephemeral vehicle by which the Swedish immigrants eventually became fully Americanized, it also resulted in the formation of permanent presences, the largest of which were those religious, social, and educational institutions that constituted the Augustana Synod.

Swedish immigration was not at all constant and uniform, varying in strength and direction, and social, economic, and political events in Sweden and America affected its course greatly.[2] Though tens of thousands of Swedes immigrated to North America between 1850 and 1920, there were three peak periods: 1868–1873 (104,000 people), 1879–1893 (452,000 people), and 1900–1913 (280,000 people). These thirty-five years represent up to 75 percent of the total immigration.[3] Sometimes events in the "old country" exerted pressure on Swedes to leave, such as the famine of 1868 or the labor troubles of 1879–1880 and 1891–1893. Other times immigration was dampened by outside events, such as the American depression of 1893 or the beginning of the First World War in 1914. Since there was such an extensive connection between Swedes in Europe and those in North America, news and opportunities were quickly transmitted from one side of the Atlantic to the other, causing the flood and ebb of immigration from year to year. For detailed charts on the Swedish immigration, see the Appendix.

What is called Swedish America is constituted by the immigrants themselves and their children, or as they are referred to in the language of the United States Census, "foreign-born" and "children of foreign-born," respectively.[4] This community of first- and second-generation Americans peaked at more than 1.5 million people in the decade between 1920 and 1930, though as might be guessed, the numbers of the first generation peaked in 1910, while the second generation did not peak until 1930. If the numbers of the second generation peaked in 1930, one could well assume that the numbers of the third generation might well have crested in the period from 1950 to 1960. The dramatic decline in immigration was evident after the First World War; only once after this time did immigration numbers ever reach their pre-war heights, with a surge in immigration in 1923 of 25,000 people, perhaps rushing to enter the United States before Congress passed dramatically restricted immigration quotas.

Early immigration consisted largely of entire families who settled in the rural areas of the Midwest, while later immigration was comprised of single young people looking for work in American cities. Initial immigration followed the expanding contours of the North American frontier and the availability of new farmland, with immigrants in the 1850s and 1860s settling in the Upper Mississippi River valley—northern Illinois, southern Wisconsin, and eastern Iowa and Minnesota. By the 1870s and 1880s, Swedish America pushed onto the prairies of the Great Plains—western Iowa and Minnesota, the Dakotas, Nebraska, and Kansas—as well as into the northeastern United States. From the 1890s to the 1910s, immigration had expanded into the Pacific Northwest and Canada. There were other areas of Swedish immigration into California, Texas, and Florida.[5]

Besides the direct migration of Swedes into these areas, Swedish Americans often moved internally within North America in "stage migration," changing locations several times to find increased opportunities in waves of secondary and tertiary migration. H. Arnold Barton observed how "there was a remarkable amount of moving around, right from the earliest days. One is repeatedly impressed how many times the same individual moved since leaving the old home."[6] For example, the secondary "colony" of Halland in southwest Iowa was formed in the 1870s by Swedish Americans who had settled initially in eastern Iowa and Illinois. During the 1890s, a group from Halland moved south to Florida, where they formed the town of Hallandale, and ventured into citrus farming.[7] Instances like this were often repeated in other areas, as Swedish Americans moved out of the American Midwest in search of opportunity. During the twentieth century, the Augustana Synod expanded out of its base in the Midwest to follow these streams of restless Swedish Americans.

The migration from rural areas to urban areas was another major contributor to the geography of Swedish America, especially into the twentieth century. After the Civil War, cities in the United States expanded with a startling rapidity, and many Swedish Americans were drawn to these growing urban areas. The percentage of Swedish Americans living in urban areas rose steadily throughout the twentieth century, rising from 56 percent in 1910 to 65 percent in 1930;[8] this is low compared to other American immigrant groups, but higher than other Scandinavian American groups, especially the Norwegian Americans. The largest number of Swedish Americans lived in the Midwestern cities of Chicago, Minneapolis, and St. Paul, but significant numbers also lived in cities on the East and West coasts, including New York, Los Angeles, and Seattle. All told, 72 percent of the first generation Swedish Americans (430,000 out of 595,000 people) lived in just twelve major American cities. (For a detailed listing of cities and their Swedish immigrant populations, see Table 3 in the Appendix.)

Augustana had to organize new congregations to meet the rising urban population, but even here, Swedish Americans were still mobile and restless, moving into more desirable areas within the cities or into newly developed suburbs as their social and economic situations improved. Synodical congregations often moved to follow their members or established "daughter" congregations in the new areas.

Home Missions Activity

Managing and encouraging the growth of the synod was difficult, not only because of the flood of immigrants and the mobility of their descendants, but because the synod often lacked the resources (money and pastors) to keep up with the need. In the first generation, the individual pastors often left their new congregations for long periods of time to "ride the circuit," bringing worship and the sacraments to scattered groups of Swedish settlers who lived beyond the reach of established Augustana congregations; many new congregations were formed out of preaching points these traveling pastors served. After some ineffective attempts to bring a little coordination and resources to this work, the synod in 1870 constituted a Home Missions Board, with five mission districts that were actually the five conferences at the time.[9] The board as a whole oversaw and financed some independent home mission and extension activity, but generally the conferences managed this activity in their own territory. This was at a time in synodical life when the conferences were gaining strength at the expense of the synod, and this arrangement would stay in effect until well into the twentieth century. Nevertheless, the arrangement did seem to be useful, as the size of the synod and its regional presence expanded throughout the end of the nineteenth century. Occasionally the board would also attempt mission work among Native Americans, African Americans, and Swedish-American Mormons in Utah, but only the last of these efforts was ever carried out with much regularity.

Each conference had home mission leadership of its own and full charge of evangelism and church extension within its own geographical boundaries. The central synodical board was only in direct charge of so-called mission districts, areas beyond the reach of one of the conferences, such as the congregations in the Southeastern United States that formed the Florida district. The board's constitution, adopted in 1906, specified that it would control foreign missions as well, and only do missionary work within the boundaries of a conference, "with the sanction of the conference concerned." During the first fifty years of its existence, the Home Mission Board spent approximately $250,000 on its work, while the conferences as a whole spent almost $600,000,[10] showing the relative strength of the two efforts.

As a part of the General Council of Lutherans in North America, which Augustana joined in 1869, the synod was able to coordinate its own home missions work with other American Lutheran groups, something that was relatively easy to do as long as it was simply a matter of dividing American

Lutherans by ethnicity and language. But as the nineteenth century came to a close, and as some Swedish Americans began to push for English-language congregations, the situation became more complicated and conflicting. Other members in the General Council were establishing English-speaking congregations in what Augustana considered to be its territory. Augustana wanted control over these congregations especially in the Upper Midwest. A number of these congregations contained mixed groups of English-speaking Swedes and other American members and did not fit well into the Swedish-speaking Augustana Synod. The temporary affiliation with Augustana proved unsatisfactory, and so in 1893 many of these congregations formed the independent Synod of the Northwest and joined the General Council. This action infuriated many in Augustana, especially in the Minnesota Conference, leading to Augustana's decision to pull back from the General Council. It also helped the development of an Augustana Association of English Congregations, formed in 1908.[11]

In the twentieth century, as Augustana began to take on a more centralized and organized denominational structure, the power and responsibility for home missions and expansion came back under synodical control. In 1928, the Iowa Conference petitioned the synodical convention for the establishment of a new centralized board that would direct and finance all home missions activity. This plan was considered for a number of years, but did not move forward until 1935, when Iowa Conference president P. O. Bersell was elected synodical president. In 1937, Augustana approved a centralized entity, the Board of Home Missions, to take over all home missions and extension activity, with a national board and full-time administrative staff that began work in 1939. It was renamed the Board of American Missions in 1949.[12] This new board was thus in place and ready for the rapid expansion of American religious life that came after World War II, and it was able to marshal synodical funds to meet the rapidly growing needs in the postwar period. The board was able to organize 257 congregations from 1939 to 1962,[13] granted aid to 450 more, and spent more than $5.6 million on the effort. Funds for this activity came from the synod that, since 1948, had organized an annual appeal—the "Augustana Mission Advance"—and from the Woman's Missionary Society (later Augustana Lutheran Church Women), who contributed $1.8 million over the years.[14]

Synod Expansion

The growth of the Augustana Synod held steady through the years of immigration, though it never came close to reaching all the Swedish immigrants and their descendants. In the early twentieth century, the synod's official membership comprised about 15 percent of all Swedish Americans[15] although its "range of influence" within the immigrant community has been estimated at upwards of 50 percent, counting those Swedish Americans who had contact with synodical congregations or institutions, but did not belong to one.[16] The voluntary nature of American religion was foreign to new immigrants, and the idea of having to join and directly pay for Lutheran congregations was alien to many. About 6 percent of Swedish immigrants joined other Swedish ethnic denominations, such as the Mission Covenant, Free Church, Methodists, or Baptists.[17] Some Swedish Americans celebrated their new American identity by joining "English" congregations, that is, English-speaking American churches (Lutheran or other denominations), while others decided that in the United States freedom of religion meant for them freedom *from* religion. Even so, the relatively low numbers of Swedish Americans who were directly affiliated with Augustana was a source of great concern and anguish to synodical leaders, leading them to plan for ways to reach the "lost" Swedes. Though their numbers were not as they would have wished, the Augustana Synod was still far and away the largest and most influential single organization within the Swedish-American community.

Regional growth of the Swedish-American community, and by extension growth of the Augustana Synod, can be seen in the expansion of its regional conferences. When Augustana began in 1860, it consisted of two conferences, Mississippi[18] (Illinois and Iowa), formed in 1853, and Minnesota, formed in 1858. By 1870, the synod had five conferences; by 1893, it had eight; and by 1923, it had expanded to a total of thirteen (see Table 5 in the Appendix). Various temporary mission districts were also established from time to time, especially in the South and West. Of the conferences, the largest were in the Midwest; Minnesota always had the most members, followed by the Illinois Conference.[19] The New York Conference was next in size, followed by New England, and by 1960, the West Coast Conferences of California and Columbia had grown to a substantial size. From the relative size of the conferences (see Table 6 in the Appendix), a number of conclusions can be drawn. The two largest—Illinois and Minnesota—always accounted for at least half the membership of the synod, and the long-running rivalry between the two conferences can be explained well by this fact. Since the Illinois conference had on its territory the synodical college and seminary, as well as the publishing house, this conference tended to represent the centralized, "official" element of Augustana. The Minnesota conference, on the other hand, often tended to represent the critical opposition, supporting its own colleges and newspaper, as well as the Lutheran Bible Institute in Minneapolis. During the presidency of P. O. Bersell, the synodical headquarters were established in Minneapolis, thus decentralizing some of the power of the synod away from Rock Island, Illinois.

The growth and shifting size of the conferences also reflect the fluctuation and regional development of the synod. Augustana grew rapidly through the late decades of the nineteenth century and up to about 1920. From 1920 to 1940, synodical growth leveled off, due to the end of immigration and the depression of the 1930s, but growth resumed after World War II, with an aggressive home missions program and the baby boom of the 1950s. The early growth in the synod was, of course, in the Midwest, but after 1900 there was substantial growth first on the East Coast and then on the West Coast. In 1960, half of the synodical members lived in the Illinois (Central) and Minnesota Conferences, but there was a substantial membership on both coasts. There were 75,000 Augustana members in the two West Coast conferences (Columbia and California) and 100,000 members in the two East Coast conferences (New York and New England), so almost one-third of all synodical members lived in the four "coastal" conferences. By the 1960s, Augustana truly was a national denomination, with congregations in thirty-five U.S. states and five Canadian provinces.

The synodical membership also shifted over time from rural areas of the country into urban areas, following a national population trend in the period from 1865 to 1940. In 1950, the synod had a total of 1,173 congregations; by its own classification, 610 of these were in rural areas and 563 were in urban areas, for a ratio of 52 percent rural to 48 percent urban. By 1960, out of a total of 1,255 congregations, 713 were urban and 542 were rural, for a ratio of 56 percent urban and 44 percent rural (see Table 7 in the Appendix).[20] In that one decade, from 1950 to 1960, the synod added 150 urban congregations and lost 68 rural congregations. This trend toward urban congregations was most pronounced on the coasts and least apparent in the Upper Midwest. Rural congregations were, on average, significantly smaller than those in urban areas, and it is clear that the main growth for the synod in the twentieth century came in the cities and suburbs.

The shift from rural to urban was filled with difficulties for the Augustana Synod, as rural congregations traditionally had been a strong part of its existence. The decline of rural areas meant an over-abundance of churches; a 1938 study concluded that, "perhaps half a dozen small, dependent, struggling congregations have had to compete for the loyalty and support of a community that could best be ministered to by, at most, two or three congregations."[21] In 1944, A. D. Mattson surveyed 144 rural congregations within the synod and found that as a group they had declined slightly in membership from 1900 to 1940, while the rural population had actually increased (though the rural percentage of the country had greatly declined).[22]

Economic and social changes, along with increased expectations and mobility, meant that many were leaving the rural areas, and those that remained behind were suffering from the loss. Mattson suggested to the synod in 1944 that a broader, social-based approach would be beneficial, not just looking at the immediate congregational needs but also at the larger forces changing the context of rural congregations.

Besides dealing with the matter of a declining rural population, the synod also faced tensions between rural and urban churches over the issue of home mission work and extension, as well as the transition in language from Swedish to English. A historian of the Minnesota Conference, reflecting on the fact that the synod was slow to build churches in urban areas, lamented, "For the successful prosecution of the home mission task there was need of mutual understanding and sympathy between city and country, and co-operation for the common welfare of all. However the unpalatable fact is that many congregations failed to do their duty."[23]

The Synod Expands Outside the Midwest

The Augustana Synod expanded in concentric circles out of its initial small grouping of congregations in the Synod of Northern Illinois during the 1850s. Initial expansion remained in the Midwest, in Illinois, Wisconsin, Minnesota, and Iowa, and these areas would continue to be dominant numerically in the synod throughout its history. The next wave of expansion was west into the Great Plains and east into New York and New England. But the Swedish immigrants were restless people, always in search of new lands and new opportunities. By the late nineteenth century significant settlements of Swedish Americans were found in Florida, Texas, California, the Pacific Northwest, and western Canada. Given its limited resources, the synod struggled to reach these Swedish-American communities and help them form congregations. In these areas, far from the most populous regions of the synod, Augustana congregations interacted more freely with other Lutherans and, out of necessity, with other Christians, bringing new ideas into the synod.

Swedish Settlements in the South—Texas and Florida

The first prominent Swedish immigrant in Texas was S. M. Swenson, who came to the state in 1838 and became a wealthy landowner. He soon brought much of his family there, including his uncle, Swante Palm. Other immigrants soon followed, and a small colony was formed in the rural areas around Austin. Though Swenson affiliated himself with the Protestant Episcopal church,

Palm and others formed Swedish Lutheran congregations. Eventually these independent congregations were linked to the Augustana Synod by means of home missionary visitors such as S. P. A. Lindahl and L. A. Hocanzon during the 1870s, and congregations were formed in Austin and Round Rock.[24] Land companies and immigrant bureaus attracted many of these immigrants to Texas after the Civil War, and they worked as contract laborers in order to repay the cost of their passage. Beginning in the 1890s, groups of Midwestern Swedish Americans moved south into rural Texas, settling at such places as Hutto (1892), El Campo (1893), Lund (1897), and Ericsdale (1906), among others. Urban congregations were formed in Austin (1872), Galveston (1892), Houston (1898), Fort Worth (1905), and Dallas (1906). These congregations first organized as the Texas district of the Kansas Conference in the 1870s and then petitioned, in 1922, to become an independent conference. At its inception, the Texas conference had 3,150 baptized members; by 1950 there were 4,800 baptized, and by 1960, there were 6,511 members in twenty-five different congregations. Of these congregations, thirteen were developed after World War II, mainly in urban and suburban areas of Texas. In 1906, Augustana Lutherans in Texas developed Trinity College, an academy in Round Rock, to educate their children, because Bethany in Lindsborg, Kansas, was seen as being too far away. Trinity College lasted until 1929; some of its assets and staff were incorporated into Texas Lutheran University in Seguin.

The history of the Augustana Synod in the Southeastern United States is much the same story. The first Swedish settlements in Alabama and Florida were rural colonies of internal immigrants who prospered in fruit farming, especially citrus in Florida. The first congregations formed in Florida were at Pierson (1884), Upsala (1892), and Hallandale (1906); and in Alabama, at Thorsby (1884), Fruithurst (1895), and Silverhill (1905).[25] The first urban congregation was formed in Miami in 1915, followed by Fort Lauderdale in 1924, a second Miami congregation in 1925, and one in Orlando in 1940. These small congregations struggled to survive; by 1926, the eight remaining Augustana congregations had less than 500 baptized members, and many of these congregations eventually closed or transferred to other Lutheran bodies. A student canvassing for the Home Mission Board in 1929 suggested that although the report of his three little congregations in central Florida was "not particularly pleasing," he was sure that if "consolidated" congregations were formed "in the bigger centers of this particular section of Florida," there could be considerable growth.[26] There was not much growth during the Great Depression, but with the population shifts during and after World War II, the migration of Northerners into the South helped revitalize Augustana in Florida. Twelve new Augustana mission congregations were formed in Florida during the 1950s, mainly in urban and suburban areas. The congregations in the Southeast, initially part of the Southeastern Mission District, formed the Florida district of the New York Conference in 1938.

Augustana on the Pacific Coast

Initially, the story was the same for Augustana along the Pacific coast, with small groups of wandering Swedish Americans, itinerant pastors traveling many miles to gather them together into congregations, the struggles to maintain congregations and provide pastoral leadership, and the slow growth of institutions. Yet with the surge of Americans westward in the twentieth century, these Pacific states saw in mid-century the development of larger and more successful numbers of Augustana congregations than in any other area outside the Midwest. By the end of the twentieth century there were more Americans of Swedish descent in California than in any other state of the Union, including the traditional strongholds of Illinois and Minnesota. Here, too, Augustana Lutherans learned the necessity of inter-Lutheran cooperation that would make possible the institutions necessary for their growth and success.

During the 1870s and 1880s, missionary pastors from the Midwest, including Peter Carlson, John Telleen, and others, made tours along the Pacific Coast, and held services and gathered congregations in areas from San Francisco to Seattle.[27] In 1882, Telleen organized a congregation in San Francisco, followed by San Jose (1884), Oakland (1887), Templeton and Kingsburg (1887), Fresno (1904), and Turlock (1912) in northern California, as well as a congregation in Los Angeles (1888). Peter Carlson, who was one of the founding pastors of the Augustana Synod in 1860, left his parish in East Union, Minnesota, in 1879, to serve as the synodical home missionary in the Pacific Northwest. He developed congregations in Portland and Astoria, Oregon. Over the next eighteen years he traveled thousands of miles, organized nine congregations, and prepared the way for many other congregations. Early congregations in this area were in Lenville, Idaho (1880), Spokane, Washington (1880), Tacoma, Washington (1882), Marshfield, Oregon (1884), Moscow, Idaho (1884), and Seattle (1885). Other pastors came west to serve in these congregations and do further mission work. In 1883, these mission congregations were constituted into the West Coast Mission District of the Augustana Synod, and in 1890, it became the Pacific Conference, with twenty-two congregations and 1,000 members. Transportation difficulties made meetings of the new conference impractical, and in 1893, it divided into two separate groups—the Columbia Conference and the California Conference.

The growth of these conferences was steady but not spectacular during the early twentieth century. There were seven Augustana congregations in California in 1890, fourteen in 1906, sixteen in 1916, and twenty-four congregations, with 5,200 members in 1926. In Washington, Oregon, and Idaho, there were a total of fifty-two congregations and 8,400 members by 1926. There were a few agricultural colonies of migrating Swedish Americans, such as Turlock and Kingsburg, California, founded in the late nineteenth century. At the time of his death in 1904, Bethany College president and land promoter, Carl A. Swensson, was working on a proposed Swedish-American colony for the San Joaquin Valley.[28] But most of the Swedes along the Pacific Coast lived in towns and cities, or worked in the mining and forestry industries; it was more the immigration of single young adults seeking work than families looking for farmland, and such communities were often less stable and less inviting for the formation of religious congregations. In light of these dynamics, the formation of more than seventy-five Augustana congregations by 1926 was quite impressive.

Much like other areas away from the Augustana heartland, the largest problem was providing enough pastors to serve the small and scattered congregations. Augustana Lutherans on the West Coast realized that education was key to a continued and stable success, and they began to plan for educational institutions. The Columbia Conference opened Coeur d'Alene College in Idaho in 1907, but it was never strong and closed during World War I. This was one of at least six different Lutheran educational institutions that were begun in the Northwest at that time, none of which survived very long.[29] In the 1880s, Senator Leland Stanford had some correspondence with the Augustana Synod about the offer of land for a college in Palo Alto, but this never came to fruition. Lutherans began to realize that if they were going to develop Lutheran education along the Pacific Coast, they would need to involve the cooperation of many different Lutheran groups. In 1931, representatives of Pacific Lutheran College (founded in 1891 by Norwegian-American Lutherans) appealed to the Columbia Conference for its support of the struggling college; the Columbia Conference agreed to help, and in return for an annual contribution, the conference received the ability to elect three trustees to the college's board of directors.[30] This began a cooperative relationship between Swedish and Norwegian Lutherans in the Pacific Northwest, somewhat akin to relationships in Texas and Canada to support joint educational institutions. By the time that California Lutheran College was begun in Southern California in 1959, these lessons had been well learned, and in the formation of this institution, the Augustana Synod joined with four other American Lutheran groups to make California Lutheran a reality.[31]

During World War II thousands of Americans moved to the Pacific coast for wartime jobs in defense industries, rapidly swelling the populations of local communities. Along with other Lutherans, Augustana attempted to meet the needs of these new transplants and to begin preparations for a postwar expansion of congregations. The expected postwar growth was not a mirage, as both the California and Columbia Conferences experienced rapid growth. The Columbia Conference grew from fifty-nine congregations and 23,000 baptized members in 1950, to sixty-eight congregations and 38,000 members in 1960. In California, the growth was even more pronounced, as the conference went from forty-five congregations and 16,000 baptized members in 1950, to seventy-seven congregations and 37,000 members in 1960. By 1960, 75,000 of Augustana's 605,000 members were residents in the two Pacific coast conferences. The rapid growth was made possible by energetic Augustana leaders, such as Carl W. Segerhammar, president of the California Conference from 1950 to 1962, who pushed the synodical board of American missions to devote considerable resources to the development of new congregations, and who oversaw the doubling of the California Conference in a decade.

Augustana in Canada

The bulk of Swedish immigration to Canada, whether directly from Sweden, or in a secondary migration from the United States, centered in the prairie provinces of Alberta, Saskatchewan, and Manitoba, beginning in the 1880s and 1890s. Much of this migration was an extension of the push northwest from Illinois and Wisconsin, the same movement that brought Swedish settlers to the Dakotas and Montana, as the railroads opened up new land for farming. After scattered home missions visitations in the 1880s, two congregations were begun, the first at New Stockholm, Saskatchewan, in 1889, and in Winnipeg, Manitoba, in 1890, where Svante Udden became the first resident Augustana pastor in Canada.[32] This home missions effort was mainly the work of the Minnesota Conference, and the scattered Swedish congregations came under the jurisdiction of that conference; in 1907, L. P. Bergstrom was appointed as the mission superintendent for Canada. The Augustana presence in Canada was hampered by a number of different factors—size, economic depression, and lack of pastors: "The congregations were scattered over a territory more than 1,500 miles in length. During the nineties economic conditions were depressed. Immigration almost ceased. Udden (the first resident pastor) stayed in Winnipeg until 1898. Several pastors of the Minnesota Conference visited the Canadian field, and theological students gave temporary service."[33]

In 1913, Augustana congregations in Canada numbered thirty-nine with 2,900 members, but only a total of nine pastors. While additional congregations were formed on the western prairies, other congregations were created in western Ontario, at Kenora (1894), and at the head of Lake Superior at Fort William (1906), Port Arthur (1906), and Fort Frances (1919). Urban congregations were attempted in Toronto (1914) and Montreal (1918), but there was only a small and transitory Swedish immigrant population in the east.[34] There were two Augustana congregations formed in British Columbia, at Vancouver (1903) and New Westminster (1909), but they belonged to the Columbia Conference.

In 1902, a young pastor named Per Almgren was sent to Alberta as the sole Augustana pastor in the province; he served at seven congregations and twenty preaching points, ministering to an estimated 10,000 Swedish immigrants, of which 175 had associated with Augustana congregations.[35] Pioneer pastors faced often brutal weather, grinding poverty, and tremendous distances to serve a few struggling congregations. In 1920, there were a total of fifty-four congregations in western Canada, but only twelve pastors to serve them.

By 1913, the congregations in western Canada had gained enough strength to consider forming their own organization, and in that year the Canada Conference of the Augustana Synod was formed, with continuing financial support from the Minnesota Conference. The conference struggled through the early 1920s, losing members and pastors. Times were difficult for building churches, as one church historian noted: "The immigration into Canada was decreasing, and the Lutherans in Canada who had lived there for decades without having any church connection . . . were poor material indeed from which to build a congregation."[36] Still, in the late 1920s the conference slowly began to grow, and baptized membership reached 4,600 in forty-six congregations in 1950, and 9,800 in forty-eight congregations by 1960. Much of this growth came in the development of urban congregations, which increased from seven in 1950 to twenty-one in 1960. Yet even with mid-century growth, the Canada Conference still lagged behind in the number of pastors; in 1950 there were still only eleven pastors serving forty-six congregations. In 1948, an Augustana publication admitted that, "The Augustana Synod has always had to face the difficulty of providing ministerial leadership for its congregations in Canada. [Pastors] from the states . . . are reluctant to become Canadian citizens and, after a few years, return South."[37]

The Manitoba Synod of the United Lutheran Church in America (ULCA) had already formed a college and seminary in Saskatoon, Saskatchewan, early in the twentieth century, and in 1939 the Norwegian Lutheran

Church in America, in cooperation with the ULCA, established a school in Saskatoon. The Augustana Synod joined these two efforts in the late 1940s, and in 1947, it gave approval and funding for a cooperative Lutheran seminary in western Canada, for the training of Lutheran pastors.[38] This development not only began to alleviate the chronic lack of Lutheran pastors in western Canada, it also began the process of inter-Lutheran cooperation that eventually would result in the formation of an autonomous Evangelical Lutheran Church in Canada, formed in 1985.

Augustana gained more than just new members in its push into new areas such as Canada, the Pacific coast, and the American South. Besides gathering in the immigrants and wandering Swedish Americans, energetic home missionaries pushed Augustana to expend resources to grow the synod, both geographically and numerically. In going beyond the traditional areas of Swedish-American settlement, the synod gained a greater interaction with different North American regional cultures, and learned further how to adapt and flourish in new areas and situations. Augustana also learned from experiences in these areas practical lessons of how to work together with other North American Lutherans, lessons that were a precursor to the merger negotiations of the middle twentieth century.

PART 3
THROUGH 1935
75TH ANNIVERSARY

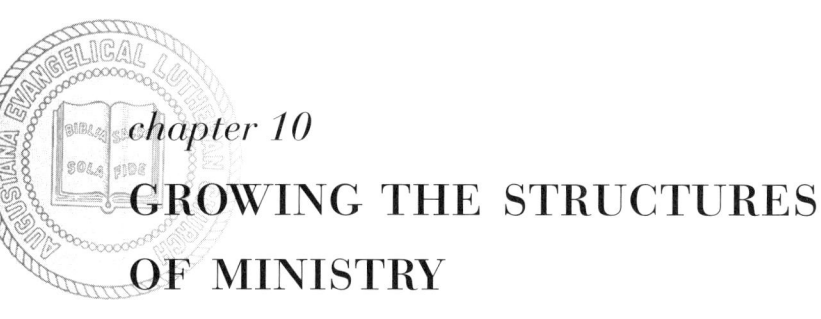

chapter 10

GROWING THE STRUCTURES OF MINISTRY

IN TERMS OF ITS BAPTIZED MEMBERSHIP, the Augustana Synod doubled in size from 1890 to 1920, and doubled again between 1920 and 1960. This kind of growth transformed the synod; not just in sheer size, but also in the very nature of the synod itself. As a religious denomination grows in size and complexity, its character changes as well, from being a kind of large extended family to a complex, multi-layered, bureaucratic organization. In some respects this transformation was inevitable, as the sheer growth in size demanded a more sophisticated structure to maintain its programs and functions. But in other respects, Augustana was following the lead of its kindred American Protestant denominations that, in the mid-twentieth century, were adapting new corporate and business models of organization for themselves. Religion took on the feel of business, with corporate headquarters, boards and committees, professional managers, and layer after layer of structure. To be sure, ties of family and affiliation continued to be extraordinarily important to the running of the synod; there were many ties within the leadership of Augustana forged in the church colleges and especially in the common experience of training at Augustana Seminary. But with the growth of the organization, both numerically and geographically, old ties could not be maintained with the same intensity. There was something gained and something lost in the transition, and people in Augustana both cheered and mourned the transformation.

The Growth of Educational Institutions

In Sweden the local parish congregation was usually charged with the additional mission of providing for the education of children and the support of those who needed assistance. In the United States, Swedish immigrants found a very different situation than the one they were accustomed to in their homeland. On the one hand, primary education in America was the business of local government, and free public schools sprang up as quickly as land was settled. Secondary education, however, often lagged far behind, and collegiate education was mainly in the hands of private organizations until well into the twentieth century.

Swedish immigrants were by and large very supportive of American public education, and there was little enthusiasm in Augustana for parochial schools. Local congregations often provided supplemental education for children in religious subjects and in Swedish language and culture, but these efforts were sporadic and occasional at best; confirmation and Sunday school education along American lines were a standard part of every congregation. Synodical leaders put their time and effort into secondary schools and colleges, usually because of the initial lack of such institutions in the areas where the immigrants settled and because of a need to provide educated leaders for the new church.[1]

When Augustana was formed in 1860, the synod had one struggling educational institution, Augustana College and Seminary, eventually located in Rock Island, Illinois. This institution consisted of three separate departments: the secondary school, the college, and the seminary. For many years the secondary (or high school) department was the largest part of the institution, and it remained in operation until the early twentieth century. Augustana College and Seminary was supported financially, at least in theory, by all the conferences of the synod. In addition, as a synodical institution Augustana College and Seminary also was subject to the control of the entire synod, and much of the business of this institution was transacted at the annual synodical convention, which at times resulted in a great deal of debate and occasional attempts at micro management and mischief.[2]

As the Swedish immigrant population grew and the synod expanded, there were many attempts to expand education, attempts that reflected both regional growth and the relative power of the conferences over and against the synod during the late nineteenth century. The school that would become Gustavus Adolphus College in St. Peter, Minnesota, was founded in 1862 as St. Ansgar's Academy and was the project of the Minnesota Conference. From 1880 to 1910 came the academy movement, when no less than eleven different educational institutions were founded by conferences, districts, or even by groups of local leaders, all of whom perceived a need for a school of their own. According to George Stephenson, himself a partisan of Augustana College, this "'college mania' that beset the Augustana Synod in the eighties and nineties was a symptom as well as a cause of the trend toward decentralization [i.e., of the synod]."[3]

Most of these eleven schools were begun on shoestring budgets, and operated primarily as academies or private secondary educational institutions, even if they had the term college in their title.[4] Even with the growth of the synod, it was clear to most that Augustana could not support all of these schools, or even a fraction of them. Many were begun on regional pride and precious little resources, and they soon came to an end. Schools that did not close within a few years of being established likely did not survive the Great Depression. Only a handful were strong enough to develop into full-fledged colleges. Those that did survive—Gustavus Adolphus, Bethany, Luther (Junior) College, and Upsala—joined Augustana as fully mature colleges, eventually dropping their Academy departments to focus on collegiate education. Later in the twentieth century the western conferences of the synod would cooperate with other Lutheran denominations in the formation and support of California Lutheran College in Thousand Oaks, California, and Pacific Lutheran College in Tacoma, Washington.

The five surviving colleges proved to be important resources for the synod during the twentieth century and a base from which it drew educated leaders—men and women who served as pastors, educators, missionaries, nurses, and lay leaders. Much of the culture of Augustana was cultivated on these campuses, and their activities became a source of pride for the synod. The competitive movement that, at least in part, instigated the founding of these colleges became more muted in the twentieth century, although there was always a healthy rivalry between the schools for students and for bragging rights. Much attention was paid to "our schools" in the pages of the synodical press, and they became symbols for the whole of the synod.

As the twentieth century progressed, the five Augustana church colleges were pioneers in moving the synod toward integration into the wider American culture, facilitated by the use of the English language for instruction, which became widespread as early as the 1890s. The English-language synodical weekly, the *Lutheran Companion* was initially begun in 1892 as an alumni publication for graduates of Augustana College.

Parents who sent their youth to these colleges wanted their children to have a solid base in Lutheran theology and Swedish culture, to be sure, but in addition, they wanted them to have good jobs in the American economy. The colleges responded with training in practical and professional areas such as business, science, and education, while also attempting to cultivate Augustana's religious and cultural ethos. They also added professional faculty with recognized university degrees and strengthened their curricula, in a move to become fully accredited educational institutions on par with other American colleges.

Along with these academies and colleges, Augustana pastors and lay leaders founded four Lutheran Bible Institutes (LBI), schools for biblical education primarily for youth, but open to all.[5] These schools were non-degree-granting institutions that usually provided for a full-time course of study in Bible, Lutheran doctrine, and practical theology, spread out over a several-year program. These schools had their roots in two related movements—the Scandinavian mission schools and the Bible school movement, an important part of American evangelical Protestantism at the beginning of the twentieth century. In Augustana's early history, the pietistic Swedish mission schools of Fjellsedt and Ahlberg were very important, providing a significant portion of the synod's first clergy. At the same time, in America, Bible schools such as the Moody Bible Institute and the Biblical Seminary of New York were developed in part as a response to the increasing liberalism of mainline American Protestantism. Both traditions were important for the Lutheran Bible Institutes, the first of which were founded in Minneapolis in 1919 by a group of Augustana pastors and lay leaders. Eventually three more Lutheran Bible Institutes were established, in Seattle, Los Angeles, and New Jersey.

The relationship of these Bible institutes to the Augustana Synod was complex; many Augustana pastors and leaders were trained in these schools, but they also often acted as conservative critics of the synod and the directions in which it was headed. The basic idea behind the LBI movement was to give youth a solid training in the Bible before they went off to college or to adult life, and to train a number of them for work in missions, broadly defined. This, however, was an implicit criticism of the church colleges and seminary, perceived by some within the synod as becoming too modern and straying from the pietistic traditions of their origins. Two of the early leaders of the LBI movement, Samuel Miller, dean of the Minneapolis Lutheran Bible Institute from 1919 to 1945, and Adolph Hult, Augustana Seminary professor from 1915 to 1943, were frequent conservative critics of modernism and liberalism within Augustana, expressing their opinions regularly in synodical periodicals. Some critics of the LBI movement have labeled it "fundamentalistic," but the label does not fit the movement well; rather, it was a conservative biblicism, with confessional Lutheran roots. The LBI movement blended the conservative biblical pietism of Augustana's roots with many elements of contemporary American evangelicalism and conservative American Lutheran theology, and often it was not too far away from the prevailing theology within the synod at the time. Miller, Hult, and other LBI leaders were honored by many within the synod for their work, even if their criticism did become, at times, too strident for others. These Bible institutes provided a sizable number of pastors and missionaries for Augustana, and the piety of the institutions had an important effect on the synod.

Ministries of Mercy within the Augustana Synod

When Swedish immigrants arrived in North America, they found that institutions of mercy, such as hospitals and homes for children and the elderly, were not readily available, especially in the frontier areas where many of them settled. In the American system, such institutions generally were provided by private, voluntary organizations (mainly religious groups), and these institutions often were poorly financed and inadequate for the needs of their communities. There were some public charity hospitals and homes, but these were often grim Dickensian institutions that were to be avoided, if possible. Elderly people, orphaned children, and the mentally and physically disabled were generally cared for within the family, or parceled out to those within the community who were willing to care for them. Those who became ill were cared for at home, as hospitals were viewed as places for the incurably ill to await their inevitable deaths. Struggling congregations often attempted to meet local needs within the ethnic community, but they had precious few resources to deal with the disasters and diseases that were all too common on the frontier.

The first institutions of mercy organized within the Augustana Synod were children's homes in Vasa, Minnesota, and Andover, Illinois, erected during the 1860s to meet a local need for the care of orphaned children.[6] As was the usual pattern, these institutions were organized and run by local groups of Augustana people and were generally owned and operated either by an Augustana conference or by groups of local congregations. Between 1879 and 1917 an additional twelve children's homes were organized within the synod, from Massachusetts to Kansas. The homes were often small institutions housed in a single building and overseen by pastors and house parents who sought to instill in the children a strict discipline and piety to train them for adult life.

Although the older pattern of caring for the ill at home remained strong in rural areas, the development of modern hospitals as centers of healing began in urban America toward the end of the nineteenth century, and it was in the cities that the majority of Swedish Lutheran hospitals were originally located. The first Augustana hospitals were organized in St. Paul, Minnesota, in 1882; in Chicago, Illinois, in 1884; and in Omaha, Nebraska, in 1890. By 1946, seven other such hospitals were developed.[7] At their beginning these hospitals were more like skilled nursing facilities, where patients could receive more professional care and assistance than they could receive at home. To insure that there were enough skilled nurses to meet the needs of the hospitals, a number of them began auxiliary teaching programs to train professional nurses, adding to the educational institutions of the synod.

For example, the nursing school at the Lutheran Hospital in Moline, Illinois, produced many classes of nurses for synodical hospitals and overseas missions, and given its proximity to Augustana Seminary, many of these nurses married Augustana pastors. Other Lutheran nursing graduates went out to serve the mission fields in hospitals and clinics in Africa and Asia.

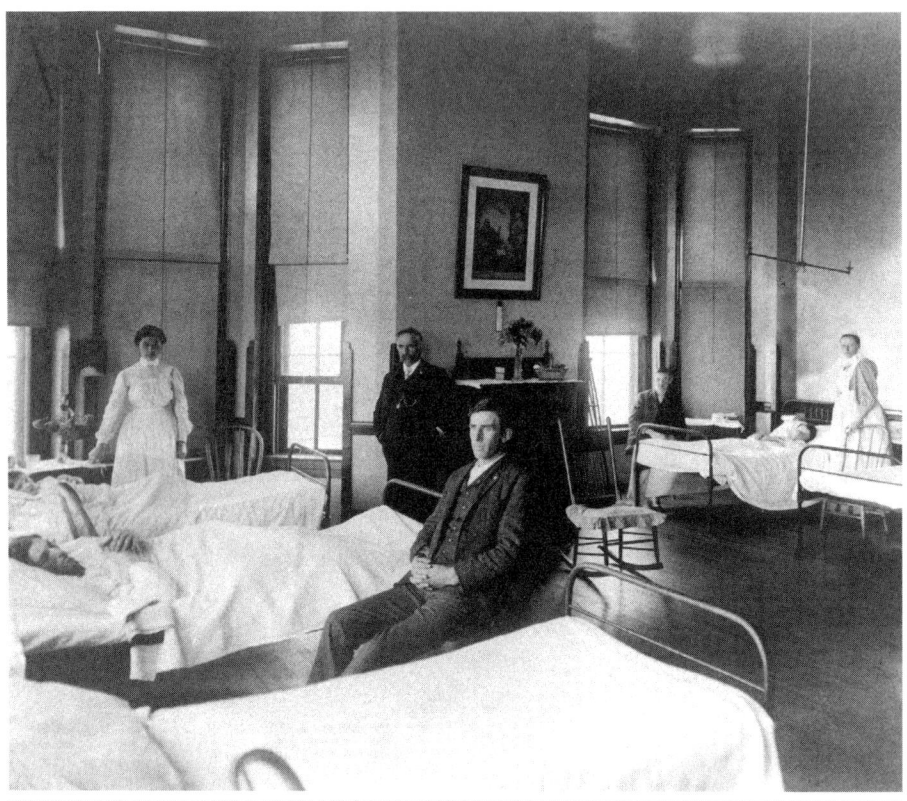

Sanatorium care at one of the synod's facilities in the West utilized the latest research on fresh air and light in the treating of patients. The photo is undated, but the dress of the nursing attendants places it between 1900 and 1910.
Photo courtesy of Evangelical Lutheran Church in America Archives.

In addition to children's homes and hospitals, Augustana groups were also responsible for the founding of at least twenty-one homes for the elderly from 1896 to 1957, a number of hospices, four immigrant and seamen's centers, and urban residences for young women, the latter under the direction of the Women's Missionary Society. All of these institutions were seen as an extension of the synod's ministry, mainly but not exclusively for the Swedish-American community. It was a point of pride for Augustana that though its membership was only about 7 percent of the total for American Lutheranism, it owned 15 percent of the Lutheran institutions of mercy in North America.[8]

Besides the Lutheran Seamen's Center in New York City, the only other synodically-owned institution of mercy was the Immanuel Deaconess Institute in Omaha, which consisted of a deaconess mother house, hospital, nursing home, and children's home. Though female deaconesses were a longstanding tradition in Lutheran Germany, they were slow to be adopted by American Lutherans, and it was not until the late 1880s when Pastor E. A. Fogelstrom established this institution in Omaha, Nebraska. The organization was operated locally for a number of years, until in 1904, the synod as a whole took over responsibility for the institution; over the course of seventy years more than 125 women were consecrated as deaconesses. Though the work of the deaconesses was generally located around Omaha, a number of the sisters worked in Augustana institutions throughout the United States, and several served as medical missionaries in India, China, and Tanzania. Another Nebraska institution of note was the Bethphage Mission in Axtell, which pioneered treatment and care for the mentally and physically disabled and was one of the few Augustana institutions to serve persons from the whole of the synod.

As with many of the other institutions of the Augustana Synod, these institutions of mercy had to grow and develop in order to compete in a world of increasingly professionalized and competitive institutions. By the mid-twentieth century it was no longer possible to operate these institutions in their original manner; hospitals and other care institutions had become highly complex medical centers that had to meet strict regulatory conditions. The demand for children's homes declined dramatically, and many of the synodical institutions either closed or took on new responsibilities, such as becoming child welfare organizations or caring for children with mental and physical disabilities. Conferences often developed social services boards to oversee the management of these institutions, and weaker ones were either closed or merged with others. The general trend among all American Lutherans, hastened by the mergers of the 1960s, was the consolidation of these institutions under local independent groups entitled Lutheran Social Services. Many of the Augustana institutions became a part of these systems, which in total represented one of the largest groups of social service organizations in the United States, after the system of similar institutions formed by Roman Catholics.

New Administrative Structures for the Synod

An aggressive campaign for home missions during the middle of the twentieth century required the development of administrative structures to support it. The surge in synodical members and congregations put pressure on the synod to develop further means of regulating and assisting the growing organization. Especially from the late 1930s on, the synod developed a complex set of administrative structures to manage the institutions and programs of the rapidly expanding denomination, and in this respect caught up with other American denominations.

Prior to 1920, the synod had a very weak form of centralized administration. Through the 1870s and 1880s, power had swung toward the conferences themselves, and some proposed making the conferences synods of their own, with Augustana as a weak federative body, along the lines of the General Council. Though the central nature of the synod as over and against the conferences was settled with the synodical constitution of 1894, there was little formal administration or coordination of efforts.[9] The synod president functioned as a part-time administrator while also serving a local congregation, and a synod council acted on behalf of the synod between the annual conventions, but there was little other administrative assistance. The boards and committees that oversaw parts of the synodical responsibilities, such as Augustana College and Seminary, home and foreign missions, pastoral pensions, and other duties, met only occasionally and had no full-time staff. There was no real budgeting process until 1927, and the financial administration was left in the hands of a treasurer who sought to disburse the available funds along the lines set forth by the annual synodical convention.

In 1911, just a year after the synod's Jubilee celebration, seventy-eight-year-old Eric Norelius retired from the synod presidency, and with his retirement went the last active pastor who had been present at the founding of the synod some fifty years earlier. Observers at the time recognized that an era in the synod's history had passed and that the course of the denomination was now to be in the hands of a new generation. The next president, Lawrence A. Johnston, was a transitional figure who led Augustana until 1918. But the real transformation of the synod came with the next two presidents—Gustav Albert Brandelle (1918–1935) and Petrus Olof Bersell (1935–1951)—both of whom, in their own ways, would lead Augustana from an immigrant communion into a twentieth-century American Protestant denomination. Brandelle was able to guide the synod through the upheavals of language transition and rapid Americanization, and helped it to gain a wider ecumenical vision. Bersell transformed the synod's organizational structure, allowing it to survive and flourish in the turbulent times during and after World War II. The last two presidents, Oscar A. Benson (1951–1959) and Malvin H. Lundeen (1959–1962), guided Augustana through the difficult years of merger negotiations and restructuring.

For the first four years of his presidency, Brandelle also served as a pastor in Rock Island, Illinois (as was the custom of his predecessors), and it was not until 1922 that he was able to work full-time as president. There was no synodical headquarters, so he conducted the work of the synod from his home, and if the presidential archives can be trusted, probably typed a good deal of his own correspondence. Rather than the synod coming to him, he went out to the synod, traveling by train a good deal of the time to visit conferences and congregations and attend board and committee meetings. Organizationally, he began to build structures within the synod; Augustana approved its fourth synodical constitution in 1922, a budgeting system in 1927, and a number of new boards and committees, including the formation of the unified Board for Foreign Missions in 1923, relieving Brandelle of direct responsibility for this area. But the important area of home missions was still not well organized, and as president, Brandelle had direct responsibility for areas outside of the boundaries of any of the conferences, such as the Southeast, Utah, and Inter-Mountain districts. In 1927, a synodical board of finance was created, with P. O. Bersell, Iowa Conference president, as chair. In 1928, a layperson, Otto Leonardson, was made secretary of finance. A General Board of Education was formed in 1922, but it achieved "nothing of consequence" and was dissolved in 1933.[10] The synodical minutes were first printed in English in 1924, and the constitution of 1922 was translated into English in 1928.

It was not so much in the area of administration, but in the areas of ecumenical relations, that Brandelle did most to transform the synod. At the beginning of his presidency in 1918, he argued that the synod should join with the rest of the General Council in the newly merging United Lutheran Church in America (ULCA). Though he lost that initial battle, he developed and maintained good relations with the presidents of the ULCA, as well as with other American Lutheran leaders. Brandelle also prompted Augustana to send delegates to the Lutheran World Conventions during the 1920s and 1930s, and he urged the synod to join the National Lutheran Council in 1918 and the American Lutheran Conference in 1930. In addition, he accepted invitations for the synod to participate in international ecumenical dialogues such as "Life and Work" and "Faith and Order"—a far cry from the emphatically negative response of Norelius to such an invitation in 1911. Brandelle could be very defensive of the interests of the synod; he tangled with the ULCA over the perceived encroachments of the Synod of the Northwest and bristled at suggestions by Missouri Synod editors that the Augustana Synod was unionistic. He also led the only Lutheran delegation to talks with the Episcopalians in 1935, though he flatly rejected the idea of the historic episcopate and often sparred with Episcopal leaders over the claims of Swedish-American Episcopal pastors.[11] Brandelle's relations with Lutheran leaders in Germany and Sweden were very good, and he managed very well the controversial visit of Swedish archbishop Nathan Söderblom to the United States in 1923.

The depression of the 1930s inflicted great hardship and difficulty on Augustana, and Brandelle managed this crisis as best he could. But he was seventy-four-years-old in 1935, when he stood for re-election, and he lost the presidency to P. O. Bersell, then president of the Iowa Conference. In letters to friends after the election, Brandelle grumbled about the introduction of "political methods" into the life of the synod, implying that Bersell had organized a political campaign to win the election. But it seemed clear to the majority of delegates in 1935 that the synod needed new leadership, and Bersell was seen as a rising star. Bersell's own genius was in building a new and comprehensive structure for the rapidly growing denomination to provide stability and resources for its mission in North America and abroad, and in guiding the synod through the difficult years surrounding World War II.[12]

It was the tradition to locate the headquarters of the synod wherever the president lived, so after his election to the synodical presidency in 1935, Bersell decided to move to Minneapolis. This was probably a calculated decision on his part, made in order to move the synodical headquarters to the territory of the largest conference within the synod; over the years a number of leaders within the Minnesota Conference had been openly critical of the influence of Rock Island and the Illinois Conference. Bersell permanently established the headquarters of the synod in Minneapolis, and in 1945, the Augustana Synod bought a building at 2445 Park Avenue, which it shared with the Minnesota Conference. It was this purchase in 1945 that required the synod to take the step of becoming legally incorporated for the first time in its eighty-five-year history, in order to own real property.

Bersell also completely overhauled the management structure of the synod, rapidly expanding the number of synodical boards and committees and engaging pastors to serve as full-time synodical leaders for these groups. This series of initiatives has been called, "The New Approach," by G. Everett Arden and has been credited by him with moving the synod "off dead center," and putting new life into the denomination.[13] The first of these moves, in 1937, was the formation of the Board of Foreign Missions, with a full-time executive director, Hjalmar Swanson. An earlier 1935 plan to create a parallel Central Board of Home Missions was delayed for a time, but by 1937, Bersell had won enough support for this board, and in 1939 it too called a full-time leader, Sigfried E. Engstrom, to coordinate these efforts. There was a new Commission on Higher Education in 1937, a new Board of Stewardship in 1942, a renewed Board of Parish Education in 1943, a new

Board of Youth Activities in 1946, and many other new commissions and boards, many of which had national staff persons dedicated to their work. Culminating these organizational activities was the synod's fifth and final constitution adopted in 1948.[14]

All these structures required resources to operate them, and the synod keenly needed the funds to maintain and expand its ministries. This was especially crucial because the level of giving to the synod had dipped dramatically during the Great Depression, from $24.43 per member per year in 1925 to $13.82 in 1935.[15] This decline in giving was also felt among the educational and social service institutions of the synod. While the synod had mounted emergency fund appeals during times of crisis, such as after World War I and during the depression, these appeals were sporadic. Beginning in the 1940s, regular plans were developed for stewardship education and appeals to increase financial giving to synodical ministries. A series of five yearly appeals, each dedicated to a different theme, led up to the Centennial celebration in 1948. This pattern was replicated beginning the next year, with a permanent Augustana Mission Advance appeal, which raised 4.7 million dollars in thirteen years, over and above regular giving to the synod.

During the terms of Oscar A. Benson (1951–1959) and Malvin H. Lundeen (1959–1962), presidential energies were devoted chiefly to the series of negotiations concerning merger, and then with the myriad details of implementation. During the late 1950s, the process of merging four Lutheran denominations into one was a daunting task, not only because of the size of the new denomination, but because of the very different denominational structures and cultures involved. During this decade, there also was a growing concern within the synod about pressing national and world issues, such as the cold war, race relations, and the rapidly changing nature of American society; Benson and Lundeen had to negotiate these difficult matters. Under the leadership of Benson, especially, the synod grew rapidly, both in North America and on the mission fields, which to him were a very important aspect of the synod's work.

One crucial aspect of the institutional development of Augustana was the growth of the church publishing house to provide the synod with books, newspapers, journals, annuals, tracts, and Sunday school and educational materials.[16] Early in its history, in 1859, the synod had begun its own Publication Society, but because of financial distress it was sold to the Engberg-Holmberg Publishing Company in 1874. Gradually the synod re-entered the publishing business, and in 1889, the Augustana Book Concern (ABC) was established. One of the chief functions of the Book Concern was the publication of church periodicals, primarily *Augustana* (1855–1956) in Swedish, and the *Lutheran Companion* (1892–1962) in English, but it also published periodicals for children and youth, about missions and other special purposes. These periodicals played an important role in uniting the members of a far-flung denomination, and served as a forum for discussion of the issues and challenges it faced. At its peak in the 1950s, the *Lutheran Companion* had a circulation of nearly 97,000 copies, ensuring that it would have a wide-ranging impact on the life of the synod. This publishing program also included annual publications, such as *Korsbaneret* (1879–1950), *Prärieblomman* (1900–1913), *My Church* (1915–1962), the *Augustana Annual* (1948–1962), and *The Home Altar*, a quarterly devotional begun in 1940 that reached a circulation of 200,000 by 1960 and continues today. There were other important periodicals within the synod not published by the ABC, including the *Missions Tiding* of the Women's Missionary Society, the *Bible Banner* of the Lutheran Bible Institute, and various conference periodicals.

The Professionalization of the Clergy and Seminary Education

Within its own self-definition, the Augustana Synod was composed of two distinct groups: the local congregations and the body of pastors who served them (the ministerium), a group totaling more than 2,500 individuals.[17] Throughout the history of the synod it seems there were never enough pastors to serve all the congregations, and it was not until 1957 that there were more pastors than congregations in the synod. Though a few of the first leaders of the synod were educated in Swedish universities and ordained in Sweden and a few more received their education at the missionary schools in Sweden, the vast majority of pastors were educated and ordained in the United States. Most of them were educated at Augustana Theological Seminary in Rock Island, Illinois. The immense needs of the early years meant that the education of pastors was often hasty and incomplete, especially for older men who decided to enter the ministry later in life. In 1877, a college degree was declared to be the normal standard for admission to the seminary, although it was not mandatory until 1932. Many of the early pastors attended the seminary for only a year or two, and then the needs of the synod resulted in their immediate ordination. Candidates who either came to seminary without a degree, or who stayed only for the minimum course were called "hospitants," who were reviewed at first by an examination committee of the ministerium, but after 1891, by the theological faculty of the seminary. Throughout the history of the synod, lay preachers without ordination or theological education also served some churches; these individuals were under the control of the conference presidents.[18]

By 1896, the synod standardized the normal course of seminary education at three years above the collegiate level, leading to a Bachelor of Divinity degree, though again this standard was often weakened in individual cases. In 1933, the seminary added a fourth, internship year to the process, both as a means of practical pastoral education and as a nod to the practical reality that during the depression the placement of new pastors in congregations was a problem. The internship program was suspended during World War II, but re-established after the war. Due to the postwar situation of older students, returning veterans, and the general need for more pastors, an alternate course of study was developed for those who did not have the usual classical language study; these candidates received a "candidate" diploma, rather than the Bachelor of Divinity degree. In 1946, Augustana created a synodical committee on examination and placement of candidates for ordination to distribute the supply of new preachers to areas of the synod where they would be needed most.

Until about 1930, theological instruction rooted mainly in the Lutheran dogmatics of sixteenth- and seventeenth-century European Lutheranism dominated seminary training, and students were becoming increasingly restless with the situation. The president of Augustana College and Seminary, Gustav Andreen, was a capable academic, with a Ph.D. from Yale University, but he was getting quite old and was burdened with spending most of his time raising money to keep the institution solvent. The rest of the theological faculty were also older, and few of them had formal graduate education. In 1930–1931, there was a large turnover among the faculty. The seminary's dean, Conrad Lindberg, died and four other seminary faculty members left or retired, leaving five vacancies to be filled. The new seminary professors were a much different group. Younger, and many with formal graduate education, they brought a renewed spirit and curriculum to the seminary, resulting in what some have termed the "Seminary Revolution." The remodeling of the curriculum and instructional methods, the addition of the internship experience, and a number of other changes spurred a new theological vision within the synod, a vision cheered as long overdue by some, and seen with suspicion by others.

The Debate over Centralization and Institutional Growth

In the 1920s, many people looked to the business world for inspiration and for a model of how organizations should be formed. This was the era of consolidations and corporations, and church groups looked to emulate or adapt these models for their own use. One editorial in the *Lutheran Companion* in 1927 heralded the virtue of "efficiency" for the synod, suggesting that efficiency was the word of the day for business, and that "[w]hat is true in the business world applies also to the work of the Church. We cannot conceive that Christ commissioned His disciples to go out into the world and found churches without demanding and expecting that they should do the work efficiently . . . [this should be] the goal of every congregation."[19]

By efficiency, the editorial meant organized and quantifiable methods of doing Christ's work, such as boards, organizations, programs, and societies. But in reaction against this trend, another correspondent wrote in 1931:

> [W]e have too many promoters, too many dreamers, and too many excursionists. We are neglecting our congregational work. Pastors are indifferent as to their parishes, and congregations are not giving pastors support. . . . We have been playing or pretending Christianity so long it is difficult for us to believe Christianity is not but play.[20]

Often, these critics were partisans of one conference or another, and naturally inclined to guard their own prerogatives. Many believed that institutional growth of the synod was necessary, and to devolve its responsibility actually weakened the mission of the church. Of major concern for some was the control of Augustana College and Seminary. "The far better way," advocated one supporter, "is to have one strong synod with one central institution of learning with three essential divisions; the college, the postgraduate university, and the seminary. And let the synod have full control of the institution."[21]

Many in Augustana agreed that to have strong institutions was key, and such could only be achieved through centralized administration and control. A church document of 1938 suggested a correlation between "the importance of expansion work in the business world and the Kingdom of God," suggesting that businesses knew the value of paying their salesmen well, and that the synod should do this same thing with its home missions pastors.[22] Others, however, claimed that the adoption of "worldly methods" was a symptom of the very problems that plagued the modern church. Living through the uncertainties and challenges of the Great Depression, it seemed to them that faith in worldly institutions was not the solution for the church. "We have listened to 'wise-cracks,' introduced 'Krueger' business methods, and generally comported ourselves in . . . an unseemly fashion," wrote one pastor at the time. "God is cleaning out the impurities of this world. Whatever is worldly, not productive of lasting good, in the Church must go."[23]

For some critics, the building of institutions and structures had been a costly experiment that had weakened the synod financially and drawn it away from its primary mission. One depression-era writer bemoaned the fact that while there were seminary graduates without congregational placements, the synod was preoccupied with saving hospitals and charitable institutions: "We have created conditions within our Synod that have brought this situation about. Some of our conferences have for a number of years bled our people in expansive institutional work. The great emphasis has been on greater buildings and better equipment."[24]

Another, analyzing the trends within the synod, especially toward evangelism and the formation of new congregations, noted a definite decline since the peak years between 1905 and 1909, and wondered, "Have we come to the end of an era of in our church history which marks the change from evangelism to ecclesiasticism?"[25] The obvious assumption was that evangelism was good, but the building up of organized church structures—ecclesiaticism—definitely was not.

The question of evangelism and home mission expansion was an important theme during the 1930s, when few new congregations were formed and a number of established ones closed. Under the direction of President Bersell, the synod moved to consider a new, centralized home missions board, under the direct control of the synod, hoping that concerted action on the issue would get things moving again. The editor of the *Lutheran Companion* wrote after the plan was adopted: "While in the past the various conferences have jealously guarded their prerogatives against synodical encroachment, it now appears that they are ready to surrender some of their functions in the hope of obtaining larger results through unified and co-ordinated effort."[26]

But boards and committees could accomplish little if the people of the synod were not engaged in the work too. Conrad Bergendoff recognized this. "How strong is the Synod?" he asked. "Frankly . . . nobody knows, because the Synod has never exerted itself to the utmost. . . . When we set rather moderate goals for ourselves and attain them, we can only say we have achieved those goals. We might have gone beyond them."[27] To Bergendoff's way of thinking, all the boards and organizations established only mirrored the will of those who organized them and of those on whose behalf they served. In his words there was a lingering sense of disquiet about the "half a million Augustana people . . . worshiping in beautiful sanctuaries, living in comfort," and a challenge for them to do better.

The disquiet about the burgeoning structures and ecclesiasticism within the synod continued until the end of its life. Certainly members of the synod were justifiably proud of their congregations, colleges, hospitals, foreign missions, and other organized efforts, and of the administrative machinery that kept all these elements at work. But even in the busy 1950s, with its rapid expansion of members and ministries, there was a certain caution, akin to the secular quiet about the "organization man." One writer reflected in the *Lutheran Companion* in 1957: "I have spent so much time in the past year attending board and committee meetings, both for the Church and civic organizations, that I begin to wonder what would have happened if we had paid less attention to the so-called 'administrative' functions of the Church and more to the soul needs of men."[28]

Another writer, with seeming concerns about the control of the elected or appointed church leadership, aggressively attacked the suggestion of hierarchy: "No dictatorial clergy clique 'runs' our Church or its congregations. In characteristic democratic fashion, the destinies of Augustana are essentially and ultimately in the complete and competent control of her members."[29] The stridency of this assertion, however, leads to the inevitable conclusion that in his mind this "fact" was either in question or that it needed to be defended in some way. Perhaps all these concerns about the increasing organizational and centralization were to be expected, for change and growth in any organization creates problems, especially for those who see the changes as being detrimental to the work of the church.

All in all, the twentieth century witnessed remarkable growth within all areas of the Augustana Synod, as it expanded into a major Lutheran denomination in North America and developed a significant program of missions around the world. Part of this rapid expansion was occasioned by simple need—there were so many Swedish Americans who needed to hear the gospel and receive the ministry of the synod—and the synod strained every slender resource to meet these overwhelming demands. Part of the expansion, too, was occasioned by the times and the cultural situation surrounding the synod; American life in the twentieth century was defined by an ebullient sense of optimism and energy, and by the building of ever-larger institutions, a spirit that naturally affected the church. During his 1923 visit to America, Swedish archbishop Nathan Söderblom commented on what he saw as the remarkable energy and activity of the Augustana Synod, although he interpreted this as the mark of a relatively young and somewhat immature denomination with many pressing tasks. But this spirit of activity is one that went back to the origins of the synod itself, and to the remarkable and audacious group of young pastors who founded it.

In 1960, commenting on this spirit, Evald B. Lawson, the president of Upsala College, reflected on the nature of the activism and energy within the synod: "Activism has always been a character trait of the Augustana Lutheran Church. This spirit is found at all levels. It pervades our conventions and meetings. Should it ever seem to lag, then it would be natural to announce a rally urging us to come to support of our good causes with renewed vigor and activity." Further, he saw this spirit of activism within the increasing structure of Augustana itself, in the pronouncements of presidents and leaders, board secretaries and committee chairs, all challenging the synod to greater commitment and achievement through its organized programs. "Today the emphasis is on the 'total program of the Church,' and the summons is directed to laity and pastors alike," Lawson maintained. "We are enjoined that we must 'sell the gospel' to all people. This is our 'kingdom business.'"

Still, Lawson saw a danger in all this organizational energy, concluding that the centrality of the Christian gospel could be lost within all the efforts: "Yet . . . our activism has done something to the soul of our Church, and has had an unmistakable influence on the average minister and his ministry. It has taken its toll."[30]

Certainly it must always be the concern of those who love the church that the temptation is always there to "play church" and become engrossed in the day-to-day organizational activities and concerns of a particular Christian denomination, to the detriment of the wider needs of Christ and the kingdom of God. Yet it does not seem that the remarkable expansion of the Augustana Synod in the twentieth century was accomplished in the spirit of hubris or institutional aggrandizement. The leaders—clergy and lay—of the synod seemed to be humble and well-grounded individuals, who sought to serve their God and God's people in the best and most effective ways they could.

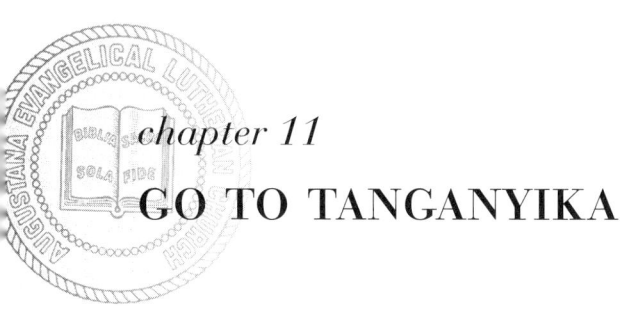

chapter 11
GO TO TANGANYIKA

WHEN AUGUSTANA'S WOMEN ORGANIZED their Women's Missionary Society, they could count on support from almost every area of the synod, since participation in the missionary movement had become a kind of seal of maturity, not only for women, but for all Protestants in America. A mission impulse was part of the originating spirit of the church, but by the turn of the twentieth century, structures were in place to direct the impulse into concerted action. Extending Augustana's ministry abroad structured the synod as a modern, American church. Augustana became a denomination, with programs, publications, and treasuries devoted to organizational expansion, and with leadership focused on a worldwide task.

Mustering adequate support for sending out missionaries proved to be more difficult than enthusiastic promoters expected. Serendipity and accidental opportunity rather than careful planning gave the synod the chance to grow its capacity for leadership and service around the world. "Go to Tanganyika" comes from the brief directions President Gustaf Brandelle gave missionary Ralph Hult in 1922. Hult's missionary path went through many fits and starts, taking detours along the way, and while other missionaries had been commissioned by the synod, he was the one who established Augustana as a church with a "field" of its own. Hult's persistent efforts gave Augustana missionaries in Tanganyika the freedom to identify their own mission focus, pursue their own mission policy, and take responsibility for developing a local indigenous church.

Early Frustrations in Lutheran Mission

In 1878, the Augustana Synod sent out its first official foreign missionary, in cooperation with the General Council—a convention of confessional Lutherans who split from the General Synod in 1867. The General Council had a mission field in India that needed missionaries, and Augustana had a candidate who was interested—August Carlson. Carlson had learned of the possibility in India from his theological studies at the General Council's seminary in Philadelphia. While in Philadelphia he also assisted in preaching for an Augustana congregation under the direction of Pastor Conrad Lindberg, who helped Carlson make the formal contacts enabling him to be ordained early, with a call to the India mission. Carlson served near Rajahmundry for four years, learning the language and going off to villages to preach. But the result was dismal. He suffered a mental breakdown and died in an asylum. Service in India would claim another Augustana missionary a decade later, when Emanuel Edman's wife's fragile health ended their stay.[1]

The formation of Augustana's Women's Missionary Society gave the synod a fresh chance to recruit someone to go to India, and Charlotte Swensson agreed to become the first single woman to be sent out from the synod. She went to India in 1895, but her health broke. In spite of these setbacks the Rev. John Teleen kept the need for missionaries before the annual meeting with words similar to his column in *Augustana*, on June 7, 1900. Millions of people were dying who had not heard the gospel, and Teleen tried the old tactic of shaming the church into service:

> In the Moravian church every 60th communicant is a missionary to the heathen. Among the Congregationalist there is one for every 2,950, the Baptists are represented by one for every 5,031 while the Methodists have one for every 12, 296. If we count student Swenson and pastor Gullander, whom of course we have not sent out, but God has led them through other paths, we have a [heathen] mission field for every 28,434 communicants. Couldn't we send, won't we send more? Let us hurry. In India between 3 and 4 million die of starvation, in China between 4 and 5 million are short of food. In the whole heathen world 30–40 million people die every year. Shall this not move us?[2]

Pastor Gullander, whom Teleen mentioned, in 1902 wrote an account of his three years as a missionary in Africa. Interest in Gullander's story was strong enough for a second printing. The account provided readers with information about the Boer War, the situation of the various tribes, and described the religious needs of the Scandinavian community in Africa. The book made a plea for sponsorship of what was really an immigrant-oriented mission. Gullander also sought funding from the Church of Sweden and from mission societies in Norway. He had begun to build a base for his mission work through his pastoral service to Swedish immigrants in Cape Town, who would, he hoped, become involved in and supportive of mission work among native people. Pictures from the congregation in South Africa and the well-appointed hotel run by Norwegian ladies there indicated that this was an urban, even cosmopolitan, place to start. Indeed, the cost of maintaining his missionary method—more than $1,000 a year for one missionary—was expensive. Gullander returned from South Africa after a short term. On his way he included a visit to the Holy Land, and vivid descriptions of Jerusalem closed out his picturesque missionary account.

Traveling to Jerusalem had by the early 1900s become a real possibility for Protestants, and this experience sharpened their missionary zeal. The opening up of Palestine to Christian business and exploration at the end of the Ottoman Empire convinced many Christians that a new day had arrived for the Christian world. They saw the finger of God moving when Jews returned to the Holy Land. German mission societies and Swedish pilgrims and American evangelical adventurers moved into Jerusalem and even lived among the indigenous Palestinian population. Some were apocalyptic in their imagination while others had more modest eschatological expectations. The Holy Land and Christian mission were part of the same spiritual landscape for most Protestants. "Christian people cannot be indifferent about who owns Palestine," remarked a Swedish priest. "It is not just a question of the places where there are holy memories, or of churches, schools and charitable places, but it is a question of a new crusade—but not with weapons—to win through Christian love Christ's earthly homeland for his kingdom on earth."[3]

Augustana's engagement with the Holy Land included a visit by an assistant professor at the seminary, Dr. Carl Elofson, who spent two years there (1897–1898) studying the area and its history. President P. A. Mattson from Gustavus Adolphus College went to the Holy Land in 1911, before becoming Minnesota Conference president.[4] Mattson took the time to visit Sweden and Europe on his way to Palestine, where he gained permission to stay at the Swedish-American Adventist colony, made popular through Selma Lägerlof's novel *Jerusalem*. By the time Mattson visited, the colony had adopted more moderate views, including the relaxation of earlier strictures against marriage. Mattson wrote only of his admiration for the hospitality, preferring not to remind his conservative readers that the group believed in a heterodox millennial theology. Mattson's popularity with young people in Minnesota made his book a favorite with them. Through it they were introduced to biblical places and historical scenes, creating a familiarity with other people around the world, in order to be Mattson's words, a "blessing for God's Kingdom."

Young People Become Interested in Missions

Augustana's young people may have responded to missionary drives in order to leave the immigrant mindset behind. It was a sign of Americanization

when students at the synod's colleges began to register an interest in foreign missions. The Student Volunteer Movement for Missions was promoted
heavily on college campuses through rallies organized by John R. Mott of
YMCA fame, and thousands of young people made enthusiastic pledges to
become missionaries. In addition, students at the synod's colleges began organizing clubs and societies to cultivate an interest in missionary work. In 1886,
future India missionary Emanuel Edman established the first foreign missionary society at Augustana College. This was the climactic year of Dwight
W. Moody's 1886 college revival in Northfield, Massachusetts that generated 100 volunteers for missionary service.[5] Edman summoned an apostolic
group of twelve. Up to this point, college societies had for the most part been
literary and debating clubs. The new mission societies had more sweeping
goals to raise money for mission and recruit candidates. The synod's Women's
Missionary Society also worked to recruit candidates. With several societies
and young people's groups together focusing on mission, by the turn of the
century, Augustana's young college students had heard the call.

In Swedish-American circles preachers circulated, spreading, like Mott,
a zeal for "the evangelization of the world in this generation."[6] In 1889, the
famous missionary Hudson Taylor announced that China needed a surge in
missionary forces of 1,000, and he challenged Protestant churches to meet
the demand. One spectacular response came from Frederik Franson, a promoter of mission in Sweden and America who did not wait for official
permission to forge ahead.[7] Franson was not Lutheran, but he was known
to Augustana people living in major Swedish-American cities. His views
had traces of the dispensationalist theories of Charles Darby, and he used
methods pioneered by Dwight W. Moody of the Bible Institute in Chicago.
Franson toured Sweden but did not waste time on detailed Bible study.
He pressed upon hearers the urgency to preach the gospel to all lands in a
hurry. Converts were not the goal; that would take too much time. What
was needed were more missionaries following God's will to just preach.
Franson's recruitment method worked in Brooklyn, Chicago, Minneapolis,
and Omaha—where, over the winter of 1890–1891, he recruited fifty volunteers. Their rudimentary training involved some medical instruction but
little orientation to mission methods or instruction in theology. The volunteers pledged to be celibate for three years and to live on a meager allowance.
In February 1881, they went straight to China, and over the next two years
200 more volunteers joined them. But China was really not ready for the
barely trained missionaries who relied on the Holy Spirit to translate their
sermons for Chinese listeners with no grasp of English.

A second competing Swedish effort was also familiar to jealous
Augustana watchers. Covenant missionary Peter Matson, after much better

training, went to China and published an account of mission work that emphasized the character of the church in spreading the gospel. "China," wrote Matson, "the last, greatest, land of the heathens, even the Gibraltar of heathendom, has been spared until our day, when the Christian congregation has developed maturity for this great task."[8] *Mission's Pictures from China* generated a different, more realistic enthusiasm based on solid experience. By 1906 Matson described two decades of work, detailing political and religious issues and showing how a missionary spent his time. Without naming names, Matson cautioned against Franson's approach, stating, "There is danger in focusing too much on quantity and not on quality," for yet another conference was calling for more missionaries. Hinting that Franson's candidates damaged the cause, Matson called for care and prayer in choosing missionaries.[9]

Augustana's Own Mission Field

Augustana members could only listen in on public discussions about strategy, as they did not yet have "their own field." Young people heard the call but a life commitment, at least under realistic conditions, was not possible until the several institutions of the church provided training. In the years before World War I, new fields opened up in China and even in Africa. Augustana members who had been growing tired of a borrowed field in India where they took direction from another church now began to hope for an area of their own. At the annual meeting in Lindsborg in 1904, the Minnesota Conference presented a resolution that the synod withdraw from the General Council. Minnesota conservatives did not trust Eastern Lutherans, and the General Council's India mission field was a less-than-satisfying project to support. The conflict in Minnesota did not directly relate to foreign mission, but ill feeling had a way of spilling over. As a member, Augustana supported the General Council's home mission efforts to conduct English language work. English-speaking pastors called by the General Council's Home Mission Board originally had joined Augustana's Minnesota Conference, thereby becoming members of the Augustana Synod, but as the work grew, these ministers formed a competing Northwest Synod whose territory overlapped the area of the Minnesota Conference. Conference pastors resented the fact that, while they had supported the India mission of the General Council, competition rather than cooperation had been the response.[10]

Synod delegates in Lindsborg did not withdraw from the General Council, citing benefits from closer association with other Lutherans, but Minnesota's independent streak found a way forward anyway. They wanted to support their own mission work and pushed ahead to develop their own field. J. G. Hultkrans, a pastor in Minneapolis, who, according to his biographer, "manifested an interest in matters just a little different from the rank and file of his brethren,"[11] prepared the way in 1901 when he hosted a meeting to explore mission work in China. The response encouraged him, and a second, official meeting occurred in September that year at Bethlehem Lutheran in Minneapolis. Two days in discussion and prayer included a lecture by Dr. C. J. Collin, on "Our Debt to the Pagan World," and then the organization of a society. Pastor P. A. Mattson, studying for his doctorate at the University of Minnesota, presided. Augustana members in Minnesota finally had the instrument to compete with the missionary work of Norwegian churches and Swedish Free churches in China.

The seventeen members in attendance elected Mattson chairman. Then the group trod carefully in drafting their purpose. The society would be independent, but draw members solely from the synod. Slowly, over the next two years, they gained members, adopted a constitution, planned more meetings, and received funds. Still, they had no missionaries, for negotiating an independent approach that maintained a friendly relationship to the synod took considerable energy. Another reason was a confusion of goals. The Mission Society tried to expedite things by linking with a local hospital to publish a monthly magazine. This gave them instant subscribers, but readers were interested in diaconal ministry rather than mission work. The society debated whether they should send a layperson to the mission field. A physician, Dr. C. P. Friberg, volunteered at the beginning of 1903, but the society felt a pastor should open the field. Friberg went to the Church of Sweden Mission in Africa instead. The society then had to figure out which field to enter—their preferred China mission, or the newer field in Africa where Dr. Friberg had gone. It took several years before the official founding of the China mission.[12]

The breakthrough came when August William Edwins, a pastor in Stillwater, Minnesota, accepted the call of the society. Having succeeded in attracting one of the leaders in the Minnesota Conference, the society had to begin to search for a field in earnest. A. F. Almer, chairman, noted that, "Our eyes have been turning to the province of Honan."[13] This was where the Mission Covenant and other Swedish and Norwegian mission societies had been working, the places Augustana people had been hearing about. Edwins left for Honan in 1905.

The China Mission Society's success now put a feather in Minnesota's cap. Minnesota pastors bristled at any hint that their experience and ideals were marginal. Living near a high concentration of Norwegians and in a center of Lutheranism, Minnesota Swedes were frustrated when their church did not build as many large churches, schools, or hospitals visible to them even though their national church supported missions and social services as impressive but farther away. Minneapolis was just not Chicago. But now they had pushed the synod in a new direction. Even though the China Mission Society carefully restricted its membership to Augustana members, by 1908 it had expanded to 600 members who supported five missionaries in the field. It had managed the difficult task of negotiating with Chinese officials to purchase property, and $3,000 waited in the treasury. At the synod meeting in 1908, the society offered its mission as a gift to the synod, which in turn created the Board of China Mission. The mission developed independent of synod or pastoral leadership. It did not come out of the contagious spread of a college culture among the youth, although all of these mechanisms would soon be enlisted in the support of mission in the synod. The growth of the China Mission Society occurred so quickly and the support was so substantial that it was clear that missionary work appealed to the broad grassroots of the church.

Gaining a Foothold on the World Scene

Mission promoters in Minnesota mustered a progressive, organized missionary spirit and helped Augustana launch its missionary work just in time. During the next three decades Lutheran missions around the world suffered multiple shocks from world wars. German mission societies—Basel, Berlin, Leipzig, Hermannsburg, and Rhenish—were cut off from their "fields." In the parlance of the day, the missions were "orphans" needing rescue, and American churches found themselves involved in international work on a new, complicated level. Augustana discovered a confident American identity in the process. In China, India, and Africa, missionaries faced daunting challenges. Sometimes they failed to seize opportunities. Missionaries were not trained as statesmen but as simple servants of the gospel. That they managed to salvage so much during a time of such upheaval was remarkable.

Missionary Oscar Larson and his wife Lilie went to India in 1905 when mission work there benefited from "a new day" in missionary preparation and service. Upon his retirement, Oscar wrote a short history of his ministry. When he started his service, Oscar recalled, Protestant missions had gained experience to recognize "perils of overwork, overexposure, and overzealous independence."[14] Work had been "reformed" through mutual consultation at missionary resorts and recreational centers. Mothers were freed for missionary tasks when home boards agreed to fund a common school for missionary children. Families could be treated at modern, western medical facilities. And mission work itself became more systematic through cooperation and consultation. Health improved when families discovered the importance of boiling water before drinking it.

When mission work commended itself to the churches as a thoroughly modern enterprise, students gained an enthusiasm for a form of evangelical ministry that had before seemed extremely risky, almost a martyr's call. In the "new day" that so encouraged Oscar Larson, missionaries still succumbed to illness, but the sending churches had by then succeeded in establishing hospitals and clinics. At least sick missionaries could get medical help. Mission stations in India had comfortable houses, and there were multiple venues for employment. Missionaries were needed as doctors and teachers, nurses and evangelists. Mission work appealed now to women. Missionaries were "couples" in their work, even though wives were not formally consecrated. Larson highlighted the role of missionary wives in his history, revealing how one had been a primary school teacher in Sweden, and her expertise with women and children enhanced her husband's work. Without their wives, moreover, some of the men would not have succeeded. Larson's profile of one early missionary included the judgment that he "was not fluent in any language, but a scholar who loved his books and spent as much of his time as possible with them . . . while his wife used three languages fluently and in the practical side of his work helped him a great deal." Even wives with no particular professional training became indispensable: "A married missionary is always spoken of in the plural, because his wife goes with him and has a vital share in his work."[15]

The idealized missionary couple became an attractive model. When home on furlough, they visited churches, colleges, young people's meetings, and synod conventions. They demonstrated that a missionary's life was a way for young couples to serve together in exciting places. Young women at the beginning of the twentieth century would recognize this as a clear call also to them, whether or not they hoped to be married. Single women like Betty Nilsson and Charlotte Swensson were supported through their professional training by Augustana's Women's Missionary Society. Dr. Nilsson trained at the University of Illinois and later at Cook County Hospital before going in 1908 to be a missionary doctor in India, where she served for forty years. The women supported Charlotte Swensson beginning in 1895, and again when she needed to recoup her health, they paid for her studies at Bethany College. Women in congregations learned to know these women through their regular informative letters about mission work found on the pages of the Women's Missionary Society's monthly magazine, *Mission Tidings.*

The opening of missionary fields in China gave young people another option for service in the church. After 1906, when China abandoned the traditional Confucian examination system, Protestant missionary boards responded and began to send the larger share of their candidates to China.[16] This shift in American Protestant mission strategy no doubt influenced the synod in 1908 to adopt the Minnesota-based China mission. Positive American orientation to China mission filtered down to idealistic students who wanted to be enlisted in world-changing events. At Luther College in Wahoo, Nebraska, three students—Johan Lindell, J. W. Lindbeck, and David Vikner—aimed their career aspirations to China. After completing seminary, they joined a large contingent of eight missionaries sent out by the synod in 1912, entering the field just before the outbreak of World War I.

Augustana Missionaries View the World at War

China missionary David Vikner experienced the First World War from the perspective of the Far East, where the tragedy unfolding in Europe may have seemed somewhat distant. He viewed the missionary cause, however, as directly connected to the overarching struggle shared by armies and missionaries alike against "false ideals, defective character, and peace destroying ambitions."[17] When he wrote to the people at home, he stressed that members should recognize that prayers and support sent to missionaries contributed to establish forces of righteousness and goodwill "which must lie at [the] foundation of all permanent peace." These words from the mission field became a voice of conscience for members at home. Armed with mission stories from the "front," supporters at home rallied to increase their donations. Vikner goaded them on: "What are we going to do this year? To get together in conference and synod meetings and make motions to be put on record, and then forget it all?" While he and the other missionaries were on the field in action, he chided that at least those at home could "talk and write more about mission" and involve the laity who are more fit than the minister to "take care of the finances."

Requests from the missionaries for more money, personnel, and prayers were printed regularly in the "Missions" column of the *Lutheran Companion*, whose readership was smaller than the *Augustana* subscription list, but more informed and interested in mission than the increasingly older, Swedish readers of *Augustana*.[18] The cause of mission seemed especially to interest young people and English-speaking members. Reading about and supporting the missionary movement strengthened a sense of evangelical engagement with the world. It was also an Americanizing process, as missionaries and supporters alike recognized that their efforts overseas were part of a larger, global American presence. Missionaries like Vikner measured their church's efforts against those of other American denominations. They also met and mingled with other American missionaries in the field, especially during their summer vacations at the resort-like campuses of missionary retreat centers.

The Missionary World

Missionary families in India and China lived in a unique missionary society. Augustana missionaries, fluent in Swedish and English and a dialect of Chinese, mingled with missionaries from America, Sweden, and Norway. Their children attended boarding school at the Lutheran-run Kikungshan School. The Lindbeck, Vikner, Friberg, and Lindell families sent their children to this school located on a campus adjacent to a cluster of more than a hundred missionary summer homes, where families joined their children during breaks. John Benson's 1925 history of the China Mission exults in the idyllic atmosphere surrounding the compound: "It is a little utopia in the middle of the Middle Kingdom."[19]

Mission teaching in China in the late 1920s. Education efforts focused on women of all ages.
Photo courtesy of Evangelical Lutheran Church in America Archives.

But missionary life was hardly idyllic in China during the mid-twenties, for mission stations were in the path of several armed uprisings. Families literally had to flee to safety. No sooner had John Benson collected all the material for his history than conflict reached even as far as the school in Kikungshan. In late August 1926, many missionaries had returned to their fields, including the Lindbecks to Honanfu. George, son of missionary couple

John and Magda Lindbeck, remembered a night in his childhood when roaming militias came so near his mission station that he heard bullets, like raindrops, on the roof while his father carried him to the safety of a bunker in the basement.[20] Other families had not yet left the school area of Kikungshan, and they waited fearfully for three months as armed groups swept through villages and came ever closer to their resort compound. But the missionaries were also quite worried about their stations where Chinese Christians were in danger, so one-by-one, they attempted to get back via byways and circular routes.

China missionaries were also unwilling to leave their posts because that fall they had scheduled a celebration at the China "All Lutheran Conference" for the dedication of the main building at Emmy Evald School in Hsuchow. The head of the Women's Missionary Society, Emmy Evald, was on her way to China, arriving in time to visit with the missionaries, even though the celebratory conference had to be cancelled. Evald dedicated the building and managed to make a tour of the mission stations. The passenger trains were not running, so she had to travel by donkey cart or ride on freight trains. One night she slept in a railroad car with only a blanket for comfort, while soldiers occupied the other end. She impressed the Chinese with her age, for she was more than seventy years old. Evald wrote about how touching it was to see "her jewels," the young girls at the school lighting candles and singing Christmas hymns in spite of the unrest all around them.[21] The trip Evald took to China was part of a worldwide tour. After leaving China in January, the Women's Mission Society entourage headed to India, and then Palestine, before heading home.

The year away touring mission stations was calming for Evald, even in the context of war and revolution, because before her tour she had suffered a very public defeat in the synod. The women of the Augustana Women's Missionary Society had raised money to fund a women's dormitory on the campus of Augustana College, but when it came time to situate the building, the trustees of the college refused to listen to the society's request that it be placed off to the side of the campus, away from undue contact with male student housing.[22] Evald's society had already provided funding for more than forty buildings around the world—hospitals, schools, and homes for women—and she was not used to having her judgment set aside. The trip around the world, even if it did pass through regions of severe unrest, gave her time with a constituency that recognized and celebrated her leadership. And through her reports on the trip, the constituency at home learned first-hand about the effects of war and unrest on women and children around the world.

Africa, Where Augustana Grew Up

Evald's 1926–1927 tour did not extend to Africa even though Augustana missionaries had begun work there. The synod's missionary extension to Africa had started in 1917, during World War I, when Ralph Hult, who had been influenced toward a missionary career when a student at Luther College in Wahoo, successfully convinced the synod to call him to go to the Sudan. Inspired by Augustana's work in China, Hult also wanted to be a pioneer. Hult had grown up in Kearney, Nebraska, and had attended the same congregation as China missionary John Lindbeck. While Hult was a student at Luther Academy in 1907, he heard a pastor make a plea for mission work in the Sudan, which inspired the eighteen year old. After finishing at Augustana College in 1913, he spent time in Utah and Arizona as a colporteur for the American Bible Society. Hult's experience as a distributor of Bible tracts ended after only one year, when he began his seminary education at Chicago Lutheran Theological Seminary in 1914.[23] Hult spent two years in Chicago, and then returned to Rock Island, where he got involved with the Augustana Foreign Missionary Society and helped them send a resolution to petition the synod's board of missions to study the possibility of establishing a synod mission in the Sudan. On June 17, 1917, Hult was ordained with the rest of his class with a call to be a missionary. His missionary zeal had time to mature when war made it impossible for him to begin. Sent to a congregation in Hartford, Connecticut, he enrolled at the Kennedy School of Missions.

In the spring of 1919, Hult completed the two-year course. He wrote to Augustana's mission board's president, O. J. Johnson, on the faculty at Gustavus Adolphus College, that coming to the school at first had been a disappointment, but "*now* I thank God that I didn't get to go at that time, unprepared as I was to meet the special difficulties of a field like Africa, where we will have to deal with the Mission on one side and the raw pagan on the other."[24] The Kennedy School was linked with the Hartford Theological Seminary, a Congregationalist school that Hult described as "interdenominational." Mission studies happened under different departments, depending on the area of the world, and Hult was proud that the school had an international reputation. Two students from Denmark, ten from Norway, and a woman from Sweden were classmates. He was impressed with the faculty: "[They] represent the best scholarship that money can buy," drawing students also from the mission fields. "I have been helped very much personally in hearing these men tell of their experiences in coming out of heathenism into Christianity." Hult characterized the school as "conservative," though two men did not fit that description. Luckily, he said, they were not at the school of missions.

Augustana's mission theology did not stretch beyond the basic conservative orientation that divided the world as Hult did into heathenism and Christianity. In the years before the Hocking Report,[25] when liberal views made inroads into Protestant mission theology and introduced the idea that the historic religions of China and India may not have been all that bad, Augustana missionaries held an uncritical, practical, service-oriented approach to mission. Like P. A. Mattson who visited the American Colony in Jerusalem, Hult seemed also willing to blend in, take in what was useful, and decline the opportunity to criticize others. Hult saw mission as a pragmatic enterprise, and he did not busy himself with making theological distinctions either at school, or in the field, or at least for O. J. Johnson at Gustavus Adolphus. Hult's correspondence was instead filled with reiterations of his desire to minister to the "dark'" continent, and to follow the "call" the synod issued in 1917. Hult took this call as a divine summons and was earnest in heeding it.

In 1919 he received authorization to plan his travel to Sudan, which at the time was a field much larger than the present-day, including countries located all across the northern half of Africa. He booked passage to Nigeria, but the synod felt it unwise to send his wife Leona with him. In November 1919 while aboard the ship *Bereby*, Hult wrote to the man who had first inspired him to seek a call to Africa, telling him what his wife planned to do in the meantime: "[S]he will be in Omaha at the Deaconess Institute to gain experience in caring for the sick."[26] Gertrude Hult clearly anticipated that she would be professionally involved in the mission work.

There was as yet no settled place for Hult to serve. The next two years were spent in negotiation with the mission board over whether he should work under the Sudan United Mission in a tiny bounded corner of Nigeria, or move into the French colonial areas where there would be room for growth. The correspondence includes rather sophisticated arguments over the relative merits of English versus French territories, and the status of Protestant missionaries especially in areas that would be dominated by Roman Catholic missions. Finally Gertrude joined him at the end of 1921, and they settled in a small area of Nigeria in the Sudan United Mission field, and began to learn the language and establish relationships. The arrangement was short lived, however, for in the aftermath of World War I colonial arrangements in Africa were disturbed. German mission societies were affected by the Allied victory, and this meant a crisis for Lutheran missionary work farther east, in Tanganyika.

Ralph Hult was affected by this turn of events almost as soon as he arrived in Ibi, Nigeria, because the Augustana Board of Missions was approached by the German Berlin Mission Society with a request that they supply missionaries to oversee mission fields in Tanganyika. The British colonial authorities had ruled that German missionaries were not welcome. When Augustana's board wrote to Hult in December 1921 to ask whether he would be willing to be transferred, the news hit him hard, but he replied, "Here we are; send us."[27] Four months elapsed with no word, but in March 1922, a cablegram arrived from Augustana's president, Gustaf Alfred Brandelle: "Go to Tanganyika."

Ralph and Gertrude Hult accepted the new instructions, but not without reservation. "Perhaps we have been in self-chosen ways during these last five years," they admitted in a letter to seminary professor C. A. Blomgren, revealing an inner struggle. "If that be so, we can surely know now that we are not going the ways of our own choosing.—'God's plans are often other than our plans.' That is certainly true, although *we may fail to understand* it." The major disappointment for them was that the Tanganyika mission work had already been established by the Germans, and Hult yearned to advance the gospel where it had never been heard. "It is quite impossible to see *why* we should be asked to leave this part of the Dark Continent, where there are but a few outposts of Christianity in the face of the advancing hordes of Islam, and go to another part where the light of the Gospel has been shining for many decades."

In the six short months Ralph Hult had spent in the Sudan United Mission he had experienced what it was like to break what he called "virgin soil" of mission: "We shall never cease to thank God that we were permitted to have this little share in direct mission work in this dark part of dark Africa." But six months had not really been enough time for Ralph or Gertrude to enter sufficiently into the life and culture of their new surroundings to cast off the rhetoric of superiority, either.

Ralph Hult's letter provides hints as to his mission theory. Establishing a school for children indicated his adoption of pragmatic methods to win the trust of villagers. Mission theorists debated whether it was more important to begin with schools or with preaching, and whether Christianity depended on teaching civilization or whether the gospel message should be proclaimed, letting native people continue to live as they had. These debates had largely been conducted during the middle decades of the nineteenth century in relation to mission work done by the American Board of Foreign Commissioners for Mission (ABCFM) and by other British and American mission boards. The "culture versus Christianity" debate also arose in relation to the work of women in mission, since they did the "civilizing" forms of Christian mission, teaching children and modeling for native women a Christian home life and a monogamous marriage.[28]

Many of these debates arose within the context of devising a Christian mission strategy for India, where the caste system challenged Protestant and American sensibilities.[29] Hult's studies at the Kennedy School in Hartford certainly exposed him to these debates, and also to the result of several decades of mission experience. His choice to start with a school put him on a reforming, civilizing path rather than a pure evangelizing approach favored by conservatives. But Hult also indicated that he was aware of the dangers of too much education. He emphasized that more than half of his instruction went to religion, calling it, "breaking the ground and sowing the good seed." He introduced western notions of time, however, because he felt hampered when "we could not get the people together at one time, since they have no way to telling the time except by the sun." To that end, Hult asked Augustana students to use the money they had raised for him toward the purchase of a bell to call the people together at the same time.

Missionaries and the Worldwide Church

Much more could be written about the internal debates over mission strategy that Ralph Hult reflected on in his letters to the mission board, friends, and family. His reluctant move into Tanganyika's German mission fields conflicted with his desire to "break virgin soil." But Hult did start work in Northern Tanganyika, ably supervising the work of the Leipzig society. During the short period between world wars, when German missionaries were again allowed to return, Augustana missionaries who had joined Hult agreed to move aside in order to begin work in their own smaller field in central Tanganyika, an area that previously had experienced only exploratory visits. Hult's strong preference for laying a foundation for mission and then being able to apply some consistency to the work gives insight into the resistance that emerged when Augustana's missionary corps in Tanganyika were asked to rescue the work of several German mission societies again during the Second World War. Gustav Bernander, a Swedish missionary in Tanganyika, wrote a detailed study of the way the Augustana Lutheran Church came to the assistance of Lutheran missions when German missionaries were interned during the war. By the time of that emergency, Augustana's personnel numbered twenty-two, men and women included, while the total number of German missionaries that had to be replaced numbered more than 150.[30]

The small Augustana contingent faced the daunting task of extending themselves far beyond their own field in the central district of Iramba. Augustana was virtually the only American church in the region. Missionaries from Scandinavia were hard to reach. Nazi occupation made it impossible to even communicate with church leaders and mission boards in Norway, Denmark, or Finland. Lutherans faced the needs of orphaned missions in India and Southeast Asia as well, again to assist German societies. Repeatedly, cooperative Lutheran agencies in the United States, and especially the International Missionary Council, worked to bring the untended mission fields before members of American churches. The stakes were high: school buildings and hospitals, dormitories and missionary dwellings, could be confiscated by the colonial authorities.

Augustana's mission director, George Anderson, sent letters to other U.S. Lutheran denominations, but none were inclined or able to help. In the end, the only assistance came from missionaries serving in other fields, or on furlough. Ray Cunningham, a missionary from India on furlough in the United States, agreed to come, explaining, "The call to help save these young churches which had no educated leadership at the time appeared far greater than the call to India with its more than one hundred trained and ordained pastors, and its hundreds of other Indian workers in different branches of mission service."[31] Others who had once served in China also came to Africa, including the Friberg and Lindell families.

Help finally came from Swedish missionaries working with the Swedish Evangelical Mission Society in what was then called Rhodesia, now Zimbabwe. Then, the Church of Sweden agreed to free some of their personnel in South Africa to send them to Tanganyika. This involved considerable expense, however, because British colonial authorities demanded that any personnel assigned to the German missions first be certified by the National Lutheran Council in New York City, who interviewed them to certify that they would serve under American supervision. Gustav Bernander and his wife came from southern Rhodesia, while Bengt Sundkler came from South Africa to the Bukoba region, later serving as its first bishop. In addition, the involvement of a few missionaries from Australia and Norway supplemented the Augustana and Swedish Church rescue effort.

One especially dramatic episode in this saga came late in the summer of 1941, when the internment of German missionaries had begun, but before America entered the war. Ralph Hult, who had founded Augustana's efforts in Tanganyika, had returned to America in 1926 to stay, after Augustana's mission board had refused to send him again to the Sudan, where he stubbornly insisted God had called him. Now he was asked if he were willing to return to Tanganyika. He accepted and booked passage to Africa with several American missionaries on the *Zamzam*, an Egyptian steamer. Attacked on the open sea, the boat sank. After spending a harrowing night in the water, all the passengers were rescued by the German ship that had attacked them. Among the Augustana families was Lillian Danielson and her six children who were traveling to join her husband and their father. After the captured passengers were brought by German ship to Portugal, they were sent back to the U.S. The story of the *Zamzam* rescue captivated missionary supporters throughout North America, but Elmer Danielson, waiting in Africa for his family and reinforcements, was left in uncertainty for many months. While he waited, he wrote what must have been white-knuckle letters to colonial authorities protecting the right of the church to their properties and asking the central mission board for more help, immediately.[32]

The crisis pushed missionaries to identify African men who could be cursorily trained and pushed into supervisory roles. Some who had been capable evangelists were ordained, but a more extensive training program was needed right away. The pressing need for teachers and medical personnel could not be met by the present missionaries, or through the new Tanganyika recruits. The missionary educational system was not developed to supply these needs. The urgent requests seemed not to get through to synod leadership, who felt obligated to respond only to requests from Augustana's own, smaller Iramba field. In fact, missionaries that the church did send resented being asked to attend to the wider problems of the struggling churches in the German fields, preferring the more removed, less developed, and more manageable Augustana fields.

These overwhelming problems resulted in numerous complaints and difficulties. Augustana's work in what became Tanzania, however, gained respect from the other churches, who recognized the difficult conditions and the real losses suffered. Ralph Hult did return to Africa after the *Zamzam* disaster, but died of malaria following a tour of schools and mission sites around Dar es Salaam in the spring of 1943. He did not live to see the result of Augustana's wartime sacrifice to serve the churches.

World War II brought American churches into a broader cooperation with struggling European mission societies and into a stark recognition that missionary work needed to become cooperative church work. African missions also needed to become African churches, a process that unfolded in the years before the Tanganyika colony became the nation of Tanzania. In America the place of mission in the life of the church changed as well. When two wars interrupted the designs of the young and enthusiastic missionaries, the church at home gained a new level of sophistication in administration and developed leaders who realized the expanded scope of the church's responsibilities. The Augustana people saw the results of this maturation in their colleges and at the seminary, and especially in the young people who emerged from this training ready for the needs of a changing world.

ASSIMILATION: "CONDENSED IN THE LAST HOURS OF A LONG DAY"

The United States Congress took action to restrict immigration in 1924, reflecting feelings about immigrants that were increasingly hostile. A widely read screed purporting to scientifically establish reasons for a retreat from immigration came from Henry Pratt Fairchild in *The Melting Pot Mistake*, a book advancing the notion that the racial foundation of America was in danger. The democratic and capitalistic system that America needed had been the result of racial factors, he argued, as much as economic and geographical fortune. The racial background of America's original settlers replicated that of England, where Nordic, Mediterranean, and Alpine races had combined. But this was no longer the case, given the nature of the new immigration from Southern Europe and beyond. Swedish immigrants were not considered a threat to preservers of America's racial purity—the problem was that there were not enough Scandinavians to maintain the desired optimum level of Nordic traits. According to Fairchild, too many Alpine, Hebrew, Negroid, and Mongoloid strains threatened to sully the conglomerate "germ plasm" of the nation.[1]

Augustana's leaders were not innocent of these ideas. They seemed pretty well acquainted with their "favored" status among Americans, and at times even reveled in their supposed natural advantage over other ethnic groups. During the 1880s, annual Midsommar picnics were occasions where speakers extolled Viking heritage, deeds of valiant soldier kings, and the virtues of a Swedish home life. Boston pioneer pastor, the Rev. Carl F. Johansson, became by 1883 a sought-after speaker at Swedish "fests" in New England. His papers include well-worn copies of talks on Gustavus Adolphus, Martin Luther, the famous Uppsala Meeting, and other heroic themes.[2] His words celebrated the contributions that the fair-haired children of the North would make to their adopted land. All the paeans to a heralded Scandinavian heritage, however, must be heard within the context of nostalgic remembrance that circled these fests like a gathering mist. Swedishness as a component of Lutheranism was no longer fluent, but condensed in the last hours of a long day.

Even the colloquial pages of *Korsbaneret* give evidence that immigrant language and experience needed to be recorded in order to be remembered. In 1923, John A. Edlund related the story of his parents in "Traces from the Immigrant's Ranks." The account needed to be brought before a new readership, since living memory of the great migration was soon to disappear. Stories of immigrant life were a far cry from the vaunted narratives of history-making figures that filled the popular immigrant press and fueled a nationalist sensibility, stories of great men, great ideas, and noble deeds. John A. Edlund's father's story was typical instead of a counter narrative. His father left Värmland after the famine years of 1866–1869 when a railroad speculator offered work in

Mississippi. After two years, he sent for his family and had modest success at farming in Illinois, until another speculator induced him to travel further west for more land. Crop failure after crop failure in western Nebraska made for unending labor and pure frustration. But the oldest son had become the pastor who recorded the history. Memories were endangered not only by the passing of generations, but also by the excessive focus on abstractions like a Nordic identity.

Sven Gustaf (S. G.) Öhman, leader in the Swedish-tending New England Conference, sought to deepen an awareness of Sweden and so wrote an article titled "Our Swedish Heritage" for the 1924 *Korsbaneret*. It would take volumes to account for everything, he said, so he limited himself to riches of "spiritual, intellectual and physical wealth cultivated through many generations and which has made the Swedish folk so towering and robust, healthy and strong. This is nowhere more evident than in this cosmopolitan country. Here you have the light of comparison, and in this light the Swede is among the best. . . . With great gifts come great responsibility."[3] Öhman's article commented on the distinct combination of Nordic, Protestant, and pioneering elements that had defined an ethnic church culture for a generation. But by the 1920s, when "Our Swedish Heritage" appeared, the readers of *Korsbaneret* were no longer the younger generation. American culture had become xenophobic. Promoting a Swedish heritage in 1924 was controversial even within the synod.

Hyphenated identities had long been suspect among the "native born," and even within ethnic communities

the emphasis shifted decidedly in the direction of the American part of the equation. World War I inaugurated a cultural mood that could only be called hyper-Americanism. Augustana's people responded by distancing themselves from their language and cultural traditions. English language advocates established themselves as leaders in the synod through the same channels as had been used by C. A. Swensson, Matthias Wahlstrom, Olof Olsson, and Carl Evald. The next generation of leaders began by starting a newspaper for young Augustana readers called *Youth's Companion*. Like *Ungdomsvännen* and *Korsbaneret*, it sought to reach a generation that would otherwise be lost to the church. As *Youth's Companion* gained readership, the name was changed in 1911 to the *Lutheran Companion*.

The shift away from Swedish involved both a theological reorientation and an enlargement of the church's social responsibility. Adopting English was slow and relatively smooth for congregations, occurring when a new pastor would arrive or through the gradual adoption of separate English language services. But the shift involved dramatic consequences in the style, focus, and content of publications. Switching from Swedish to English entailed more than a pragmatic adaptation to the linguistic needs. The older Swedish language carried associations with the religious life of Sweden. It conveyed an inner reflectiveness and a pious and serious orientation to the world.

The language transition took place in every home, congregation, and public occasion. Immigrants spoke two languages, and children learned to speak Swedish at church and home while using English at school and in the neighborhood. Swedish gave way bit by bit, but never disappeared entirely. At the synod meeting in 1927, President Brandelle's opening report gave a dim sort of praise for the 790 pastors in the synod who were handling the transition. "We thank God that the rank and file of the clergy have been faithful," he began. But recognizing that these faithful warriors were weary, he continued, "Some find the work rather irksome by reason of poor health, advancing years, and insufficient knowledge of the English, still others are laboring under financial stress." The purely practical was however manageable: "Changing conditions in one way or another often bring difficulties and trials, but we are grateful to God that our clergy are holding out as well as they do."[4]

Brandelle's report revealed that the English language was on the march everywhere, even affecting Swedish-speaking pastors who needed some command of English to have an effective ministry. In the words of the president they were "holding out." Brandelle was American-born, but his language betrayed his mother tongue. In Swedish, to *hålla ut* was to endure, to persevere, to complete a task until the end. In English, however, the meaning of the very similar sounding phrase "holding out" contains the added notion of resistance to change. The president slipped a "Swediomatic" phrase into his otherwise natural English. Even those born in America succumbed to these confusing linguistic mistakes. Brandelle's presidential report would not have passed muster with E. W. Olson, writer of the Augustana Brotherhood columns in the *Lutheran Companion*, the synod's English paper. Olson examined and expunged Swediomatic usages in synod publications. He was fighting against those who, even inadvertently, assisted the synod's Swedish language "hold outs."

chapter 12

RECONNECTING WITH THE CHURCH OF SWEDEN

LATE IN THE SUMMER OF 1897, a group of ministers and their wives trudged up a hill in the diocese of Härnösand and prepared to eat a picnic lunch. They had walked all morning and needed refreshment. The party included the Rev. Carl A. Swensson and his wife Alma, who were on their second trip to Sweden and visiting the northern diocese. The more energetic and trim Swedes waited for the heavyset Swensson to catch up, and then they all enjoyed an afternoon of food and amusement. To honor their guests, the Swedes entertained the westerners with an "Indian" reenactment. The Swedish dean of the cathedral proclaimed himself chief, called for his wife to get out the food, and commanded his "braves" to sit in a circle. The forested hills around Härnösand became the wild frontier.[1]

While it may seem offensive to the modern reader, this "American" moment during C. A. Swensson's 1897 visit recalled the familiarity that reigned among Swedes and their Augustana counterparts in the 1890s and reflected the interest the Swedes took in "all things American," especially the church on the American frontier. Carl and Alma Swensson felt at home in Härnösand and knew Bishop Martin Johansson well; he was an old friend of Carl's father Jonas Swensson, even considered one of Carl's "cousins," and a congenial supporter of Augustana's version of churchly piety. He was a proponent of the more evangelical, low-church wing within the Church of Sweden associated with the university faculty in Uppsala.

Martin Johansson's election as bishop in 1889 strengthened Augustana's relationship with the Church of Sweden. After his election, Johansson put in writing his belief that "no other denomination in America deserves to be called Swedish Lutheran but that, which, organized in the year 1860, bears the name Scandinavian Evangelical Lutheran Augustana Synod."[2] This endorsement of Augustana came along with the endorsements of all the Swedish bishops, who sent official letters to the synod, complete with wax seals and brief statements. Augustana leaders regarded these as necessary for their work among Swedish immigrants. The American Episcopal Church had begun to do active mission work among Swedish immigrants, claiming to be the closest church to the Church of Sweden since it also had bishops. Augustana leaders had, of course, had their moments of criticism of the Church of Sweden, having arisen out of the revival movement, but now through these official signs of support, they began to realize that the Church of Sweden had begun to appreciate, or at least would no longer disparage, their simple evangelical and churchly piety.

A letter from Archbishop U. L. Ullman of the Church of Sweden, dated January 18, 1892, attesting to his recognition of the Augustana Synod over that of any other Swedish Lutheran church body. Similar letters were sent by each of the Church of Sweden bishops to the seminary in Rock Island. The letter scan is courtesy of the seminary archives at the Lutheran School of Theology at Chicago. For a transcript, see Table 10 in the Appendix.

At the end of the nineteenth century Augustana and the Church of Sweden renewed their ties through personal contacts like those between Martin Johansson and Carl A. Swensson. Swensson, the American-born son of an immigrant pastor, was a representative figure for the new Swedish American, and he wrote often, effusively, and effectively to young people and a wide circle of Augustana readers about his conception of the Swedish-American culture. Now, through his active pursuit of transatlantic friendship he established a way for American Swedes to approach their Swedish heritage on new terms. Several Augustana pastors made high profile visits and published them later as travelogues through the Augustana Book Concern.[3] C. A. Swensson's visit was so widely known that it functioned as a public encounter between Augustana and the Church of Sweden.

Visits on four different occasions during the years between 1893 and 1925 impacted the Augustana Synod. Two involve Augustana visitors—Carl and Alma Swensson and later L. G. Abrahamson, and two involve the Church of Sweden—the bishop of Visby, Knut Henning Gezelius von Schéele and Archbishop Nathan Söderblom. The visits could almost be called public pilgrimages; three of the tours were published as churchly travelogues. The Swedish bishops who visited churches in America became celebrity figures and their touring schedule was announced to the synod through *Augustana*, and later to English readers through the *Lutheran Companion*. Augustana visitors in Sweden usually found themselves in more intimate surroundings, but their presence also registered on the popular imagination of Swedish citizens.

The public addresses and travelogues were condensed moments that do not reveal the whole story of the encounter between complex entities like churches, but the visits and the publicity nevertheless changed the tone of the relationship between the churches. Those who, for various reasons, held back from participating in public ceremonial occasions also expressed criticism and even overt hostility. The internal diversity of theological and political opinion within Augustana became evident especially during the visit of Söderblom, but this ecumenical pioneer and modern churchman also had a winsome personality. On both sides of the Atlantic, neither theological argument nor practical example seemed to move church leaders as much as the welcome they felt when they visited each other. Hospitality fostered closer friendship. It provided the opportunity for influence.

The Kansan in Sweden

Carl A. Swensson's tour to Sweden in 1897 quickly became the subject of another of his many publishing ventures. In an exuberant introduction to his travelogue, *Åter i Sverige*, Swensson hailed the new Sweden to an imagined reader who, like the author, had grown up in America. Swensson practiced a special form of Swedish-American tourism: that of visiting the Church of Sweden. He encouraged readers to develop the same sympathy for the mission of the Church of Sweden as they had for the Augustana Synod. By allying themselves with the church of the old country and imagining its prospects in terms familiar to an American, denominational mindset, Swensson projected onto the Church of Sweden a familiar, more evangelical role than most of the older immigrants at least would have remembered it having. Younger readers used to Swensson's tutelage took him at his word. Swensson assigned the American nomenclature to the Church of Sweden's priests and bishops. They were "leading men" or "prominent friends." Even more practical for Swedish Americans was the way that Swensson envisioned the Church of Sweden as a destination that provided hospitality for those who otherwise felt alienated with their homeland. This was just one more synod meeting, except that it happened across the ocean.

When he wrote about his feelings toward Sweden as homeland, Swensson conveyed his sense of being at once familiar and unsure of himself. He likened clergy gatherings to the meetings of Augustana clergy, but Swedish dinners, even those hosted by churches, included wine and beer, beverages never served at Augustana functions. Swensson's temperance convictions made him uncharacteristically shy when he was asked to make a toast. His momentary embarrassment passed when he found the object for his impromptu speech: he lauded the Christian Swedish woman, our mother and spouse, our sister and daughter. Extolling the piety of the Swedish woman, in her many important roles, permitted Swensson to draw attention to the shifting, ambivalent, but still close relationship between Swedish and Swedish-American churches.

Augustana writers addressed the overlapping and dynamic ties between Augustana and the Church of Sweden using women's lives and roles as the metaphor. The turn to feminine categories for understanding these ties can explain why the question of Augustana's influence on the Church of Sweden, of the daughter on the mother, really did not come up. Instead Augustana leaders worried about recognition. Did the Church of Sweden acknowledge her daughter, the Augustana Synod?

Carl's wife Alma Swensson, who helped Emmy Evald organize the synod's women in 1892, served as the society's secretary for twenty-two years.[4] Women's leadership in the synod contributed greatly to its survival and success, but this reality had so far made little impact on the minds of church leaders in Sweden. Carl's role as president of Bethany College impressed them more. Bethany was a much vaunted but struggling educational institution;

it frequently stood at the brink of financial collapse. But Carl Swensson was so well versed in the language of the future, of optimism and progress, that Lindsborg, Kansas, loomed large in Swedish minds. Many know the joke told of the immigrant who came to New York, probably after reading one of Swensson's descriptions: "If this is New York, what must Lindsborg be like?"

Carl Swensson's expansive projects and remarkable use of the college to promote a refined Swedish-American Christian culture point to Swensson's probable ambition to be the cultural leader of Swedish America. Other Augustana men were understandably jealous of Swensson's reputation and complained.[5] The flamboyantly pious Swensson had few peers in America, but he did have a counterpart in the colorful bishop of Visby, Knut Henning Gezelius von Schéele, who during the 1890s was the envoy of the Swedish Church in America.[6] Von Schéele made three visits to America—in 1893, 1901, and again in 1910 for the synod's fiftieth Jubilee celebration. His first visit coincided with Augustana's commemoration of the Uppsala Meeting of 1593. The bishop also published a vivid account of his trip in *Hemland-stoner*, a book that described and interpreted Swedish America for Swedish readers.

Lindsborg, Kansas was a pivotal stop where von Schéele strengthened his friendship with Carl Swensson and celebrated an emotional reunion with an old school friend, Erland Carlsson. Carlsson and von Schéele had studied together in Växjö but had not seen each other after Carlsson immigrated to Chicago. While at Carlsson's summer retreat near Lindsborg, the bishop heard first-hand accounts of the early years of church work and stories of starvation and desperation that marked Carlsson's first years in Illinois. Moments with students at Bethany College, on the other hand, made him aware of the cultural advances of the immigrant community. The visit in Lindsborg showed von Schéele the entire progress of Swedish emigration, from the pioneer years to the culmination of Augustana's cultural achievement: the four-year college.

Von Schéele noted that this vibrant and progressive community emerged during his lifetime, determining that at Bethany College the Swedish-American people had "come of age." Von Schéele used the term in a double sense—not only had students there come of age but also the college itself was a cultural monument of the Swedish-American people.[7] Carl Swensson's Swedish world in Lindsborg was touted to Swedes as a place where the best of Swedish culture had been preserved.

As the synod's leadership passed to those born and educated in the United States, Augustana's preservation of its Swedishness understandably began to receive notice from Swedish visitors. On each of his three visits in

1893, 1901, and 1910, von Schéele applauded the role of colleges in promoting the study of Swedish. He expected that the potential for any kind of
salutary influence upon Augustana by the Church of Sweden was dependent
on a shared literary, theological, spiritual, and devotional culture. Von Schéele
did not imagine that cultural influence would flow in the other direction.
Though Augustana's young people increasingly spoke English, he hoped that
a lively interest in Swedish music, hymnody, and literature would continue
to thrive at the colleges. Otherwise, he feared that contacts between Sweden
and the Swedish Americans would become merely sentimental.

Carl Swensson and Bishop von Schéele had large personalities and an
instinct for garnering publicity. Each attained, at least within church circles,
the status of a celebrity. Because they could speak eloquently and seemingly
without preparation, they were able to charm their listeners. They sought to
evoke a feeling of kinship between two populations—Swedes and Swedish
Americans—who had almost become strangers to each other.

Members of the Augustana Synod needed to become reacquainted
particularly with the Church of Sweden, which had, by virtue of sending a
bishop to the synod, certainly begun to recognize the immigrant church in a
new way. Bishop von Schéele, in turn, came to think of himself as Augustana's
man in Sweden. One result of this feeling was that von Schéele immediately
raised formal objections to Anglican overtures to the Church of Sweden that
were presented in 1909, out of fear that this might strengthen the hand of
Episcopal proselytizing among Swedish immigrants.[8] Von Schéele's defense
of the synod demonstrated to Augustana that visits a bishop made to them
were not just social calls but were important for the synod's evangelical strategy among their own immigrant population.

An Ambivalent Partnership

Von Schéele's third visit in 1910 honored the synod's fiftieth anniversary.
Most of the celebration focused on the past, as a kind of final tribute to the
heritage from Sweden and the pioneer years in the rural Midwest. The emotional high point came when Eric Norelius, the last of Augustana's patri-
archs, stood on the platform. Norelius embodied the original evangelical
piety of the synod and had chronicled the synod's humble beginnings. Those
who listened to the speeches and sermons at the Jubilee knew that the pioneer days were gone. Now, within the synod, there were tensions between
the older pastors and younger leaders who wished to lead the synod away
from the narrow pietism of the early years.[9] Confronting Augustana leaders
were new realities, particularly modern biblical criticism and liberal theology, influences that the synod had so far been able to resist, partly through

retaining Swedish language worship and instruction that kept pastors and church people isolated from American theological movements, and partly by fostering the old revival pietism that distanced itself from the theologians and liberal tendencies in the Church of Sweden.

Concern about the course Augustana would take as it met the currents of liberal thought were not uppermost in the minds of those at the anniversary, but von Schéele's presence signaled that the future of the synod would still be bound with the Church of Sweden. The spirit of kinship that von Schéele exuded reassured both the passing patriarchal generation and a new cadre of pastors who wished to push for a more rigorously educated ministry. Von Schéele's appreciation for the pioneers honored the older pastors, but the bishop's connection with Uppsala's theological faculty and his steadfast support of the interests of the Augustana Synod in Sweden encouraged younger leaders. What made von Schéele almost perfect to all sides in Augustana's internal debates was his international reputation as a strong confessionalist. This heartened diehard traditionalists among Augustana's ministerial ranks, who suspected liberal tendencies in the new churchmen in Sweden.[10]

Augustana's more vocal conservative pastors, especially in Minnesota, worried more about a theologian on the faculty of the University of Uppsala, Nathan Söderblom, who, in 1897 sponsored a scientific conference on religion. Several of Augustana's up-and-coming leaders had attended the event, encouraged by the fact that von Schéele was moderator. Carl Swensson was one who attended, and he resolved the tensions between his more familiar conservatism and the new ideas he heard by stating that the liberals at the podium were such poor speakers that they would probably not do much damage to the evangelical cause.

The official report on the conference for *Augustana* came from Lars G. Abrahamson, who communicated stark displeasure with the event. Like the World Parliament of Religions that had been held in Chicago in 1893 and was studiously ignored by the synod, the Stockholm Conference presumed to set side by side the religions of the world and historic Christianity. God's revelation in Christ should never be compared with any other religion, Abrahamson wrote. Learned men could discuss disputed questions, but no one should suppose that Christianity needed to be proved. He noted that the secretary of the conference, Nathan Söderblom, gave a questionable address entertaining the demands of socialists, but otherwise Abrahamson gave little attention to the personalities who had inspired and shaped the conference.

L. G. Abrahamson may have been worried about Uppsala's theological faculty, but he shared Carl Swensson's enthusiasm for the Church of Sweden and appreciated the challenges the church faced in the new century.

He communicated his sympathy more discreetly, with less of the Kansan's exuberance. Lacking Swensson's magnetic charm, Abrahamson nevertheless gained the confidence of Swedish church leaders. When Carl Swensson died suddenly in 1904, Abrahamson became the chief interpreter and contact between Augustana and the Church of Sweden. Probably the main reason for Abrahamson's assumption of that role was that since 1893, he had been the synod's man in charge of arranging the tours and accompanying visitors from the Church of Sweden, so he was well known.

In 1908, after Abrahamson assumed the editor's position of the synod's newspaper, *Augustana*, his opinions began to shape the conversation within the synod. The previous editor, S. P. A. Lindahl, was by some accounts an autocrat who had steered the synod in a low-church, pietist direction.[11] Abrahamson represented a more churchly (as opposed to pietistic) and broad-minded leadership, one eager for freer exchange of views in the paper and within the church. Abrahamson's tenure as editor spanned thirty years, straddling the time when the church moved from Swedish to English. As the church became more American in its language and ethos, it seemed more eager for formal ties with the Church of Sweden.

Meeting the Charming, Modern Church of Sweden

L. G. Abrahamson represented the Augustana Synod at the consecration of Nathan Söderblom as archbishop in 1914. The new archbishop asked Abrahamson to make a public address that presented the work and mission of Augustana to the gathered priests of the Church of Sweden. Abrahamson recognized his momentous chance to gain the recognition for the once dismissed immigrant church and opened his remarks with this assessment: "I deem this task, to present to the mother church the work of the daughter church, to be a great privilege that will be recognized by Augustana and by all of Swedish-America."[12]

Abrahamson knew that many Augustana people in America reading his travel accounts viewed the new Swedish archbishop with wary eyes. They suspected the archbishop's intellectual rigor and his quest for a modern theological language would take the Church of Sweden away from its confessional moorings and out into the sea of uncertainty. Conservatives believed that modern theology needed to be resisted mightily, especially in America where liberal voices dominated university and divinity faculties. In the competitive Lutheran environment in America, any perceived slip in confessional faithfulness created occasion for accusation, especially from the self-appointed guardian of Lutheran purity, the Missouri Synod. The debates among Lutherans intensified as they began to adopt the English language, and in the intense inter-Lutheran environment of Minnesota, Augustana leaders were intensely self-conscious of the way that their synod was viewed. Abrahamson used his position as editor of *Augustana* to steer the synod in a more moderate direction, but it still gave voice to the fears of Adolf Hult, a teacher on the faculty of Augustana's seminary, who wrote for the Minnesota-based *Bible Banner*, the organ of the Lutheran Bible Institute. Hult warned readers about the threat Söderblom posed to the synod.[13]

L. G. Abrahamson must have entertained these reservations himself, at least early on. In a short reflection he wrote after the archbishop's death in 1931, Abrahamson disclosed that his earliest acquaintance with Söderblom at the Scientific Conference on Religion in Stockholm in 1897 was not positive. His very critical report of that conference and its planners even singled out Söderblom for censure. Abrahamson's opinion changed during his visit in 1914, when he was invited to stay in the archbishop's residence. During this extended visit, he learned to know the private and spiritual side of Söderblom, disclosed in the moment of personal prayer.[14] The visit also gave Abrahamson the ear of the archbishop, who seemed genuinely eager to learn the nature of the Augustana Church.

Augustana's People, a Chosen People

Abrahamson's informal account of Augustana to Söderblom no doubt conveyed the humble piety of an individual Swedish American, but his formal address to the gathered clergy of the Church of Sweden was more confident, and assured. His topic—Augustana's peculiar calling—needed to be communicated with political sensitivity, but Abrahamson took a chance, too, and stated boldly that Augustana had realized some advantage over the Church of Sweden through immigration. First, he acknowledged the controversy of emigration, while he flattered his audience by rehearsing the American preference for immigrants of Nordic stock. He suggested it was providential that Northern European Protestants settled in America and not emigrants of Southern Europe. Expanding on his nationalist theme, Abrahamson ventured the proposition that emigration was itself proof of chosen status. He compared God's call to Abraham, to go and settle in Canaan, to the calls that came to Lars Gustaf Esbjörn, Tufve Nilsson Hasselquist, Erland Carlsson, and Jonas Swensson. Well aware that these preachers had championed pietism and were for that reason forgettable figures among Swedish churchmen, Abrahamson stated that the founders of Augustana "laid the foundations for a spiritual home that houses your children, and will house coming generations."[15]

After describing the struggles of a pioneer church and citing facts and figures that proved its success, Abrahamson noted that statistics could not convey the heart and soul of the synod or indicate to his listeners the true extent of Augustana's role vis-à-vis the immigrant population. Since Augustana was a free church, it did not boast membership numbers that the Church of Sweden might expect. Abrahamson explained that synod pastors had finally realized that unless a person was driven by a religious need she or he would not seek church membership. Free church membership required what Abrahamson called a "positive spiritual interest."[16] Unfortunately, this interest was not always present among the emigrants that the Church of Sweden was sending out.

In describing the kind of church Augustana tried to be, Abrahamson portrayed its unique Lutheran spirit that resulted from pioneer years when the church had assumed a missionary role among the Swedish immigrants. Augustana had been forced to find its own way since it did not get pastors or money from the homeland. While treading on sensitive ground, Abrahamson quickly claimed that he did not ultimately blame the Church of Sweden for Augustana's difficulties, and that the neglect was in fact providential. The lack of support had created a more resilient church. It had been difficult, however, for the Augustana people to accept the fact that the Church of Sweden had taken so long to recognize their church as the Swedish church in America. Both churches now faced a new situation in their ministry and work. Many Swedish immigrants had no part in Augustana's church world, and this fact was well known to the Swedish priests who sat listening to Abrahamson's address. Augustana's less-than-successful experience with retaining the loyalty of Swedish immigrants did not bode well for the church at home in Sweden.

Abrahamson used the conclusion of his speech to exhort the listening clergy. He stood as a partner and asked church leaders in Sweden to bear responsibility for the success of the immigrants' church. The "soul" of Augustana, its positive spirituality, was now threatened by indifference. Abrahamson wanted Sweden's pastors to know that the spiritual state of more recent immigrants was a lot less positive than it had been before. Even though pastors were putting in more effort and energy, results were more meager than ever. "The immigrants a decade ago were hardly models of piety," Abrahamson said, "but at least they had some respect for the holy, with which we could find a touch point. Some could even respond to a spiritual awakening." Those now arriving were overcome by bitterness against the church, against the homeland, and against organized society. Pastors had a very hard time reaching them and had to be satisfied with the possibility of reaching their children. "Send us better material and we'll give you better results!" he pleaded. The ocean, he warned, would not change a person's heart.

"What did you go out to see?"

After Söderblom's consecration, the First World War disrupted all travel across the ocean, suspending personal visits between Augustana and the Church of Sweden. Particularly disappointing for Augustana was the disruption of plans for a visit by Söderblom or one of the diocesan bishops to coincide with Augustana's 1917 celebration of the Reformation.[17] It wasn't until 1923 that Archbishop and Anna Söderblom finally accepted the long-standing invitation to come to America. Abrahamson took personal hand of the arrangements and also the diplomatic task of negotiating Söderblom's itinerary. Leaders of the Federal Council of Churches had also invited the archbishop. They understandably expected the ecumenical leader to spend the greater portion of his time with them. The difficulty caused by Söderblom's perhaps naive acceptance of mutually conflicting invitations was finally resolved when Abrahamson pointed out the difficulty to Söderblom, who then made a choice for Augustana. Söderblom's resulting itinerary combined the two tours, giving him an exhausting speaking schedule. He delivered lectures to university audiences based on his research into the development of theism, addressed ecumenical audiences, and delivered sermons at Augustana congregations and schools.[18] Söderblom no doubt hoped that personal diplomacy might lead to wider levels of support among American Lutherans for the ecumenical cause, and he did not begrudge the time he would spend among the Augustana people.[19]

Aside from the official reasons that Söderblom went to America, another more personal quest animated him and involved his wife as well. Nathan and Anna Söderblom went out to see, as Anna so vividly put it, "where the Swedes had gone."[20] Abrahamson, as host, guide, and interpreter, gave them the opportunity to see the diverse circumstances in which immigrants worked and made homes in America. Anna's presence on the trip presented the opportunity for Abrahamson to arrange for more intimate and familiar contacts with the life and piety of Augustana's people. Coupled with the archbishop's many lectures, sermons, and dinner speeches were visits in the homes of Augustana pastors, giving the Swedish visitors a chance to understand the domestic setting of the Augustana Church.

In order to demonstrate to Söderblom the high regard that these ordinary Swedish settlers had garnered in America, Abrahamson arranged dramatic receptions by civil authorities in several cities. In Chicago, a mounted police escort, in which Anna Söderblom discerned many Swedish faces, led them to the mayor's office. While the men went in to meet the mayor in City Hall, their wives waited outside in the car. The exposure of the couple to

Swedish and American life gave them a vivid picture of the place of Swedish Americans in American society. The couple became ambassadors when they addressed the American university or ecumenical audience, where Söderblom enjoyed formal recognition. Their high profile visit gave Augustana people a reason to boast, while the intimate and less public domain of the respectable Augustana parsonage and congregation became a domestic sphere where the representative of the Church of Sweden became familiar with the people of Swedish America.[21]

Augustana's members knew of the archbishop's reputation as an ecumenical leader and religious scholar, but his personal engagement and the spiritual passion that underlay his commitment to Christian unity was not so well known. This was the side of Söderblom that Abrahamson wanted Augustana's people to see. By providing congregations with the chance to hear the archbishop in their pulpit and by introducing the synod's pastors, one by one, to the disarming charm of the chief pastor of the Church of Sweden, Abrahamson provided the kind of face-to-face encounter that not only warmed the heart of an episcopal-wary Swedish America, but also enabled the archbishop to truly "see" the Swedes and where they had gone.

In the conclusion to the travelogue Söderblom wrote after his trip, he reflected on the character of America-Sweden, as he had decided to christen the population. He commented on the national traits of Swedish immigrants in the context of the current racial debate in America; Söderblom had read Madison Grant's ecstatic utterances on the Nordic race and knew that there were many in America who welcomed Swedish immigrants for this reason. Söderblom was dismayed by the tone of current racial arguments, but he still could not escape an occasional resigned musing on the eventual fate of all the blue-eyed, tow-haired immigrants who would merge into the American people. Perhaps most indicative of the reservation Söderblom felt toward assimilation were his comments about the fate of the Swedish language in America. He was bothered that the Swedish spoken by immigrants had been corrupted by Americanisms. He hoped that Augustana would keep the Swedish language pure, and in this way promote a spiritual and cultural coherence for the immigrant community.

Söderblom's reflections on the immigrant church focused on the positive, though Augustana's free church polity seemed to him to make pastors overly dependent on the goodwill of a congregation.[22] Söderblom could nevertheless list four aspects of Augustana's church life for consideration. He first noted the energetic involvement of laymen. The organization and mobilization of women that almost dominated Augustana's congregational life eluded him, but the figure of the quiet, unassuming industrialist, who helped fellow immigrants through magnanimous and anonymous charity, seemed to Söderblom to give the American Swedish man a model to emulate. Contrasting the cultured churchly businessmen with the flamboyant Swedish American more popularly known, Söderblom suggested that Augustana had grasped the secret of how to involve men in the congregation, and this was the more necessary lesson for the Church of Sweden than mobilizing the women of the church.

Other dimensions of church life that appealed to Söderblom included the Sunday school, the many church choirs, and musical events. Finally, the spirituality of Augustana's congregations drew comment. Here the archbishop touched on a particularly sore point for the Church of Sweden. Augustana's communing practices contrasted markedly with that of parishes in Sweden. He thought that the immigrant congregations regarded the communion table as the center of their worship and congregational life while he ruefully acknowledged that there were whole regions in Sweden where people felt the sacrament was a once-in-a-lifetime experience.[23]

Mutual Understanding

Söderblom's prosaic listing of the quartet of practices and disciplines to be emulated by the Church of Sweden could hardly be called inspiring or visionary. Instead, they represented his acknowledgment that the American example involved the hard work and energy of many nameless and ordinary people. The spirit of Augustana did not reside in a few exemplary or flamboyant individuals, nor could any one man personify the life or spirit of the synod. If there were any representative men, they were those who worked in relative obscurity.

During Carl Swensson's 1897 trip to the diocese of Härnösand, when the exotic possibilities of a Swedish-American life were imagined by the picnicking tribe, a freely ranging playfulness characterized exchanges between church leaders. There were problems and challenges within the life of each church that Swensson and his Swedish hosts enumerated and discussed, but whether they focused on the growing indifference of the typical parishioner or on the difficulty that the church faced in the cities and industrial centers, Swedes and their American visitors were optimistic. Challenges were surmountable.

In 1923 Archbishop and Anna Söderblom found a different mood; postwar disillusionment characterized the spirit of America's churches. The meetings that Abrahamson arranged for the archbishop with Augustana's people were still perceived by them as occasions of special moment, but what was remembered was the personal, the private, and intimate encounter, rather than stirring speeches to large throngs at a rally. Söderblom himself did not come out to see great moments of immigrant culture or imagine the large vision that von Schéele powerfully shared with Carl Swensson. Instead, guided by Abrahamson, he looked for the ordinary believer, the patient pastor, and the hardworking Sunday school teacher.

Archbishop Söderblom enjoyed many face-to-face encounters, meeting his long ago emigrated brother, his godfather, and hundreds of anonymous Swedish Americans, but a separate reception that he did not attend, held for women only, where Augustana's women gathered to greet Anna Söderblom, revealed best the kind of face-to-face meeting that occurred. In a suite of rooms in the Women's Missionary Society's Emanuel Home, Emmy Evald and Mathilda Peterson, who represented the W. M. S. Board, introduced the archbishop's wife to a room packed with members of the society. In Anna's vivid account, the reserved formality of the meeting—handshakes and introductions to nearly 700 women with the title Mrs.—became revelatory of the inner spirit of the Augustana Swedish-American woman, and of the synod itself.

Mrs. Peter Peterson, wife of the Illinois Conference president, took hand of the introductions. While she stood next to Anna Söderblom, whose title in Swedish, *Ärkebiskopinnan* translated literally as "Archbishopess," Mrs. Peterson spoke of the work of individual women within their congregations, and gave their names. Anna recounted it with some humor: Mrs. Johnson, Mrs. Nelson, Mrs. Swanson, Mrs. Johnson, now and then a Gustafson, maybe an Ekblad, and then back to the regular rhythm of Johnson, Nelson, Swanson. Anna, like her husband, tried to discern the inner spirit of these women. She gazed at each person, making a personal effort to see who she was. Trusting to some intuitive power, she felt she could grasp a residual Swedishness in each person, though sometimes it seemed buried beneath American forms. Anna strained to see the woman behind the faces of the many types of Swedish Americans: the flapper, the matron, the office worker, and the young mother. All these women were proud titles, of anonymous names, of their married status in a democracy. Now, they could be a "Mrs." to the *Ärkebiskopinnan*.

After greeting them, Anna rose to address her kinswomen and helped them reminisce over life in Sweden. In the faces of the older women she thought she discerned a stark longing for home. She felt she knew the question on the minds of her listeners: What does Sweden look like? Mrs. Söderblom sketched a portrait of golden-haired children walking hand in hand down a country road to school. What does Sweden look like? New families live in the old homesteads. Much has changed, but still the white church spire rises above the lake. Nevertheless, she cautioned those who wished to go back: it is hard to go home, Sweden has gone forward, and it is a heavy thing to walk through graveyards.[24]

She saw in the women before her a church that had gone forward but that had still preserved elements of a common folk spirit. The bond that united these women, and their independence, elicited from Anna Söderblom an affectionate, maternal admiration. When she retired for the evening, the names stuck with her, helping her float off to sleep. Mrs. Johnson, Mrs. Swanson, Mrs. Nelson. These American wives, proud of Swedish anonymity, told her that in the Augustana Synod they belonged to something worthy of their lives and their devotion.

The Söderbloms' visit came at a time when large Swedish audiences in America could still understand and enjoy hearing Swedish spoken. The more informal gatherings also occurred in the context of a residual shared language and piety, so that the Augustana people and their Swedish visitors could imagine that they discerned the inner life and spirit of the other, and even appreciate a kinship they discovered and made. This visit by the Söderbloms was bittersweet, however, for it probably was the last time that Swedish Americans and visitors from the Church of Sweden could really see eye-to-eye and appreciate what they saw. In the next year, 1924, Congress passed the Johnson Reed Act, stipulating strict quotas on all immigration. This had an immediate effect on emigration from Sweden. Additionally, the language bond that, in 1923, still enabled the archbishop and his wife access to the inner world of the immigrant church, was broken when Augustana next turned its energies to building an English-speaking church. Still, bonds of culture and spiritual kinship had been forged through many meetings, and these made possible or at least sustained a receptive attitude between Augustana Lutherans in America and the Church of Sweden.

Signs and Symbols

One gift that came to Augustana after the exchange of visits was not happily received. In 1930, Archbishop Söderblom sent to Augustana Synod President G. A. Brandelle a bishop's cross similar to the ones worn by the bishops in the Church of Sweden. Brandelle included the letter that he received from the Swedish archbishop in his report to the synod at the June meeting that year:

> Dear Brother:
>
> On behalf of the Swedish bishops in session I have the pleasure to deliver to you a cross of gold, similar to that cross which belongs to the official garb of the Swedish bishops. This cross is delivered by the archbishop and bishops of Sweden to our Swedish American brother, and

we beg that the episcopal servant of the Swedish Church in America, the president of the Augustana Synod may carry it and that it may like the crosses of the bishops in Sweden be carried by one after the other of those who succeed him in this office. This symbol is intended to strengthen the bond of union between us, a union that is deeply rooted in descent, language, and history, but which is still more deeply rooted in our common holy faith. When about one hundred and twenty years ago the golden cross was established as belonging to the official garb of a Swedish bishop, the desire was expressed and emphasized that this emblem was ever to remind him of what is central in our Christian faith, to wit, our Saviour's work of redemption which he who carries the cross is called to bear witness to in his life and teaching. Wishing God's blessing and the power of the spirit upon the Augustana Synod, all its members and congregations, and its trusted servant, I am on behalf of the Swedish bishop's convention, your affectionate brother, Nathan Söderblom.

The synod meeting in 1930 came at a time of significant transition for the synod. A coalition of Midwestern Lutheran churches had created the American Lutheran Conference, and many of the members of this group, especially in Ohio, were critical of Augustana's ties to the liberal archbishop. The synod meeting also received news of a dramatic change of personnel on the seminary faculty, and these concerns far outweighed any concentrated interest in strengthening symbolic ties to the Church of Sweden.

The official response of the synod to the gift was curt, and escaped being more brusque only through the intervention of Brandelle, who worked behind the scenes to soften the synod's language. The resolution in response to the gift finally read:

That we appreciate with sincere gratitude and brotherly affection the gift of the archbishop and bishops of the Church of Sweden in bestowing upon the president of the Augustana Synod a gold cross as a token of their desire to strengthen the bond of fellowship between the two churches; and that, although we do not hereby adopt any episcopal insignia to be worn by the incumbent of the presidential office, we will cherish the gift as a symbol of unity of purpose between two independent Lutheran Churches.

President Brandelle's own view concerning the purpose of the Augustana Synod may have maintained a more cordial place for the ties of affection and unity between the churches, but he was now leading a church that sought closer relationships with their American Lutheran counterparts and recognition and respect first and foremost on the American scene. The place where this changed orientation to the American context made itself most evident was at the synod's seminary in Rock Island, where students and a younger constituency of pastors had begun to exert pressure for a new engagement with pressing issues of a modern day.

chapter 13
MEETING THE CHALLENGES
OF A NEW CENTURY

As the Augustana Synod matured during the twentieth century, it increasingly lent its voice and opinions to the external national debates on pressing issues of the day, such as science and evolution, the authority of the Bible and ways of understanding it, liberalism and modernism, and questions of war and peace. Indeed, the members of the synod had long expressed their opinions on topics such as these, going back to the beginning of the synod and the national debates over slavery and the Civil War. But as Augustana matured as an American religious denomination, it had more time, energy, and seemingly more confidence to address these and many other national issues of the day. Though essentially careful and generally conservative, Augustana leaders and members sought to enter these grand, national debates and to suggest solutions to these problems on the basis of their own theological understandings.

Science and the Question of Evolution

One of the most important issues of the early twentieth century was focused rather narrowly on the question of Darwin's theory of evolution, but it brought with it a host of other scientific and religious questions that spiraled out from its center. In the narrow sense, the questions involved the scientific plausibility of the theory of evolution, and immediately, its relation to the biblical story of creation in Genesis. In a broader sense, the controversy did (and still does) call into question the nature of biblical truth and scientific truth, the idea of divine agency in the world, and the ability of human beings to make determinative judgments about ultimate reality. The older science of the Enlightenment, as typified in Newtonian physics, was essentially deistic in it orientation, believing in a creator God who set the world into being and provided it with rational laws, laws through which one could determine the actual Creator. Since this deistic science left room for God, those who held to supernatural religion could be in some harmony with it or at least make their accommodations. But the new science of the nineteenth and twentieth centuries was much less hospitable to traditional religion; God as a starting point for a universe that was run by divinely ordained natural laws was not a starting point for these ways of thinking. In the new science, religion was often viewed as antithetical to its aims or at least irrelevant; science had no need for the "God hypothesis." The social controversies between the old religion and the new science troubled American society for most of the twentieth century.

The first and primary controversy between science and religion was over the theory of evolution, first suggested by Charles Darwin in the 1860s. The theory—and Darwin himself—was not specifically directed to challenge either traditional theism or theological anthropology nor was it to discredit the Christian Scriptures. But the theory proved extremely troubling to traditional Christians on two accounts; first, that it invalidated the literal reading of the Genesis creation story, and second, that in the randomness and chance of evolution there was no room for a God to direct and guide the process. Some American Protestants, tending toward a more liberal position, believed that Darwinism and the creation story could be brought into some harmony; they suggested that "evolution was God's way of doing things." But more conservative Protestants saw evolution in particular, and modern scientific learning in general, as direct threats to traditional religion, and they made Darwinism the whipping boy for all the sins of modern secularity. This campaign against Darwin and evolution peaked in the United States in the 1925 Scopes Monkey Trial, to which a national audience listened with rapt attention.

As Augustana was moving more definitively into the world of American religion after 1900, questions such as the nature of evolution and the place of science and religion came to be discussed with greater frequency within the synod. Initially, at least, synodical opinion was squarely on the side of traditional theism and against evolution. Typical was the editorial comment by G. A. Brandelle in the *Augustana Journal* in 1897, where he ridiculed the idea of the evolution of human beings. "It matters not how long this earth of ours has been in existence," wrote Brandelle. "But it makes a tremendous difference whether I am to believe that man was made directly by God and in his own image, or has . . . evolved from a monkey."[1]

Yet other voices began to be heard within the synod. While continuing to hold to the divine creation of the world, they believed that this could be held at the same time there was a belief in some form of evolution. In an open letter printed in the *Lutheran Companion* in 1913, a writer expressed his belief that a Christian could hold to evolution since both ". . . geology and

Scripture tell us that there was a gradual ascent from the lower to the higher. Now if careful research should lead us to believe that the ascent was more gradual and more closely knit than we had supposed, what of it?" The letter writer here seemingly had abandoned the idea of a 6,000-year-old earth and referred to evolution as "God's method of creation."[2]

Other voices soon entered this debate within the synod and expressed a variety of views on the topic. I. O. Nothstein, the scholarly librarian at Augustana College and Seminary, expressed his contempt for evolution in a 1914 article, suggesting, "Evolution is a theory of creation which has never been proved, and under the circumstances of the case, cannot be proved. . . . The gaps between the animal, vegetable, and mineral kingdom are gulfs which nothing can cross except God himself by definitive progressive creation, which is not 'evolution.'" In the same piece, he lauded a campaign by the Lutheran Joint Synod of Ohio to "uproot this fad" from American public schools.[3]

Yet only one month later, in the same periodical, his editorial colleague, C. J. Södergren, countered with an article of his own in which he pushed for the harmonization of evolution with traditional Christian belief, stating, "The time has arrived, it appears, for someone to say that the theory of evolution is not necessarily atheistic, and that it may be quite consistent with the Christian belief in God as the Creator of heaven and earth." Södergren warned about those who would "compel faith by the methods of the inquisition," by forcing a particular view of the subject as the only Christian manner of belief.[4]

One area of anti-evolutionist strength was in Minnesota, where Baptist pastor William Bell Riley was a strong, fundamentalist leader. When Riley pushed efforts in the early 1920s to restrict the teaching of evolution in Minnesota public schools, many Lutherans, including many members of Augustana, were in support. The Minnesota Conference adopted a resolution in 1923 that, while not aimed against evolution directly, protested some of the ways in which evolution was taught in public schools. The resolution concluded:

> We respectfully request all school boards to eliminate from the schools under their jurisdiction textbooks that inculcate an anti-Christian interpretation of the evolution theory . . . and urge them to restrain teachers from spreading this or any other religious philosophy antagonistic to the Christian faith.[5]

Behind this resolution was a battle between two of the early leaders of the Lutheran Bible Institute (LBI) of Minneapolis, C. A. Wendell and Samuel

Miller. Wendell was more open to evolution, while Miller, dean of LBI, took a much harder line on the subject; the two traded arguments in print during the early 1920s, and Wendell eventually withdrew from any position in the LBI movement. Wendell was on the committee that developed the Minnesota Conference resolution, and Miller, while appreciating the sentiment of the resolution, believed that it did not go far enough to oppose evolution. Miller worried that the resolution, which he saw as a form of "Christian interpretation of evolution" was confusing, and not clear enough on the biblical position. "I am of the opinion that those who hold modified views of the evolution theory make a grave mistake . . . ," wrote Miller. "To construct a theory which includes God and creative miracles and still call it evolution simply causes confusion." He ridiculed the effort to "construct some sort of harmony between the revelation of God and the theories of scientists."[6] To him, and a number of others within Augustana, evolution and theism were incompatible.

In a 1927 article in the *Augustana Quarterly*, Emil Johnson agreed, stating, "[I]t is dangerous to accept the theory of evolution. Its philosophy leads to a gross materialism which will tolerate no divine interference in human events. . . . No compromise between the idea of evolution and the Christian religion is possible, and any concession to the one involves a betrayal of the other."[7] Some of these opponents of evolution would willingly adopt the label "fundamentalist," as long as they could be "Lutheran" fundamentalists, and distance themselves from the dominant Reformed version of Fundamentalism.[8]

One arena in which these battles over evolution were played out was in church-related schools and colleges. Synodical members might not be able to do much (besides passing resolutions) to influence the teaching within the public schools, but they certainly could determine what was being taught in their church schools and colleges, and often these schools did become a battleground over the issues, especially in areas of the natural sciences such as biology and geology. It seems that the colleges of the Augustana Synod were somewhat more open to the natural sciences than were the schools of other Scandinavian American Lutherans; both Augustana College and Gustavus Adolphus College established their departments of geology early in their history, while the Norwegian American colleges did not establish such departments.[9]

Joshua Edquist, who taught biology and geology at Gustavus from 1887 to 1926, frequently repeated a lecture on "The Theory of Evolution," concluding with a quote from the great American historian John Fiske, who invoked not the "theory" of evolution, but "the doctrine" to say: "The doctrine of evolution destroys the conception of this world as a machine. It makes God our constant refuge and support, and nature his true revelation; and when all its religious implications shall have been set forth, it will be seen to be the most potent ally that Christianity has ever had in elevating mankind."[10] It is hard to imagine a more ringing endorsement of the modern scientific view. Edquist's lecture notes refer to the debate on evolution and consistently support the theory. He wrote that even without proof the student should "give the evolutionists the benefit of the doubt," and concluded another lecture—"The Antiquity of Man"—by saying, "While at the present time it is impossible to say that man has lived on our planet so and so many years, there is strong evidence which favors the opinion that he has existed here much longer than is indicated by any written record. It may be 100,000 yrs [sic], or it may be only 10,000 years." While the Minnesota contingent at Gustavus had Edquist quietly teaching his science classes supporting the theory of evolution, in Rock Island, prominent geologist Fritiof Fryxell reassured students and pastors with his competent teaching on the subject and a very public devotion to the church. Both teachers seemed confident enough in their positions to teach what they felt Augustana's young people should learn.

Still, some within the synod sought to suppress the teaching of these new ideas within the church schools, seeing the main purpose of education as the transmission of received doctrines and ideas. In a 1928 exchange on the question, "Are Modern Pursuits of Knowledge Dangerous to Loyal Lutheranism?" A. S. Segerhammar argued the affirmative, suggesting, "The Church of Jesus Christ is the bulwark and repository of truth. . . . Individual ideas and opinions are not the arbiter of truth . . . and freedom of opinion and individual interpretation may not take upon itself the authority to change our doctrines and teachings."[11]

For others, the idea of a static repository of truth posed a major problem for the church. Arguing against a blanket theism in the debate, Otto Bostrom argued, "If loyal Lutheranism is endangered in our modern era of great intellectual advancement, the danger lies rather in a prevailing perverted view of the Bible as a compendium of all knowledge, both scientific and religious." Further, he warned, the future of the church would be imperiled if "no room for growth has been provided, indeed, no room for growth has been recognized."[12]

The larger issue, then, was how to reconcile the theistic worldview and the permanent truths of Christianity with the modern scientific worldview that questioned all received truths and seemed to hold a mechanistic and material view of human life. On the contrary, argued some who taught the natural sciences at the synodical colleges, there was no essential conflict between the two. Biologist J. A. Elson of Gustavus Adolphus argued that the problem was mainly with theology, rather than science. "Our church should not regard science as an enemy but as an ally and best friend," suggested Elson. "Our Lutheran church is conservative but not too conservative for scientific thinking. Perhaps the chief cause of the apparent conflict is that science progresses but theology lags." Still there was no apparent difficulty between the two disciplines, rightly ordered and understood.[13]

Another scientist, Luther Anderson, writing in the *Lutheran Companion* in 1933, saw a new-found humility in science, and a recognition in many scientists for a need of religion to provide meaning and insight:

> In these troubled times people feel the need of religion more than ever. Sensing its value as a cultural asset they are not going to allow themselves to be bluffed out of their faith by any claims of infallibility on the part of religion . . . religion stands firm from generation to generation while science changes its dogmas from year to year.[14]

Anderson saw no need to harmonize the two, as they were "separate languages," each able to provide truth.

In 1957, chemistry professor H. Bradford Thompson told students at a Gustavus Adolphus College chapel service that modern science, far from taking the mysterious and miraculous out of the world, rather deepens the mystery of the world for faith in a creator God: "Our Christian faith does not fundamentally depend on the pillar of fire or the parting of the sea. Our faith involves the miraculous in a far more fundamental way." The chapel talk was subsequently printed in an edition of the *Lutheran Companion*, where the editor E. E. Ryden lauded it as "an excellent example of the reverent approach which characterizes scientific teaching at our Christian colleges."[15]

One of the key points of the discussion within the synod revolved around the question of whether the worldview of science was in itself an ideology that served as a substitute for religion, or whether there were forms of scientific inquiry that left room for the traditions of the Christian faith. In a 1933 editorial, C. J. Bengston derided the hubris of scientists who claimed to know things they had no way of knowing. "If we are asked to believe the wildest theories of men who claim to know, why not rather believe the simpler and more reasonable accounts of the world and life on earth given us in the Word of God?" he asked rhetorically.[16]

E. E. Ryden, while reflecting on the claim by a contemporary psychologist that faith was a basic need of human existence, suggested that, "We have always contended that there is no real conflict between religion and true science. When science, in its search for truth, finally arrives at the objective for which it has been seeking, its conclusions will always be found in accord with the revealed Truth of God." Ryden scoffed at scientists who would deny religious truth, calling them "pseudo-scientists, men of small mental calibre."[17]

On the basic level, several writers asked the fundamental question of how Christian theology ought to proceed in a world that was dominated by scientific thinking of a purely mechanical and materialistic variety. Pastor Axel Berg suggested in a 1941 article that whereas theology had dominated all other forms of knowledge in the Middle Ages and Reformation, now science predominated, and that both theology and science in turn became a "dominant theory that would tolerate no opposition." Berg argued that the hubris of science, seen especially in the theory of evolution, was idolatry, putting human beings in the place of God: "There is no need of a Supreme Being since man by his own power and genius can attain the heights of perfection and racial immorality. But this self-confident, intolerant philosophy has received severe jolts during recent years."[18] Berg was obviously referring to wars, the depression, and the rise of totalitarian regimes, when suggesting that the hubris of scientific materialism and idolatry would be its own destruction.

In a slightly earlier article, Karl E. Mattson (then a graduate student, but eventually president of Augustana Seminary), reflected on the challenge of this situation for the work of Christian ethics. He suggested, "Modern science has possibly had more of an effect on man's life that any other one influence," a situation that he believed led to a naturalism that made God and theology irrelevant. Furthermore, he continued, "The organization of modern life on the basis of a scientific world view . . . denies the Christian estimate of human worth." In such a world, according to Mattson, the human being who has taken on this world view has "lost the sense of a world that is to be explained by God . . . [and] finds very little comfort and help in nature." The essential challenge for Christianity is to help such people to find their essential connections with God and others around them.[19]

Many in the Augustana Synod sought, during the first half of the twentieth century, to make sense of modern science, and especially its larger influence on the society around it. Though the question of evolution was a key and early issue, one that captured the imaginations and fears of many North Americans, the question soon became larger. Some dealt with this issue simply by rejecting or ridiculing science, suggesting that it was nothing more than wild speculations based solely on unprovable theories. Others seemed serenely confident that there was no real issue between science and religion, if the two were rightly understood. In this way, then, scientific inquiry would lead to the strengthening of religious faith, rather than its destruction. Both ideas were present among the members of the synod, and both were routinely expressed. But there were problems with both approaches; simply rejecting science would not work in a world increasingly dominated by it, and a serene confidence that the two could be harmonized did not adequately take into account the serious challenges that science posed to traditional theism. Some in Augustana came to see that though science was an established fact in the modern world and though religion would have to take this into account, science could not solve the evident social and moral crises that kept rolling through the century. Christian theology would have to change substantially to meet the challenges and inadequacies of modern science head on.

Understanding the Bible and Its Authority

Evolution and modern materialistic science were enough of a challenge in and of themselves, but they also led to internal conversations within the synod about the direction of modern theology and in the nature and authority of the Bible as a source for theology. In all the arguments and debates, the Bible was, for Augustana Lutherans, as well as for all Protestants, the final authority and arbiter of truth. Even though the Word of God had not often been the means of unity among disparate Christians, it was, especially in the nineteenth and twentieth centuries, a center of dispute and debate. The challenges of modern science and learning had further questioned the authority and veracity of the Bible, and Christians were internally divided and externally defensive about biblical authority. For American Lutherans, the Bible was still central to all truth, but they differed about the correct way to express this confessional idea, especially as they were translating their theological ideas into English. Did the new terminology gaining ground among some American Protestants, most notably the terms *inerrant* and *infallible*, express the nature of biblical authority that they had assumed from the Lutheran Confessions. Or were some of the new scholarly approaches to the Bible, known as "higher biblical criticism," the vehicle through which the Bible could be freshly interpreted for the modern world?

The traditional Lutheran idea, expressed in the Lutheran Confessions, was that the Bible was the revealed Word of God, and the source and norm for all Christian theology. The reformers of the sixteenth century based their Reformation on the idea that scripture alone was the ultimate source of authority; yet Luther and others could be very selective in their use and understanding of the biblical books. By the early twentieth century, American Evangelical Protestants, in their battle with modernism and science, had concluded that in order to save biblical authority from complete erosion, they had to declare the entire text of the Bible as inerrant and infallible, a complete edifice that needed to be believed literally in every detail. American liberal Protestants, on the other hand, believed that though there was eternal truth in the Bible, it was mixed with dated understandings of the world that could and must be jettisoned in order to make the Christian faith relevant to the modern world. Liberals believed that critical tools of biblical study could separate the two, and bring the eternal truths of Christianity to a modern and scientific world.

Augustana Lutherans were suspicious of this new critical approach to the Bible, since some of those who employed this method seemed bent on destroying biblical truth rather than making it relevant. Critical study of the Bible seemed to undermine the divine nature of the document and weaken the reverence of the faithful for the book. Typical of the early attitude of Augustana toward the new criticism was this editorial comment of 1900 by G. A. Brandelle: "The destructive critics are making a whole lot of noise, but that will in the end accomplish very little. Those who still believe in it as the revelation of God to humanity are neither idle nor wavering in their faith."[20]

A few years later, however, another editor could allow that critical methods, if not in too much variance with the intent of scripture, might even lead the critic to some form of divine truth: "To treat the Bible as a literary production is indeed a mere picking at the bark and rind of truth . . . still [the interpreter] may eventually find the kernel and come to realize that this is the essential part."[21] Still, as late as 1929, when then synod president Brandelle was replying to an inquiry about evolution and the Bible, he evidenced a rather literal attitude: "I have always been given to understand that the story of the human family goes back something like six thousand years."[22] This attitude, while not fundamentalist, shows a rather pre-critical literalism about the Bible that was fairly common in the synod of that day.

Even though there was precious little of the modern biblical criticism in the Augustana Synod in the first decades of the twentieth century, this did not stop conservatives from roundly condemning their ideas and worrying that new methods might find a home in the denomination. When an author in the synodical *Bible Study Quarterly* dared to assume that Isaiah, chapters 40–66, were not the product of the historical prophet Isaiah, seminary professor Adolf Hult heaped scorn on the idea, concluding, "The crashings and clatterings when a critic came thundering on impress no more. God is confusing human dunderheadedness and self-complacency in Liberal theologians. Their denials are too simple for skeptics of our day and useless for believers of any time."[23] Writing in the *Lutheran Companion* in 1927, O. N. Olson rejected the ideas of a modern theologian that the Bible is not "inerrant and infallible," and suggested that while biblical scholarship had its place, ". . . it gives no finality to our hope that will be satisfying in the hour of death. Here my appeal must be to the infallible Word of God, which liveth and abideth forever."[24]

Pastor Emeroy Johnson, writing for Luther League study groups in 1933, suggested that the Bible was "divinely inspired," and that a "remarkable unity" ran through the whole book. Further, he stated, "He who is vitalized by the Scriptures has an inner conviction that they are truly holy, God's inspired Word."[25] Words like *inerrant* and *infallible* were routinely used as a way of explaining the authority of the Bible; human criticism was seen as a way to doubt scriptural authority. LBI dean Samuel Miller agreed with the assertion that the "infallibility of the Bible as the Word of God" was the foundation of the whole Lutheran doctrinal edifice, and without this idea it would collapse.[26] As late as 1940, Pastor Victor Tengwald wrote that the books of the Bible were "literally the very words wherein God has spoken. . . . The holy men whom God used to write these books were guided in such a way that they were supernaturally so guarded from all mistakes."[27] If not exactly the wording that American Fundamentalists of the day would have used, these passages express much the same ideas in much the same way.

However, others within Augustana strongly resisted this use of fundamentalistic language to describe the nature of biblical authority. One common argument was to go back to the ways in which the Lutheran reformers, especially Luther himself, used scripture and understood its authority. In his controversial 1930 chapter, C. A. Wendell worried that, "Our very veneration for the Scriptures may lead us to excess." Further, he wrote, "A stilted veneration for the Word betrays an inward weakness rather than a virile faith, and out of it proceeds a nervous anxiety to prove the 'complete inerrancy' of the Bible. . . . This may be good Fundamentalism but hardly good Lutheranism, for Luther was not of that type."[28]

In examining Luther's "standards of canonicity" in a 1936 article, George Hall wrote that Luther understood the authority of the biblical books to be in the proportion that they "drove Christ," and that it was the contents of each book that determined its value. Further, he argued, "The Word of God is within the Scriptures. Some books to a greater extent than others have this Word. . . . Within the apostolic books the differentiation must be made."[29] Using this idea of "canon within a canon" was a way in which the insights of higher biblical criticism might be employed while still maintaining the overall authority of scripture for the believers.

When, in 1930, changes took place at Augustana Seminary, the newer generation of professors began cautiously to employ the ideas of modern biblical scholarship in their writings and in their teachings. While still holding to the authority of the Bible as the Word of God, the "standard and norm" of all theology, they believed that not all parts of the Bible were literally true, and that this idea in no way negated the Bible's truth or authority. A. D. Mattson wrote in 1938:

> The Bible nowhere claims verbal inspiration for itself, the facts do not substantiate the theory. . . . The Spirit of God quickened and guided human souls and thus inspired the Scriptures, but this does not imply verbal dictation. . . . Neither does it insure from errors of memory, accuracy of historical detail, or scientific fact.[30]

Seminary Biblical scholars such as Eric Wahlstrom began to use the new critical methods in their scholarship, and others used these new ideas to counter the rise of fundamentalistic tendencies within American Lutheranism. Augustana College professor Hjalmar Johnson fired such a salvo in 1939, when he wrote to other American Lutherans: "You sometimes hear conscientious Lutheran pastors make the statement that unless you accept the verbal inspiration theory you are not a consistent Lutheran. . . . such statements are by no means a defense of Lutheranism, but on the contrary constitute a lapse from it."[31] Language such as this, of course, further split the synod theologically and suggested to other, more conservative Lutherans in the American Lutheran Conference that the Augustana Synod was theologically suspect. The battle over the nature of biblical authority, like those of evolution and science and modern theology, would not be soon easily solved.

Militarism, Isolationism, and Pacifism, 1914–1941

One of the major external questions facing the synod early in the twentieth century was that of growing European militarism, and the eventual outbreak of war in 1914. Traditionally, Swedish-American Lutherans had a close affinity for Lutheran Germany, a distrust of English and French imperialism, and an inclination toward isolationism and pacifism.[32] England represented to them all the mercantile power of a vast empire, and its dominance of the world economy was often linked to its militarism. One Augustana writer even suggested, "Who has decided England's policy? The 'God Mammon,' whom the world worships and loves. There can be no other cause for England's enmity to Germany, no other reason why for many years she has planned her neighbor's destruction."[33] The real enemies, in the minds of many Swedish Americans, were the hated Russians, and many saw the battle in terms of a "Slavic" attempt to overrun the heart of Protestant Europe.

The editor of *Augustana* was one of the most prominent of the supporters of Germany, extolling: "With its people . . . [and] high culture, and not least with its Protestantism, Germany constitutes a wall which has held back the pan-Slavic, semi-barbaric drive toward the West."[34]

Although they were generally more inclined toward Germany, it is probably better to say that Swedish Americans were rather more opposed to England and especially toward Russia. In this matter, the *Lutheran Companion*, representing the younger, Americanized generation of the synod, though no less in opposition to England and Russia, was also much more wary of imperial German aims. Editor Bengston remarked in 1915 that God was on no one's side in this conflict, but that God's ". . . smile is equally benignant on all His warring children, whether they be German or English, French or Russian."[35]

As Americans, however, the Swedish immigrants tended toward isolationism, and they were generally opposed to military action and expenditures, seeing all of this as not only a tremendous waste, but also as evidence of the power of evil in the world. The war was seen as the result of European immorality and disrespect for traditional religion: "[B]rutal competition, social injustice of all kinds, and shameful disregard of the laws is always incipient anarchy. For sooner or later selfishness and lust means murder. 'Sin, when it is finished, bringeth forth death.'" If American Christians did not mind the lessons of European decadence, they would surely follow in this path, because "America . . . [was] not far behind."[36] Christians were urged to pray for peace, because peace was God's plan, though the chastising and cleansing hand of God was at times seen even in the horrors of war. Most synodical leaders wanted to avoid an American entanglement in this "European" war, though some, as American citizens, thought that limited military preparedness was justified.

The outbreak of World War I proved to be difficult for many American Lutheran groups, including the Augustana Synod. The anti-German hysteria of the war years soon extended to a xenophobia that attacked many foreign-speaking groups and institutions in the United States, and Scandinavian American Lutherans were often as much of a target as their German American counterparts. American entry into the war in April 1917 occasioned a great deal of popular hatred and scattered official actions against anything "foreign" in the United States, including foreign language worship and education, both of which predominated in the Augustana Synod at the time. This widespread sentiment against "foreignness" led to the acceleration of the language transition already underway in the synod, and to attempts to show that Augustana people were "100 percent Americans." One writer presented the case this way:

Let us wage war as a united country. Let us dispense with everything that tends to weaken the fabric of patriotism and nationalism. Let us make America a safe place to live. . . . We must make war upon those forces within and without our borders until the struggle is brought to a successful termination.[37]

Augustana periodicals of that time were filled with notices about the service of Augustana members in the military, and President Gustav Andreen of Augustana College and Seminary sent a telegram to the White House in September 1917, stating that 70 students from Augustana had enlisted in the war effort.[38] Augustana periodicals and official organizations such as the Lutheran Brotherhood frequently urged readers to buy as many Liberty bonds as they possibly could afford, and urged compliance with the various rationing requirements that the government had put in place.

On the other hand, synodical leaders decried the efforts being made against foreign groups in the United States, especially Lutherans, who were suspected of being pro-German. One editor wrote:

It cannot be too strongly emphasized that we Lutherans in America, who are to large extent naturalized citizens, must demonstrate to the country and the nation that we can and do practice what we preach . . . the nation will discover before the war is over the loyalty of the rank and file of the Lutheran Church is beyond question.[39]

Augustana members were proud of being American Lutherans, and doing their part for their new country.

After World War I, opinion in the synod seemed to revert to traditional isolationist position. In 1927, the *Lutheran Companion* suggested, "The Christian churches . . . can scarcely do anything else than align themselves with the peace movement" and evidenced strong support for the League of Nations and the World Court.[40] In 1933, an Augustana professor wrote the members of the synodical council, advocating: "The war against war is a *holy war*. Should not the Augustana Synod engage in it in some effective way . . . to rid the world forever from that monstrous evil . . . ?"[41]

The synod did address the issue several times in convention, in 1924, 1934, 1935, 1937 and 1939. In 1937, Augustana reaffirmed its opposition to "aggressive warfare" and urged the government to institute strict regulations on the manufacture of war materials. In 1939, the synod called war "a particular demonstrative of the power of sin in the world, and defiance of the righteousness of God. . . . no justification of war must be allowed to minimize or conceal this fact." The same convention opposed the sale of war materials to combatant nations, a major concern as World War II was beginning.[42] In 1937, the *Lutheran Companion* repeated some of the anti-British attitudes of the pre-World War I period, when it suggested the English actions were "Tricking America into Conflicts," and submitted, "It was greed for profits from sales of supplies to belligerents that paved the way for our entry into the World War; but America has learned that temporary prosperity based on war profits is poor economics."[43] Although the synod did evidence a similar degree of sentiment for neutrality and against England, it did not have the same degree of pre-war sympathy for Germany, especially under the control of the Nazis.

As the European situation turned darker toward the end of the 1930s, some in Augustana joined to form a group to encourage pacifism generally, and to support specifically the young men who wished to register as conscientious objectors to military service. Gustavus Adolphus professor Edgar Carlson began to circulate a proposal in 1938 that eventually resulted in the formation of the "Augustana Lutheran Fellowship of Reconciliation" at Augustana Seminary in 1941, although the group received no official recognition or support.[44] Besides Carlson, Emeroy Lindquist at Bethany College and A. D. Mattson at Augustana Seminary were prominent leaders in this pacifist movement. In 1938, Edgar Carlson wrote an article entitled, "If War Comes. . . ," in which he suggested the pacifism in peacetime was easy, but needed to be sustained through periods of war to be consistent. "God keep [war] from us," he wrote, "but if it does come, the Way of the Cross may lead through sacrifice and death, but never through murder and bloodshed."[45] E. E. Ryden, the editor of the *Lutheran Companion* from 1934 on, was aggressive in supporting this pacifist tradition. However, Ryden did not represent all of Augustana, whose leaders worried about his more extreme views. Editor A. T. Lundholm of *Augustana*, the other synodical publication, consistently assailed pacifism as unrealistic: ". . . absolute pacifism is neither possible nor even thinkable for a Christian in such a world as this in which we live. Evil must be fought."[46]

Where Ryden, in the *Lutheran Companion*, sharply criticized American efforts to aid Britain militarily, Lundholm, in *Augustana*, supported the efforts of the Roosevelt administration in this area. Overall, the general position of the members of Augustana, and that of Swedish Americans in general, was much more toward isolationism than it was toward pacifism. The group of pacifists within the synod was prominent and vocal, but not particularly representative of the attitude of the whole.

Augustana and World War II

Although in the late 1930s Augustana was generally predisposed toward isolationism, and some of its leaders held pacifist positions, the synod could not help but be affected by the encroachments of World War II. While it sought to remain aloof from war and politics and supported a strict American neutrality, events were rolling toward an explosion that would involve the whole world. As young men from the synod went off to military service, and the whole country mobilized for war, Augustana struggled to understand and cope with these earth-shaking times.

At least one Augustana congregation was embroiled in the turbulent political winds of the late 1930s, as it resisted pressures from pro-Nazi sympathizers in Chicago. Concordia Lutheran Church, on the north side, had invited Professor A. D. Mattson to speak, which caused the local Nazi organization, the "Silvershirts," to warn them against promoting communism. Concordia pastor Carl Lund-Quist contacted the FBI and Augustana President Bersell, and sent a letter to the head of the local German-American Bund, refusing the organization's request to rent the church for one of its meeting. Lund-Quist wrote: "[T]he German government today is opposing the things that the Christian Church will always hold sacred and eternal. Any attempt on the part of Americans to promote such a system would meet with our disapproval." In reply to Lund-Quist, President Bersell suggested that though all political activities should be off-limits in a congregation, this was especially true of the Bund, "because of international and religious complications and involvements."[47]

As the synod struggled to maintain its position against war; the synod convention in 1940 adopted a resolution commending "all Christian efforts in behalf of peace," and urged that all Christians work and pray to resist "the temptations to hysteria [that] increase through war propaganda."[48] But other voices were sounding less isolationist; in early 1940, the dean of LBI in Minneapolis, Samuel Miller, wrote to express his approval of the growth in American defense: "We hope that it shall all be short of war for us . . . If, however, our growing defense program and aid to Britain [sic] program does not eventually break the morale of the Axis powers, then we must eventually meet them in war."[49]

After Pearl Harbor, when the national sentiment for war was stoked by the Japanese attack, the synod moved to support the war effort as far as it could, but saw the conflict as a spiritual failing on the part of all nations. the *Bible Banner* resisted a call from President Roosevelt for a day of prayer, asking, "Shall we pray for victory? It is better that we pray for humility, for repentance, and for faith in the true and living God." In a similar tone, the synod convention in 1942 called the war "a disaster," and urged synodical members to "withstand all propaganda of hatred and revenge," while reminding them to work for the "spiritual needs of the men in the armed forces of our country."[50]

The war also had a deep and dramatic affect on many of the missions and ministries of the synod. Pastors were needed to act as chaplains, and nurses also left synodical hospitals to serve in the military. Enrollments at Augustana Seminary plummeted as the seminary program was condensed into three years, and few new ministerial candidates entered. At the church colleges, just then beginning to recover from the loss of funds and students during the Great Depression, the war meant a drastic loss of male students. At Gustavus Adolphus, the college opened its facilities to the Navy, which installed a V-12 training program on campus. This use of the college proved to be very successful, though initially opposed by members of the college's board, who feared the potential effects of "outside" military men (not subject to the college's moral discipline) on female students.[51]

The war brought a tremendous disruption to Augustana's foreign missions, as China and much of Asia were overrun by Japanese forces, and missions in India and Africa suffered from isolation and lack of support. As in World War I, the synod again was forced to take over the "orphaned" German missions in Tanganyika, even though it had few resources in personnel and funding to do so. At home, the massive migration of workers into new defense industries created major social problems. One pastor who had toured the West Coast observed: "The shifting of twenty-two million people . . . to government defense areas creates a grave national problem. . . . [F]ifteen out of every hundred have a definite Lutheran background [and that creates] a grave church problem." Even the social dislocations of war were addressed, including a letter from one Augustana seminarian urging against wartime discrimination, especially against African Americans and Japanese Americans: "If we fail the Negroes and the Japanese-Americans, we *all* lose. . . . This is the hour for real Christian attitudes and actions in the realm of these minorities."[52]

Within the synod, many saw that the war itself, with its horrors and trauma, might eventually shock humanity into a new era of peace and goodwill. Secular movements such as those that would result in the formation of the United Nations in 1945, and postwar ecumenical movements such as the Lutheran World Federation (1947), the World Council of Churches (1948), and the National Council of Churches (1950), represented for some the long-desired catalysts for social and political change. In response to one correspondent, President Bersell wrote in 1944: "It is my prayer that when this terrible war is over with the Christian Churches might find a common basis for action that will prevent future wars. . . . I am not so hopeful with reference to this, but we should not cease to pray and work for such a consummation."[53]

Seminary professor Adolf Hult was, however, skeptical that human plans, secular or ecclesiastical, could change the fundamental disposition of humanity. "If all externals be changed, the things of the spirit will not be changed *fundamentally*. . . ," argued Hult. "There exists hidden to a large extent a craving for the Biblical solidities in place of the rampant present niceties and prettinesses of religious fancy in the pulpit or out of it."[54] Dean Samuel Miller at LBI suggested that the unleashing of great military forces in the world might even be the immediate prelude to the apocalyptic coming of the Anti-Christ, and the end of the world: "Are these consummations near at hand? We cannot yet tell. It all depends on the present situation. Perhaps we might even say it depends on the outcome of America's present aggressive defensive actions."[55]

Communism and the Cold War

Since Augustana was exposed to the troubles of the wider world, especially through its missions in Asia and Africa, the world's political tensions were often in the synodical view. The rise of communism as a world movement was a direct threat to the synod's work in China, and the communist takeover of that country in 1947 to 1949 was reported widely in Augustana publications. The historian of Augustana missions wrote: "Under Communistic anti-Christian rule the bamboo curtain now excluded all foreigners. . . . Only God knows when this curtain will disappear."[56]

The atheistic threat of communism was the subject of synodical resolutions adopted annually from 1949 to 1952. Communism as a threat to the world, and more specifically to Europe and the United States, was also a common topic, especially how Eastern European Lutherans were being treated by communist regimes. In 1947, professor Conrad Peterson suggested that though the church was not tied to any particular social or economic system, "The kind of socialism represented by modern so-called communism does constitute a decided menace to peace and to the highest human values." Another writer, in 1953, made the bold assertion that God was more powerful than Joseph Stalin, and that "evil [could] be overcome with good." An editorial in 1957 rejoiced in the "decline" of communism, as Western European communists lost power, and predicted "the revolt against Red rule in Hungary . . . will undoubtedly be . . . the decisive turning point marking the decline of Soviet power."[57]

Opposition to communism, however, was also marked with a skeptical attitude toward the anti-communist policies of the United States government. Traditionally opposed to war and militarism, synodical writers tended to oppose a military build-up and the strategy of trying to "contain" communist encroachments. The continuance of peacetime conscription was decried as not only a repudiation of efforts toward peace but also as the principle source of the moral pollution of young men. One letter writer in 1953 suggested that the menace of communism was greatly overstated by politicians and the military, who wanted to scare Americans so as to maintain their grip on power. An editorial in the *Lutheran Companion* in 1957 criticized the fact that more than half of the federal budget went to the military, suggesting that people will soon tire of supporting "the greatest military establishment on earth."[58] The peril of atomic weapons and warfare was routinely deplored; typical was the opinion expressed in an article in 1957: "The Christian conscience of America is deeply shocked over the possibility of an atomic conflict that may spell disaster for the whole human race." The writer urged all governments to "turn their genius and energy and resources" to peaceful enterprises.[59]

The American crusade against communism, and especially the McCarthy hearings in the early 1950s, also received negative attention in the synod. Pastor Thomas Basich wrote in support of an editorial against the tactics of the anti-communist crusaders: ". . . certain religious sects have directed the charge of 'Communism' against church people, seminaries, and Bible translators, to conceal a *theological* attack on persons and institutions whose biblical views are at variance with their own."[60] Synod pastor Ralph Hjelm inquired of president Oscar Benson his opinions on a proposed resolution against the McCarthy hearings. "I have been convinced that it is imperative that the Church express itself unequivocally in the struggle for the maintenance of freedom of thought," wrote Hjelm. President Benson in return told him that he was "intensely interested" in the problem, and said, "That such a threat exists at the present time can hardly be disputed."[61] Though the synod never formally attacked the McCarthy hearings, it seems that at least some in the synod were very uneasy about them.

The leaders and thinkers of the Augustana Synod had a keen interest in the religious, social, and political issues of the world around them. They were never completely closed off from these controversies, but from the beginning of the twentieth century onward, as they were making the transition to becoming a truly American denomination, this interest grew and developed. Oftentimes these controversies sought to divide the synod, as individuals and groups took divergent positions on the issues of the day. This was, to a great extent, a part of the process of acculturation and change, as the leaders and people of Augustana were forced to confront issues and ideas for which they, as full participants in American society, had responsibility.

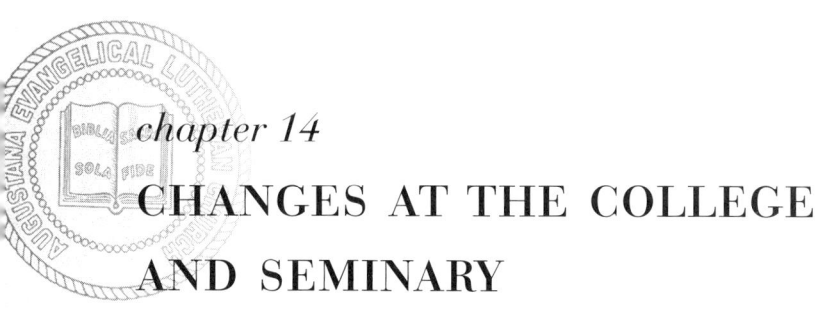

chapter 14
CHANGES AT THE COLLEGE AND SEMINARY

WITH THE INTRODUCTION OF AN ENGLISH LANGUAGE HYMNAL IN 1925, pent-up energy for change was released, only to increase tensions within the synod. Synod meetings had always been places of intense debate, but the focus shifted from the cultivation of piety to a more self-conscious engagement with the question of Augustana's place within a broader Lutheranism in America and in the world. To turn the synod outward involved a transformation of the internal politics of the church. Many eagerly sought to lead the synod as a whole in a new direction. Whether Augustana would align itself with Midwestern Lutherans holding conservative views of biblical interpretation or join ecumenical and progressive Lutherans in the Eastern United States was really up for grabs. Augustana had advocates who pushed the church to be part of a conservative Lutheranism devoted to the cultivation of piety along almost fundamentalist lines, but the synod also had proponents of an ecumenically minded, progressive Lutheranism that engaged modern critical scholarship.

The Crisis of Modern Methods and Modern Thinking

Augustana did not have a pitched battle between modernists and fundamentalists like the well-known battles in the Presbyterian, Methodist, and Northern Baptist churches. It is worth remembering that in the more public debates over evolution and biblical criticism that were waged within other American Protestant churches, the modernists, when attacked by the fundamentalists, invariably held on to their institutions. They retained control of missionary boards, schools, and seminaries, and the denomination. It was the fundamentalists who withdrew.[1] Such was also the case for Augustana's institutions of learning. No public attack by conservatives jeopardized the teaching of geology at Augustana and Gustavus Adolphus College, for instance, where instruction included a clear affirmation of the theory of evolution. Even with support from the colleges, however, evolution remained a flash point in the synod for several decades. In 1939, after reading a heated editorial in the *Lutheran Companion* that took aim at the theory of evolution, Pastor C. A. Wendell wrote to geology professor Fritiof Fryxell at Augustana College: "I don't blame you for taking it seriously. It hits right home at your life work. But—and here's my grandfatherly advice—don't let it upset you. Do as Darwin did. How they thundered and yelled and roared around him, yet he went about his business as calmly as if he had no knowledge of it. Do likewise. Let them fuss."[2]

In responding to science and the modern world, Augustana theologians had to decide on a strategy for meeting these challenges—whether to continue to hold the old ideas and fight the new ones or modify theological approaches and strategies in order to be more relevant to contemporary society. There were dangers and promise in either approach. If Augustana kept to its usual conservative nature and simply rallied the forces around traditional theological ideas, there was always the danger that the synod would find itself increasingly distant from its own members and be seen as irrelevant in a modern world. But theological change was a severe wrench for this immigrant denomination, and there was a danger in moving too far too fast, and away from its theological base.

Though many of the first leaders of the Augustana Synod were deeply rooted in the pietism of the nineteenth century Awakening in Sweden, they remained confessionally Lutheran. Their attachment to the Lutheran confessional theological tradition was strengthened in North America because of the impact of religious pluralism and the battle with other, non-Lutheran Swedish-American denominations. This combination of confessional Lutheran theology and awakened pietism was distinctive in the synod and provided the pivot around which it was oriented. In the "second period" (1890–1923) of Augustana's history, Lutheran confessional theology was taught through the lens of the seventeenth-century Lutheran scholastics, mainly through the influence of C. E. Lindberg.[3] Other new influences were from American-born teachers such as Adolf Hult, who combined a deeply conservative Lutheran pietism with strict Lutheran confessional identity, and C. J. Södergren, who was much more open to the social issues confronting American society at the beginning of the twentieth century.

Although the question of liberal or "modernist" theology was debated within the synod during the late nineteenth and early twentieth centuries, this conversation was rather sporadic in nature. There were, however, two major controversies within the synod after World War I that illustrate the existence of the fault lines: the controversy surrounding the visit of Swedish archbishop

Nathan Söderblom in 1923, and in 1930, the publication of a volume titled, *What Is Lutheranism?* with essays by two Augustana writers. Both events had synodical conservatives up in arms over their possible implications, worrying that they were the harbingers of liberal or modernist theology within the synod.

Söderblom was problematic to synodical conservatives for several reasons, primarily because of his active leadership in ecumenical affairs and because of his scholarship into the history of non-Christian religions. Söderblom's own theology was difficult for many to pin down exactly; it sounded to some like a version of European liberal Protestantism, tinged with mysticism and a history of religions approach. Söderblom himself called Christianity a divine revelation, unique among the world's religions, but critics were not satisfied by his claims to Christian and Lutheran orthodoxy.

During his trip to America, the archbishop visited Augustana congregations around the country, dedicated a new seminary building in Rock Island, and assisted in the re-installation of synod president G. A. Brandelle. In response, conservatives within Augustana and among other Lutheran denominations loudly denounced him and the synod for receiving him. They worried aloud about Söderblom's orthodoxy and commitment to confessional Lutheranism and saw the synod's enthusiastic reception of him as a sign that liberal or modernist theology had invaded Augustana. Dean Samuel Miller of the Lutheran Bible Institute in Minneapolis heard Söderblom preach; he admitted that the archbishop was a "great and wonderful man," but found that the sermon was "full of beautiful generalities but contained nothing positively and specifically Christian." Further, he explained:

> The Archbishop of Sweden is not standing openly on the side of the liberals, but it is evident from what we heard that he does believe in mediating stands with the group which seeks to find some point of contact between the two. And it is not difficult to see that that group really belongs among the ranks of the liberals.[4]

Seminary professor Adolf Hult was less polite in his denunciation of both Söderblom and of those in Augustana who welcomed him. Calling the archbishop the "most skillful evader of the issue," he echoed the judgment of Ole Hallesby[5] that Söderblom was the "most dangerous man of the Lutheran Church." Hult also blasted the synodical press for their praise of Söderblom, writing, "But our Augustana Synod keeps on in a chorus of rapt praise. Shall our Synod be the door to rationalism in the American Lutheran Church?"[6]

Though the archbishop was well received in most synodical circles, it did not appear that his theology was ever very influential in the synod. Even Conrad Bergendoff, who was invited to Sweden to study and work with the archbishop from 1926 to1927, later judged that Söderblom was not a great theologian, although "he was a great Christian Churchman."[7]

A number of writers continued to argue against modernist theology in the synodical press. Professor Hult kept up the attack on modernism and liberalism throughout the 1920s and 1930s. There were not many signs of this kind of theology within the synod itself, but he kept a watchful eye on incipient moves in that direction. He saw modernism as a pervasive sickness with the culture of his day, and a sickness with which the theologians were "well versed," to their detriment.[8] In a later article he blasted the "professors of creed [i.e., the Lutheran Confessions] who engage in time-fretted incertitude, unionism, and an anaemic [sic] doctrinal state . . . [who] experiment with both God and themselves."[9]

Oscar N. Olson rejoiced at the failure of theological modernism in a 1927 article. "We should be glad. . . ," he wrote, "that a religion of denials and negations is barren. While unitarianism is at a standstill, churches with a positive faith are making progress."[10] The danger, it seems, was not so much that the Augustana Synod was full of those who held to a liberal or modernist position, but that they were not sufficiently hostile to liberal theology and to those who professed it; this was the sin of Söderblom and his supporters. Even centrists, like Conrad Bergendoff, who was hardly an ally of Hult, could be strongly critical of theological liberalism. In a 1937 article, Bergendoff wrote that "the present leaders in American theology of the liberal type are dealing with a Christianity that is something different from what used to be called Christianity. Consciously or unconsciously they have cut themselves off from those Christians who look on Christianity as a revelation and as historical."[11] This type of theology was rarely to be found within the synod during this time.

Augustana and the Question of Ecumenism

Söderblom's visit also raised for Augustana questions over the ecumenical path the church should pursue. Should it enter into contemporary theological debates, and in effect open itself to the ecumenical movement that had emerged after World War I, or should it take a more cautious route toward a stronger Lutheran witness? Söderblom already had played an important role in the development of ecumenical relationships among world church leaders, especially in Europe where the ecumenical movement functioned more as a peace movement. American participation had so far been limited to

so-called liberal churches. American Lutherans were lukewarm toward ecumenism, which many derided with the outmoded term "unionism," named
after the effort to form a Prussian Union Church in the early nineteenth
century. Augustana's stance remained quite hesitant when Söderblom visited,
because they realized he hoped to entice them to participate in the upcoming the Stockholm Conference on Life and Work in 1925.[12]

Participating in the ecumenical movement was a loaded question for
American Lutherans because it signaled readiness for relationships that
conservative Lutherans like the Missouri Synod would brand unortho-
dox. Lutherans in America wished to be perceived as Lutherans by other
Lutherans, simply put. Instead, Lutherans were judged by the company they
kept. Ecumenical friendship was a taint. So was association with the liberal Lutheranism in the Eastern United States and in Europe. Midwestern
Lutheran churches wanted to avoid liberal influences at all costs. Since so
much else was changing, many Midwestern Lutherans argued for conservative theology to go along with modernizing American practices. The change
ensuing from adopting the English language was offset by the founding of
Bible schools, for instance, substituting the language of biblical inerrancy for
the pious idioms of Swedish, Danish, German, or Norwegian.

Lutheran conservatives had much in common with fundamentalists, but
they could not rest easy in schools and networks founded by non-Lutherans.
Lutheran young people signed up for classes at the Moody Bible Institute
in Chicago and at other Bible schools. Everywhere conservative Lutherans
turned they saw a threat. They worried that students would take in too much
Reformed theology along with their biblical study. They recognized that it
was incumbent on the Lutheran church to provide for its own.

In 1918, Augustana leaders in South Chicago had initiated a Lutheran
Bible school based on Moody's school. Missionary promoter John Teleen
and Carl Emil Bergquist got the school off the ground but soon left the
Chicago area, where there was not as much support for a separate Lutheran
school as was possible in an area with a higher Lutheran concentration—
Minneapolis. A longer lasting effort by a broad coalition of Lutherans there
had formed the Lutheran Bible Institute (LBI) in 1919. This kind of cooperative work received significant leadership from Augustana pastors. The
dean of the school was the pastor at Messiah Lutheran Church, Samuel M.
Miller, who was popular with youth because of his work in the Bible camp
movement. All the leaders in the early Bible schools were also involved in
promoting English language in the synod.[13]

The shift to English did not entail theological modernization. Conservatives in the synod championed a Bible-based Americanization as a way to resist
influences toward liberalism. Visits by modernizers like Archbishop Söderblom

were a threat. Professor Adolf Hult, the most conservative on Augustana's theological faculty, was a regular contributor to the conservative newspaper the *Bible Banner* of the Lutheran Bible Institute in Minneapolis. When he organized youth work early in the 1900s he pioneered English youth conferences and just as consistently defended theological conservatism. A capstone summary of his views about Swedish bishops in general came when he wrote a heated letter to synod president P. O. Bersell after he heard that Swedish bishops had nominated a Swedish scholar to the faculty. "I have not full trust in Swedish bishops. They have through fourty [sic] years put in men that were not true to the Word of God. And we of our land can not nowadays have a European in our Seminary, except as a guest. We are through with that Scandinavian control, in our country, if we shall live at all."[14] Hult's dismay at these dangerous European and Swedish ties was shared by others in the orbit of the LBI in Minnesota. Still, it was not always clear what aspect of the older Swedishness of the synod conservatives wanted to be purged, or retained, or reinterpreted. As Augustana shifted its theological education and its official church language to English, modernizers came from the left and the right.

English language worship, publications, and teaching spread within all the other Lutheran ethnic churches. Germans in Ohio and Iowa united as the American Lutheran Church in 1930. Efforts to form alliances among Lutherans formerly separated by language sometimes stretched even to the isolated Missouri Lutherans but never succeeded. Instead, the remaining Lutherans began to form associations. The large Evangelical Lutheran Church (Norwegian), Augustana, and the United Evangelical Lutherans (Danish) and Suomi (Finnish) joined with the American Lutheran Church to form the American Lutheran Conference in 1930 to pave a middle way toward Lutheran unity. Augustana shared this church political theological vision at first. The way forward for these Lutherans was to courageously stick to the middle between the extremes of Missouri and the liberal East Coast Lutherans. Augustana conservatives responded to this positively since it provided an "ecumenical" Lutheranism to counter the broader cooperation pioneered by Söderblom and his supporters. In reporting on the opening of the American Lutheran Conference at the premier ELC English Congregation, Central Lutheran Church in Minneapolis, the editor of the *Lutheran Companion* saw the conference as the wave of the future: "Conservative Lutheranism will win the day in America as in the world at large."[15]

Progressives Moving Forward

While Augustana conservatives cheered the advance of the Lutheran Bible school movement and the launching of the American Lutheran Conference,

Augustana's progressives sought to strengthen their position within the governing structure of the central institution of the church, the seminary in Rock Island. The upheavals of the early twentieth century, including the Progressive Era, World War I, and the boom and bust of the postwar period, led to some dissatisfaction with the rather traditional Lutheranism of many seminary instructors. Some thought the prevailing theology was not open enough to the challenges of the modern world, and they sought to explore new options, including theological modernism and neo-orthodoxy; a number of Augustana theologians sought education and employment outside of the synod. Others felt that modernization should come in a traditional restatement of orthodox theology and traditional piety in the direction of American evangelicalism; this might well be seen in the Lutheran Bible Institute movement.

Progressives used the language transition as an opportunity to rewrite, recast, and retell the synod's history to a new generation of readers. Young people in the synod certainly had gotten used to history lessons. It had been the favored way of Olof Olsson and Carl A Swensson, who had founded *Korsbaneret* and *Ungdomsvännen* for an earlier generation in the 1880s. Now, in the pages of the *Lutheran Companion*, and through an expanded participation by Augustana leaders in inter-Lutheran projects, readers got new fare. Instead of stories regaling the exploits of heroic Swedish kings or extolling the humility of the pioneers, the new history focused on the founders and saw mistakes and errors, misjudgments and sorry calculations. Historical critical research had come to the Augustana Synod, and the subject of examination was the synod itself.

Young history professor George Stephenson from the University of Minnesota was one of the modernizers, and he supported continued strong ties to Sweden, particularly with scholars. In 1927, the first of his extensive studies of the Augustana Synod came out, entitled *The Founding of the Augustana Synod*. It focused on the confusing years of Augustana's founding as a separate denomination. Before gaining a degree in history Stephenson had studied at the seminary but he did not become a pastor. Stephenson had family roots in one of the oldest of the synod's congregations in Iowa, but as a modern historian he placed the history of Swedish Lutheranism in a broad, ecumenical, and critical context. He belonged to a generation that aspired to bring Swedish-American culture out of the protective cocoon of a Swedish filio-pietism and into the critical and scientific realm of the modern twentieth century.

"Filio-pietism" was a technical term that denoted historical remembrance that praised the valor of faithfulness and used historical evidence to inspire church leaders. Pushing for an objective and critical use of these sources, a new generation of historians placed decisions, persons, and events in religious history under a critical lens. The story would not be aimed at a limited, loyal church following, but instead at a wider, critical readership. When the history of the synod was examined critically, with motives and personalities and mistakes of the founders scrutinized, these scholarly elites hoped to turn churches in a new direction.

Stephenson and other scholars, including Eric Wahlstrom, Conrad Bergendoff, A. D. Mattson, and Vergilius Ferm, began their academic careers in the late 1920s, during a time when historical investigation of religion was unchallenged in university theological faculties, but was only beginning to influence denominational seminaries like Augustana. In 1928, Shirley Jackson Case, a teacher at the University of Chicago where Conrad Bergendoff got his degree in that same year, wrote the preface for a book of essays honoring the retirement of his Yale teachers, Frank Porter and Benjamin Bacon. The opening essay "The Limitations of the Historical Method," by Ernest Scott summed up the modern method: "Instead of reading history in the light of the Christian message we have learned to interpret the message in terms of history."[16]

Stephenson applied these methods to Swedish immigration, and to the Augustana Synod. His book, *The Religious Aspects of Swedish Immigration*, was published in 1932 and remains an important treatment of Swedish immigration and religion. Stephenson was even-handed in his treatment of Methodists, Baptists, and Covenant groups among the Swedish immigrants. His candid treatment of Augustana's early leaders, and critical assessment of Augustana academic standards, startled synod leaders because of his blunt and dismissive treatment of the church. This dismayed the loyalists, but Stephenson's approach was welcomed, even embraced, by progressives in the synod. He was elected to the seminary's board of directors in 1930.

Institutional Direction

During 1930, a very public debate on the future of Lutheranism was being conducted on the pages of the *Lutheran Companion*, due to the publication of *What Is Lutheranism?*, a controversial book of essays by prominent Lutheran leaders, including some liberals. The volume was edited by Vergilius Ferm, an Augustana pastor and professor at Wooster College in Ohio, who had earned his doctoral degree from Yale in 1925. Ferm was also the author of *The Crisis in American Lutheranism*, a book detailing the mid-nineteenth-century confessional dispute in the Lutheran General Synod, in which the departure of the Augustana Synod in 1860 had played a role.[17] In this new publication, Ferm called for the reinterpretation of the Lutheran theological tradition in light of contemporary reality: "Luther, we believe, would have been one of the very first to reinterpret and reevaluated that large group of Protestants that today carry his name. We hardly believe that he would answer modern problems by merely citing pages from his own writings."[18] Another contributor, C. A. Wendell, pastor at Grace Lutheran church near the University of Minnesota, called for a Lutheranism that was neither modernist nor fundamentalist, but that held to the Lutheran Confessions "not as cement walls for man's incarceration, but as a witness to the faith of the fathers and a guide to their followers."[19] Both writers sought a Lutheranism transformed by a continuing interaction with the modern world, and one in which the Lutheran confessional documents were a guide, but not necessarily a final arbiter.

In response, Samuel Miller, dean of the Minneapolis LBI, began an unsuccessful push to have both Wendell and Ferm thrown out of the synod. Writing in the *Bible Banner* in response to the Ferm and Wendell essays, Miller rejected their idea of the place of the Lutheran confessions as historical guides to faith; rather, Miller believed, "The Confessions are therefore not only a witness and declaration of faith of those who wrote them, but also a witness and declaration of those who subscribe to them."[20] He also rejected Wendell's stance against biblical literalism and his assertion of "flaws and contradictions" in the Bible.

Adolf Hult was even more adamant in his defense of the Lutheran Confessions and his rejection of the approach of Ferm and Wendell, arguing emphatically, "[O]ur Confessions constantly insist that only the Word of God dare make articles of faith, no man, no 'light of modern perspective,' no psychology, no philosophy, no criticism,—no, and not the Church itself. Only the Word!"[21]

In the spring of 1930, George Stephenson reviewed *What Is Lutheranism?* favorably, just before the synod meeting that elected him to the board. He also reviewed all the harsh criticisms of his colleague's work in a personal letter to Ferm. Miller apparently had called for the "expulsion of Ferm and C. A. Wendell" from the synod, and the battle over pure doctrine raged further; in Lindsborg, Kansas, pastor Alfred Bergin at Bethany Lutheran Church blasted the book and called for a heresy trial. It was apparent that Ferm had entered a battle. Stephenson, however, felt a kind of freedom: "I never pay attention to anything the dean [Miller] says or writes. I recognize the fact that I am in a different position from you ministers. In my case there is nothing to 'discipline.'"[22] By September, when these exchanges took place, Stephenson had already made his influence felt on the college and seminary board, for in addition to pushing for academic standards in theory, a death on the faculty had made possible actual changes in personnel. While this possibility excited men like Ferm and Stephenson, it alarmed the conservative watchdogs.

Ferm and Stephenson recognized that they stood little chance themselves of landing a faculty position and they were open about their unpopularity. "What little I may have contributed to the synod has been in the role of an 'agitator,' and this species of animal makes few friends, although I suspect a number may say that they admire his courage," wrote Stephenson.[23] He realized that if conservatives suspected he had personal ambitions it would weaken his position on the board. He had other goals in mind. The more important change had to do with the seminary, where there was an immediate possibility for change of a fundamental character.

As these battles over one edited book raged in the presses, Conrad E. Lindberg, who had been on the faculty of the seminary since 1890 and its dean for almost thirty years, suddenly died. The newly elected college and seminary board now had an immediate task before it: electing a new dean for the seminary. Stephenson recognized the opportunity for a fundamental change of direction. At an August meeting, the man who seemed to satisfy everyone was Conrad Bergendoff, pastor at Salem in Chicago and graduate of the University of Chicago with a doctoral degree in history.

A Modern Church Historian

After his ordination in June 1921, Conrad Bergendoff began a ten-year ministry at Salem Lutheran Church on the south side of Chicago, following in the footsteps of L. G. Abrahamson, who had once served that parish. Because the Swedish population had declined near the church and the church was near the University of Chicago, Bergendoff was able to devote time to his studies, completing a doctoral degree in history in 1928. The congregation did not wither under his leadership, however, and during the 1923 tour of Archbishop Söderblom and his wife, Bergendoff hosted the couple. Söderblom extended an invitation to the young pastor to spend a year in Sweden, serve as his secretary, and work on his thesis. During Bergendoff's year in Sweden in 1926, Söderblom wrote a letter of introduction to German libraries for the young scholar, giving him access to previously unstudied material in Wittenberg on Olavus Petri, the key leader in the Swedish Reformation. Bergendoff argued in his thesis that the Swedish Reformation had independent origins and was not a derivative of one or another German theologian. His book was published in 1928, and it established Bergendoff as a historian with a promising career. His international research had also gained for him invaluable ecumenical and international connections.

On August 7, as soon as the board acted to call Bergendoff as dean, George Stephenson wrote to him: "From the time you were proposed to your formal election, it was unanimously agreed that you were the man for the place. For my own part, I have followed your work and have looked forward to the day when you would be in the seminary, but I never dreamed that I would have the pleasure of voting for you as a member of the board." [24] Stephenson had much more to say to Bergendoff, however, than mere congratulations. "You know what the seminary situation is," he wrote. "Fortunately, to a man the board is fully aware of it and I believe you are the man to reorganize the curriculum and faculty." Stephenson's approach was to purge the existing faculty: "We are in the most fortunate situation of having every member of the faculty, with two exceptions where they can be retired if we see fit."[25]

Bergendoff also had two other offers in front of him, for he had attracted attention wherever he had studied. Charles Jacobs, president of the Philadelphia Seminary, wrote in March with an offer of a position, as they were seeking to strengthen their faculty. Getting Bergendoff to come would add academic as well as political strength to their seminary. In a series of four letters Bergendoff expressed his uncertainty: "Your letter put me in a quandary from which I have not yet emerged," he wrote at the end of March. In June, he wrote: "For almost a month I have struggled to arrive at a decision in regard to the call which the Board of your Seminary extended to me. I have sought honestly and sincerely and prayerfully to come to the right conclusion. Much as I would like to accept the call, I cannot do so." He was asked to reconsider, and in August, he wrote again: "You will probably recall that in my last letter I expressed doubt that there would be any radical reorganization of our seminary at present. I did not then foresee what has since happened. Least of all did I expect that I would be asked to succeed Dr. Lindberg."[26] A third option also beckoned: to stay at Salem and teach in the history department at the University of Chicago.

Deciding whether to accept the offer as dean of Augustana College and Seminary took time. Bergendoff certainly knew the synod; his father served congregations in Nebraska, New England, and Philadelphia. But the younger man represented a new type of leadership. He had pursued academic studies alongside his seminary work at the University of Pennsylvania. Bergendoff also had personal experience with the old guard at the seminary, for the Rock Island faculty had insisted he leave graduate work and finish in Rock Island with the seminary class of 1921. Bergendoff's time in Philadelphia had, however, given him intimate friends and important connections among the Lutherans in the East.

Even with these liberal and therefore suspect connections in Philadelphia, Bergendoff had impressed leaders in the Midwest, particularly

Minnesota conservatives at the Lutheran Bible Institute because of their past contact with him through youth conferences. In the fall of 1920, after Bergendoff, then secretary, sent notices inviting young people to come to Rock Island the next year for "The First Annual Christian Conference of the Young People of the Augustana Synod," he received a letter from the dean of LBI, Samuel Miller. "We are, of course, as yet such a small institution that we could not swell the numbers very much but we could do that which I believe to be of still more importance—swell the volume of prayer ascending to the throne of grace for such a convention." Miller had other thoughts about Bergendoff that he passed on in the letter: "Ever since we began our work here at the Bible School we have had you in mind, hoping that some day you might work with us. I have mentioned this in prayer to God many, many times and I cannot help but believe that He would bless both you and us if you could be won for our work."[27] He described a possible call to a local parish where English language work was needed. Bergendoff knew that he had friends throughout the synod in all the various camps. He had not identified himself as a "party" man, one who took sides.

Conrad Bergendoff, new dean of the seminary, stands in the pulpit of the chapel in Augustana's Old Main.
Photo courtesy of Special Collections, Tredway Library, Augustana College.

Equipped with strong personal ties to eastern Lutherans and to the ecumenical pioneers of his day, and with some support also among conservatives, Bergendoff's hesitation during the summer and fall of 1930 seemed to hinge on the consideration of where he might do the most to advance Lutheran unity. In writing his final reply to Jacobs at Philadelphia, he asserted that his ultimate aim was not to disappear into an isolated orbit but to bring about closer ties. "I have become convinced that any influence that I might be able to exert for a better understanding of the ULC [United Lutheran Church] in the Augustana Synod would come from within rather than without. Remaining in the work of our Synod I shall nevertheless seek to bring closer the day when the Lutheran Church in America shall be one."[28] In October 1930 he accepted the position at Augustana and requested a year of preparation to assume the role of dean in the fall of 1931.

In the meantime the board began work to overhaul the faculty. The seminary in particular had faculty who neared the end of their effective influence over a younger generation. Setting the stage for the shifts to come, Stephenson wrote several essays covering the history of Augustana's educational efforts for readers of the *Lutheran Companion*. These appeared in the spring of 1931. He argued that, given a long history of inadequately funded and sub par educational offerings, the seminary should now be "a graduate school, with a faculty fortified with years of preparation in the best graduate schools in this country or Europe."[29] Stephenson soft pedaled his criticism in the synod's newspaper, but he had more negative opinions of the faculty recorded in a book ready to come out in 1932: "None on the seminary's faculty in the first three decades of the twentieth century had written a distinguished book, and only one had a graduate degree."[30] The seminary and college boards changed that when they met during the 1930–1931 school year.

A Short Window of Opportunity

Those ambitious for higher standards at the seminary clearly believed that the synod had potential for being a leading church in America, otherwise they would not have agitated so vigorously for change. They felt that the future viability of the church was at stake. Stephenson had support from the board for the hard work ahead, and also from leaders on the college faculty, influential pastors, and a raft of dissatisfied students. The board had also received numerous written complaints about the teaching of these men from students, who had finally orchestrated a protest demanding that the faculty be improved and specifically that men with advanced degrees be brought on to teach.

The goal was to bring about the departure of four seminary faculty, creating the opening for new professors. Those who lost their positions in 1931 were Sven G. Youngert, who reached a technical retirement age, and three recently hired teachers—Oscar N. Olson, John P. Milton, and A. T. Lundholm—who had contracts up for renewal.[31] These relatively new faculty had come with substantial parish experience and synod wide leadership credentials, but without extensive university training that Stephenson and others were now demanding.[32]

Information about this critical period in the seminary's history is almost nonexistent in the seminary archives, but correspondence between George Stephenson and Vergilius Ferm, who shared Stephenson's modern academic training and outlook, provides an interesting insider perspective. Already at the August meeting, Stephenson reported that he had staked out his ground, that the seminary needed scholars. "I said that since the death of O. Olsson [1901] there hasn't been a single first rate scholar on the faculty. Only one man took issue, and I squelched him. I took Brandelle to task for trying to make out a case for O. N. Olson, and the board liked it." The board voted to investigate the whole teaching program at the seminary. Stephenson with a committee would visit the seminary classrooms in advance of the November meeting. His own plans for the meeting were clear and he shared his conclusions about what he would find with Ferm on October 12:

> Don't you envy me for having the privilege of visiting the classes of the inimitable Adolf? I have been reading seminary catalogues to learn what real institutions require of their men. If I have my way Olson and Lundholm will be looking for a congregation pretty soon; and I am not so sure that Milton would do the cause more good in a congregation. I have heard that he has become possessed of the idea that he knows a lot and is emulating the example of another professor who passed away some four or more years ago.[33]

Ferm wrote about the theological professors and revealed the essential problems with the two professors Olson and Lundholm: "As to the Seminary profs. I sometimes ask myself what is it in the climate of Rock Island that when men get down there they seem to get 'cuckoo.' Olson and Lundholm must at all costs go. As you know the students themselves have had enough. They have been treated in the class room like an ill-informed deacon treats a men's Bible class."[34] Essentially the problem at the seminary had to do not only with academic training but also with teaching ability.

In his book, *Augustana Heritage*, G. Everett Arden wrote about this period in the seminary's history both as a historian and as a participant. He was a student at the time of the changes, and his account gave weight especially to the student complaints and their frustration with the board of directors.[35] Stephenson wrote to Ferm that students had submitted a second petition to the board asking for the removal of Olson. The accumulated pressure from the students, together with the determination of some of the board to make changes, resulted in an upheaval. When Stephenson wrote to Ferm in December he described an almost complete victory by the new forces on the board. "The spirit of the committee and board was good and showed a determination to take the bull by the horns. . . .[T]here was no disposition to temporize and action was taken without fear or favor. Everything I favored went through." Stephenson probably magnified his own role in the transition as he reported on events to Ferm,[36] but there is no mistaking the powerful impact that a recognized academic well versed in Augustana's history wielded in the committee.

Stephenson's and Ferm's ambition went further than replacing a few seminary teachers. In his October 17 letter, Ferm included details about the academic backgrounds and teaching abilities of candidates the board had discussed for president of the college. This position was not yet open, but the two men had shared ideas about potential changes throughout the summer. Stephenson's critical assessment of Augustana College and Seminary to Ferm—"the entire institution is a rudderless ship"—had been communicated more widely, and now, having intervened into matters, the board would have a new role beyond criticism: it had to begin to take positive action and build a faculty.

The Aftermath of Criticism

Stephenson and Ferm shared confidences and strategies about how they hoped to press forward a progressive Lutheranism. The old guard—a pietistic, orthodox crowd of pompous clergy—seemed to them to have commandeered the pulpits, columns, and classrooms for too long. Their worst invective was reserved for the college and seminary president, Gustav Andreen, who they felt had "waffled" on important matters. In the final paragraph of Stephenson's long report on the consequential board meeting in November 1930, he denounced the state that the seminary and college had fallen into, and revealed a level of personal bitterness. Adolf Hult wrote a column in the *Lutheran Companion* that warned against a layman taking over the presidency of the college and seminary. Even though Stephenson was careful to keep his own ambitions private, his letter hints otherwise:

> All I have to say is: God help the next president of Augustana. He will have to be a man of steel. Who wants that job! Augustana hasn't had a president for thirty years. . . . Well, it is comforting to know that the old guard is frightened and is aware of the fact that something is happening. I suspect that I am the most cordially hated man in the synod among a certain element.[37]

Since the changes initiated by the board in the fall of 1930 were so dramatic, it is tempting to suppose there had been longstanding plans afoot, with candidates in mind, to replace the underachievers. The correspondence between Stephenson and Ferm reveals, however, that as soon as the board managed to secure the departure of Lundholm and Olson, offered a stringent set of terms to Milton, and accepted the permanent retirement of Youngert, they were left with a problem. They had expectations, but no organized plans. Ferm listed possibilities in his private advice to Stephenson, but neither of these two men would determine the outcome. Even if they would have had the power to put a favored candidate forward, it is not clear that they would have found anyone to their liking. Every person they could think of had liabilities. And Ferm was especially sensitive to political forces. Whenever he noted that some of the men probably had ambitions for the positions, he cautioned that they should be watched. But then he did not have much confidence in those left after the politically ambitious were dismissed. He worried that men who were more humble may not have the necessary steel to withstand the scrutiny they would face from fundamentalists in the synod. Certainly Ferm was going to be hard to please. But he did not have any official position in the synod and would remain on the outside.

The official members of the board now seemed to wake up to their responsibilities. They consulted with Conrad Bergendoff, who had managed so far to keep clear of the internal politics. He certainly did not write to Stephenson and Ferm, though there were no doubt face-to-face meetings when the board was in town. Bergendoff had been listed as a possible candidate for president or seminary faculty on one of Ferm's early lists, together with the assessment that his teaching was less than adequate, or "dry as dust." But now this dry as dust person had the task of assembling a faculty that would satisfy the exacting demands of the self-appointed experts.

Two committees of the board tackled the job of getting new faculty. Stephenson reported to Ferm on the letdown he felt after the committees met in Chicago in mid-December 1930: "Nothing definite resulted. Bergendoff met with us and we had an opportunity to look him over. Naturally he was very cautious."[38] Everything that was going to happen next would be in accordance with the seminary constitution and official procedures. The revolution had slowed. Stephenson voiced frustration with the committee on the presidency:

> I believe that Brandelle and Ekblad [synod president and board president] are holding back for some reason, but I don't know what it is. I asked them what they have heard from the constituency, and both replied that they had heard nothing. Of course, that cannot be true; but if it is, it reveals a sad state of affairs. They ought to be sounding out every possible person and ought to be sensitive to every vibration. Of course, it is notorious that Augustana committees are do nothing. Perhaps if we sit down and twiddle our thumbs, a president will descend from heaven.[39]

People stopped talking to him and Stephenson's influence waned. He wrote to Ferm about supporters in Chicago who approached him about the presidency of the synod. These few believed that the "anti-machine" element was growing. The continued correspondence between Ferm and Stephenson, however, noted that matters had now gone into proper hands or into "the machine." The remaining faculty members were now to be consulted on future appointments. The heady days of dismantling the old guard were over.

At the next board meeting in February 1931, the first of the new appointments was made: A. D. Mattson, a teacher in the college who had support from the seminary faculty, including the conservative Adolf Hult. Stephenson, who supported Mattson's appointment, reported, "I was severely silent when Mattson was discussed. I knew that my recommendation would cause him to be suspect."[40] When the synod meeting in June approved the Mattson appointment they gave the treasured faculty position to a known teacher who had gained his S.T.D. degree at the seminary, so he was familiar as an insider. Still, the seminary was on its way to rebuilding in a new direction. Stephenson became much less active in this new phase since he was "up to my ears in proof for my book *The Religious Aspects of Swedish Immigration*."[41] He had consequently been out of touch. But he had been visiting the Rock Island campus, at least in order to do research. He could report to Ferm, "It seems that the seminary has taken on a new lease of life. The spirit is entirely different. Several students testified to that, and several members of the college faculty offered the same testimony."[42] Ferm was glad to hear the news: "It is still a far cry from a No. I institution; but, perhaps it is now in a stage of transition."[43]

Augustana's national network had enabled Vergilius Ferm in Ohio to write and conspire with a historian at the University of Minnesota about the college and seminary in Rock Island. The educational reform that they promoted also benefited Augustana's women who, increasingly holding a college degree used their skills in organizing to develop strong ties to other Lutheran women through their missionary society. The colleges in Minnesota, Nebraska, Kansas, New Jersey, and Illinois prepared young people for wide ranging careers and produced students willing to continue their studies for the ministry from all sections of the country. With only one seminary for the whole church, students from across the country came to know each other personally. This gave Augustana leaders advantages in the emerging, and merging, Lutheran scene in America. They had congregations and people across the country, with personal ties to East and West Coast communities. While Augustana held its own in the upper Midwest among the numerically dominant Norwegian Lutherans, the synod had strong congregations in Western conferences. President G. A. Brandelle, had come to the presidency of the synod from successful ministry in Denver, Colorado, and knew intimately what the new frontier of American Lutheranism looked like, where mission to the American people took center stage.

In the end, the critics Ferm and Stephenson, for all their talk of academic standards and tough and rigorous critical examination, made their judgments about a suitable Augustana professor on much broader terms than scholarly credentials. They too were looking for something more elusive and incalculable: a spirit on the campus among students that allowed for freedom, critical reflection, and something like an open-minded commitment. The change of mood that Stephenson, Ferm, and other progressives felt when they came to the Augustana campus cheered them on in their own work to promote an ecumenically minded, open Lutheranism. They felt at home at headquarters, now, and could spend their time talking about theology and world events, rather than complain constantly about in-house dynamics. Leadership was soon to change in the synod, as well.

PART 4
THROUGH 1962
MERGER

chapter 15
NEW VOICES WITHIN THE SYNOD

As clergy leaders cautiously led the Augustana Synod through the transition from being an immigrant group to becoming an American religious denomination during the first part of the twentieth century, there were other momentous social changes happening within the synod itself, as women, youth, and lay people sought new ways to influence the life and direction of their church. Since Augustana was led predominantly by those who were male and ordained, there were times during which the expectations of these other groups clashed with this leadership, sometimes creating tensions or conflicts. If women, youth, and laymen did not always find the opportunity to participate fully in the life of the synod, they were very inventive in creating alternative ways of contributing, in very substantial ways, to its life and direction. Women and laymen, especially, used their organizational and economic power both to ensure the growth and mission of the synod, as well to attempt to influence the direction of its policy. Since the young people of the synod represented its future, their interests and activities were often a high priority, and much of Augustana's resources were employed to see to that they were educated in the faith and brought into its congregational life.

Most of the time women, youth, and laymen did share the general values and suggestions of the clerical leadership of the synod, and the groups worked in general harmony. But those who were not ordained did not automatically acquiesce to clerical leadership, and there were important instances where the two interests did diverge. At these points, much as the extended family it was, the synod worked through the issues and often managed to come to some sort of accommodation between the disparate interests. In turn, the synod often gained immense energy and many new ideas from women, youth, and laymen, who were an indispensable element in the growth of Augustana itself.

The Changing Role of Women in the Synod

Swedish immigrants to North America came from a society where the role of women was tightly defined and limited to a traditional and subordinate position. In the double transition to a new hemisphere and to the twentieth century, women found that there were many new and wider opportunities available to them, although these openings were often slow to appear in conservative immigrant organizations such as the Augustana Synod. But the women of the synod were not to be denied, and if they were not to find opportunities within the traditional boundaries of the synod, they would make new opportunities of their own. Women found vocational opportunities as deaconesses, nurses, missionaries, and teachers, as the wives of pastors and missionaries, and in the formation of powerful church auxiliaries, such as the Woman's Missionary Society, that provided training for Christian service and leadership.

One important feature of the immigrant experience was the economic and social role of women in the transition to American life. Women's economic contributions were a key element in the survival of the immigrant community, whether it was their labor on farms in the rural areas or their employment as domestic and industrial workers in the cities. Their contributions eventually suggested to many women that they had a right to a voice how their support was to be used, and many of them, especially in the urban areas, came into direct and significant contact with the wider American culture. Young immigrant women, an increasingly significant portion of total immigration, found that there was a great freedom in this experience. One immigrant historian has observed that "domestic service offered a steady means of transition to the outside world, providing a far greater contrast in lifestyle than that experienced by their male peers. . . . The importance of this . . . cannot be overemphasized, particularly its power in assimilating young girls into American culture."[1]

Besides traditional women's employment, some women used education in the synod's academies and colleges and service to the institutions of the synod as vehicles for independence and vocational fulfillment. However, the synod itself was slow to acknowledge the contribution of its women members, and to grant them a significant voice in synodical business. In 1872 and 1901 the synod voted to prohibit local congregations from allowing women to vote in congregational meetings, and in 1894 it issued a stern warning against "women preachers."[2] This was in reaction to an invitation in 1893 of prominent temperance and suffrage leader Anna Shaw, an ordained Methodist minister, to address a meeting of the Augustana University Association.

The invitation had caused quite a controversy within the synod.[3] In 1907, the synod voted to reverse the previous, restrictive action, and allowed for congregations to decide for women's franchise, although there is no record that this was done on a wide basis. The editor of the *Lutheran Companion* wrote approvingly of this decision: "[W]e are of the opinion that the change was proper and reasonable. No Lutheran or Biblical principle is violated in granting women this privilege."[4]

In 1910, the annual synodical convention was thrown into a uproar when a congregation in Utah sent a woman as a delegate to the national meeting; this one woman was allowed to vote,[5] but soon the conservatives pushed through a series of measures to prevent the occasion from ever happening again. Women were prohibited as conference and synodical delegates in 1915 and 1921, and they were not allowed to serve as board members by actions in 1915, 1926, and 1927.[6]

However, women were an increasing presence in the life of Augustana, and they would not be shut out of decision-making for long. In 1924, the foreign missions board invited the Women's Missionary Society (WMS) to send two "advisory" members to their meetings, and in 1941, they became voting members, a reasonable (and long-overdue) move, since the WMS contributed a major share of the board's budget. In 1929, the synod voted to place a woman on the board of Augustana College and Seminary, and slowly, women became members of other synodical boards and committees.[7] Increasingly, women were allowed voting privileges, but the question of leadership was still unresolved, especially on the congregational level. There were proposals during the 1930s and 1940s that women be allowed to serve as trustees in local congregations, but this was not approved until 1951, and it was only slowly implemented. By 1960, "less than 100 congregations [had] accepted this amendment," and probably many fewer had actually elected a woman as a trustee.[8] In 1953, synodical president Oscar Benson replied to a local pastor, who inquired about this change: "If the majority of your members is convinced that it ought to have women as trustees, that ought to settle the matter. Of course, there are arguments against having women on the Church board, but they are practical rather than theological in my opinion."[9]

Slowly and cautiously, the synod began to allow for a greater degree of participation by women. In 1952, Augustana College president Conrad Bergendoff argued that there was no biblical basis for denying women leadership in the church: "[T]he place of men and women in the service of the Church may vary from century to century . . . changes . . . should be made in a spirit of love and devotion to the Church and by common agreement among those concerned."[10] And by 1958, the editor of the *Lutheran Companion*, responding to the controversy in Sweden over women as priests, could write: "[I]f a woman has truly heard the call of God to become a minister of the Word, what Christian has a right to say that she should not be permitted to respond to that call?"[11] Women were indeed allowed to study theology at Augustana Seminary, by means of board action in 1957,[12] but in a denomination where fewer than 10 percent of the congregations even theoretically allowed women to be trustees, the idea of allowing women pastors seemed distant, indeed.

Because the synod and its congregations were slow to recognize the leadership of women, many Augustana women went ahead and carved out positions of vocation and leadership wherever they could find them. Since many synodical colleges had been coeducational from the beginning, the synod had a large pool of educated women, committed to the service of God and church, who could go out into the world as teachers, nurses, or missionaries into areas of local culture where men would simply not be allowed. Some of the first foreign missionaries sent by Augustana were women: Charlotte Swensson was sent to India in 1895, and Betty Nilsson, who had earned a medical degree in America, was sent to India in 1908. Deaconess Sisters Ingeborg Nystul and Magda Hallquist were sent to China in 1906 and 1910, respectively, and Annette Wahlstadt was the first woman missionary to Puerto Rico in 1910, supported by the WMS. Of the 275 Augustana missionaries sent out up to 1962, fully 125 of them were women. If one were to include missionary wives, who often played a significant role in the missionary endeavor, it is then clear that women accomplished a substantial amount of Augustana's foreign missionary work.[13]

Besides the foreign mission fields, there were many areas in North America where Augustana women served their community, especially through the institutions of mercy and the schools of the synod. One of the first organized efforts in this direction was the establishment of the Immanuel Deaconess Institute and its social and medical ministry in Omaha, Nebraska, in 1889. Patterned on similar ventures in Sweden, Germany, and among eastern Lutherans, its first sister, Botilda Swensson was consecrated in 1891. The Immanuel sisters served not only the local Omaha institutions, but some were sent to foreign mission fields, while others served as parish workers and teachers in local congregations. The synod accepted this ministry in 1901 as an institutional part of the synod itself, and in 1902 the Minnesota Conference established a second Deaconess home and training school at Bethesda Hospital in St. Paul. By 1935, some 168 women had joined the deaconess service of the synod; of their ministry in Omaha, historian G. Everett Arden wrote: "Although the number of deaconesses was never large . . . this corps of dedicated, unsalaried women made possible the greatest single institution of mercy in the Augustana Church, the Deaconess Institute in Omaha."[14]

The deaconess movement reached its peak during the 1920s and 1930s, but declined thereafter; in 1954, the synodical convention authorized a study of the diaconate, and this study led to an extensive modification of the program in the late 1950s.[15]

For young women who wanted a medical career, but not the restrictions of deaconess life, many of the synodical hospitals began nursing schools to recruit and train nurses for their staffs. These nursing schools generally offered a three-year course leading to the R.N. degree, or if located near a cooperative college or university, the addition of a bachelor's degree. The Lutheran Hospital in Moline, Illinois, for example, utilized the educational resources of Augustana College; and many theological students at Augustana Seminary found wives from among the student nurses. Proponents of these nursing schools sought to cast the profession itself as a Christian calling; typical was one article in the *Lutheran Companion* in 1952: "The Church of today has a definite responsibility in the preparation of young women for the nursing profession. To secure nurses who give Christian leadership, we look to our church-affiliated schools."[16] A number of these nursing graduates also served the synod in medical missions abroad.

The greatest organized presence of women in the synod, and perhaps the most effective and powerful organization in the synod itself, was the WMS, organized in 1892 by fifty women meeting during the synodical convention in Lindsborg, Kansas. Ever since the founding of the synod, women had organized themselves in local congregations to support each other and the work of the congregation, but the establishment of the WMS on a national level was a step further. The leaders of this new movement were the wives and daughters of the leaders of Augustana and thus had some indirect access to power through their husbands. A prime example of this type of new woman leader was the founder and prime mover of the WMS, Emmy Evald, herself the daughter of pioneer synodical leader Erland Carlsson, and wife of C. A. Evald, a prominent Augustana pastor in Chicago.

The new organization grew quickly and soon established an elaborate structure within the synod; besides the national WMS board, a WMS board was established in each of the conferences, and in almost all the districts of the synod. A publication, *Mission Tidings* was launched and supplemented by other publications, notably for children. The backbone of the organization was the local society—WMS women in a particular congregation or location. Later, separate societies for younger women and children were added. By the time of the organization's fiftieth anniversary in 1942, the organization could claim more than 1,700 local societies, with 57,000 members that had raised over 2.9 million dollars for the work of missions.[17] Volunteers ran most of the organization, though there was a headquarters in Chicago with a small number of paid staff. For a period of time through the 1910s and 1920s, the WMS had a larger annual budget than the synod itself.

The Augustana Women's Missionary Society assembles for a group photo at a meeting in 1929. The candid and relaxed posture of the college women in the upper window contrasts sharply with the earnest attention of the society women.
Photo courtesy of Evangelical Lutheran Church in America Archives.

The resources of the WMS were focused on both home and foreign missions. In the area of foreign missions, the WMS cooperated with synodical missions in India, China, Tanzania, and Puerto Rico, as well as cooperating with other Lutheran women's groups in these efforts. In general, the WMS provided funds for schools and hospitals, recruited young women to enter the mission fields, and supported them financially through their training and work abroad. They had a special interest in mission work among women and children. In the area of home missions, they supported synodical efforts, especially in Utah, as well as missions to migrant workers and Mexicans in California, efforts toward conversion of Jews, and efforts to track Augustana members as they moved within the country. The WMS also supported homes for women in Vancouver and New York City, the Deaconess

Institute in Omaha, and the Bethphage Institution in Axtell, Nebraska, as well as occasional appeals for special synodical causes.

The WMS proved itself to be a rather independent organization; although it raised a significant amount of money for synodical purposes, it also sponsored many of its own independent activities. When it did give money to synodical organizations, it had no small input as to how the money was spent. In recognition of its contributions, and implicitly of its power in the synod, the WMS was granted the right to nominate women for two positions on the synod's foreign missions board in 1924, and the home mission board in 1938, as well as one position on the deaconess board and the board of the Bethphage mission.

The Work of Laymen and the Augustana Brotherhood

Although from the beginning lay men and women had always been active in the Augustana Synod, it must be said that on the whole, leadership of the synod generally was provided by ordained clergy. Lay delegates to conference and synodical conventions always had a strong voice, especially in practical and financial matters, but the ministerium of the synod generally guided the religious affairs of the denomination. In the earliest, immigrant phases of the synod, the clergy had a virtual monopoly on advanced education, and the lay delegate would often defer to them on many issues, maintaining the traditional Swedish respect for the clerical estate. Indeed, to become a pastor or to marry a pastor was generally seen as becoming upwardly mobile. The social gap between clergy and lay was much less in the Augustana Synod than it was in Sweden, though a lingering attitude of deference may well have been due to the short supply of clergy within the synod.

As an element of the acculturation and Americanization of the synod, one indicator must be the rise of the role of laymen in Augustana, especially as the members of the synod were moving up in the social world of America. Here again the church colleges were of great importance, as they produced not only ministerial candidates but also educated men and women who were trained for professional careers within the Swedish-American world. The academies and colleges of the church had always been intended to prepare students for secular professions, but as time progressed, they faced popular pressure to offer an increasing range of "practical" subjects to fit students for successful careers. At Augustana College in the 1880s, for example, nearly half of the students moved toward eventual ordination, but between 1910 and 1914 only 20 percent of students finally entered the seminary.[18] The Augustana Synod was increasingly producing a large class of educated, professional men for its congregations; the question remained, how would they utilize the talents of these men?

One of the first tasks usually handed to such a group of men was that of raising funds to support the work of the church and the subsequent administration of such financial efforts. In 1915, with the realization that the synodical ministerial pension fund was seriously underfunded, the synodical convention asked a committee of laymen to raise $500,000 to meet its needs. As one source reported: "In the face of indifference and opposition in some quarters of the Synod, they continued their campaign until at the Synodical meeting in 1922 they were able to report that the amount promised had been raised."[19]

In 1917, another, larger crisis loomed with the entry of the United States into World War I, a crisis for which the nation and its churches were woefully unprepared. The Lutheran churches were faced with the immense task of ministering to thousands of servicemen around the country and overseas. In order to coordinate this work and pay for it, a group of Lutheran laymen organized the "Lutheran Brotherhood" on November 13, 1917. This was a pan-Lutheran organization, and Augustana laymen were involved, especially in fund-raising activities and building "Brotherhood buildings" that served as centers for chaplaincy and outreach efforts at Army training camps.

After the war, Augustana laymen continued to be involved in the Lutheran Brotherhood, and chapters of this organization were formed in some synodical congregations. In Iowa, for instance, they were formed into a Conference Brotherhood. In 1919, some of these groups petitioned the synod to form a synodical men's organization. This took several years to negotiate, because of the question of affiliation with the national Lutheran Brotherhood of America. In 1922, the national Augustana Brotherhood was formed as an official group within the synod.[20] The group focused mainly on encouraging stewardship, raising funds for special needs and projects, and working with boys and young men. The initial military work was soon taken over by other groups within the synod, but replacing it was a new focus on boys' organizations. The Brotherhood initially suggested the formation of boys' clubs within congregations, under the title of the "Christian Citizenship Program." The program seems not to have been very successful, however, and in its place many local brotherhoods turned to the sponsorship of Boy Scout troops in congregations, and eventually the Brotherhood formed a synodical scouting program in its place.[21] In 1942, the Brotherhood was instrumental in pushing the synod to form a stewardship committee, headed by a synodical executive secretary for stewardship.[22] Since it began later than other ancillary organizations, the Augustana Brotherhood grew more slowly than the others, though by 1935, it consisted of 328 Brotherhoods and 19,000 members.

Youth Culture and Organizations

As has been seen earlier, many of the language and cultural transitions within the Augustana Synod were driven, at least in part, by the desires and demands of a younger generation of synodical youth, loyal to the synod but impatient with the rate of change. They really wanted a place of their own within the synod, and pushed to make this happen, either within the confines of the synod or, if necessary, by creating new structures and institutions, much as women did in the formation of the WMS. While this was not really a revolution, it was a movement for full inclusion in the life of the synod. Taking their models from other American religious youth, they organized themselves into groups and young people's societies—literary, musical, and debating groups; missionary societies; athletic clubs, fraternities, and sororities—all of which practiced "becoming American" without that ever being the stated or perhaps even the intended purpose.

One of the crucial functions of the ethnic congregations was to provide a social and cultural forum for the immigrant communities, and this was certainly the case for immigrant youth. Within congregations, groups of young men and women began to gather themselves into organized groups for a variety of purposes; in one congregation it might have been a choir, in another a literary or mission society, and in yet another a social grouping. The definition of "young people" was fairly elastic; since young people generally left school and began work in their middle teens, the definition of the group could encompass a range of ages from post-confirmation through about the age of thirty, although they usually included only unmarried persons. Some of the earliest congregational young people's societies were organized in the 1870s and 1880s, in Des Moines, Iowa, Free Mount, Kansas, and Moline and Andover, Illinois. The one in Moline was generally regarded as a model for organizations in other congregations to follow, and the one in Andover was distinctive for allowing women to take an equal role in the society, which was not surprising, since the pastor's daughter, Emmy Carlsson (later Evald) had a guiding hand in its organization.[23] Following the lead of these early examples, similar young people's societies were formed in quite a number of synodical congregations.

Given the inclination toward further organization common in society and in the synod of this time, it was not long before local groupings of young people's societies were formed within various conferences. At the same time, this kind of grouping of young people's organizations was going on in other American Lutheran denominations too. These groups, increasingly calling themselves "Luther Leagues," were forming state and national federations. In

1895, the Luther League of America was organized. Within Augustana, this movement caught on rapidly with the formation of Luther Leagues at the conference level, beginning with the Kansas Conference in 1903, and continuing until there was one such organization in each of the thirteen conferences.[24] The next and logical steps were the formation of a synodical Luther League organization to oversee this work on a national level, and affiliation of the Augustana group with the Luther League of America.

In 1905 and 1906, the question of the Luther League was brought to the synodical convention, which, characteristically, created a committee to study the issue. The committee brought a proposal to the 1907 meeting, and the convention considered the question in 1908.[25] Obviously, this proposal was one that created more than a little controversy in some corners of the synod, as it required almost five years to come to conclusion. Some people in the synod had long been suspicious of these youth societies, fearing that they would become de facto congregations themselves within the local congregation and pull away from the synod. Given that organized groups of youth had often been pushing for changes within congregations, such as greater use of English and other refinements, this perhaps was an understandable concern, though in reality it did not appear to have generally occurred. It is true that some of the early breakaway "English" congregations within the synod were composed partially of younger members who were impatient with the rate of change within established congregations, but these new congregations remained within the synod itself. Other critics of youth societies feared that they would be frivolous organizations, generally bent on amusements and social entertainments, to the detriment of more serious and religious purposes. Finally, some Augustana leaders worried about the proposed affiliation with the Luther League of America, since this organization included a large number of youth organizations from groups whose Lutheran orthodoxy was in question within some parts of Augustana.

Advocates of the Luther League responded to these charges with their own assurances that the main intent of such a movement within the synod was to strengthen the work of the synod among its young people, and that it was in no way sectarian or schismatic. One young Augustana member wrote about the activities of the Young People's Society in her congregation:

> Are our Young People's Societies of any benefit to our church? What can a league whose attendance roll averages seventy-five members accomplish? Stop and think what such a body of young enthusiastic workers can do and have accomplished within the past few years. . . . Each meeting of the society brings something new.[26]

As to the larger issues of affiliation and direction, one of the members of the synodical committee, Adolf Hult, asked rhetorically in 1907, "[S]hall we of the Augustana Synod provincially isolate our young people . . . and develop only our own Swedish Lutheran Augustana Synod lines, in the self-centered conviction that we have all we need within ourselves, as churchly and spiritual lenders, but not borrowers?"

In 1910, the synod convention approved the constitution of the new synodical Luther League, which was organized in Chicago in December 1910 as an official part of the synod.[27] As to the final product, one observer suggested that it was a half measure, "a compromise rather than a whole-souled, organic proposition." He lamented, "And still we had little choice. There were two rather divergent ideas pushing at us from two sides: The out and out Swedish national and the distinct Luther League, with all that the latter includes."[28] But a majority of the synodical delegates did approve of the new plans, and in 1916, the convention even came out strongly urging the youth of the synod to join the new organization.[29]

Banquet held at the First Annual Christian Conference of the Young People of the Augustana Synod, February, 1921, Rock Island, Illinois. Conrad Bergendoff was on the committee organizing this youth conference, which was designed to promote the mission work of the synod among young people. Photo courtesy of Special Collections, Tredway Library, Augustana College.

The local Luther League, along with the conference and synodical organizations, grew during the next decades, though, as a historian of the organization observed, "[Y]oung people's work is also difficult at times. . . . One year we can have a splendid League, and the next year . . . it seems to have vanished." The reorganization and redevelopment of youth activities in the synod will be seen in a subsequent chapter.

Another most important area of youth culture within the Augustana Synod were the organizations and activities of the academies and colleges of the church. As has already been seen, these educational institutions were often more open to American influences than other parts of the synod, and the youth at these institutions often organized themselves into groups along the lines of those found in other American schools and colleges.[30] During the late nineteenth century, students at Augustana, Gustavus Adolphus, Luther, Bethany, and Upsala formed debating and literary clubs, mission societies, Bible study groups, prayer fellowships, and all kinds of student musical organizations. These activities led to a rich campus life and initiated students into the world of American voluntary organizations, though their teachers were heard to grumble that there were so many activities and ancillary groups that the student's attention to academics was curtailed. In 1923, the Lutheran Student Association held its organizing convention at Augustana College, and chapters of this group were later organized at the other synodical schools.[31] Synodical college students even defied their teachers and administrators and formed social, "Greek" fraternities and sororities, whose resemblances to forbidden secret societies caused much controversy. At the turn of the century, students at Gustavus Adolphus formed at least a dozen of these forbidden groups, and maintained them for long periods of time despite the prohibition.[32] Although one writer in the *Lutheran Companion* suggested that college fraternities were "doomed," and that in the synodical schools "wherever this snake's-nest sticks out . . . [it] is promptly chopped off," the societies in question managed to survive and even thrive.[33] As one observer in 1932 suggested, "Greek letter societies, however, have come to be accepted as necessary evils, and even students headed for the ministry display fraternity pins with pride."[34] Whether by petition or resistance, college students tended to get their way.

Though youth at the synodical colleges were generally well committed to the aims and means of the synod as a whole, they also at times helped push the boundaries of synodical attitudes. This has already been seen in the language transition; it also was fairly clear when it came to social attitudes, such as the role of women in society, and elements of popular culture, such as music, dancing, theater and movies, and other amusements. Though synodical college students were hardly radicals, they often were more open-minded on these issues than were their elders. Conrad Bergendoff observed:

> The increasing numbers of college graduates in the ranks of . . . the churches was itself a modifying influence . . . to longstanding tradition. . . . An unwritten chapter is the cultural influence of [the colleges] on the Swedish immigrants to the United States as they became Americanized and adopted attitudes toward culture in general and higher education in particular.[35]

One example of this was student reaction to a decision in 1905 to ban intercollegiate athletic teams at the synodical colleges.[36] Conservatives, worried about the rates of injuries in such sports and the possibility that they were detracting from the religious and educational aspects of the colleges, pushed through this ban. Students reacted strongly against it, staging a "disturbance" at Augustana College, where students protested loudly to the college's board members. They also presented petitions to the synod meeting in 1908. The culture of American education was strong among students in the colleges, and they saw that intercollegiate athletics were an integral part of that culture. Eventually all sports but football were restored in 1910 (football was allowed in 1916); in 1910, one writer applauded the reversal, saying, "To have athletic contests with students in good standing is certainly far better that to have such contests with secret-society members, brewery employees, and even members of the YMCA."[37]

But athletic events were not the only concern of these students, and a new generation of Swedish-American collegians were not shy about speaking their minds. In 1926, Augustana College students had urged the faculty to pay more attention to the opinion of students on religious matters; when the professors voiced their objections, the editor of the student paper demanded that they apologize. Conrad Bergendoff observed that this new generation of students was "interested no less in religion, but not hesitant to disagree with what seemed only traditional and ultra-conservative. Their lengthening list of organizations gave these students a feeling of solidarity in their attempts at more freedom in expression and action."[38] The increasing restiveness of seminary students during the 1920s, especially against the entrenched conservative members of the theological faculty, must also be seen in this light.

The church colleges were also an important vehicle in the development of the Swedish-American religious culture that was such an important part of the synod from 1890 to 1930, and in whose formation the youth of the synod were so vital. Dag Blanck has suggested that by the period of 1890 to 1917, this Swedish-American identity no longer came as a natural part of growing up in the immigrant community, but was "an ethnic identity" that "had to be learned."[39] One perhaps trivial aspect of this was the effort to reform the surnames within the synod: there were too many Johnsons, Olsons, and Petersons to keep straight. In 1910 one writer suggested: "There are too many Swedes having the same names . . . our young 'Johnsons' . . . should find a name that has a Scandinavian origin . . . and then make an early change."[40] A more organized effort along the same lines was urged by five Swedish-American college presidents in 1923, who held up a similar movement by the Swedish government for the reform of surnames. Speaking for the group, Gustav Andreen stated that the names "were not in the least objectionable *per se*. . . . Many of them have been borne by men of highest distinction and worth in America and Sweden. But . . . these names are so common that they do not serve . . . to distinguish one family from another."[41]

What is so interesting here is that the intent was not to change names in order to meld the young into American society, but rather, by taking new names that were distinctively Swedish, they would be seen as part of a unique ethnic and religious culture in America, one not simply to be born into but to be chosen and nourished as a voluntary part of one's own carefully constructed identity. In large part, this was the journey of acculturation and Americanization in the Augustana synod from 1890 to 1930, and in this journey, the younger generation in the synod took the lead in exploration.

An American Model for an Immigrant Church

One of the most striking changes in almost any religious tradition reestablished in the United States by immigrants is its own transition to the realities of American forms of voluntary religion. This idea, formed by sixteenth- and seventeenth-century Protestant immigrants to North America, and codified in the American constitution and legal theory, says that any religions formed in this country are voluntary organizations, dependent on the support of their members, and not supported financially by government in any way. This means that the clerical leadership of religion (backed by State support) so common in other parts of the world is not possible in the United States. If clergy leaders wish to establish and grow their religious traditions in America, it will only be possible with the help and support of those who are not ordained, professional leaders—in the case of Augustana, lay women and men and youth. The American system of voluntary religion, then, theoretically places a tremendous amount of power within the hands of the laity, without whose assistance organized religion in the United States simply is not possible.

In the case of the Augustana Synod, the "gap" between clergy and laity was often less than it was in Sweden, where the traditional orders of society and of clerical dynasties made for rigid social distinctions. The clergy leadership of Augustana was, quite to the contrary, drawn mostly from the ranks of the immigrants themselves, and closely related to the lay women and men they served. Augustana Lutherans, like other American religious groups, established a renewed context and use for Luther's idea of the "priesthood of all believers" that made a great deal of sense within the context of American voluntary religion. Even though there were tensions at times, the synod could not have grown as it did without the tremendous contributions of lay women and men. They certainly contributed the bulk of the material support that made possible the synod and its institutions, often at a great sacrifice to themselves. But beyond this, lay members of the synod—men, women, and youth—were often in greater daily touch with the changing world of twentieth-century North American society, and it was their important contribution to see that the synod maintained the vitality of its mission by continuing to evolve with the new challenges and realities of contemporary life. Lay members of Augustana were devoted to their synod, enough at times to push it toward important and necessary changes.

Early in 1932, as the financial depression settled in on the churches and colleges of the nation, the students in Birger Sandzen's second year art appreciation class at Bethany College in Lindsborg sat down to write their final examination on the theme "Beauty and Life." While the students were busy recording their thoughts, Sandzen took out his pen to write to his younger friend and supporter, Fritiof Fryxell, the up-and-coming geologist at Augustana College in Rock Island.

Sandzen had several possible paintings he could offer to Fryxell, who had commissioned a work of art to add to the collection of Augustana College's Art Association, which he chaired. Fryxell had provided Sandzen with photos and sketches of scenes from the Grand Tetons that Sandzen had transformed into several large canvases. This time, however, Sandzen proposed that he would sell a 30-inch by 40-inch painting of a Kansas theme: "Creek with Cottonwood Trees" for less than half its asking price of $1,000. In addition, he would also donate another painting to the association along with the purchase. The depression had greatly reduced the income that Sandzen had been able to garner from his paintings and prints, but his letters contain no complaints. Instead he records for Fryxell that his own art had begun to be recognized even beyond the ocean, in his homeland. He reported that the famous Swedish artist Carl Milles now owned six of his paintings.

Sandzen came to Bethany in 1894 at age 23 after studying with the Swedish artist Anders Zorn and completing the required stint in Paris. He joined a faculty where Olof Grafstrom led the department, and worked alongside another artist, Carl Lotave, to cultivate appreciation for art in the Swedish-American community. Grafstrom's altar paintings showed many congregations that art could inspire devotion, and his work came to adorn over 200 churches. Sandzen ventured further in his art, and used the West itself as his subject. Early in his career as an American artist he spent several months traveling in Mexico, and he wrote to his fiancée about his fascination with a floral exhibition in the San Angel district of Mexico City: "The whole city was adorned with flowers. We went first to the old cathedral. There were flowers from floor to ceiling. Over the altar there was a cross of violets and white lilies. And outside there was an exhibition the likes of which I have never seen and the many beautiful colors and strange flowers that only the South can offer."[1]

The college in Lindsborg saw many of its best faculty move north to Rock Island, but unlike Olof Olsson, J. A. Udden and Olof Grafstrom, Sandzen stayed in Kansas. The Western landscape, with its intense colors and vast open spaces, captured Sandzen's imagination and heart. He used the scenes around the Smoky Valley and the colorful mountain views further west and south to inspire his students and stimulate their sense of beauty. At the high point of his career, when he began correspondence with Fryxell, he used the opportunity to explore the meaning of his art in the context of the changes facing the whole nation. Sandzen thanked the younger geology professor for his interest and his prompt payments and noted, "The best thing we can do in these serious times is to work away as usual and do the best we can."[2] He felt that a complete social reorganization was in process. Even politicians were thinking seriously for once. The changes also touched on his own vocation, for he felt that people were finally discovering the essentials in life, and this would help society solve the great social problems. His hope was that "We may have culture and intelligent enjoyment of life without wealth."

Sandzen produced many prints featuring the creeks, rivers, bluffs, hills, valleys, and trees of the area around Lindsborg. These were displayed alongside other art works during the annual Messiah performances in Lindsborg, giving attendees the chance to participate in an art exhibition, and to become collectors themselves. The mountains and streams of the West entered the homes of hundreds of church members. Home décor, however, was only a small part of the way that Sandzen's art influenced the church. His fascination with the austere beauty of the West had also become lodged in the imagination of many leaders. He could not follow Fryxell into the sublime heights of the Grand Tetons, but he promised, "I will be sketching there at the Timberline and be there when you come down."[3]

The relationship between the two men continued to deepen. Fryxell

Birger Sandzen's print of Olof Olsson's house in Lindsborg was made in 1922. Olsson and his family lived here from 1871 to 1877. Print courtesy of the Birger Sandzen Art Museum archives, Lindsborg, Kansas.

named his son John Birger after his artist friend, and they carried on a mutual campaign to work to improve the cultural scene at Swedish-American colleges. Sandzen hoped that "our colleges could become fine, noble centres of broad culture and real vision," and commiserated with the reality that "unfortunately, too many small, narrow, uncultured ministers and influential laymen have a perfectly pitiful conception of Christian culture." Fryxell had encountered much resistance from these same conservatives because he attempted, through geology, to explain the majesty of God's creation as an evolutionary process. Sandzen's support encouraged the young geologist and art connoisseur in these years of controversy: "Life is short. Why make it narrow, sad and hard instead of beautiful, kind, joyful and *forgiving*." He quoted the Swedish author Victor Rydberg, the romanticist who wrote, "The work of the human being is to dream and to think."[4]

chapter 16
AUGUSTANA'S YOUTHFUL EDGE

IN 1939, THE REV. WILTON BERGSTRAND, YOUTH DIRECTOR, traveled 36,500 miles and gave 202 talks to 55,000 youth. He spoke at six Luther League camps and five conference Luther League conventions. These statistics from his first year of service as executive secretary of the Augustana Luther League were included in the synodical report for the year. The report also measured office output, so when the president of the synodical Luther League council had tallied miles traveled and words spoken, he added: "Pastor Bergstrand also wrote 6,000 personal letters, 8,000 circular letters, and contributed 175,000 words for the readers of the *Lutheran Companion*."[1] The report did not mention another important worker, Bergstrand's sister Lorraine, who typed, filed, and compiled all this data and also entered a career of service in the youth office. The two Bergstrands made the youth office professional. Youth work had become typically American. The various departments of the church worked as a cohesive system and were an efficient and successful operation. Organizationally and culturally, the synod reshaped itself, communicating to members in a reassuring language borrowed from politics and business.

While younger people were enthusiastic about the new efficiencies that Iowa Conference president P. O. Bersell introduced when he became president of the synod in 1935, others resisted as organizational machinery expanded. The modernization of women's leadership and the systemization of youth-related programming was a profound and important transition, changing leadership from a paternalistic or maternalistic system honoring seniority into a system that rewarded skills needed to run a democratic, initiative-taking enterprise. Even though Lorraine Bergstrand's contribution in the youth office did not register as publicly as that of her executive director brother, the synod increasingly depended on the practical ability of women and young people, who stepped into less heralded but crucial workers, missionaries, and camp directors. While these forms of ministry did not bring political clout at conventions, the multiplication of programs that these talented leaders provided created opportunities for many young people to imagine new ways to serve their church. Young men and women got a new message from their church when they went to camp or to a conference gathering. Bergstrand's leadership focused on harnessing the potential of the young people in the church. He gave them a consistent message: we will work with you so that you can become active leaders in the church and in the world.

Bergstrand's example and others show how the Luther League became the vehicle used to shape Augustana's youth as future leaders. At Bible camps and leadership conferences the relational network that provided the historic foundation for trust and leadership in the synod was refashioned. By drawing young people into this new, expansive, and exciting inter-Lutheran program, and helping them form friendships and gain skills in leadership, the synod built capacity for change in the church.

Leadership for an American Church

Augustana's Luther League was affiliated with the inter-Lutheran Luther League movement founded in 1895. Early youth advocates had been prominent in advancing English language work, and the Luther League absorbed the older youth society programs, with their libraries and literary recitations, turning these debating societies into programmatic units that could advance the church's expanded efforts to build a denomination. The same emphases that captured the enthusiasm of synod delegates now were on the agenda of the Luther League: missions, stewardship, effective group process, and social reform.

To teach Luther Leaguers how to organize local chapters and run interesting and effective programs, the synod's Luther League Council through Chicago's Lutheran Bible School published *The Manual for Luther Leagues*. The first volume came off the press in 1925 and provided 300 pages of important information, beginning with the history of the synod's Luther League work—mostly a series of organizational dates—and organized by chapters describing many facets of church life. The manual had lesson plans, sample dialogues, and a series of debate topics. Several focused on stewardship, as in: "Resolved that the voluntary pledge system is preferable to the stipulated communicant fee system." Judging from the wear on the copy handed down to the author, a frequently used section was one that listed "One Hundred Hints for Your Social Meeting."[2] The topics covered gave Luther Leaguers a well-designed script educating them to be leaders in rapid

Americanization. Augustana's young men and women had been targeted for leadership, and they responded with enthusiasm.

The popularity of youth programming created a constituency that pushed within the synod for the creation of a new department and the selection of a full-time director. One obvious way for this to happen was for the Luther League itself to become a department in the church structure, which eventually occurred, albeit through several organizational steps. As the youth program grew and local leagues became organized as part of district and conference structures, church members felt the increasing influence of this new dimension of church work. They could follow the progress by hearing official reports at synod conventions and through reading regular columns in the synod newspapers. By the 1927 convention, the proposal for a full-time director was ready for delegate action.

Breaking through the "Old Guard" Thinking

Getting a full-time director for youth did not seem like the obvious next step to delegates at the synod meeting, however, for in 1927 they rejected the proposal. Synod delegations in the late 1920s were all-male, clergy-dominated, and practiced in the routine of dismissing requests for new initiatives by auxiliary groups. The synod was also handling the transition from Swedish to English at the time, and tensions about that shift also delayed approval for women's voting rights, expanded college programs, and progressive initiatives like a pension fund for pastors.

Even though the official synod meeting was able to fend off modernizing features like full-time executive directors of programs, the infrastructure of these initiatives was being created on the local level. The programs advanced by younger leaders in the synod focused on youth, women, and laymen, who, in the process of organizing, created a network of influence and gained skills in leadership that slowly but surely challenged the older patterns of decision making.

The most dramatic confrontation testing the decidedly paternalistic system of leadership in the synod had been waged for several years between the Women's Missionary Society Board and the Augustana College and Seminary Board of Trustees over the location of a new women's dormitory at the college. Emmy Evald mustered the signatures of 40,000 other women who had, at the official request of the synod, raised money for a completely modern and suitably refined women's residence hall. In the meanwhile, their wishes had been stymied by the board, which had selected a site for the building that the women vehemently rejected. In addition to being an ugly site near an industrial scrap pile, the women feared the dormitory would be too close to the men's dormitories, something that, according to their peti-tion, was forbidden by a relevant Pennsylvania statute.[3]

They presented their petition to the church at its convention in Phila-delphia in June 1926. The women asked that the sentiment of the 40,000 members of the Woman's Missionary Society on behalf of the young women at the college be heard. The petition came at the end of a five-year struggle. Two years previously the women had taken a more modest course, appro-priate to the conventions of the paternalistic culture that prevailed in the synod. Their request merely asked for permission to address the synod meet-ing. It drew from Evald's impressive Bible knowledge and cited a scriptural precedent:

> When the daughters of Zelophehad, thousands of years ago, had been denied their rights in having a share in the division of the land [Num-bers 27:1–8], they were granted the privilege of speaking for themselves. They stood "before Moses, Eleazar the priest, the princes, all the con-gregation, at the door of the tabernacle of the congregation" with a plea for consideration. When Moses "brought the cause before the Lord," the Lord approved their action, saying "The daughters of Zelophehad speak right." Give them their rights and give them their shares.[4]

The women chose to address the male delegates as a modern-day Moses and Eleazar, an over-the-top gesture of honor and respect necessary in order to reassure the men that they were not stepping outside of their assigned female roles. The request continued: "May not then the mothers and daugh-ters of the Augustana Synod be heard sending a plea for consideration, not for themselves, but for the betterment and welfare of the womanhood at our college. Should they not have a share in that work?"

Frustration with the guardians of the campus at Augustana College and Seminary grew after two defeats. It was stoked among the mem-bership in regular articles in *Mission Tidings*, and in 1927 a new strategy emerged. To mend relations, the Alumni Association of Augustana College and Theological Seminary petitioned that the synod elect a woman gradu-ate to the board of directors. It did not take much discussion for the 1927 delegates to respond: "[T]he Synod is of the opinion that there is no real demand for a woman member on the board of directors of the Augustana College and Theological Seminary, and, hence, that this petition be not granted."[5]

To be fair to the delegates at the 1927 convention, besides the women's request, many other issues loomed on the horizon, including unrest in China that forced the mission board to remove missionaries from the field, the opening of a new mission field in Iramba, Tanganyika, language transition that affected the older pastors, and the introduction in congregations of the synod's new 1925 hymnal. It is not surprising then that the request of the Luther League to install a full-time director might be buried in the midst of other important concerns. The growth of so many of the synod's initiatives in higher education, home and foreign mission, youth, publications, and women's work severely strained the decision making structure of the church convention.

Persistence Pays Off

The synod's Luther League responded to the 1927 setback by enlisting a modern polling technique and mailed a survey to all the Luther Leagues within the synod. Needless to say this was hardly a representative sample since Luther Leagues could certainly be counted on to support a full-time director for their program. The survey could not possibly give an objective assessment of the opinion, but surveys were still a new idea, and therefore the report of results made quite an impression, enough to sway the 1928 delegates. Out of 150 delegates, 144 voted to create a formal position of Director of Youth Activities.

Advances for youth went along with other new initiatives in the synod that delegated responsibilities that had before been stewarded by the convention as a whole. Leaders in the synod also responded to the accumulated pressure of women's activities, not by giving the women any access to voting rights, but by giving them public recognition. President Brandelle, at the sixty-ninth annual convention in Des Moines, Iowa, hailed the women's persistence: "The work of the women of the Church is one that is old and well established. Despite the fact that three and four generations are now in it within our Church they do not seem to tire of it."[6] The old guard of men at the helm of the synod recognized the emergence of an expanded leadership structure in the church, and the challenge ahead of them was to keep new leaders fully connected to the whole church.

The first executive secretary of the Augustana Luther League was Pastor P. N. Sjogren who started work in 1929. Then economic depression struck the country and severely constricted any thoughts of expansion in the church. Funding sources dried to a trickle. Yet youth activities remained at the local and conference level and continued at the popular summer Bible camps. The Great Depression taught leaders that youth work would have to grow from the grassroots, drawing on local leadership, particularly the pastors. In effect, a decade of slow growth with dependence on pastoral leadership resulted in a youth ministry program tightly connected to congregations. An additional decade of language transition in the congregations also helped to create a positive climate for youth work. The Luther League became more firmly established in congregations simply because it provided a social outlet when other entertainments were rare.

The Augustana Luther League grew along the same lines that had shaped the growth of the Women's Missionary Society in the synod. Luther Leagues in each congregation joined district and then conference structures. At district and conference levels, larger gatherings of young people made it possible to promote the colleges in an efficient way, and this helped congregations prepare youth for a liberal arts education. The younger pastors in the synod and a network of interested leaders provided programming for youth meetings, conferences, and Bible camp weeks that soon became a regular part of the summer. The Bible camp program extended the influence of the Lutheran Bible Institutes to hundreds of young people who would otherwise not have attended the schools in Minneapolis, Chicago, New Jersey, or Seattle. In Illinois, the organizer of the first Luther League Camp, Joshua Oden, recalled that, "We followed the Chautauqua program, with an early morning sunrise service, breakfast, and then a Bible study, a practical hour, and brought the forenoon sessions to a close with a program of an inspirational nature."[7] Bible camps provided a way for local Luther Leagues to retreat to an outdoor setting for intensive Bible study. A more concentrated opportunity for social mixing with other Luther Leagues came at conference-wide youth conventions, also held in the summer months.

A Career of Summer Programs

In 1930, S.J Sebelius, who taught church history at Augustana Seminary, spoke to New England youth gathered at the large and still mainly Swedish-speaking Maria Congregation in New Britain. New England's conference president, Sven Gustaf Hägglund, had asked Sebelius to emphasize the Swedish language and culture as "Our Heritage," a concern characteristic of Hägglund, who made a career out of promoting Swedish. Sebelius, who hailed from the more evangelical and Americanized Midwest, had no patience with this request. "Naturally I refused," he wrote. "'Our Faith Heritage' is more important." Three years later, Sebelius was a popular speaker at events in both Nebraska and Kansas. In Kansas, he found himself critical of the intense concern about personal salvation that led to an "emotional element" in the meetings. He concluded that it was "best to teach the Word without resort to mechanical devices to stir feeling. The reaction is not good." Sebelius's tour of duty as a speaker put him in contact with the various regions of the synod, where it was clear that the programming provided for young people reflected the concerns of pastors serving in those areas.

By the middle of the 1930s, July had become the month of Luther League conventions all across the country. The *Lutheran Companion*'s opening editorial for July 7, 1934 announced that youth "from Lake Winnepesaukee in the green-clad hills of New Hampshire to Fortune Lake in the wilderness of Michigan and Mt. Hermon in romantic California will gather for annual Bible Conferences."[8] The outdoor settings for summer conferences provided a popular vacation opportunity. Summer camp was an invention of the YMCA, and although it was designed as an extension of the work of the Sunday school, Augustana's use of the program highlighted the power of worship in the out-of-doors: "The influence of religious worship . . . under sunset skies or amid rosy dawn, is more lastingly powerful than many other religious experiences." Augustana leaders used this program to foster a "religious experience" for its young people. This method was followed by many other Lutheran camps, and by 1948 more than fifty Luther League camps in the synod followed this type of Bible-centered youth program. These experiences, whether they occurred in Texas, California, Kansas, Illinois, or Minnesota, were reported in the Luther League section of the *Lutheran Companion*. The Red River Valley Conference sponsored their first Bible Conference in 1934, and the success of their venture attested to the familiarity even young people in Northwestern Minnesota and the Dakotas had with the concept: "The attendance was greater than the planners had dared to expect. Young people, eager to study God's Word, gathered in this beautiful locality became better acquainted with each other and had great benefit from the Christian fellowship."[9] Luther Leaguers in the Colorado Rockies enjoyed the beauty of the mountains, casually waiting for coffee around a campfire. Formal New England Luther Leaguers sat in the pews to learn the principles of the Lutheran faith. Kansas youth delved into the subjective pious feelings that characterized their founding communities in Lindsborg and McPherson.

While hundreds of youth might attend a conference-wide gathering, even larger numbers were attracted to the biennial "Youth Conferences" held every other year beginning in 1929. The first four of these gatherings were held at Bethany College, Gustavus Adolphus College, Upsala College, and Augustana College, but beginning in 1937, they became too large for the colleges to accommodate. Youth activities continued to outgrow the institutional structures that the church had pieced together. A full-time director had been approved in 1928, but because of the Great Depression had seen little success. By 1937, the economic situation had improved and new leadership had emerged. It was time for a full-time director to oversee the future development of this aspect of the church's program.

Finally at the Modern Stage

When Wilton Bergstrand finally was able to open an official youth office in 1938, President Bersell and the executive board of the synod could not guarantee a budget for the work. Wilton and his sister Lorraine developed what they called a "prayer budget" and trusted that if they communicated their hopes, the money would come in. It did. Wilton Bergstrand held the position, with various titles but increasing prominence for the work, for twenty-five years until the merger that formed the Lutheran Church in America.

Wilton Bergstrand in his youth director office. Photo courtesy of Evangelical Lutheran Church in America Archives.

Lingering in the piety and culture was an aversion to the new system of budgets, reports, committee meetings, and formal resolutions. Bergstrand was a son of a pastor; he understood and practiced a form of piety adapted to the new structural order. By adopting a prayer budget and asking for the prayers of the Leaguers, he may well have elicited contributions from reluctant church members who learned in this way to understand the "youth office" as a place of consecrated service and not as a division in the corporate headquarters. A prayer budget also signaled the importance of the Bible Institutes in the organizational development of the youth program.

Wilton Bergstrand's resort to prayer budgeting was not just a forced choice. It represented a particular method familiar to Bible Institute supporters. The rapid growth of famous institutes like the Moody Bible Institute in Chicago and the dynamic expansion of missionary ventures like the China Inland Mission relied on novel fundraising techniques that deliberately avoided the taint of fundraising. Prayer budget methods were used in many fundamentalist-oriented Bible schools in emulation of the methods of George Muller, who had founded and sustained orphanage work in England in the mid-nineteenth century through praying for support. In order to project confidence that "God will provide," these methods focused on prayer rather than monetary appeals. Some fundamentalist readings of scripture furthermore emphasized that the world was soon ending, and this orientation kept many leaders of Bible schools very wary of budgeting, building funds, or any kind of future planning.[10] Bible Institute leaders in the Augustana Synod were not promoters of end-times scenarios and other fundamentalist schemes, but they did have a vibrant culture of prayer. Bergstrand's reliance on prayer as a means of communication not only with God but also by example was a sincere gesture of confidence in the ministry he now began in the youth office. His emphasis on his own reliance on God also kept the new department spiritually set apart from the developing bureaucratic structure of the synod.

Bergstrand's use of the prayer method to expand the church's ministry with youth was not unique in the synod either. Jonathan and Paul Lindell turned to prayer-based budgeting when their request to enter Nepal as missionaries was turned back by the synod's mission board. Through prayerful negotiation with the South American Mission Prayer League in 1940, the organization expanded their focus beyond Latin America and became the World Mission Prayer League. Though this mission effort remained independent, Augustana men and women were its key leaders, and the venture created an outlet within the synod for members frustrated with a developing business-like professionalism. Prayer budgets represented a stream of piety that softened the hard edges of the emerging business model in denominations.

Though Bergstrand's prayer-budget initiative may have revealed an old-fashioned piety to those who were familiar with Bible school culture, it was a sign of the times. Bergstrand was also a more complicated figure than this one example would reveal. He was an exceptionally fine speaker and had a competent theological mind. While a student at Gustavus Adolphus College, he shared a national title in debating with partner Edgar Carlson, continuing the synod's tradition of debating excellence and speaking prowess among collegians. When the *Lutheran Companion* spread the news and the fame of Bergstrand and Carlson, church members expected that they would turn out to be future leaders of the church. Bergstrand's quarter-century career as director of youth work, like Carlson's future responsibility as theologian and president of Gustavus Adolphus College, depended on the ability to shape an argument, inspire a crowd, and win trust. What Bergstrand accomplished in his career in youth work was to enlist support from almost every conceivable faction of the synod, from social justice-minded progressives to fervent Bible pietists. The youth office thus functioned as a bridge to keep various factions in the synod together as the church made difficult choices about its theological and political alignments within American Lutheranism.

Bergstrand's success was already evident in 1941, at the first synod-wide conference that he planned and executed. Registrations for the event in Rockford, Illinois, topped more than 3,700 young people. The event was held at a hotel, since none of the church's colleges were large enough. So many extra people came that fifteen members of the hotel staff gave up rooms to delegates. Even this was not enough. Six young people took turns sleeping on three beds at the local hospital and marked on the registry that they had been treated for insomnia.[11]

Important memories were formed, and youth created their own church culture, complete with traditional practices passed on and enhanced at each gathering. One of these was the "Singspiration." The Rockford Conference was again the pioneer in incorporating the love of singing into what became a series of biennial conferences. Youth became practiced at singing, impromptu, in public places during these week-long conferences, joining in harmonic singing at train stations, in hotel lobbies, and in the parks. A particularly memorable event occurred in 1953, when a "Singspiration" was held on a boat sailing on the Charles River, in Boston. The whole event was reported in a special youth edition of the *Lutheran Companion*. The manager of one of Boston's hotels

Luther Leaguers arrive by train at a synod-wide conference, sometime in the 1940s. Signs indicate that the enthusiastic youth came from all over the synod.
Photo courtesy of Evangelical Lutheran Church in America Archives.

sent a personal letter to the youth board, thanking them for sending such wonderful models of Christian youth. It was reported that after the "Bean Feed" on the Boston Common, the park director gathered a crew of 100 to clean up, but dismissed them when they saw no litter.[12]

Social Consciousness

The work of conferring was not all fun and games, for the delegates to the national youth conferences also faced the difficulties of the world in their meetings. From early on, the conferences were designed to provide information and frank discussion of the problems in the world. In the first years of the biennial conferences, Leaguers were aware and concerned about growing tension as war threatened in Europe. Luther Leaguers in Rockford passed a resolution calling for peace: "We believe that war is a particular demonstration of the power of sin in the world and a defiance of the teachings of our Lord and Savior, Jesus Christ."[13] In registering a strong opinion against war, they also expressed their own complicity: "We recognize the failure of society to find a solution to this great social sin, and also recognize our share in this failure. We therefore plead for national, church and personal repentance for our indifference and apathy." The resolution went on to recognize also that even within their own conference there were differences of opinion about the "right course to follow," but their stance against war clearly identified the young people as committed to the kind of pacifist positions that had been advanced by theologian Edgar Carlson, who was then theology professor at Gustavus Adolphus College. In 1947, he assumed the presidency also of the Luther League, a position that was typically given to one of the pastors in the church.

Edgar Carlson provided strong leadership, along with E. E. Ryden, the editor of the *Lutheran Companion*, for Midwestern Lutherans who were against war. These representatives joined similar efforts for Eastern Lutherans by the United Lutheran Church pastor the Rev. Alton Motter who convened a group of pastors supporting a Lutheran pacificist position in Gettysburg, Pennsylvania.[14] Pacifism espoused by the synod's younger theological leadership demonstrated an increasing openness to engaging the church in critical social reflection. While pastors were debating this issue on the pages of the *Lutheran Companion*, and in longer articles in the *Augustana Quarterly*, Luther League gatherings became venues where these leaders brought this message to the youth. The strong pastoral leadership for youth work provided a time for youth to engage in Bible study and also, through conferences, to confer together about the social questions that faced the church, especially war.

The late 1930s and early 1940s were a brief window of opportunity for anti-war views. In the October 10, 1940 issue of the *Lutheran Companion*, Eric Wahlstrom, professor of New Testament at Augustana Seminary, wrote a column outlining a Lutheran theological position on pacifism: "Law, Gospel, and Peace." He argued, "The Christian recognizes that war is sin, just as much as he recognizes other sins in himself and in the social order. . . . The Christian soldier knows that war is due to sin, and is sin, but he also knows that in upholding the authority of government and law he is doing the will of God." Wahlstrom resolved this terrible conflict of principles by invoking the "forgiving grace that covers all of life." Then he drove home the point that would push against the quietism of the older piety: "But to stop at that point would be to use grace for an excuse to sin. The Christian must fight sin, the sin of war as well as sin in himself and in the community."[15]

The focus on pacifism in the fall of 1940 coincided with the enforcement of a new military conscription law requiring all men between the ages of twenty-one and thirty-five to register with the government. Editor E. E. Ryden also supplied information on conscientious objection, informing readers that the new law opened the status of conscientious objection to individuals who on their own were opposed to war in any form, even if their church body had not taken an official position against war. The older Selective Service Act of 1917 reserved this status only for members of religious bodies with an official pacifist position in their confessional statements. The *Lutheran Companion* wanted its young men to know that Lutherans could be conscientious objectors even if their church had not taken a principled position against "war in any form." It was not long before the United States was drawn into war again, and statements supporting pacifism like the resolution at the Youth Conference in Rockford, Illinois, would disappear also from the pages of the *Lutheran Companion*.

The wide framework that young people adopted in wrestling with the question of war and peace gave these young people strong convictions about how their faith should be lived out in service. Loyalty, commitment, service, and consecrated living became watchwords for the youth program during and after World War II. Long before the protest culture of the 1960s radicalized the young people in churches, Luther League conferences were places where young people took the problems of the world seriously and believed that through the church they could respond to God's call to participate in world changing activities.

Youth on the "Front Burner"

In the middle of the 1940s the synod prepared to celebrate the founding of the first Swedish congregation in Iowa in 1848. Even though the synod had not been founded until 1860, the 1948 "centennial" celebration provided an opportunity for a reiteration of the story that had brought the synod into being. A churchwide stewardship emphasis accompanied the centennial to help support ministries and respond to the enormous needs on the mission field and in Europe after the war. The celebration would involve all the various boards of the church, and the youth board was no exception. Even though youth work was considered the wave of the future, Bergstrand knew, as generation after generation of historically minded youth leaders had discovered, that the way to the future was paved by laying down the stones of history in a telling pattern.

By invoking the past and celebrating it, leaders knew they could deepen the commitment of members to the ongoing work of the church. The support that was sure to be generated would extend the influence of the church to a new generation of Lutherans and to new communities created in the postwar economic boom. Martin Carlson, later a stewardship leader, wrote the story of Augustana's youth program. One of the people consulted about the pioneer years understood how to "use" the occasion of the anniversary for promotional purposes. Immigrant pioneer pastors and the settlers had come to America as young people, so the synod was itself a youth movement. The cover of *Forward in Faith: A History of the Augustana Synod Luther League* fastened on the image of the Swedish pioneers as quintessential American pioneers. Roughly etched portraits of nine founders appeared to swirl like a great cloud of witnesses over a prairie schooner. The oxen and pioneers stood on the wide-open prairie, over the traditional Lutheran seal.

In the hands of the fundraising division of the church, Augustana's history threatened to become cliché, but Bergstrand and his staff aimed at something more. When Bergstrand communicated that youth ministry was for the church, not just for the youth, he expected that he would get a generous response. The flip side of the message was that the church needed to be "for the youth." The result was that youth programming was not seen as transient, focused only on a life stage or the work of an auxiliary or a movement with a fleeting lifespan. The catch phrase that captured this principle was that youth work was to be "on the front burner" of the church. That meant enough staff, enough funding, and public support from all levels of the church's leadership.

The Luther League retained its connections with the inter-Lutheran movement through several administrative adjustments and became an official part of the budget and structure of the synod, which in 1948, changed its name to The Augustana Lutheran Church, referred to by the new fashion of acronyms as TALC. The shift from the old nomenclature coincided with other Americanizing developments, including greater financial capacity.

With increasing support for youth work, more staff was added and youth programming became more professional. The leadership for youth work was in experienced hands. The investment paid off in better programming and exciting adventures. When the Lutheran World Federation and the World Council of Churches were getting off the ground, Bergstrand served on planning commissions for international, ecumenical youth work.

In the following decades, young American Lutherans joined international delegations to visit Lutherans in Eastern Europe, Scandinavia, and Germany. The international opening brought Bergstrand out of the upper Midwest. He recalled what it was like to take a delegation of youth with him to Lund, Sweden: "One beautiful summer evening I invited Hans Lilje to come down to the restaurant to meet with these young people. Dr. Lilje was describing the great air raid on Berlin by American planes one night when he was a prisoner of the Gestapo. Suddenly one of the youth, Otto Bremer, cried out, 'I was a tail gunner in one of those planes that night!' Dr. Lilje threw up his hands and said, 'I'm glad you missed me!'"[16] The opportunity made Bergstrand an early promoter of international ecumenical exchanges for youth. His report on the initial meeting of the Youth Department committee for the World Council of Churches, after it met in Oslo, Norway, in 1946 showed his communication skills, as he outlined a Lutheran basis for ecumenical work:

> There is a minimum ecumenism—a childish ecumenism—which calls all cats gray, even though we know well enough that they are not all gray—an ecumenism which would throw all our differences out of the window. But there is a maximum ecumenism—a child-like ecumenism—which recognizes the differences and permits the Spirit of God to make these tensions fruitful. It recognizes that God has given to every church a treasure—a vessel. Then we together dip into the oceans of the riches of the grace of God with the measure God has given to each of us.[17]

Bergstrand's intelligent and informed theological leadership for youth created a deep reservoir of trust among the pastors and lay people. The youth office continued to refine its work with training youth for leadership in their congregations, for the "work of Christ's Church on earth." Youth who had been selected for leadership training—an often-heard rule was "the best fruit is hand-picked"—were invited to leadership schools. In the instructional manual written for 1955–1956, the purpose of the program made it clear that leadership meant responsibility. Unlike the camps that were intended for the great mass of young people or the youth conferences that "knocked out the sidewalls and gave the youth the sense they were part of a big team," leadership schools "[gave] intensive leadership training to a small select group of young people. The courses . . . accentuate[d] the practical, dealing specifically with League methods and thoughtful churchmanship." And the methods were entirely modern: "The entire school is conducted according to the latest findings of Group Dynamics—buzz groups, cell group Bible Study, socio-drama and role playing," and so on.[18] One innovative program that emerged out of leadership training gained a kind of legendary status.

"Caravaning" involved teams consisting usually of four select young people, who, after completing ten months of Bible study and personal reflection, gathered for an intensive seven to ten days of training. Then they visited congregations during the summer months to work with local Luther League leaders to strengthen their programs. By the middle of the 1950s, the full range of youth programming had been developed, from Bible camps, youth conferences, leadership schools, and caravaning, to international youth exchanges. All the programs strengthened in young people a commitment to the work of the church, locally, and at the national and international level. The young people who signed on for such a summer were serious about their commitment to the church.

Youth having a lively discussion at one of Augustana's summer youth conferences, sometime in the late 40s/early 50s.
Photo courtesy of Evangelical Lutheran Church in America Archives.

Sharon Anderson, Luther League president at Augustana Lutheran Church in Washington, D. C., wrote to friends she had made across the country. In a letter from her friend, Marcia, who was attending Gustavus Adolphus College, Sharon heard about her friend's idea to "donate" one of her summers to the church. Another friend in New Jersey, Ken, wrote for advice about leading a successful league: "I just want to thank you for your lovely Christmas card and I was wondering if you could send me some information on activities for a Luther League, for our League is in a disorganized state. P.S. Let's hope I become President."

Luther League president responsibilities brought Sharon to Chicago for a churchwide conference. She wrote to these new friends about her own character development, her loyalties, and her commitments. She also knew how to be grateful. On her way to attend a new kind of youth leadership experience at Work Camp, she penned a thank-you letter. "Pastor Woods guided me through confirmation and served as a source of strength for me in my days as Luther League President," she wrote. "I cannot begin to tell you what a guide and inspiration he has been. I am now looking forward with great anticipation for this new and wonderful experience as a serving Christian."[19]

Sharon's pastor, Wayne R. Woods, also brought a new reality to Sharon's congregation. He had been trained for ministry at the United Lutheran Church seminary in Gettysburg and not at Augustana Seminary. The years of Sharon's presidency were the years of Lutheran merger, and her gratitude for her pastor is evidence of the confidence that leaders, young and old, had for the future of ministry in the bigger Lutheran Church in America (LCA). Woods served on the Inter-religious Committee on Race Relations in Washington, D. C., and apparently he brought a social justice orientation to his advising of the youth. Sharon's League saw the Lutheran Film Associates movie, *Question 7*, about the struggles of the church in East Germany. Another film, *A Time for Burning*, produced by the Lutheran Film Associates, focused on race relations in Omaha, Nebraska. These difficult questions were very much a part of the work that Sharon's Luther League worried about in the 1960s.

Enthusiasm for the merger did not reach all quarters of the youth office at the headquarters in Minneapolis, however. As the planning meetings progressed, Wilton Bergstrand began to be concerned, especially with the basic question that he heard again and again from his cadre of local leaders: "Will there be strong youth work in the emerging L.C.A.?" He wrote to Martin Carlson, who unsurprisingly had become the director of stewardship and finance, to seek help in getting beyond the "blueprint" stage to actual budget planning, where crucial things were at stake. He was concerned that the United Lutheran Church in America (ULCA), with which Augustana was moving toward merger, needed to catch up to Augustana's standards. The ULCA had just started with four League leadership schools, but to serve the 6,000 congregations the new church would need 120, and provision for counselor training. He had compiled the statistics on the status of the Luther

League in the ULCA also and found that of 2,500 future LCA congregations that had not yet organized a league, 2,300 of them were ULCA. Next
he noted that the teenage population was exploding: "The new L.C.A. will
start out with over a half million youth, going on to a million youth by
1973."[20]

Bergstrand heard from members of the four merging bodies who had
commended him on youth work. It was a contribution that would enrich
the new church, but only if the level of support Augustana had given to
youth ministry could be maintained, if not increased. As the merger planning
went forward, Bergstrand grew more concerned. He wrote a five-page brief
called, "What's the Score re: The Youth Work in the L.C.A.?" sometime in
1961, and it contained a clear expression of frustration felt within the Board
of Youth Activities as their carefully built programs faced a kind of extinc-
tion through absorption in the merger. It did not seem that the leaders of the
new LCA were going to maintain a commitment to youth that would put
youth ministry on the front burner. The opening statement of Bergstrand's
brief makes clear what negotiators were up against. According to Bergstrand,
"To understand what has happened in the youth work of the LCA you
must keep this clearly in mind: Dr. Fry has had a dictatorial stranglehold on
every comma of the negotiations that must be experienced first hand to be
believed; and Dr. Fry has a notorious and long-standing blind spot when
it comes to youth work."[21] In the planning documents, the staff would go
down, youth leadership schools would be planned by youth in the Leagues
rather than by professional staff, "caravaning" would be cut back, and funding sources would be severely cut back. In effect, the new church would not
provide the leadership for youth work that Augustana's people had come to
expect.

Wilton Bergstrand had spent his entire adult career in youth ministries
and had clearly expended himself in a long, drawn-out struggle through
the merger process. The brief that was written to explain what was finally
worked out also contained a long paragraph of gratitude for Bergstrand's
selfless leadership:

> [We] find that the things he has told us have been prophetic. . . . Five
> years ago he predicted almost down to the last detail the way things have
> worked out. We have appreciated above all his honesty. . . . His public
> and his private utterances have been consistent . . . [and] few if any of
> us who would be willing to be expendable as he has been. Only a very
> deep concern that Augustana's operation not peter out but keep going
> strong through '62 could lead him to stay as long as he has. [O]ther
> creative youth assignments here and abroad have been repeatedly

seeking his services. . . . [H]e has known for a long time he was black-
balled by Fry for going to bat for the things that we as a Board and
Council have asked him to contend for. . . . [H]e made it clear that he
was not at all interested in being a candidate for the kind of restricted
desk job the Youth Directorship of the L.C.A. has shaped up to be.[22]

When Bergstrand retired from service in 1963 he had served for twenty-
five years. His skill in communicating with different factions, or sections,
of the constituency made his program effective in rural congregations in
Minnesota as well as urban neighborhood congregations in Washington,
D. C. The pastors in the church trusted his leadership, but the familiar network of the synod/church, did not carry over into the larger realm of the
new LCA, where the various factions of that church could afford to exist
separately. Bergstrand's successful role as a bridge between different factions
in the Augustana Church—his comfort with Bible Institute promoters and
with ecumenical leaders in his church—did not make him a trusted man
in the ULCA, where Augustana's Midwestern language of Bible piety was
foreign to church leaders.

When Bergstrand had reported in 1946 on the notion that each church
was an earthen vessel, one that could be used to scoop up the riches out of
the ocean or stream of Christ's revelation, he invoked a biblical image familiar to readers of the letters of the Apostle Paul. In the Bible studies that stood
at the center of training for young people, these images could be used, played
with, and expanded to touch on new realities because youth were immersed
in Bible study in their congregations, in their League work, and whenever
they went anywhere to a church event. Even though the leadership schools
used new pedagogical methods, the Bible study retained its pride of place.

Tensions between conservative and activist factions in the synod had
often been mitigated through a discovery of a shared piety, but now the
merger brought Lutheran churches together based on their public commitments, rather than on the basis of their interior, private sensibilities.
Augustana people had developed a familiar interior culture to go along with
their public commitments, and this inner spirituality depended on habitual,
regular reiteration for its survival. In the new LCA, structures and relationships could permit the same ministry to continue, but this would depend on
the initiative of leaders at the local level. The new executives, sitting as Bergstrand expected at a desk job, would not be able to instill the same spirit in
the program. So the retiring Board of Youth Activities knew they had ended
their work, but they also knew they had trained many, many people how to
be leaders for this new church.

chapter 17

AUGUSTANA'S ECUMENICAL VISION

THE SWEDISH IMMIGRANTS WHO FOUNDED THE AUGUSTANA SYNOD in the nineteenth century were people with a wide knowledge of the Christian world and an engagement with many sectors of religion, both in America as well as in other countries. Besides their contacts with the Church of Sweden and their fellow American Lutherans, Augustana leaders also reached out to other American Christians for support and encouragement, such as the early help given to the synod by the Congregational American Home Mission society. Wider ecumenical ties were of interest to Augustana's leaders but were not the most important issues for the young synod. Augustana's most pressing needs during its early years were immediate ones: building congregations and institutions, training pastors and leaders, and recruiting immigrant members. It seemed that there were never enough resources to fully accomplish these tasks, and they consumed nearly all of the synod's time and effort. But as the Augustana Synod grew and matured in the twentieth century, many of these earlier concerns became less pressing, and the synod began to enter into a series of ecumenical relationships with Lutherans, both American and European, as well as with other Protestant groups here and abroad. Augustana not only participated in many of these ecumenical relationships but also assumed a distinctive leadership within many of these processes and organizations.[1]

Throughout its history, the Augustana Synod struggled with two conflicting positions from which it dealt with religious groups outside of its own boundaries. As a Lutheran, confessional body, the synod believed that achieving theological agreement and uniformity with other churches was so important that it was willing, for example, to suffer the loss of the "free church" portion of the synod over the atonement controversy of the 1880s. Yet Augustana also strongly held to the idea that Christians ought to cooperate with each other to the fullest extent possible, and the synod was often in the forefront of such efforts, especially with fellow American Lutherans. Swedish scholar Hugo Söderström observed this as a defining characteristic of the synod during the nineteenth century:

> Throughout its history the Augustana Synod oscillated between confession and cooperation. Through adherence to the Lutheran confessions and cooperation and conflicts with other denominations the Augustana Synod found its individuality, the structure and polity that its leaders regarded as the most truly Lutheran and best suited to serve the Swedish immigrants in the New World.[2]

At times these two inclinations caused tension within the synod, as Augustana struggled to define the boundaries of both confessional identity and inter-Christian cooperation, wanting to avoid both artificially rigid confessionalism and promiscuous cooperation, but not always agreeing internally how to make this happen.

Contacts with Other Lutherans in America

The immigrant leaders of the Augustana Synod came to a new country with a bewildering array of religious groups and options and a completely new system of church organization and religious practice. The wild pluralism of the American system of voluntary religion was far different from that of Sweden, with its monolithic State Church and smaller dissenting groups. Although there was some initial assistance to Augustana from other American Protestant groups, by far the most important help was given to the synod by other American Lutherans, first the General Synod, and then the General Council.

The affiliation with the General Council in the nineteenth century was a source both of support and tension for the Augustana Synod. The General Council provided Augustana with not only support and a congenial theological partner, it also gave the synod an entry into the larger world of American Lutheranism. Augustana participated in a number of General Council activities, especially home and foreign missions. Yet the affiliation was not without serious difficulties. Structurally, the General Council consisted of a number of smaller, regional synods that tended not to overlap geographically, while Augustana was a large, national ethnic denomination. Most of the meetings of the General Council were held first in German and then in English, and that limited participation and interest on the part of Augustana. Most importantly, in areas such as education and home missions, the General Council became a perceived direct threat to Augustana's own growth and institutions. When the General Council merged together with the General Synod and the United Synod of the South in 1918 to form the United Lutheran Church in America (ULCA), Augustana declined to enter into this merger.

Augustana and Other Swedish Ethnic Denominations

Augustana was not the only Swedish-American denomination at work within the immigrant community, and its relationships with these other religious groups were often filled with conflict.[3] A significant portion of the Mission Covenant (1885) and the Evangelical Free (1884) churches had roots in Augustana, and the theological rifts that resulted in the formation of these denominations were very damaging to the synod; friends, families, congregations, and whole communities were split over theological and ecclesiastical issues. Augustana mourned the loss of these individuals and congregations, but it became an opportunity for the synod to come to a clearer theological and organizational identity. Swedish-American Baptists and Methodists were also early competitors with the synod, and Augustana pastors quite regularly debated with their leaders, both in person and in print. A number of other small religious groups active in the Swedish-American community included Mormons, Pentecostalists, Seventh-Day Adventists, and Episcopalians. Though these churches numerically did not pose a danger to the synod, Augustana leaders felt that it was necessary to counter their perceived threats to its theological legitimacy. Augustana saw itself as *the* church for Swedish Americans, and it guarded its territory jealously. However, as immigration waned in the twentieth century and as Augustana began to mature institutionally, ties between the synod and other Swedish-American denominations did improve somewhat.[4]

Augustana and the Episcopalians

One church group—the Swedish-American Episcopalians—represented a larger on-going ecumenical conflict for the Augustana Synod, due to their relationship with the Protestant Episcopal Church. The Episcopal Church, like many other American Protestant denominations, sought to reach out to any number of different immigrant religious groups in their midst, both to assist them, and at times, to recruit from among them in order to bolster their waning share of the American religious sector.[5] The synod often viewed the Episcopal Church, and especially its mission to Swedish Americans, as an intrusive form of proselytizing. The Episcopalians insisted that their only concern was with unchurched Swedish Americans, though reports from Augustana pastors in the field suggested that some Swedish-American Episcopal priests were trying to persuade Augustana members and congregations to join the Episcopal Church by questioning the very legitimacy of the Augustana Synod and its status as the true successor to the Church of Sweden in America, especially calling attention to the fact that the synod had no episcopal structure and was therefore not a "true" church. Writing to an official of the Episcopal Church in 1921, Augustana president Brandelle inquired: "[W]hy do the agents of the Episcopal Church put forth every effort to make our congregations their mission field with this as the burden of their preaching: 'The Augustana Church is not a Lutheran Church, it is only a sect. We alone are the true Lutherans.' If this is not proselytism, what is it?"[6]

Though the Swedish-American Episcopal congregations struggled for existence and never reached a level of numerical significance, the rhetoric of their immigrant leaders was a source of much concern to the synod. Augustana leaders responded forcefully to this rhetoric and strongly opposed Episcopal overtures both to the synod itself, as well as to the Church of Sweden. Regular contact would be initiated by the Episcopal Church toward the Augustana Synod, but synodical leaders responded to these overtures with coolness and caution, often chiding Episcopal leaders for the more intemperate rhetoric and actions of their Swedish-American Episcopalian priests.

During the first part of the twentieth century, however, Augustana began a continuing series of ecumenical contacts with the Protestant Episcopal Church in the United States, although these contacts were sometimes less than cordial.[7] Given the difficult past history between the churches, it was somewhat surprising that the Augustana Synod, through its Commission on Comity, accepted an Episcopal invitation to ecumenical discussions in 1935; it seems that Augustana leaders were the only American Lutheran group to accept this overture. Although the two groups agreed on many doctrinal issues, the 1935 discussions broke down over the question of the historic episcopacy, and its role in church life and cooperation.[8] The Episcopal delegates insisted that this Episcopal structure must be the basis of closer work and cooperation and suggested that Augustana could receive the "gift" of the historic episcopate either from them or from the Church of Sweden. The Augustana participants held that though they were free to adopt the episcopate if they found it to be helpful, a demand that such a structure be adopted before closer communion could be established was completely unacceptable to them. President Brandelle told the Episcopal negotiators, "I am perfectly willing for those to have the Historic Episcopate that have it and want it, but . . . I am certain that the Lord never ordained it. . . .[I]f you are going to insist on this . . . the Augustana Synod would never, never, never go with anyone on that point."[9]

Although there were scattered voices throughout the history of the synod that called for the implementation of the episcopate, this was never really a serious movement within Augustana, and it seemed that the majority of the synod felt no need for it. The synod was absolutely consistent in its belief, expressed in 1935 by Brandelle and others, that the adoption of the episcopate as a precondition to intercommunion and recognition of ministries was absolutely unacceptable.

Augustana and International Lutheran Cooperation in the Twentieth Century

While American Lutheran groups were struggling to find paths toward new forms of cooperation and unity amid their ethnic and theological diversities, there were larger currents of ecumenical movement among Christians in the United States and in the world, currents into which the Augustana Synod would move during the first half of the twentieth century.

At the end of World War I, Lutherans in Europe and North America began to cooperate more closely in areas such as war relief and world missions, and these efforts led to calls for a greater degree of Lutheran organization to meet these needs and to bring together Lutherans from around the world. The first conference was held in Eisenach, Germany, in 1923, and that conference led to the formation of the Lutheran World Convention. Augustana sent President Brandelle and two other delegates to this meeting, which resulted in not only the formation of an organization but the development of a common statement on faith and practice that would lay the groundwork for further efforts. Augustana also sent delegates to a second meeting at Copenhagen in 1929, and to a third meeting in Paris in 1935. The outbreak of war in Europe led to the cancellation of a scheduled fourth meeting in 1940, and plans for augmenting and strengthening the institutional structure of world Lutheranism were abandoned for a time. But the ties that had formed between American Lutheran groups and Lutherans in Europe remained strong and were the basis of much informal work undertaken before and during World War II. The pages of *Augustana* and the *Lutheran Companion* were filled with accounts of this activity, keeping Augustana members informed about Lutheran work around the world.

World War II led to tremendous upheaval and destruction, and as with the previous war, American Lutherans were called upon to mobilize for military chaplaincy and service to the troops, for participation in the war efforts, to care for "orphaned" missions, and to aid in postwar relief and the reconstruction of Europe. The National Lutheran Council initiated a fund-raising campaign in 1941, called "Lutheran World Action," that eventually raised more than 250 million dollars over twenty years. After the war, teams were sent to Europe to aid with relief effort, refugee resettlement, and the rebuilding of the devastated churches of Europe. More than 90,000 refugees and displaced persons were settled in North America alone, many of them sponsored by local congregations.

After World War II, Lutherans around the world gathered to resume the cooperative work begun in the inter-war years, and in 1947, in Lund, Sweden, the Lutheran World Federation (LWF) was formed. The Augustana Synod was represented at this formational meeting by its president, P. O. Bersell, five other delegates, and numerous visitors. The LWF took over the efforts of the Lutheran World Convention and began by coordinating much of the postwar relief work in Europe and expanding and directing mission efforts and other cooperative work. To accomplish these goals, LWF decided it needed a larger and permanent presence, so an LWF office was established in Geneva, Switzerland. At the 1952 meeting in Hanover, Germany, the federation elected an Augustana leader, Carl E. Lund-Quist, as the executive secretary of the federation; he was re-elected to this position in 1957 in Minneapolis and served the LWF with distinction until he was disabled by a stroke in the late 1950s. Lund-Quist gave exemplary service to the LWF, but he was not the only Augustana leader to do so; a number of Augustana leaders served in important positions within the LWF throughout the 1950s and 1960s.

Ecumenical Partnerships with Other Christians at Home and Abroad

While working for greater cooperation and fellowship with fellow Lutherans in the United States and around the world, Augustana was also strongly involved in efforts here and abroad to bring together all Christian groups for fellowship and cooperation, efforts that eventually resulted in the formation of the National Council of Churches in the United States and the World Council of Churches. Augustana led most of the other American Lutheran denominations in their commitment to these ecumenical organizations.

In 1908, when the Federal Council of Churches (FCC) had been formed, the only American Lutherans to participate were from General Synod; this informal cooperation lasted only until the formation of the ULCA in 1918. Augustana, like the other Lutheran groups, was not happy about what they saw as a loose and undefined theological character of the organization, and did not join the FCC, though it did cooperate in a number of its efforts, especially those involving social ministry and relief programs. There was a distrust of these efforts among those in the conservative wing of the synod; typical was the voice of Professor Adolf Hult, who wrote to President Bersell in 1938: "Will the Protestant Unionists . . . again take up the battle at Synod? . . . . As we Protestantize we *de-Lutheranize* in progressive ratio. That is historically provable."[10]

The Federal Council was hardly the only ecumenical group at work in the United States, and the Augustana Synod was a member of such cooperative groups as the Foreign Missions and Home Missions Conferences and the International Council of Religious Education. In 1945, Augustana voted to explore a more formal relation to the FCC, but this was delayed by the fact that other Lutheran partners in the National Lutheran Council had reservations about the move and by the fact that the FCC was already planning its own reorganization and expansion. When the Federal Council and twelve interdenominational agencies formed the National Council of Churches (NCC) in 1950, Augustana was one of twenty-nine charter member denominations and the first Lutheran group to join the NCC. The synod ratified this participation at it convention in June, 1950, in Washington D.C., resolving that it was "desirous of continuing relationships which our church has already enjoyed in agencies now merging into the new Council, the Augustana Lutheran Church join this Council."[11] This was a momentous step for both Augustana and the rest of American Lutheranism, and soon the ULCA and some other American Lutheran groups would also join the NCC.

In a pattern similar to that of the ecumenical situation in the United States, World Christianity was also coming into more formal ecumenical relationships during the twentieth century. An ecumenical world Conference on Life and Work was convened in Stockholm, Sweden, in 1925, led by the energetic and controversial Archbishop of Sweden, Nathan Söderblom; Augustana president Brandelle was invited to the meeting as a personal guest of the Archbishop. In 1924, Brandelle had written to ULCA President F. H. Knubel, stating, "I am inclined to believe that were an invitation extended to the Synod on the part of the Archbishop to take part in this conference, the opposition to an acceptance of this invitation would not be great."[12]

Brandelle delivered one of the major speeches at the conference, and reaction to the meeting was generally positive. The *Lutheran Companion* editor C. J. Bengston wrote:

> What interests Evangelical Christians most to-day, however is a universal agreement on what is termed "life and work". . . . [W]hy can we not as living Christians still work together for the outlawry of war and for the prevention of those things that bring human misery and woe, and for the hastening of Christ's kingdom of peace?[13]

Although this was a notable breakthrough for Augustana (fifteen years earlier President Norelius had curtly dismissed a similar invitation), there were still those among the synod who were uneasy about this conference and the larger ecumenical implications. Professor S. J. Sebelius argued, "Personal salvation is the one thing every human being needs, and it is the blessing the Gospel has to give—It were a tragedy for the Church to neglect its chief business for something which is altogether secondary. . . . Where do we as a Synod stand in this matter?"[14] Though there seemed to be no major opposition to this invitation (perhaps because it came from the Swedish archbishop), there was little further ecumenical participation on the part of the synod in the next decade, nor was there much reflection on the nature of the synod's ecumenical position.

A second "Conference on Life and Work," along with a conference on "Faith and Order," met in Edinburgh, Scotland, in 1937. Augustana was represented at both meetings by a delegation headed by Conrad Bergendoff and several other Augustana leaders. The synod did not act directly on the invitation to these conferences, but empowered the executive committee to send delegates. In their report back to the synod, the delegates recounted: "Both at Oxford and at Edinburgh it was felt that there was something inconsistent about a variety of ecumenical movements when the very principle of ecumenicity is oneness. . . . [T]he original divergent programs of the two movements have tended more and more to coalesce."[15]

But there were those in Augustana who felt that the synod might be moving faster in these areas than was comfortable for their other Lutheran colleagues. In early 1942, President Bersell expressed his concerns to Conrad Bergendoff about moving too quickly:

> Personally, I am in favor of greater latitude and I believe that the Lutheran church must to some extent change its tactics so as not to be accused of Pharisaical isolationism. But for that very reason I believe that the best strategy is to move cautiously so as not to cause a break within our own ranks.[16]

Plans were developed to bring these two ecumenical movements, as well as other affiliated groups, into a proposed World Council of Churches, and the synodical convention in 1940 approved Augustana's participation in these discussions. World War II disrupted these plans, however, and it was not until 1948 that the World Council of Churches was formed at a meeting in Amsterdam, the Netherlands.

Augustana was an important leader in this process, both by urging other American Lutheran groups to participate in the discussions, and by leading the group in signaling its willingness to join the organization, assuming confessional and structural issues could be satisfactorily solved.[17] Augustana was not interested in joining ecumenical organizations simply for the sake of joining, and would at times take strong positions on theological and structural issues. But the synod and its leaders were willing to join with other Christians for cooperative work at almost any time, assuming that the work and the organizations had theological and ecumenical integrity. A series of articles in the *Lutheran Companion* throughout the summer of 1948 gave synodical readers a detailed description of the foundational events of the new group. In one article, however, President Bersell (a delegate to the proceedings) gave a decidedly mixed reaction to the proceedings. After listing the difficulties and achievements of the formational meeting, he wrote:"The World Council of Churches is now a fact but nevertheless the ecumenical movement is still in a state of flux. The next decade will be quite determinative as to its development and functioning."[18]

Augustana College president Conrad Bergendoff and Swedish Archbishop Erling Eidem at an ecumenical gathering. Photo courtesy of Special Collections, Tredway Library, Augustana College.

This next decade was, however, to be a busy one for the synod, with the formation of both the National and World Council of Churches and the various movements toward Lutheran unity in the United States. Augustana would continue to participate in the WCC by sending delegates and reporting the proceedings to its members, but it did not always have the ability to go farther than this.

Ecumenical relations had given Augustana a window to the wider Christian world and a group of Protestant Christian partners with whom it could carry out its ministry on a wider and more effective scale. Of all the Midwestern ethnic Lutheran denominations formed in the nineteenth century (German and Scandinavian), Augustana was clearly the most adventurous in terms of its participation in formal and informal ecumenical ventures, and it led the way for the rest. Many in Augustana were quite proud of their synodical participation in the ecumenical movement, and this became a distinctive part of the synod's identity. At times, the attempt to be both confessionally Lutheran and involved in ecumenism was not easy, and the Augustana Synod did not enter into some areas of the movement because of its own theological preconditions. Yet the leaders of the synod tried to balance the confessional and ecumenical impulses, so as to keep both poles of the synod's identity in harmony. "[T]he Synod ventured forth in the second half of its existence," reflected Conrad Bergendoff, "and learned how to cooperate with other churches, both Lutheran and non-Lutheran."[19]

chapter 18

THE SOCIAL PURPOSE
OF THEOLOGY

IN 1948, THE AUGUSTANA SYNOD MARKED THE CENTENNIAL ANNIVERSARY of the establishment of its first congregation, and in 1960, it celebrated the synod's own centennial. The little more than a decade in between those celebrations marked a particularly robust period when Augustana's church leaders realized that they would play a unique role in the effort to bring Lutherans at home and abroad closer together. P. O. Bersell's presidency brought him out of Minnesota and onto a world stage, while Augustana leaders at the seminary, particularly Conrad Bergendoff, pushed for stronger relationships with other, like-minded ecumenical Lutherans in America.

These theological leaders were joined by pragmatic churchmen who committed themselves to ecumenical efforts for practical reasons. Augustana's official leaders came into office with pastoral and political sensitivity rather than theological creativity or sophistication. Seeking to demonstrate for the constituency of the church that they were men of decisive action and skilled in negotiating a way around conflict, Augustana's presidents of the mid-twentieth century came to see an ecumenical Lutheranism in America as a positive good that would advance the church in the world. They tried to foster a church culture that kept theological and academic discussion at the seminary and not on the floor of synod meetings where it might obstruct decision making. They guided a church from its quietist backwaters to join the mainstream. There was urgency, both theological and practical, in rescuing Lutheranism from the crisis of culture and religion that had enveloped the church in Nazi Germany.

Augustana's Cooperative Profile

Americans had developed a language of shared but distinct responsibility through their work with the National Lutheran Council, created in 1918 to coordinate military chaplaincy and to attend to the urgent needs of Lutherans in Europe during World War I. After the war the partnership expanded to facilitate relations among Lutheran churches that were growing into each other in cities, towns, and rural areas, especially in the Midwest and Northwest. The National Lutheran Council provided the venue for church leaders to find ways to work together despite theological differences. National Council meetings became laboratories in church diplomacy where spokesmen slowly came to recognize how to both represent a constituency and define objectives on which they could work together.

For Lutheran leaders, the middle part of the twentieth century represented a transition not only in language but also in the activities and programs of the church. Lutheran unity movements were premised on an American future, and Lutherans were challenged to update their programs, youth activities, and worship to be fresh, relevant, and modern to meet the needs of the ever-growing youth population. Often self-conscious of their immigrant backgrounds, the Lutheran churches of the mid-twentieth century were eager to shed what might not seem to fit within the modern American culture. Meanwhile, theologians and church executives assumed the task of articulating how their church, in spite of these new modern appearances, continued to uphold the confessional traditions of Lutheranism.[1] The Lutheran Confessions did not give much guidance here, however. The American context presented challenges that the confessions did not address, chief among these being modern biblical criticism, lodge membership, and scientific advances that challenged traditional conceptions of the world.

Two very distinct approaches to Lutheran cooperation emerged, with one side extending the hand of fellowship to all who subscribed to the Lutheran Confessions, and the other taking a cautious, biblicist route, harboring a hope that the Lutheran Church–Missouri Synod might somehow participate. The American Lutheran Conference, organized in 1930, hoped to find a middle path.[2] Members of the conference pursued unity through agreement on theses drafted and presented to the churches for their adoption. These theses insisted on biblical inerrancy, they prohibited lodge membership, and stated plainly that ecumenical involvement should wait for full theological agreement. Augustana participated in the American Lutheran Conference, but also maintained relationships with the more open and ecumenical United Lutheran Church in America. Augustana's stance in the middle made the synod suspect to more conservative Midwesterners, and created tension within the ranks of Augustana's own people too. Through their experience in both of these circles, Augustana leaders slowly moved into the more open and ecumenical posture of the ULCA that basically advanced the view that Lutherans could already enjoy fellowship with each other on the basis of their acceptance of the historic confessions and not through the adoption of new standards. The basic question on biblical inerrancy had become a sticking point for conservatives, however, and they resisted ecumenism because of it.[3]

Augustana's mediating position between conservative and ecumenical Lutheranism could be described as a compromise, or it could be attributed to patience or wisdom or the absence of dominating leadership. However it may have started, the resulting, strongly ecumenical stance derived from a process of ongoing discernment among many leaders. It is clear that more liberal and moderate voices at the seminary influenced the process toward an ecumenical future for Augustana. Getting there, however, was not always such a smooth process. Augustana had vocal conservatives who complained about the influential liberalism at the seminary. Efforts to push in a more conservative direction would surface as a factor in elections, and would sometimes erupt publicly.

The Seminary as a Proving Ground

One example of the balancing act preceded the election of a new professor of theology at the seminary in the late 1930s and again in the mid-1940s. President P. O. Bersell had been elected synod president because of his organizational ability and also because conservatives hoped he would clean up theological vagueness at the seminary. Correspondence in Bersell's papers indicate that he heard from those who hoped for a new decisive (and conservative) Lutheran spirit at the seminary. They felt that the school lacked a certain something, but exactly what was not explicitly stated. This vagueness was also a signal of the modern age: Bersell was a full-time executive, self-conscious that his letters would be part of a record, and they reveal less than full candor. Conservative Adolf Hult, for instance, commended Bersell for leaving Rock Island after he was elected and moving to Minneapolis, where he was free from Rock Island's entangling vines.

Living in Minneapolis, however, placed Bersell in the midst of other entanglements, especially surrounding the Lutheran Bible Institute, where Samuel Miller was a bulwark against liberalism. Miller's success in drawing theological students to LBI created a constituency familiar with his verbal inspiration theory, who, when going on to the seminary became confused by a different approach to scripture. The scholar Hjalmar Johnson, after almost two decades of teaching first at Gustavus Adolphus and later at Augustana College, joined the faculty at the seminary in 1944 as professor of the history and philosophy of religion. Johnson was on record in an article in the *Journal of the American Lutheran Conference* that questioned directly the "verbal inspiration" theory taught by Miller at LBI.[4] To conservatives, Johnson's appointment signaled that an "ingredient" in the faculty seemed to be missing,

In 1945, those who had long hoped for a renewed spiritual emphasis at the seminary advanced Miller's name to the board of directors as the right choice to fill another faculty position. A senior member of the faculty was nearing retirement, and supporters of Miller hoped that he could join the faculty. The possibility of having the leading conservative critic of the faculty as a colleague was a bit alarming to the others, but to their credit they kept pretty quiet in public. Bersell, however, got mail from Conrad Bergendoff, who attempted to explain why Miller would not be a successful faculty member at the seminary. Miller's academic record was not in line with standards set when Conrad Bergendoff was selected as seminary dean, but powerful voices pressed the board to nominate Miller anyway. These efforts mostly consisted of lobbying efforts directed at Bersell, who endured long personal meetings that convinced him Miller would not attack other faculty members.

Faculty opposed Miller because they believed his use of scripture was flawed. Ethics professor A. D. Mattson claimed he would leave if conservatives succeeded in getting Miller to Rock Island. He wrote to Bersell that the real push at the seminary should be to reclaim the dynamism of Luther: "There is vitality there. Everything else is subordinate. We cannot reclaim the genius of Lutheranism by any emphasis upon verbal inspiration, by any emotional ebullitions, or by reading History in advance out of the Scripture. The fathers of our Synod had it even when their scholarship was not very great."[5] In arguing over Miller, conservatives and progressives alike emphasized that somehow a vital and unified Lutheranism was yet to be reclaimed, and was urgent.

Bersell attempted to assure that Miller's candidacy would not run into public opposition by asking for Bergendoff's opinion on the matter and also whether he cared about the relationship between the seminary and the church. Bergendoff's response was direct. He explained that he cared for the relationship between the seminary and the church and for high standards and cooperative relationships. "My reference to harmony and academic standards pertains to the specific problem raised by Miller's candidacy," wrote Bergendoff. "On the item of academic standards he is definitely lacking. . . . And on the matter of harmony . . . Miller's adherence to verbal inspiration is apt to divide the seminary."[6] Bergendoff indicated that his personal wishes were less important than the good of the synod and he was "willing to leave the matter to the Board which has jurisdiction, and will seek to do my duty as the Board decides. I know there is not unanimity, and in the nature of the case no hope of unanimity. That is why in my letter I deplored the fact that repercussions will be serious no matter what happens."

Miller did not get the job.

Bergendoff had warned Bersell that no matter what the decision, there would be serious repercussions, and indeed, within three years it would dramatically affect Bergendoff himself, as the college and seminary were separated in 1948. He was given a choice of presidency—either the seminary or the college—but not both. The idea to separate the two institutions certainly could get a lot of support from leaders at the colleges in Minnesota, Nebraska, New Jersey, and Kansas, but also from those who thought that the seminary could perhaps become more "spiritual" if it had its own separate, and maybe more church-controlled leadership. The teaching of theology at the synod's colleges and increasingly at the seminary stimulated a good number of students to push ahead with their studies and to interpret the Bible according to modern historical critical methods.[7] Graduates from colleges in the Augustana Synod and some seminary graduates were continuing their graduate work at Yale, Harvard, Chicago, and Union, participating in ecumenically stimulating graduate degree programs, and readying themselves for academic careers in universities and colleges beyond the more narrow orbit of the Augustana Synod.[8]

These signs of encroachment from the world outside the church alarmed conservatives who continued to push at Bersell to do something about the liberals. One of the more radical, but not very active members of Augustana's ministerium, was Vergilius Ferm, who had spent his scholarly career at the College of Wooster in Ohio. He did not teach at an Augustana school, having spent his time at a Presbyterian college as a teacher of philosophy. Ferm remained well known as a scholar and somewhat of a publicist, but with a longtime position in Ohio, he was literally off the radar screen until he requested permission from President Bersell in the fall of 1946 to serve an Augustana parish during an upcoming sabbatical year. Bersell knew many Augustana pastors who suspected Ferm's orthodoxy, so he wrote back and asked Ferm point blank if he still held to Augustana's Constitution, article II, which read:

> As a Christian body in general, and as an Evangelical Lutheran body in Particular, the Synod accepts and acknowledges the Holy Scriptures as the revealed Word of God as the only infallible rule and standard of faith and practice, and accepts and confesses not only the three oldest Symbols [the Apostolic, the Nicene, and the Athanasian] but also the unaltered Augsburg Confession as a brief but true exposition of the fundamental doctrines of Christianity, said Confession being understood

in accordance with the further development of these doctrines as contained in the other symbolical books of the Lutheran Church.

Ferm wrote back and said "of course he did." Then he added, "I am
amazed at the breadth of this doctrinal statement which permits wide range
of theological thought within the framework of the fundamental doctrines
of historic Christianity. . . . I note too that the doctrinal article of the synod
permits one to study the Scriptures with an open mind."[9]

Indeed, the function of the constitutional statements that American
Lutherans used to outline their confessional stance did permit wiggle room.
This helped the church avoid endless debating and allowed it to get on to
the task of doing things together. Bersell acknowledged that Ferm's letter
gave him "great satisfaction and assurance." He wrote, "I appreciate what you
say about the breadth of the doctrinal statement of our Church which permits wide range of theological thought. . . . [I]n my opinion the Augustana
Synod is the most ecumenically minded of any of the general Lutheran bodies in America and I stand on that."[10]

Ferm's liberal views were accommodated, but Bersell had also solicited
opinions from the president of Wooster College, as to Ferm's orthodoxy.
Hearing that there was some vagueness there, Bersell wrote back to say that
he felt that theological openness was all right, as long as it was contained in
the seminary, or other academic realms. It just didn't belong in the congregation.

Ferm mentioned studying scripture with an open mind, and indeed,
on the seminary faculty there were some who flourished above the fray. A.
D. Mattson enjoyed the freedom of the church to advance progressive views
about the prophetic role of pastors and the church in the public realm. He
broke deliberately with quietist pietism to advance the view that the church
needed to understand the plight of the working man, speak for justice, and
use its influence to change society. Mattson retrieved the voice of the prophet
to critique theological seminary study that spent too little time on sociology.
He felt that by neglecting the social-ethical aspect of theology the student
wouldn't acquire the social attitudes necessary for the church to make a vital
impact on society.[11] Mattson advocated a change in consciousness, so that the
church would be imbued with a spirit, rather than a program. Rather than
writing the name of Christ into the constitution of the land, argued Mattson, "we are concerned that the church might serve as a leaven for human
thought and action to the end that the spirit of the Christian faith might
permeate the social order and its programs."[12]

Those then who wanted a new spirit at the seminary were using the
same language about vitality and dynamic work, even though they were not

really advancing the same agenda. But neither did they want to fight it out. They instead hoped that a vital spirit and a resulting social action would flow out of a church as long as it was not debilitated or embroiled in theological polemics.

While the debate and the skirmishes at the seminary literally drained the energies of church executives, dramatic battles were being won overseas, creating an entirely new set of challenges for American Lutherans. The end of World War II made the internal politics of the Augustana Church quite parochial, indeed, for the needs of the devastated people in Germany and in Asia and Africa became immediately evident. Conservatives who wanted to build a fortress for piety were not needed for this task. The ecumenical and more scholarly orientation of Augustana's academically trained leaders now appeared to be quite an asset.

In 1951, President Bersell wrote to the Rev. Karl Mattson, brother of seminary ethics professor, A. D. Mattson, for his advice on a sensitive issue. Admired for his pastoral instinct to compromise and avoid overt conflict, Karl Mattson understood the value of calm communication and was able to give clear advice to others who lacked his diplomatic talent. The matter facing Bersell involved Vergilius Ferm, who once again had been discovered by conservatives, and written about in what Bersell called "one of the fundamentalist magazines," where he was attacked for his heresies, and his ties to Augustana were prominently pointed out. Bersell sent Mattson a copy of the *Crozer Quarterly* from 1946, in which the offending passages noticed by fundamentalists had been published. Now Bersell wondered whether there should be a heresy trial. "In spite of the bad aroma which always accompanies such a procedure it might be well even for our ordained pastors [to be] checked on some of their utterances," wrote Bersell. "That would go a long way in the re-establishment of confidence in the orthodoxy of the Augustana Church, which is now challenged in some parts." Bersell must have been tired of defending Augustana's orthodoxy over and over again, and also tired of Vergilius Ferm, whom he dubbed a stormy petrel. "I have read it and re-read it and mulled over its contents and with my limited intellectual and theological capacity I cannot for the life of me reconcile the statements and the whole temper of this address with Ferm's letter to me just a few years ago," where he had asserted his commitment to Augustana's statement of faith.[13]

Mattson wrote back with calm caution, making six clear points. First "to bring up an article written in 1946 and revive it, when it is deader than a door nail, and of no interest except as an historical curiosity, seems to be of no avail." He noted that even those who are negative on the Augustana Church would fail to be impressed for they would wonder "where were we in the meantime?" Mattson also noted that there could be nasty consequences since

Ferm had wide contacts and a facile pen. His sharper point, however, contained a moral argument about leadership: "using one man as an example stings my conscience a bit. Again it seems that our responsibility as leaders in the Christian Church compels loyalty to the principle that as far as possible we judge each man as a man and though it may be necessary to use men as a means to an end, we should never consciously do so." Mattson did give Bersell a loophole to use: since Ferm had not been in a "living" relationship with the Ministerium for many years, some provision should be made in the constitution for "plugging this hole."[14]

Bersell's deliberations on the problem of bringing heresy charges based on one extracted statement in an article helped him agree with Mattson, and he let the matter be. The rules governing the ministerium and the membership in the synod would have to be more rigid than they were if he were to try to remove the liberal Ferm from membership in the Augustana Church. He held warm personal feelings for the man, even though he felt sorry for someone with such a "wobbly faith." Bersell and Mattson, however, shared distaste for dwelling on theological minutia leading nowhere. Their deliberations mirrored the lesson learned by the synod's treatment of Olsson, in 1889, when leaders realized that theological charges of heresy had led to painful regret.

So when Bersell and Mattson weighed the problem of Vergilius Ferm, they recognized that it was their responsibility as leaders also to protect freedom. Their deliberations about how to respond to the attacks of conservatives showed that they had learned some lessons about the value of restraint. Augustana became a bigger church, one with more room for theological study and critical insights, through these behind the scenes decisions by administrators. The organizational, administrative abilities of men like Bersell, who shared leadership decisions with others, kept theological innovation from disrupting their larger purpose. Mattson stated this very cogently to Bersell: "Our ultimate trust must still be in the God who judges, leads, guides, and directs His Church, and our weapons are good will, patience, and our faith in the power inherent in the Gospel. . . . It is infinitely better if our boys can leave the Seminary with an inner sense of the truth and power of Lutheranism than with a fearsome sense of external compulsion."[15] Heresy trials, declarations, statements, and reassurances would not be the lasting legacy of Augustana. Instead the church relied on inner strength and the dynamism of its many "boys" who would extend the truth and power of Lutheranism.

The American Accent

The formation of the Lutheran World Federation brought Lutherans from around the world together for the first time since the end of the war. Students from the Lutheran Student Association in the United States participated in this historic gathering in Lund, Sweden, and witnessed the restoration of ties between European churchmen and also the new role that American Lutherans now were playing on a world stage. A student who witnessed the arrival of German leaders—among them Bishops Hans Lilje and Otto Dibelius—at the train station in Lund, noted that they seemed uncertain about how they would be greeted.[16] The welcome they received from their hosts restored fellowship with Lutherans in Norway, Finland, Sweden, and Denmark. The Americans who attended noted in their letters home and also in their published remarks that a state of dependency on the part of Americans had passed away in the period after the war. Americans no longer acted the part of younger children in the Lutheran family, waiting for direction from European elders. Now the Americans joined as full partners in the work of theology for the church, expressing their own point of view.

For Augustana, news of the exciting proceedings came from P. O. Bersell, who sent his own impressions to readers of the *Lutheran Companion*. Of the opening session held in Lund's twelfth-century cathedral he wrote: "There were no less than 40 archbishops, bishops, presidents of churches, and those of equal rank present at the convention, not to mention an imposing array of other ecclesiastical dignitaries. The academic procession at the solemn service of worship in the 800 yr [sic] old magnificent cathedral on Friday evening was a brilliant spectacle."[17] The thrill of the moment did not overwhelm him for he noted also that "it was difficult to keep one's thoughts away from the sad background of starving, persecuted, dispersed millions of Lutherans in Europe." Reminders of the ongoing persecution came from bishops of Latvia and Estonia, who were still living as exiles.

In his account of the business of the assembly, Bersell revealed himself for the American that he truly was, noting, "The plenary sessions were more or less satisfactory," and then describing the various study sections the executive planning committee had designed. The theme of the assembly addressed the postwar crisis. "The Lutheran Church in the World Today," was to be addressed in three study documents. A Scandinavian committee was given the topic "Confessing the Truth in a Confused World." The American committee's topic revealed the activism that Americans were known for: "Performing Her Mission in a Devastated World." The German document recognized their unique status as having emerged from repression: "Facing the Problems in a Troubled World." If the titles were not revealing enough, Bersell went on to make his impatience clear: "After revisions by the sections these documents were again read and discussed in the plenary sessions. This made for much tiring repetition and waste of time in academic, dogmatic, and platitudinous discussions and left little time for discussion of practical problems and matters of policy and immediate action."[18] The study sections were places for extended theological discussion; this is what the theologians from Scandinavia and Germany came to do. But Americans were given the task of writing a document that focused on what the churches could do, and how they could best perform their task.

The German document read in the smaller study sections received such heavy criticism that it was replaced by a concise statement drafted by the American Frederick Nolde. Reporting on this surprising turn of events for the January 1948 *Augustana Quarterly* was Clifford A. Nelson, who had witnessed the event. Nelson, an Augustana pastor who served as the assistant to Sylvester Michelfelder and helped prepare the groundwork for the envisioned Federation, explained the replacement of the German document by stating that it did not resonate with those who needed a theological rationale for concerted action. Nelson hoped that "in the shuffle of getting papers together, the original study by the German men will not be thrown into the discard basket entirely. It contains a masterly description of the powers of materialism, secularism, and nihilism."[19]

P. O. Bersell was self-consciously American. He held a place of honor on the program, serving as master of ceremonies at the banquet, a task quite familiar for a president of Augustana, but again he seemed impatient with the necessary protocol, and his penchant for efficiency again came through:

> Four languages were used, English, Swedish, German and French. Greetings from three kings and many officials from various parts of the world were read by the dean of the cathedral. 42 eminent personages were introduced to take a bow and receive an accolade. 25 speeches were made by representatives from as many countries. It lasted until 11:30 pm, but we were not seated until 8:30, so at that the time element will compare favorably with typical American banquets. Incidentally, may it be mentioned that the shortest speech was made by President J. A. Aasgaard, who represented the US.

It was at the banquet that it finally dawned on Bersell that this event was more than a platform on which to present the latest form of American superiority; it was, indeed, a truly historic occasion:

> As the greetings from the various countries continued there was unfolded to us a panorama of church history: a modern drama of martyr testimony, of heroic resistance, of patient suffering, of Christian faith and unprecedented benevolence. Eyes were suffused with tears and hearts were thrilled as we sat face to face with the men who

will go down in church history as makers of history. One said the next day that it felt as it must have felt to the participants of the post-persecution Council of Nicea in the 4th century. All were gripped by the consciousness of the fact that this was a unique and epochal reunion of Lutherans, a union of hearts and a meeting of minds in a new consecration to the great mission of the Lutheran Church throughout the world.[20]

The emotional impact of this parade of witnesses seemed to push Bersell to a new, personal, ecumenical vision. He saw a union of hearts as well as a meeting of minds. Where theological "ponderosity" had failed, the personal testimony of speaker after speaker moved the assembly to renewed energy and purpose. For Augustana, a longstanding personal tie with the Church of Sweden was strengthened and placed on new footing. The assembly elected theologian bishop Anders Nygren as first president of the Lutheran World Federation and Swedish theology instantly became better known to Lutherans around the world.

Augustana's image and position among other American church bodies stood to gain from the popularity given to Swedish theology after the war. Augustana's theologians had long maintained an interest in Swedish theology and church life even when ideas from Swedish theologians rattled conservative Lutherans. A generation earlier, Söderblom's scholarship and his ecumenical enthusiasm had become flash points for conservatives who wanted nothing to do with theological work coming out of Europe. Augustana's leaders were then worried to protect their Lutheranism as biblical and soundly confessional. Now the ascendancy of Swedish theologians to the leadership of World Lutheranism made these anxious hearts subside.

While conservative Lutherans in America had spent the interwar decades positioning themselves on a spectrum of orthodoxy, Augustana's theological leaders had deepened ties with the Church of Sweden, and found themselves pulled in a more ecumenical direction. Other Augustana pastors trained during this period were influenced by Swedish theology to move beyond the propositional theology of the conservatives and become open to scientific study of Christian faith and scripture, and to efforts towards Christian unity. Conrad Bergendoff, as dean at the seminary and president of the college, had encouraged ties with the Swedish theological faculties. Filling a position at the seminary in systematic theology in 1938, he had influenced the choice for Carl Gustaf Carlfelt, who wrote a dissertation at Chicago on Swedish scientific study of the New Testament. Bergendoff had sent him to Sweden in 1938 for a year of preparation in Uppsala and in Lund. In his later teaching, writing, and lecturing around the synod, Carlfelt promoted the work of contemporary Swedish theologians Gustaf Aulén, Einar Billing, and Gustaf Nygren.[21]

Contact with the Church of Sweden had not been disrupted even during World War II, because Sweden remained a neutral country. In contrast, other ethnic Lutherans were more directly affected by the war and had not been able to maintain personal contacts that Augustana experienced; during the 1930s and 1940s, Norwegian, Danish, and German American Lutheran churches had weak ties with theological faculties in their respective home countries, as those countries were under occupation or at war. After the war, however, American Lutherans were ready for renewed contact with Europe. The message about Europe was cooperation, assistance, and rescue. European liberalism was not characterized as a threat.

Those who planned the work of the Lutheran World Federation recognized the unique contribution that the organizationally proficient Americans could bring to the work of reconciliation. The world stage of Lutheranism had expanded: it was no longer a simple one act struggle between "liberal" Europeans and naive Americans, but a drama of several churches coming out of isolation into active engagement with each other for concrete purposes in the world. The totalitarian threat demanded that German, Scandinavian, and American Lutherans work together to "Face the Problems, Confess the Truth, and Perform Her Mission," in a confused, troubled, and devastated world. Communism was now a bigger threat than liberalism.

Rediscovering Luther

The postwar period provided Lutherans in America with an opportunity to engage in significant theological reflection with theologians around the world, and Augustana's Swedishness made them more than a little receptive to the contributions of the Swedish theologians who had assumed such prominence. Lund theologian Anders Nygren took advantage of his opportunity as president of the Lutheran World Federation to provide a theological vision for the future of Lutheranism. His own work belonged to a theological movement called the Lundensian School, named after Lund University where he taught. The Lundensians—Anders Nygren, Gustaf Aulén, Ragnar Bring, Einar Billing, Yngve Brilioth, and Gustaf Wingren— were church-centered theologians. The Lundensian School reexamined Luther and the Reformation and articulated the distinctive theological insights of Lutherans as over against Reformed or Catholic views of salvation and the church. At the rival Uppsala University, Swedish biblical scholars were also gaining international reputations, particularly Anton Fridrichsen who lectured on primitive Christianity.[22] Swedish theologians and students were returning to the sources, participating in a widespread Luther Renaissance.

Theological students at the colleges and seminary of the Augustana Synod had long been familiar with the names of Swedish theologians, but after the war other American Lutherans were interested as well. Carl Rasmussen, professor at the Lutheran Theological Seminary in Gettysburg, was a member of the United Lutheran Church. In 1946, as the agent of the United Lutheran Publication House of Philadelphia, he toured Scandinavia to find books to translate for English readers. Danish, Swedish, and Norwegian theologians sent him their books, entertained him, and kept contact with him over the next decade. One of the first books to be published in English was Gustaf Aulén's basic text on Christian theology, *The Faith of the Christian Church*, translated by two Augustana professors, Eric Wahlstrom and G. Everett Arden. Aulén then helped Rasmussen find new writers excited to produce work that might find an English-speaking readership. Gustaf Wingren wrote to him from Åbo, in Finland, in the winter of 1947: "I am very glad to hear, that my book on Luther possibly can be read in English. If it should be so, then I know, that you are the man, I in the first place have to thank for this happy event"[23]

The new direction that Nygren and other Scandinavian theologians provided for members of the Lutheran World Federation was the challenge to research and articulate the meaning of Luther for the modern world. Luther's reemergence on the theological landscape after World War II was in stark relief to the co-opting of his image and name by the Nazis, and Nygren's initiative, "Forward to Luther," became an invitation to all Lutherans in every nation to renew their acquaintance and understanding of his theology.

Luther needed to be reintroduced, especially to American Lutherans, who had been largely indifferent to the Reformer before the twentieth century.[24] Interest in Luther created a means for cooperative theological work among all the branches of the Lutheran church, including the Missouri Synod. In conjunction with this worldwide initiative, Concordia Publishing House in St. Louis and Muhlenberg Press in Philadelphia cooperated in producing the American Edition of *Luther's Works*, in fifty-five volumes. Luther would no longer be known only in German, or only to those familiar with Medieval Latin, according to the general editor, Jaroslav Pelikan. The effort of scholars to get Luther to speak English wrenched him out of cloistered academic arenas and made his thought available to Lutherans from Africa, Asia, and America who needed to develop an indigenous understanding of the tradition.

Organizational Devotion

The task of creating the structure and articulating the vision of a new international Lutheranism would depend on financial and material investments that American Lutherans were uniquely able to provide. During the decade after the war, American Lutherans could not avoid or resist invitations to abandon their isolation. Whether asked to join other Lutherans in practical relief, aid, or mission, every American Lutheran church faced an ecumenical decision. Augustana's weekly newspaper brought news of the significant relief efforts that American Lutherans had undertaken to rebuild Europe and its churches. Lutheran efforts to help went beyond physical needs to recognize the communal and spiritual impoverishment of refugees, motivating a team of student volunteers from Lutheran colleges and seminaries to go to Europe to organize spiritual care for refugees in camps. All of these efforts involved a considerable amount of planning and negotiating with military supervisors and provisional governments. The credibility of the churches had also been damaged in Germany by association with the corrupt German Christian movement that virtually had replaced the Lutheran Confessions with loyalty oaths to Hitler. Americans had to be direct and clear in their language, pressing for access to pastors and people. A coordinated effort was imperative if any help was to get through. In reports back to the United States, the refugee work was carefully linked to the efforts among American Lutherans to rebuild congregations and churches that had also been damaged.

Americans impressed the Europeans with their organizational expertise, efficiency, and tireless industry; the American Lutheran leader best exemplifying this was ULCA president Franklin Clark Fry. Known for his parliamentary skill and mastery of the detail of constitutional procedure, he led the Americans in the work to overhaul the tattered remnants of the dormant Lutheran World Convention and invent the structure of the new federation. After his death in 1966, European Lutheran leaders reminisced about his long and dominant leadership, revealing their keen observations also of American style and verve. Bishop Bo Giertz thought that Fry's ability to shape resolutions and lead a meeting demonstrated to Europeans how organizations could get effective results. "Fry and his American friends had a capacity for work which often left us Europeans breathless. After long days of taxing negotiations, sub-committees often had to work into the late hours of the night. The next morning, Dr. Fry appeared seemingly rested and efficient." Americans also exuded a kind of friendliness and candor that seemed exhausting to the more circumspect bishop: "A European does not say half as many friendly words during a day as a normal American does."[25]

Bishop Hans Lilje, a German church leader, remembered Fry's genius in conducting a meeting. Lilje was a seasoned observer of the American prowess in constitutional maneuvering, and Fry was usually the victor when it came to a contest, except for one time, when Augustana's president showed that there was a depth to American expertise when it came to drafting resolutions and understanding how they would work. Dr. Bersell questioned Fry, who was chair of a meeting, as to his ruling on how a recently passed resolution should be interpreted. Lilje noted that "Bersell apparently acquiesced in the explanation. But on the next day Bersell raised a question over a similar point, referred to the resolution of the previous day, and asked the chairman to explain how the resolution could be reconciled with the former one. None of us had paid much attention to this inconsistency." Europeans did not attend so carefully to the minutia of constitutional language and procedure and also practiced a deference that Americans who came to these meetings did not observe. Lilje was startled to watch the persistence of Bersell, who zeroed in to challenge Fry. None of the other participants thought "to impale Dr. Fry on this incongruous statement. Dr. Bersell, himself a master of parliamentary procedure, did not shun this gentle, friendly clash." Fry, Lilje noted, was visibly shaken, since he so seldom had this happen to him.

Organizational competence emerges in these descriptions as a characteristic American contribution to the work of international Lutheranism, and this expertise was not limited only to constitutional discussions. Both Bishop Lilje and Bishop Giertz commented that the Americans knew how to turn language into action, to make ideas effective. The Americans who participated in this work were not so interested in refining ideas; they had encountered the devastation of the war and were filled with a sense of urgency. Augustana's representatives focused on what needed to be "done," rather than how to "think" about theology or the role of the churches in the aftermath of the war.

The ardor kindled when Lutherans around the world met and discovered their unity and began to realize the potential for Lutheran service around the world, did not stay bottled up in memories. The leaders who came to Lund and who were enlisted in the creative work of establishing world Lutheranism were just as active at home—meeting, organizing, shaping, and establishing networks of cooperative Lutheranism. The decades following the war were days to seek unity in America as well. Augustana entered this process with enthusiasm, looking forward to a future where all Lutherans would recognize each other as fully Lutheran.

chapter 19

THE ROAD TO LUTHERAN MERGER

Up until World War I (1914–1918), American Lutheranism was fragmented along many ethnic and confessional lines, but the beginning of this decade saw the first major period of institutional merger and realignment, changes that resulted in the formation of the Norwegian Lutheran Church in America (1917–1960), the United Lutheran Church in America (1918–1962), and the American Lutheran Church (1930–1960). The catalyst to these mergers came from earlier efforts at closer cooperation between Lutheran groups over such areas as home and foreign missions and the celebration of significant Lutheran anniversaries. Though the story of the changes during this decade would involve all these areas, the initial activity was the planning that led to the celebration in 1917 of the 400th anniversary of the Lutheran Reformation.

In 1909, the General Synod invited all American Lutheran groups to a meeting, the goal of which was a joint celebration of the Reformation anniversary. Though the leadership of this group, the Joint Committee on the Celebration of the Quadricentennial, came mostly from Lutheran groups in the eastern part of the country, it awakened in many Lutheran denominations, including Augustana, a desire to celebrate this significant milestone. For Augustana, and for the rest of American Lutheranism, this major celebration was not only a chance to exhibit some confessional pride but also an opportunity to work together as American Lutherans for a common goal. Though for a number of reasons the celebration of the anniversary fell far short of its goal, it began to pull many Lutherans together for a common purpose and actually did lead to some of the mergers mentioned above.

The actual celebration in 1917 was muted by two features: first, the fact that many Midwestern Lutheran groups, including the Augustana Synod, refused to participate officially in the work of the Joint Committee, and second, that American entry into World War I, in April 1917, made the celebration of any significant event in German history to be inexpedient at the least. Nevertheless, there were some significant celebrations of the Reformation in 1917, and in New York City, Augustana lay leaders and pastors played a significant role, mixing with New York Lutherans across denominational lines.

Augustana leaders also worked together with other American Lutheran groups to provide ministry and relief for American soldiers and sailors involved in the war. America was unprepared for war, so the mobilization of chaplaincy efforts needed to be rapid; in October 1917, the "National Lutheran Commission for Soldiers' and Sailors' Welfare" was formed. Augustana participated fully with most other American Lutherans in this effort, establishing Lutheran outreach to uniformed servicemen both in the United States and in Europe. Local Augustana laypeople worked with other Lutherans in the Lutheran Brotherhood to bring ministry and relief to local military camps around the nation, and Augustana members contributed funds to this work, which from all Lutherans totaled 1.5 million dollars by the end of 1918. Augustana historian G. Everett Arden commented: "What theological debate and doctrinal discussion failed to accomplish, catastrophe achieved, namely, galvanizing Lutherans in America into common action, and creating out of their divided ranks a common front."[1] The experience of cooperation in the National Lutheran Commission led directly to the formation of the National Lutheran Council in 1918.

Augustana and American Lutheran Efforts toward Greater Unity

At the beginning of the twentieth century there were a dozen major Lutheran denominations in the United States, along with many smaller groups; some of the major groups were themselves confederations of smaller synods without significant central organization. This new century would see three major waves of merger and consolidation leading to the eventual situation where 95 percent of American Lutherans belonged to one of two major denominations—the Evangelical Lutheran Church in America and the Lutheran Church–Missouri Synod. For much of the last fifty years of its independent existence, the Augustana Synod was deeply involved in the complex and often tortuous negotiations that led to this result, and at points, the synod played a key defining or mediating role in determining the course of these negotiations.

Augustana had been a member of the General Council since 1870, but it did not always have an easy relationship with the Council or the other synods that constituted this body. Many of the other synods were smaller, regional bodies that had been in existence since the colonial period, or were ethnically German synods from the Midwest. Augustana's real conflict with the General Council began, however, when the Council began to expand its English language home mission efforts into the upper Midwest during the 1880s and 1890s.[2] As English-speaking Lutherans from the East began to move west during the final decades of the nineteenth century, there was a strong need for English language congregations to serve them. Pastors George Trabert and A. J. D. Haupt organized congregations in the upper Midwest during the 1880s, and these pastors and congregations initially affiliated with the Augustana Synod. But this arrangement did not last, and in 1891 these English language congregations entered the General Council as the Synod of the Northwest. Augustana perceived this move, and others by the General Council, as a direct threat to its existence, and the synod began to distance itself somewhat from this organization.

The General Council was one of three denominations established by the descendants of Lutherans who had come to America during the colonial period, heirs of the traditions established by Henry M. Muhlenberg in the eighteenth century. At the beginning of the twentieth century the three groups were on a convergent course, and it seemed to most that they would merge together sometime early in the new century. This development posed a dilemma for the Augustana Synod: Would it follow the rest of the General Council into a larger merger, or would it refuse to enter the new organization and continue its independent existence? When serious merger negotiations began among the three Lutheran groups in 1917, this issue occasioned a lively discussion within Augustana. A spirited debate erupted in synodical publications and meetings, with sides drawn generally (though not exclusively) along generational and geographic lines. Supporters of Augustana's entering the new merger were often younger, English-speaking pastors and laypeople, or those of the synod outside its Midwestern center, especially in the East, who had long and positive experience with these eastern Lutherans. Generally opposed to entering the merger were many of the older, Swedish-speaking members of the synod, and those in the Midwest who resented the competition of the General Council. In 1914, the editor of the *Lutheran Companion*, C. J. Södergren, wrote, "The present writer has arrived at the conclusion that the Augustana Synod ought to sever its *present* relations with the General Council. And if for no other reason . . . that it proves to be in the interest of each and every phase of our present cause."[3] He cited especially his concern for Augustana's own home and foreign missions, which he believed would be strengthened by the split.

The debate also broke along theological lines, as the confessional orthodoxy of the more liberal General Synod was still suspect in some quarters of Augustana, while others in the synod appreciated the new ways in which eastern Lutherans were engaging theologically with the contemporary American situation. In the middle of the First World War, one Augustana pastor seemed to hint that theological modernism, which in his mind came from Germany, had "Prussianized" parts of American Lutheranism. "How will the 'theological attitude' react on the 'merger?'" he wrote. "How will it affect the political aims and ideals of our own nation? Is it not time that the Lutheran Church say something official on whether Social Darwinism shall be taught in its press or not? Which shall it be: Christ or Darwin?"[4]

Others believed that "Eastern Lutheranism" was of a different sort than that of the West (that is, Midwest): "[These are] two great *American* groups, representing two big types of American Lutheranism. . . . [N]either represent total American Lutheranism."[5] For this writer, merging into the new eastern church would be unnatural for Augustana, and a form of capitulation.

Those who thought that Augustana should enter into the merger negotiations stressed the long history of synodical engagement with these other Lutheran denominations and suggested that the merger was a way for Augustana to enter more widely into contemporary American life. They feared that if Augustana did not enter the new denomination, it would be isolated and regress into an ethnic and linguistic ghetto. One writer suggested, "[R]efusal to enter into the United Church would put us back historically, and further, there is strength in union, especially when this union has as its center Jesus Christ our Savior."[6]

Newly elected President Brandelle addressed the synodical convention in 1918, strongly urging Augustana to enter into this new denomination: "For a long time the need for greater Lutheran unity in our country has been apparent, and in our present circumstances it has become particularly imperative. . . . Those who are along from the beginning will be privileged to have a part in arranging the organization."[7]

But many others were hesitant to move into this new organization. While resentment of the General Council and not a small amount of ethnic pride were sometimes motivating factors, there were other substantive arguments against proceeding in the merger. A common argument was that the synod needed to maintain its own independence in order to continue its Swedish-speaking ministry to the older generation as well as to a new wave of immigrants who were expected into the country after World War I.

Others suggested that the merger was at the same time too drastic and too limited a development; too drastic in that it was a leap forward into an organic union when a more federative approach was better, and too limited, in that it did not involve many of the other Scandinavian and German Lutheran denominations in the Midwest. Resenting criticism of refusal to enter into the merger, Adolf Hult wrote: "[T]he witful independence and strength of principles in the rank and file of the Synod had its own ideals and realities in plain view when it voted for the 'federation' plan of uniting the whole Lutheran Church in America."[8] The merger would, it was suggested, pull Augustana away from its relationships with its natural Midwestern partners, and toward the Muhlenberg groups in the East. These were arguments that would continue to ring through the synod during the rest of its independent existence.

Though Brandelle and others represented a new generational wave of leadership in the synod, Augustana was, in 1918, not yet ready to join the new Lutheran denomination, the United Lutheran Church in America (ULCA). During the synodical convention of 1918, it was apparent that the synod was not ready to take this step toward merger, and so a compromise resolution was adopted by the convention, stating that while the synod was not willing to enter negotiations at the time, they were indeed in favor of a "confederation of Lutheran church bodies in North America."[9] The synod also voted to request that the General Council allow it to withdraw from that body, a request that was granted in November 1918.

At the same time as the ULCA was being formed in 1918, there were organized efforts underway to formalize and expand the cooperative efforts of American Lutherans that had begun during the First World War. The experience of the National Lutheran Commission on Soldier's and Sailor's Welfare had indicated to many Lutheran leaders that it was necessary to form some sort of permanent organization to coordinate many national efforts such as military chaplaincy, home and foreign missions, social service efforts, and to provide for publicity and literary enterprises. The new organization, the National Lutheran Council (NLC), formed in September 1918, represented most of the American Lutheran denominations outside of the Synodical Conference, which was dominated by the Missouri Synod. The Augustana Synod was closely involved in many of the projects of the NLC, including the question of "orphaned missions" and relief efforts in postwar Europe, but in general Augustana representatives to the NLC did not take strong leadership roles in this new group.

In its formation, the National Lutheran Council was not the kind of federative body envisioned by the Augustana convention resolution of 1918, but there were many in contemporary American Lutheranism who thought that the NLC could serve as a vehicle to such an organization. However, steps toward a closer federation of American Lutherans also brought to the surface deep divisions and tensions within American Lutheranism about how such a body should be formed and the theological basis that would underlie it. Within Augustana, some questioned the proposed scope and limits of the NLC: former editor of the *Lutheran Companion*, C. J. Söder-gren, wrote President Brandelle a sharp letter on the development of the new group, stating, "I wish to correct your impression that the National Lutheran Council makes a Federation of our church bodies in the Middle West superfluous. I know that this is the idea of the N.L.C., with which you have identified yourself from the start. But this is not at all the idea of the Augustana Synod."[10] Efforts toward closer cooperation within the National Lutheran Council were complicated by the insistence of representatives of the Norwegian Lutheran Church of America, backed by other conservative Midwestern Lutherans, that all theological and confessional questions must be settled before there was any effort at common work. During the 1920s the NLC was preoccupied with theological debates over these questions, and it divided into two different positions. The more conservative position, expressed by H. G. Stub of the Norwegian denomination, held to a strict confessional position and the need for absolute theological agreement before proceeding into closer relations (the Stub Theses). The more ecumenical position, articulated by Frederick Knubel and Charles Jacobs of the ULCA, sought an agreement on essential doctrines, but suggested that other elements need not be hammered out before closer cooperation would begin (the Knubel-Jacobs Theses).[11] Augustana representatives were not the primary leaders in this battle, and at times sought to act as a bridge between the two positions. Augustana did sympathize in some part with the concerns of the Norwegians and conservative Midwestern Lutherans and did have theological and ecclesiastical reservations about some elements within the ULCA. On the other hand, Augustana had a long history of cooperative relations with many constituent parts of the ULCA and a disinclination to the kind of theological approach of the Stub Theses.

The leaders of the conservative faction within the NLC decided it was necessary to form a confederation of their denominations, perhaps leading to a close union, and this led to the formation in 1930 of the American Lutheran Conference. In preparation for this organization, representatives met in 1925 and laid out a theological position, an expansion of the Stub Theses, named the Minneapolis Theses, which restated and strengthened a conservative confessional position on closer cooperation. Augustana was not directly involved in these initial discussions, but in 1929 it was invited to join the group working toward the formation of the Conference, and at its 1930 annual convention, the Augustana Synod approved this relationship, and by extension, the Minneapolis Theses.[12] At that convention, the synod voted that "we as a Synod join together with the American Lutheran Conference. . . . We also heartily endorse the proposed constitution and by-laws of the American Lutheran Conference."[13] The Augustana Synod became a constituent part of the new American Lutheran Conference, and over the course of its existence, cooperated closely in the activities of the Conference itself.

However, the synod was also involved at this time in talks with the ULCA about closer cooperation, and at the same convention in 1930 that approved the relationship with the American Lutheran Conference, the synod also passed a resolution to continue discussions with the ULCA. This put Augustana squarely in the middle of efforts for Lutheran union in the United States, but this middling position within these negotiations often resulted in conflict within the synod as to ecumenical and cooperative strategies. Augustana seemed to want to have it both ways; good relations with the ULCA and the other denominations in the American Lutheran Conference, while it was clear that the rest of the Conference was very suspicious of the orthodoxy of the ULCA, and the ULCA was not willing to join with the Conference on the basis of the theological position of the Minneapolis Theses.

The Beginnings of American Lutheran Merger Negotiations

During this time, it became widely assumed that Augustana and the other ethnic Lutheran groups would be merging together sometime in the future. But the question was not really if these Lutheran groups would merge together, but which of them would merge, and when and how these rearrangements would happen. Thus began a protracted period of positioning and negotiation between American Lutheran groups, with shifting alliances and plans toward merger running in many different directions. The formation of different organizations, such as the National Lutheran Council and the American Lutheran Conference, were in one sense a way to bring about closer cooperation between the various Lutheran denominations, but in another sense they were also a means of positioning the various denominations for possible merger and a way to exclude other groups from merger. The publication of theological position papers, such as the Knubel-Jacobs Theses and the Minneapolis Theses, served a similar purpose of defining both positions and opponents. In the shifting winds of merger activity, Augustana would often find itself caught in the middle, between other groups who did not always agree.

The basic dynamic of all this merger activity consisted of two poles, with a shifting set of players in the middle. On one end of the spectrum was the ULCA, which argued for the inclusion of all Lutheran groups in the merger process; this would involve only the agreement on essential theological details as a precondition. On the other end of the spectrum was the Lutheran Church–Missouri Synod (LCMS), which insisted that there needed to be full and complete agreement on all points of doctrine before there could even be fellowship between these Lutheran denominations, let alone merger. Anything that involved fellowship before full agreement was "unionism," a dangerous erosion of Lutheran principle. It was clear that these two denominations represented dramatically different views of how any future merger might happen; the question for Augustana and the remaining Lutheran groups was which principle should guide the negotiations? If negotiations were structured in an open way that would include all Lutherans, even the ULCA, then it was difficult to see Missouri participating in the movement. If, however, things were organized in a way that Missouri found acceptable, it would necessitate the exclusion of the ULCA.

Since Augustana had a long tradition of affiliation with the General Council, it was, of all the Midwestern Lutheran denominations, most sympathetic to the ULCA position, although there were elements within the synod, often represented by those in the sphere of the Lutheran Bible Institutes, who were more in line with the LCMS approach. But in general, Augustana stood for the principle that merger negotiations should be open to all American Lutherans, without preconditions. The formation of the National Lutheran Council in 1918 had been envisioned by some as a possible framework for this kind of merger negotiation, although the NLC was soon bogged down in theological discussions and writing theses that inhibited such an approach.

The formation of the American Lutheran Conference in 1930 was an attempt to bring together various Midwestern Lutheran groups into an alliance that many hoped would off-set the power and position of the two large denominations on opposite ends of the spectrum, especially for many participants, to counter the ULCA, which was not invited to participate in the Conference. Professor Adolf Hult represented this line of thinking when he wrote in 1927: "Why should not we Middle Western Lutherans of Northern descent come together? . . . The United Lutheran Church will presumably never be . . . the body around which other groups will congregate . . . this illusion must be given up."[14]

Augustana did decide to join the Conference, showing its affinity with the other Midwestern Lutheran denominations, but its affiliation with the Conference did not seem to dampen its enthusiasm for a merger process that would include all American Lutheran groups, including the ULCA. In commenting on the formation of the Conference, editor C. J. Bengston wrote, "[T]here is one Lutheran body which, in our opinion, should be a part of the American Lutheran Conference, namely the United Lutheran Church in America."[15] In this way many in Augustana saw the synod as a bridge between the Midwestern groups and the ULCA, but it was often a difficult position to maintain, because an action in one direction would please one party but offend many others, and the reverse.

Even while joining the Conference, Augustana also met with representatives of the ULCA to explore further moves toward closer cooperation between the two denominations. Minnesota Conference President P. A. Mattson, as a member of the Augustana Committee on Church Unity, voiced his objection about this meeting to President Brandelle, stating, "[T]he seven synods [of] . . . the American Lutheran Conference, are not in favor of uniting with the U.L.C. . . .[N]ow that we have lined up with them. . . . I hold that we would not show good faith if we now confer with a body that the other Synods would not unite with. . . . Furthermore, [we] . . . are not in harmony with the practices of the U.L.C."[16]

In response to Mattson, Brandelle admitted that while his feelings "ran at first along similar lines," he suggested that the synod had authorized the meeting as a "fact finding" process. Further, he acknowledged, "[T]he Augustana Synod will be obliged to deal with the U.L.C. both on mission-fields [sic] and in the larger cities. We come into contact with [them] . . . many, many more times than with the work of the German Synods. . . . The U.L.C. influences our people in the large cities infinitely more than do the German Bodies."[17]

Augustana historian G. Everett Arden later commented on this "divided" approach to Lutheran unity: "The endeavor to face, as it were, in two directions at once, was perhaps ingenuous and naive, but . . . Augustana assayed the role of intermediary, hoping to become a bridge across which rapprochement . . . might be achieved."[18] But the role of intermediary was a difficult one in a synod that was itself divided in its loyalties to the other Lutheran denominations.

Some of the first attempts toward Lutheran union came through the process of these groups working together on common tasks, such as the cooperative efforts of the NLC and the Lutheran World Convention and then the Lutheran World Federation. Military chaplaincy, campus ministry, home and foreign missions, publicity, and planning were all ways in which Lutherans learned to cooperate and to trust each other, and Augustana was a firm proponent of such cooperative endeavors. One specific way that American Lutherans came together was through the development of hymnals for common use; historically, a common hymnal has often preceded merger activity as an important precursor of unity. Such was the case of the *Common Service Book* in the 1880s that paved the way for the reunion of the Eastern Lutherans into the ULCA in 1918. In the mid-twentieth century, most of the American Lutheran groups (with the exception of the Missouri Synod) cooperated in the development of the *Service Book and Hymnal* (SBH), introduced in 1958.

The origins of the SBH came out of the American Lutheran Conference in 1934, with an idea toward developing a hymnal for the member denominations of the Conference. Augustana had just introduced its own hymnal in 1925 (the second English-language hymnal for the synod), but the synod was at least interested enough in a common hymnal to endorse the study of such a project. The ULCA was also considering a possible revision of the *Common Service Book*, and in 1945, the two parallel processes were merged together into two joint commissions, one to suggest a common liturgy, and the other a common hymnal. This parallel process was the suggestion of Augustana, which had urged the development of both elements in a synodical resolution in 1944. The work proceeded until 1948, when the two commissions provided a detailed progress report to the member churches (now all of those in the National Lutheran Council), reports that were well received by the synod.

The work of these two commissions, in which Augustana played an important role, especially through the work of E. E. Ryden, was slow due to the sheer number of denominations involved as well as the concurrent merger negotiations that were in full progress in the 1940s and 1950s. The eventual introduction of the *Service Book and Hymnal*, though many years in the making, was a great success, in that eventually it was adopted by all eight of the NLC denominations as their hymnal; in this sense it was more successful than the merger negotiations. Augustana did adopt the new *SBH*, and the vast majority of congregations put the new hymnal into use, though many carefully stored the old 1925 *Hymnal*, "just in case." It was in many respects a move of great joy and also great loss for the synod, with both emotions reflected in letters to the *Lutheran Companion*. The synod did have to compromise on both hymnal and liturgy, and many people felt the loss of Swedish heritage in the new book. Yet the common hymnal pointed the way to unity, and this was worth some sacrifice in the minds of many.

The Final Push toward Merger

The final period of this mid-century process of merger negotiations began in November 1942 at the annual meeting of the American Lutheran Conference. At that meeting in Rock Island the delegates passed a resolution, largely authored by E. E. Ryden, P. O. Bersell, and Conrad Bergendoff, stating that the conference should open merger negotiations to *all* American Lutheran denominations and instructing the executive committee to "negotiate with all other Lutheran bodies, looking for a more inclusive organization [and for] its constituent members to invite into pulpit and altar fellowship those Lutheran groups with whom they are not now in fellowship."[19]

Though the resolution passed, the executive committee of the conference was dominated by representatives of Norwegian Lutheran denominations who "resented the 'pushiness of the Swedes'"[20] in trying to include the ULCA in these negotiations, and the executive committee sidestepped its instructions by engaging in a lengthy dispute over a theological framework for the process. The leaders of the Norwegian Lutheran Church in America and the American Lutheran Church wanted to limit the merger discussions to only the five American Lutheran Conference denominations, while Augustana leaders favored expanding the negotiations to include all eight of the National Lutheran Council groups, and Missouri, too, if they wished to participate. In an article, E. E. Ryden noted that Missouri "was not ready to go beyond its present commitments," but that the other eight groups involved "drew their lines closer and solemnly resolved to go forward together in the tremendous responsibilities and opportunities which are challenging the Lutheran Church of America in this day of world crisis."[21] But the practical realities of the Second World War itself, and divisions within the eight denominations in the National Lutheran Council stalled the march forward.

In hopes of restarting these negotiations along a more fruitful path, the synodical convention in 1948 passed a resolution attempting to shift the venue of the negotiations back to the NLC, by declaring itself "in favor of the organic union of the constituent bodies of the National Lutheran Council," and further resolving: "That the Synod initiate action asking other synodical bodies of the National Lutheran Council to approve organic union of the participating bodies."[22]

Later that year the American Lutheran Conference met and set forward a plan of moving toward greater Lutheran unity in America by means of an "All Lutheran Free Conference."[23] The editor of the *Lutheran Companion* wrote to his readers: "It was only on the question of the best manner of approach to the problem of Lutheran unity that there was any real division of opinion. . . .[The Free Conference] seemed to offer the most logical solution."[24]

On January 4, 1949, a meeting of representatives of all eight NLC groups was held at Augustana Synod headquarters in Minneapolis. Named the "Committee of Thirty Four" (because of the number of delegates included), this group proceeded to discuss either a closer federation of the NLC members or a complete organic union of the eight. The next day Augustana hosted a meeting of the presidents of the American Lutheran

Conference to discuss Lutheran unity. Speeches at the meeting emphasized the urgency: "What are we waiting for?" asked Dr. H. F. Schuh of the American Lutheran Church.[25] When put to a written ballot, all the representatives voted for merger among the churches of the National Lutheran Council, which did not include the churches of the Synodical Conference—Missouri, Wisconsin, and the Evangelical Lutheran Synod. The unanimous vote for unity was not the full story, however, for there were reservations as well. Presidents of the Evangelical Lutheran Church (ELC—formerly the Norwegian Lutheran Church in America) and the Danish United Evangelical Lutheran Church (UELC) voiced concern about insufficient orthodoxy in some of the churches, namely the United Lutheran Church in America (ULCA). They began to have talks separate from the larger effort within the National Lutheran Council to create what President P. O. Bersell called "a merger of the majority."

Talks continued over the next three years, but these discussions seemed to lead nowhere. During this time Augustana also turned over the helm of leadership from Bersell, who had strong sympathies for an American Lutheran Conference orientation, to Oscar Benson from Illinois, who had demonstrated in his scholarship and would soon show in his leadership a stronger sympathy for ties with the ULCA, which also promoted what he called societary action in its outward posture toward the world. When two options for merger eventually became clear—participating in the five-way merger with the Norwegian, Danish, and German Lutheran churches in the American Lutheran Conference, or choosing instead a four-way merger with the ULCA, the Suomi (Finnish) Synod, and the American Evangelical Lutheran Church (Danish)—Bergendoff took to the floor of the synod and articulated the rationale: "It is a fallacy of unity negotiations that we have to prove that we are Lutherans. We are not becoming Lutherans; we are Lutherans. We are never going to get anywhere in any unity negotiations if we must rewrite the confessional books of the Lutheran Church. . . . Unity is not made; it is acknowledged."[26] In 1950, the two proposals for federative or organic union were defeated, and the merger negotiations within the NLC collapsed, only to shift to another venue.

The United Evangelical Lutheran Church (UELC-Danish), in consultation with the ELC, began a process leading to organic union, and they invited the American Lutheran Church (1930–1960) to join with them in the "Joint Union Committee" (JUC). The JUC in turn invited the Lutheran Free Church and Augustana to participate in the merger negotiations, which were envisioned as an organic union of the five Conference denominations, on the basis of a theological platform entitled *The United Testimony*, an updated version of the conservative Minneapolis and Chicago theses of earlier in the century. In response, Augustana appointed its own "Committee on Lutheran Union," a nine-member panel, to study the issue of Lutheran union and to relate to the various Lutheran merger negotiations then in progress. In 1951, the Augustana Committee on Lutheran Union met with representatives of the JUC, which pressed the Augustana committee to commit to the JUC merger process. In return, the Augustana committee agreed to bring the issue to the synodical convention in 1952 for a vote and to consult with the JUC negotiations until such a time as the synod itself would conclusively answer the question. The scene was then set for a decisive vote at the June 1952 Augustana Synod convention in Des Moines where members would decide whether Augustana would merge with the other four members of the American Lutheran Conference or would hold out for a more inclusive merger process that would be at least theoretically open to all American Lutheran denominations.

Predictably, there was not a consensus of opinion within Augustana about which of the two paths toward Lutheran union the synod should take, and proponents of the two positions carried out a vigorous debate in the church media during the months leading up to the 1952 synodical convention. Those who favored the JUC plan of union set forth a variety of reasons for their position. Some thought that Augustana naturally had the most in common with the other Midwestern Lutheran denominations within the American Lutheran Conference, and that merger with this group would act as a centrist bulwark against both the Missouri Synod and the ULCA, respectively. H. Conrad Hoyer, an Augustana pastor and an NLC staff member, suggested that merger within the American Lutheran Conference would most likely take place and Augustana should be a part of that merger: "The writer is of the opinion that our participation would hasten the day of closer organizational fellowship with other Lutherans."[27]

Some Augustana voices supported such a merger, citing that the ULCA was lax on Lutheran doctrine and practice, and tolerated lodge membership, and they found *The United Testimony* to be a congenial and helpful statement of belief. E. E. Ryden, editor of the *Lutheran Companion*, who had long been active in the Conference, stressed the long history that Augustana had with its partners in the Conference: "There [are] . . . no differences in the doctrinal positions held by the five bodies. They are already united in faith . . . by reason of the Christian fellowship they have enjoyed with one another in the American Lutheran Conference for more than twenty years."[28] To these Augustana people, merger within the American Lutheran Conference was the natural way for the synod to proceed.

Those who argued against the JUC proposal did so on a number of related grounds, most of which stemmed from the perceived conservative position of the other four Lutheran denominations as expressed in the merger documents, or in protest against the exclusion of the ULCA from the negotiations. Some in Augustana rejected the idea of additional theological documents, such as *The United Testimony*, as being necessary for Lutheran union, and they argued that acceptance of the Augsburg Confession of 1530 was theological agreement enough.

Others found *The United Testimony* too theologically conservative, especially on the question of the authority of scripture, and they worried that in a merger with American Lutheran Conference denominations Augustana would lose its ecumenical contacts as well as memberships in the National Council of Churches and World Council of Churches. Still others stood on the principle that merger negotiations should be open to all Lutheran groups in the United States, and that the JUC's exclusion of the ULCA was simply wrong. In a series of articles in the *Lutheran Companion*, S. E. Engstrom argued for a larger vision of Lutheran union: "Let us decline any further participation in discussions on an American Lutheran Conference level, discussions which automatically exclude other bodies . . . because we want merger on the National Lutheran Council level."[29] Opponents of the JUC process stood on the principle that all groups should be invited to the negotiations, even though it was beginning to be clear that there would be little hope of a merger negotiation of all eight National Lutheran Council members.

In May 1952, the editor of the *Lutheran Companion*, E. E. Ryden, reported that he had attended four different Augustana Conference meetings in regions around the country. He said that while there were no formal motions, "keen interest was evidenced everywhere." Illinois wanted "total Lutheran union," while New England wanted merger of the NLC denominations, or failing that, with the ULCA. The sentiment in the others (Iowa and New York) was on the side of "bringing to a consummation the present merger negotiations between the five American Lutheran Conference bodies." In Ryden's opinion, Augustana as a church was "not altogether unanimous" about the future direction of Lutheran unity in America.[30]

At the June 1952 synodical convention, delegates did not accept the JUC's *The United Testimony*, but as a weaker substitute did declare its "substantial agreement" with the statement, and urged that it be "further studied and refined." Further, the convention adopted a resolution to reaffirm the synod's position on the widest possible Lutheran union, and to explicitly include in such merger negotiations the question of future ecumenical relations, something that the other Conference denominations were not interested in addressing. So when the JUC met in November 1952, Augustana representatives related their synodical actions of the previous summer and pressed for an answer from the rest, as to the question of wider union and ecumenical relations. The JUC would not change its basic stance or approach, so the Augustana delegates had no choice but to withdraw from the negotiations. One observer stated: "It was a solemn moment . . . as the Augustana representatives arose and walked quietly from the conference chamber. . . . A chapter in Lutheran unity strivings in America had come to an end."[31]

The JUC continued its negotiations, eventually leading to the formation of the American Lutheran Church (1960–1988), and the American Lutheran Conference quietly dissolved in 1954. Augustana's immediate future would not lie with the other four Midwestern Lutheran denominations who had comprised the Conference.[32]

Having effectively closed this door, Augustana's future was still uncertain: Would it remain independent, would it seek a pan-Lutheran merger, or failing this, would it move toward a union with Lutheran groups outside the JUC structure? The whole issue came to life again in the spring of 1955, when plans were underway between Augustana and the ULCA for a new approach to the issue of unity. That people were impatient with the pace of things is evident in a letter from an Augustana member who wrote: "Augustana should make 1955 a year of decision in the matter. We *must* choose between the forthcoming 'new' Church or the ULCA—either one or the other. The Church should not go it alone, I firmly believe."[33]

Though the range of opinion covered the whole spectrum, there was a general tone of frustration and weariness as to a lack of progress and direction. Editor E. E. Ryden decried the fact that things seemed to be no further than they were in 1944 with the "Overture for Lutheran Unity," and saw the intervening years as a "dismal failure." He suggested, "Why not begin by seeking an understanding with Missouri?"[34] Others took the position that Augustana should rejoin the JUC negotiations; typical was this letter writer's opinion: "I wish to add my agreement to those who regret we are not now in the proposed merger of Lutheran groups. . . . May Augustana confirm its friendship of the past with the member Churches of the American Lutheran Conference, and take the forward step with them."[35]

In 1955, after several years of discussions with various other Lutheran denominations, Augustana and the ULCA issued open invitations to all the other Lutheran denominations in the United States to consider a broad, organic union. Editor Ryden found this invitation "unexpected," but saw in it an opening to other American Lutheran denominations. "[W]e might venture once more," he wrote, "to ask our four sister Churches of the former American Lutheran Conference if there are any grounds for hoping that they might still alter their position."[36]

Missouri and the JUC members refused to accept the invitation, with a serious sense of annoyance on the part of the some leaders at what they saw as Augustana–ULCA "interference" in their ongoing negotiations. But the American Evangelical Lutheran Church (AELC-Danish) and the Suomi Synod (Finnish) did accept this invitation, so with these two groups Augustana and the ULCA formed the Joint Commission on Lutheran Unity (JCLU) in December 1956.[37] Although there were a number throughout American Lutheranism who saw the inherent tragedy of two separate and exclusive merger processes proceeding independently, there seemed no way around it; at that point there was no way to bring about a larger union of American Lutheran denominations.

Negotiations Leading to the Lutheran Church in America (1962–1988)

Having insisted throughout the Lutheran merger struggles of the twentieth century that there was no absolute need for further theological statements beyond the Augsburg Confession, Augustana and the rest of the JCLU did not spend much time re-examining each others' theological orthodoxy, but recognized in the four denominations a "sufficient ground of agreement in the common confession of our faith, as witnessed by the Lutheran confessions"[38] to proceed with the negotiations. According to Conrad Bergendoff, "[T]he first thing we decided was that [since] we are one in doctrine, we don't need to go further, so that we lost no time in doctrinal discussions."[39] Instead, the days of negotiation were filled with figuring out "what the church meant" and determining the respective rights of congregations, synods, and national church, as well as the roles of agencies and seminaries. One historian observed that it was "refreshing to know that . . . the JCLU members were in no mood to submit one another to some sort of extraconfessional Lutheran litmus test."[40]

Having settled on a merger of the four denominations, the JCLU representatives set an ambitious timetable for merger, hoping to complete the process by 1962. Although they agreed upon theological issues fairly readily, the practical issues involved in merging four Lutheran denominations proved to be more difficult, for in many instances the structure and culture of the ULCA was at odds with the other three groups, and being the largest of the four, the ULCA had to walk a fine line in negotiating with the others. Augustana, along with the smaller AELC and Suomi Synod, was organized as a national church body, with a large degree of centralization and weaker intermediate judicatories, that is, Augustana's conferences. The ULCA, however, had grown from eastern Lutheran traditions in which the regional synod was the primary locus of power, and the national body was in some senses a federation of synods (something along the lines of the structure of the General Council). The differences had a significant bearing on merger negotiations seeking to combine denominations with substantially different structural traditions and polity.[41]

It seemed clear that many in the ULCA sought a stronger role for the national church organization than they had in the ULCA at that time, but it was not clear exactly what this meant, especially concerning practical issues such as the ownership and control of educational and social service institutions. The JCLU decided to name its proposed intermediate judicatories "synods" (following the ULCA pattern), but gave the national church more power as compared with the synods. In Augustana and the other non-ULCA denominations, the national church had substantial control over educational and social service institutions, but the pattern proposed for the new church body was more along ULCA lines, where these institutions were supported by combinations of synods. The related perceived issue, of there being too many seminaries with not enough resources, was put off for resolution until after the formation of the LCA in 1962. Practical issues concerning publishing houses, pastoral pensions, and the location of church headquarters were also points of contention and absorbed a great deal of time and energy.

One smaller point of contention nearly derailed the merger negotiations, at least for a time; this was the issue of "lodges." Most conservative Lutherans in the nineteenth and twentieth centuries had strongly opposed membership in lodges (such as the Masonic lodge) as being inimical to Christian faith and practice. These groups believed that lodges were an alternative form of "faith," and that it was especially wrong for pastors to belong to a lodge; it was, in fact, an action that could lead to disciplinary action or dismissal from the ministry. Augustana strongly opposed lodges, as did Suomi and the AELC; the ULCA did not generally consider this to be a major problem, and it was known that in some areas any number of ULCA pastors were also lodge members. In September 1957, Conrad Bergendoff, an Augustana representative to JCLU, submitted to the group this resolution about ministerial qualifications: "A candidate shall not be ordained into the ministry of this Church who is pledged to loyalty to any organization—secret or public—which practices religious observances not in full conformity with his witness to Christ as defined in the Lutheran confessions."[42]

The resolution also suggested that ordained ministers who had joined lodges would be subject to censure or discipline. This was a sensitive issue for the ULCA, which did not want this strict of a position on the lodge issue, precisely because it knew that such a provision would be difficult to "sell" to its clergy. Yet the Augustana representative stood firm on this principle, and at the December 1957 meeting the JCLU adopted constitutional language on the issue that was substantially along the lines of the original Augustana proposal. Historians have debated about how seriously this issue might have affected the merger negotiations, but it does seem clear that at this point in the talks Augustana representatives were willing to walk away from the table if they were not able to achieve satisfactory resolution on the topic of lodges.

Even as late as 1958, there was a flurry of hope that the two separate merger tracks going on in American Lutheranism could be combined into a larger, more comprehensive Lutheran union. F. Epling Reinhartz, president of the National Lutheran Council, made an impassioned plea at an NLC meeting for the two groups to seek a larger union, to which the editor of the *Lutheran Companion* concurred:

> It is indeed true that the hour is late, and that merger plans on both sides have begun to crystallize. . . . But it is still true that the point of no return has not yet been reached. And surely, if a larger and more satisfying goal can be achieved . . . should not every conceivable effort be made to attain such a result?[43]

But this was not to be. The two mergers continued on separate tracks.

There seemed to be a sense of weariness with the course of merger negotiations that had been on the table, in one form or another for forty-five years, and a growing sense that even if not perfect, the JCLU negotiations were the inevitable next step for Augustana. Yet, some in Augustana still worried that the voice and independence of the church would be lost if it united with a much larger body like the ULCA. Professor A. D. Mattson, concerned about what he saw as ULCA insincerity on the lodge issue, suggested that the "agreement" reached was "a pretense of agreement when there is no agreement. The only agreement seems to be that there ought to be a merger. . . . After Augustana is swallowed, her voice will be silent forever. There are some things in life which are more important than ecclesiasticalism."[44]

Other letter writers however, defended the ULCA on the matter or saw no difficulties with it. One writer commented: "The results of the discussions to date would seem to indicate that the proposed merger is within God's will and purpose for the Lutheran Church and His Kingdom."[45]

After settling many of the merger issues, ignoring a few more, and leaving the rest to be settled later (for example, theological education), the JCLU brought its work to conclusion, and in 1962, brought a proposal to the four member denominations for the creation of a new church. When Augustana met in synodical convention in June 1962 in Detroit, it voted overwhelmingly to accept the merger agreement and voted itself out of institutional existence. After 102 years as a separate entity, Augustana merged itself into a newly created body, the Lutheran Church in America (LCA). In this action, Augustana brought to a close a period of intense discussion and thinking, one that had become much more complex and drawn out than Lutheran leaders had foreseen in the optimistic beginning negotiations for Lutheran union in the 1920s and 1930s. If the new Lutheran Church in America was not the inevitable end of Lutheran union, it was hoped that at least it was a large step in that ultimate direction.

In his history of the Augustana Synod, G. Everett Arden entitled his final chapter covering these negotiations toward the formation of the Lutheran Church in America, "Destiny Fulfilled." In some senses that is accurate, and in others, it might need correcting. Certainly if one sees the LCA as a milestone to a larger unity among American Lutherans, his claim is perhaps correct. But both in Augustana during the 1950s, as well as among some later observers, the question has been asked as to whether the two separate Lutheran mergers of the 1960s were not more of a mistake than an advance, more of a sidetrack than a way forward. Perhaps the timing was not exactly right for a larger merger, but by waiting, Lutheran unity might have been hindered further. On the other hand, delay and patience might have had merit. Though merger may well have been the "destiny" of Augustana, it also meant the loss of a distinctive American Lutheran culture and of a church with the soul of a family. For everything gained in a merger, there is something lost.

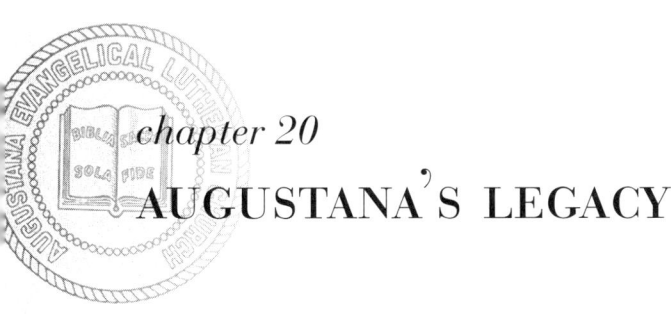

chapter 20
AUGUSTANA'S LEGACY

THE AUGUSTANA STORY IS PEOPLED WITH LEADERS who were deeply devoted to the church that shaped them. They participated in a complex denominational ecology that held in balance the ambitions and aspirations of many sections of the church. Health ministries in Nebraska and college funding appeals in Kansas were judged by men and women who also knew about the ministry to seafarers in New York City and the plan to create youth leadership schools in every conference. When delegates gathered for yearly conventions to debate the church's priorities for ministry and funding, controversy did not descend into polarization because there were systems to hem in the ambitions of others, wait for passions to subside, and create room for reconciliation. Augustana's leadership was established and experienced. Because people in congregations were well informed, leaders could wield influence without dominating. The deep reservoir of trust within the church depended on the ongoing work that had taken place, over several generations, to maintain a strong relational network within the church. This developed a capacity for leadership that made it possible for the Augustana Lutheran Church to enter the merger processes of the mid-twentieth century with confidence. The trust that Augustana's people invested in their leadership, together with an enthusiasm for extending the kind of work and service performed by the church in a wider arena, made them eager partners.

When Augustana entered into the new Lutheran Church in America in 1962, it was entering an unequal partnership with one Lutheran church body that was much larger and two other church bodies that were considerably smaller. The United Lutheran Church in America (ULCA) was, at 2.4 million baptized members, four times the size of Augustana with 600,000 baptized members. The other two denominations, the American Evangelical Lutheran Church (Danish) and the Suomi Synod (Finnish) together consisted of only 60,000 baptized members. This distribution of membership was, however, often very regionally specific, as the merger partners were heavily concentrated in different parts of the country. Augustana dominated in the Upper Midwest (Minnesota, Iowa, and the Dakotas) and in New England and in the Central Plains (Kansas and Nebraska), while the ULCA was stronger in the Mid-Atlantic and the South. In the Great Lakes region, in Canada, and on the West Coast, they came together as relative equals.

On the national level, as would seem obvious, leaders of the former ULCA had more prominence in the new LCA.[1] The headquarters of the new denomination were moved to New York City and the publishing house was consolidated in Philadelphia—both ULCA strongholds. The Board of Pensions was located in Minneapolis. Some Augustana leaders did move to the East to work in the structures of the new denomination, such as Malvin Lundeen, who became the first Secretary of the LCA, and Martin E. Carlson, who was involved with Finance and Stewardship. Some others in the existing Augustana leadership held responsibilities within institutions and agencies, but many did not make the transition to new national leadership in the denomination at the beginning. Later on there were some who did. Reuben Swanson, for example, who had been President of the Nebraska Synod, held the office of LCA Secretary from 1978 to the end of 1987 when the ELCA merger took place.

Bigger, but Not Necessarily Better

In some ways, especially in structure, the new LCA was a strange amalgam of both Augustana and the ULCA. The LCA was organized along the lines of the regional synodical system prevalent in the ULCA, and most of the institutional elements (seminaries, colleges, and social service agencies) of the new denomination depended on support from regional synods rather than from the national organization. Augustana's centralization of both power and identity was different from that of the ULCA, which had existed more as a federation of regional synods than as a strongly cohesive national church. As a result of Augustana's strong formal and informal network—its "sense of the wider church"—the LCA inherited more centralization than many former ULCA people found comfortable. In some new LCA synods, such as Minnesota, Red River, Iowa, Nebraska, and New England, former Augustana presence predominated, but in Eastern and Southern synods there was much less. Augustana people tended to dominate in the synodical leadership in the western synods of the United States and Canada. Many Augustana leaders guided synods composed of a real mix of members from all four of the predecessor denominations, and it may be that the strong cohesive spirit among the Augustana people was at work in their leadership. This was true in the Pacific Southwest Synod with Carl Segerhammer, the Pacific Northwest

Synod with A. G. "Gib" Fjellman, and the Illinois Synod, with Gerald Johnson. Other Augustana pastors who were synod Presidents or Bishops in the LCA included Otto Olson in Central Canada, N. Everett Hedeen in Central States, Raynold Lingwall in Iowa, Leonard Kendall, Melvin Hammarberg, and Herbert Chilstrom in Minnesota, Dennis Anderson in Nebraska, Karl Olander, Eugene Brodeen, and Harold Wimmer in New England, Lloyd Burke in Pacific Southwest, Walter Carlson, Carl Larson, and Harold Lohr in Red River Valley, Donald Sjoberg in Western Canada, and Theodore Matson in Wisconsin-Upper Michigan.

To be sure, both the size of the new LCA (three million baptized) and the enormous social upheavals of the 1960s and 1970s were contributing causes to the sense of dis-ease and loss expressed by many from the old Augustana. They missed the familial closeness fostered by a single seminary, a common yearly convention, national auxiliaries for women, men, and youth, and a "homey" synodical press that kept everyone up-to-date. In some sense, Augustana represented the "good old days," and evoked nostalgia for a perceived loss of identity. Reflecting on the change that occurred following the merger, ninety-two-year-old Richard Pearson, a former Augustana pastor in New England, lamented, "There was a time when nearly every pastor in Augustana knew my name and the fact that I lived in Forestville, Connecticut."[2] Such intimacy simply was not possible in a denomination five times the size of the old one.

Augustana's Institutional Legacy

Long-standing Augustana institutions of education and social ministry remained within the new church. The most important of these were the colleges: Augustana, Gustavus Adolphus, Luther (Wahoo), Bethany, and Upsala, as well as those colleges where Augustana had joined with other Lutherans, such as Texas Lutheran, Pacific Lutheran, and California Lutheran. Now, nearly fifty years after the merger, three former Augustana colleges remain—Augustana, Gustavus, and Bethany. Luther (Wahoo) merged into Midland Lutheran College in Midland, Kansas, in 1962, and Upsala College struggled financially for years before closing in 1995. The most successful of the colleges had strong local and synodical support as well as a devoted corps of alumni across the country, especially former Augustana members and congregations. Gustavus Adolphus, for example, created its very successful Association of Congregations as a way to funnel local support to the college. Upsala, on the other hand, suffered a great loss of support at the merger because many of the LCA synods assigned to support it had weak ties with the struggling institution, and the college's student body and alumni pool became increasingly African American and Jewish, rather than Lutheran.

The Lutheran Bible Institutes did not fare as well as the colleges in the merger. It seemed clear to the leadership of the LBI movement that they would have to seek accreditation and grant collegiate degrees to survive, but this change would dilute the traditional focus on Bible teaching, making the decision controversial and change difficult. In Minnesota, LBI attempted to form a liberal arts institution, Golden Valley Lutheran College, which struggled from 1967 to 1985, but eventually had to close its doors. The LBI program in Seattle recently achieved accreditation as a liberal arts institution under the name Trinity Lutheran College, and it plans to move to Everett, Washington. Since it has only a few hundred students, however, it will need significant support in order to make this transition. LBI in Southern California tried several times to achieve accreditation but was not successful; it has become a House of Studies associated with Concordia Lutheran College, Irvine, an institution of the Lutheran Church–Missouri Synod.

The core institution of the synod, Augustana Theological Seminary, did not continue as an independent institution after the merger. A study of theological education at the beginning of the LCA, led by Augustana theologian Conrad Bergendoff, found that many of the seminaries of the new church were small and underfunded. The controversial "Bergendoff Report" suggested merging them together in central locations, close to major American universities, from whom they might gain intellectual and theological vitality. As a model of what Bergendoff proposed, the Augustana Seminary paved the way by merging with four other seminaries at a new location on the south side of Chicago (across from the University of Chicago) in 1967.[3] There was diminished influence by Augustana at the new Lutheran School of Theology at Chicago (LSTC), since many of the senior members of the Augustana Seminary faculty did not make the transition from Rock Island to Chicago, choosing instead to retire. President Karl Mattson sought to continue, but he was not chosen as president of LSTC. For two years as the Chicago campus was constructed, the seminary remained in Rock Island. "Kemtone," as he was known by the students, continued as president. But he died suddenly and prematurely, before the move to Hyde Park near the University of Chicago, which finally happened in 1967.[4]

In the new system of seminaries, students who came from Augustana congregations now had the opportunity to study at several approved seminaries. Those who would have attended the Rock Island seminary did not automatically transfer their intentions to the new urban and university campus in Chicago, and chose instead to attend other Lutheran seminaries like Gettysburg or Philadelphia in the East, or Northwestern or Luther Seminaries in Minnesota instead, and even at university divinity schools like Harvard, Yale, Chicago, and Union, taking seriously the opportunity to work their way personally into the new and larger Lutheran Church in America. The enriched environment of a university setting on an urban campus did provide a rich context for committed engagement with social problems, which ought to be noted as a strong Augustana emphasis, beginning with the teaching of A. D. Mattson, and strongly advanced in the presidency of Oscar Benson, who earned a doctoral degree in religious sociology. The church culture that had obtained in the Augustana Synod had not exposed its theological students to direct public protest and community organizing, though social justice commitments had been talked about and advanced. The direct exposure to activism might have happened in any case in the old Augustana arrangements, given the radical political and theological climate of the years of student revolution and protest.

The Ordination of Women

As Augustana Seminary faced its own closing and absorption into the Lutheran School of Theology in Chicago, President Karl Mattson carried forward an active correspondence with theologians in the Church of Sweden, maintaining important personal ties. Gunnar Hillerdal, a professor at the University of Lund, kept him informed about the latest Swedish theological scholarship and issues within the Church of Sweden. At the end of 1958, Hillerdal gave a blow-by-blow account of the Swedish church's decision to ordain women. He depicted the reactions of men like Bo Giertz, the bishop in Göteborg, with some disdain, and registered surprise at Anders Nygren's initial conservatism. Only Ragnar Bring seemed to him to have taken the logical, positive position. He wrote that theologians representing the "Uppsala School" argued that, "Christ chose only men for apostles, demonstrating the created difference of men from women. The apostles represent Christ. Christ was a man. A woman cannot represent Christ. So naively—somewhat simplified—they actually reason!"[5]

Hillerdal's two-page, detailed letter about the politization of this decision, and the resulting cohort of churchmen in Sweden who refused to accept the ordination of women, certainly gave Mattson all he needed to know about where his friends in Sweden stood on the issue. Mattson wrote nothing to Hillerdal in response to the dramatic decision. He hoped that Hillerdal would apply to teach at LSTC because he wanted a Swedish influence to endure at the Lutheran seminary, but Mattson may not have been so enamored of modern Swedish theology if it meant that a controversy like women's ordination might loom in the near future. As an American churchman, the ordination of women must have seemed to him to be completely outside the area of possibility. The decision to ordain women in the LCA came finally in 1970.

In addition to educational institutions, American Lutheranism's inheritance from Augustana included hospitals, nursing homes, and social service agencies. A half-century of change in healthcare and social services has resulted in few, if any, of these institutions remaining as solo or independent agencies. Instead they minister through leveraging public monies or in association with public welfare services. Economies of scale and the necessity of a large-systems approach have greatly altered the familiar church-related feel of these institutions, but because they have been able to expand to offer social services to a wider public, agencies that Augustana's people founded now participate in Lutheran Services in America, which has become the largest charitable network of its kind in the United States.

Ministry of Hospitality

By the time of the merger, the building that housed the ministry to young women begun by Emmy Evald in the 1940s had become run down, and Augustana's ministry to sailors also needed a new facility. The women of Augustana decided to sell the Home for Women and to use the money realized in the sale to help the seamen build a new building. The Seafarers and International House on New York's Nineteenth Street, with two floors reserved for female guests, became a house for travelers where Augustana's legacy of hospitality lives on.

Augustana's Youth Legacy

Augustana's leaders may not have assumed a fair proportion of formal leadership in the new LCA, but this did not mean that they disappeared entirely. Wilton Bergstrand, Augustana's visionary youth leader, expressed dismay that the design for youth work in the new church appeared to be a decided setback. In the new LCA plan, the smaller emphasis on youth in the overall budget would result in a 75 percent cutback for youth who would have otherwise been served if Augustana had continued its program. Youth leadership training had been a major initiative for Augustana, with leadership events in every conference. Bergstrand warned that they would have to really fight to maintain even a semblance of the former Augustana youth ministry. "Franklin Fry has a blind spot when it comes to youth,"[6] he claimed, frustrated that priorities established after long study and experience were renegotiated with people who had little exposure or commitment to youth work as an essential program of the church. Bergstrand and the Augustana church had become committed to the principle that youth work was a program "for the church." Now the work looked like it would become a program of youth leadership "for youth," making it more difficult for LCA congregations to inspire in young people the loyalty and commitment to the church and the strong cohesiveness and sense of the wider church that had been so valued by Augustana. In the LCA, within ten years, the Luther League was dissolved.

Bergstrand and other senior leaders planned for ways to extend their influence in other venues. A new initiative that began during the time of merger was the purchase of a former copper mining camp on Lake Chelan in Washington state. Wes Prieb, a student at the Minneapolis LBI, sent a letter to the mine company asking them to donate the camp or sell it at a significantly reduced price. Wilton Bergstrand, together with his long-time partners in youth work Caroll Hinderlie of the ELC and Elmer Witt of the LCMS, envisioned Holden Village as an "experimental laboratory" for youth work in the West. The effort to build the camp into a retreat center involved participants from outside the LCA, including former members of the youth committee of the American Lutheran Conference, which became the American Lutheran Church in 1960. This made it possible for ideas to survive on their own merit, and not because they represented a political constituency. After Bergstrand brought sixty visitors to the remote camp, including all of the conference leaders from across the country, the Luther League Executive Committee voted in August 1961, in anticipation of the merger, to give their library and all other inventory to Holden Village.

Unlike the Luther League, Bible camps thrived following the merger. Camp Augustana outgrew its facilities in Lake Geneva, Wisconsin, and purchased acreage for a new camp in Oregon, Illinois, where programming expanded to adult retreat weekends during the fall and winter. Other camps, including Camp Calumet, in New England, also flourished by expanding their facilities to minister to adults and families. In Minnesota, the Augustana presence is still felt at Chisago Lake Lutheran Camp where campers return to the site of the first Swedish congregation in the state, at Mount Carmel Ministries in Alexandria, founded by LBI constituents, and at The Cathedral of the Pines, a camp owned and operated by Mount Olivet Lutheran Church in Minneapolis, a flagship congregation of the former Augustana Lutheran Church.

The Gift of Augustana

The formation of the Evangelical Lutheran Church in America (ELCA) in 1988, from a merger of the LCA, the American Lutheran Church (ALC), and the Association of Evangelical Lutheran Congregations (AELC), further diluted a discernible Augustana identity in American Lutheranism. Still, according to Lutheran observer Richard Koenig, "One wonders how, without something like the Augustana tradition to draw on, the merger ever could have taken place."[7] The "skittish" ALC, the "officious" LCA, and the "truculent" AELC needed a "zone" where they could find a path forward.

Herbert Chilstrom, a son of Augustana and bishop of the Minnesota Synod of the LCA, was elected the first presiding bishop of this new Lutheran church body at the ELCA's constituting convention in Columbus, Ohio, in 1987. For his installation service, attended by Lutheran church dignitaries from around the world, only the archbishop of the Church of Sweden was asked not to come forward for the laying on of hands. This request came from Lutherans who were opposed to the symbol of apostolic succession claimed by the Church of Sweden and suggested by the participation of the Swedish archbishop. Within just a few years, apostolic succession would become a major theological issue in the ELCA, especially with regard to ecumenical dialogues with the Episcopal Church. Given Augustana's rich history in ecumenical affairs, this conversation about how Lutherans understand the nature of the church brought former Augustana leaders together again, and out of this the Augustana Heritage Association was formed in 2000. This history was commissioned by the Association as part of their continued efforts to articulate clearly and maintain the legacy of the Augustana Lutheran Church within the context of Lutheranism in North America.

The Augustana Ethos

Apart from the Waldenström doctrinal controversy in the 1870s and 1880s when some congregations left to form the Evangelical Mission Covenant Church,[8] the Augustana Lutheran Church did not experience schism, did not merge with another Lutheran church body until 1962, and did not undergo traumatic leadership changes during its century of history. Instead, Augustana matured through several generations of capable and effective leadership to create a strong, cohesive national spirit, recognized by American religious historian Sydney Ahlstrom as the "Augustana ethos." Pastors, educated at the synod's one seminary, met together regularly at conference and annual meetings. Congregational lay leaders, educated at synod colleges, maintained over their lifetimes relationships fostered during their school years. The broad familiarity with the church's ministry that ordinary members of congregations received through church publications contributed further to this ethos, keeping Augustana's story active and alive across the country. Thus, twenty-first-century historians can speak of an Augustana legacy that is still recognizable in the ongoing life of American Lutheranism today.

The Augustana story is woven of relationships maintained over time. Leaders depended on a network of friendship and trust that provided a reservoir of goodwill for new initiatives. Augustana's youth were invited into a connected system of people who had known each other through several generations. These relationships did not end, but continued in the new church, in the LCA, and in the ELCA. And so the Augustana story that began in the villages and farms of a changing Swedish landscape has become an American story. In 1998, forty years after their ordination, a reunion class returned to western Pennsylvania and western New York to celebrate in the place where they had been ordained. When they returned to the Chautauqua Institution, they probably did not realize how close they had come to the place where Swedish Lutheran immigrants had first picked up the thread that wove a pattern of a church that always thought big, thought national, thought of itself not only as local congregations, but as part of the wider church.

NOTES

Chapter 1: Swedish Beginnings

1. Jay Dolan, "The Immigrants and Their Gods," *Church History* 57 (March 1988).

2. Timothy Smith, "Religion and Ethnicity in America," *American Historical Review* 83, no. 5 (December 1978): 1155–1185.

3. Gunnar Westin, *Emigranterna och Kyrkan* (Stockholm: Svenska Kyrkans Dialonistyrelses Bokförlag, 1932), 10–11.

4. C. Fr. af Wingård to L. P. Esbjörn, March 8, 1849. Letters are compiled in Westin, *Emigranterna och Kyrkan*, and arranged by date.

5. Bengt Sundkler, *Svenska Missionssällskapet 1835–1876* (Uppsala, Sweden: Almqvist and Wiksells Boktryckeri, 1937), 301ff; Bror Walan, *Församlingstanken i Svenska Missionsförbundet: En studie i den nyevangeliska rörelsens sprängning och Svenska Missionsförbundets utveckling till o. 1890* (Stockholm: Svenska Missionsförbundets bokförlag, 1964), 23.

6. Sundkler, *Svenska Missionssällskapet 1835–1876*, 260ff. The Basel Mission Society and Leipzig Mission Society trained Swedish missionary candidates, while the Islington Society in London provided training for fields in British territories.

7. Westin, 195. Letter from L. P. Esbjörn to G. Th. Keyser, February 22, 1847.

8. When the *Evangelical Fosterlandsstiftelse* (the Evangelical Fatherland Foundation) formed in 1856, both inner and foreign mission interests had an outlet. To take back some of the energy for mission, the Church of Sweden Mission was founded in 1874. Swedish debates over the proper location for missionary work—church or voluntary society—created an intense examination of ecclesiology. Gustaf Aulén, *Hundraårs Svenskkyrkodebatt* (Stockholm: Svenska kyrkans diakonistyrelsens bokförlag, 1953), passim.

9. See *A Pioneer in Northwest America 1841–1858: The Memoirs of Gusaf Unonius*, trans. Jonas Backlund, vols. 1, 2 (Minneapolis: University of Minnesota Press, 1950).

10. The biographical narratives of Erland Carlsson and Tufve Nilsson Hasselquist contain episodes detailing conflict with bishops and senior ministers. See the two biographies of Hasselquist: Eric Norelius, *Hasselquist, en levnadshistoria* (Rock Island, Ill.: Augustana Book Concern, 1891) and O. Fritiof Ander, *Life of Hasselquist* (Rock Island, Ill.: Augustana Historical Society Publications, 1931).

11. The term *priest* ought to be explained further, since in America the Augustana people used the term *pastor* to designate their clergy. One effect of the revival movement was to introduce new titles for ministry—lay preachers, evangelists, catechists, readers, and pastors—designating those who were active in spreading the movement. But the first pastors of the Augustana Church were priests of the Church of Sweden, too, and in Swedish they used the term *priest* when communicating with each other. The transformation in language was gradual.

12. Information about the New Sweden settlement is in Eric Norelius, *De Svenska Lutherska Forsamlingarnas och Svenskarnes Historia i Amerika* (Rock Island, Ill.: Augustana Book Concern, 1890), 87.

13. It would be an interesting study to compare this Swedish pattern with the demographic and geographical characteristics of other Lutheran churches founded by immigrants. Norwegian immigration to the United States began more than a decade earlier than the Swedish, before much of the transportation systems of the United States had been developed or postal systems established. See D. W. Meinig, *The Shaping of America: A Geographical Perspective on 500 Years of History*, especially volume 2, *Continental America, 1800–1867* (New Haven, Conn.: Yale University Press, 1993).

14. Norelius, *De Svenska Lutherska Forsamlingarnas och Svenskarnes Historia i Amerika*, 32.

15. Robert Ostergren, *A Community Transplanted: The Transatlantic Experience of a Swedish Immigrant Settlement in the Upper Middle West, 1835–1915* (Madison: University of Wisconsin Press, 1988), passim.

16. Timothy Smith, "Religion and Ethnicity in America," *American Historical Review* 83 (1978): 1155–1185; Oscar Handlin, *The Uprooted: The Epic Story of the Migrations that Made the American People* (Boston: Grosset & Dunlap, 1951); Ostergren, *A Community Transplanted;* Inger Selander, *O hur saligt att få vandra: motiv och symboler i den frikyrkliga sången* [Oh How Blest It Is to Wander: Motifs and Symbols in Free Church Song] (Stockholm: Gummesons, 1980).

17. Stenwall to Erland Carlsson, Berga, March 1, 1854, published in vol. 5, Augustana Historical Society Publications, Rock Island, 1935, 115.

18. *Paul Peter Waldenströms Minnesanteckningar 1838–1875* (Stockholm: Svenska Missionsförbundets Förlag, 1928), 49; etext version Project Runeberg, accessed September 2005.

19. Pietism emerged first in Germany in the middle of the seventeenth century. It spread to other Lutheran countries, where it took on distinct forms. Portions of the defeated Swedish army at Poltava experienced a revival while being imprisoned in Russia. When they returned home they brought pietism with them. The movement got its name from the writings of Philip Jakob Spener (*Pia Desideria*) and its social program from the work of Spener's son-in-law, August Hermann Franke, who established the Halle Institution near Wittenberg. Contemporary scholarship on pietism in English is increasing but still spare, though the importance of the movement for the development of American Lutheranism is well known. Pietism has generated a lively debate about definitions. A recent study by Harry Yeide Jr., "Studies in Classical Pietism: The Flowering of the Ecclesiola," *Studies in Church History*, vol. 6 (New York: Peter Lang, 1997), focuses on the programs of key German leaders. He argues that one aspect of pietism held them all together: the impulse to form small committed groups that aimed to reform or improve society.

20. Hilding Pleijel documents this network in *Herrnhutismen i Sydsverige* (Stockholm: Svenska kyrkans diakonistyrelsens bokförlag, 1925).

21. "Types of Swedish Piety," *Augustana Quarterly* 7, no. 3 (September 1928) and 8, no. 2 (April 1929). These differences appeared in a series of articles in the journal. The synod's Swedish background was no longer a living memory and was now historicized and interpreted. The effort to disentangle the many streams of pious tradition in the Swedish revival did serve to counteract a too easy dismissal of it or the rhetorical invocation of a monolithic (and probably lost) piety. Similar studies appeared in Swedish journals. The process of change in America involved the incorporation of American elements into the mix.

22. Gustaf Aulén, *Hundraårs Svensk Kyrkodebatt* (Stockholm: Svenska kyrkans diakonistyrelsens bokförlag, 1953) examines the differences in the views on ministry that distinguished different parties in the Church of Sweden throughout the period of the revival.

23. Sundkler, *Svenska Missionssällskapet 1835–1876*, 31–44, 221–223, 432–434.

Chapter 2: Making Lutheran Connections in America

1. The Eielsen Synod (Hauge's devotee Erling Eielsen) started in 1846, followed by a more clergy-oriented Norwegian Synod in 1853. Occupying a mediating position between the theologically sophisticated Norwegian Synod and the lay-oriented spirituality of the Eielsen Synod, was a small group of pastors and congregations who affiliated with the American Lutheran General Synod. Each group suffered splits, making for five Norwegian synods by the 1870s. See E. Clifford Nelson, ed., *The Lutherans in North America* (Philadelphia: Fortress Press, 1977), 185–187.

2. Happy Danes were influenced by Nicolas Frederick Severin Grundtvig, the Danish bishop, hymnwriter, and educator who advocated the development of the "folk" church, while the holy Danes advanced the views of Vilhelm Beck, the founder of the Danish Inner Mission, a pietistic revival leader who emphasized withdrawal from worldliness. The Danish churches established separate synods and schools but cooperated in producing a hymnal.

3. G. Everett Arden, *Augustana Heritage: The History of the Augustana Lutheran Church* (Rock Island, Ill.: Augustana Book Concern, 1963), 32ff. Esbjörn was accepted for support in January 1850.

4. Josiah Strong's report to the American Home Missionary Society later in the century, *Our Country: Its Possible Future and Its Present Crisis* (New York: The American Home Missionary Society, 1885) gave voice to the accumulated experience of that body in working to evangelize and "Anglo-Saxonize" the country. "My plea is not Save America for America's sake, but Save America for the world's sake." quoted in Sydney Ahlstrom, *A Religious History of the American People* (New Haven, Conn.: Yale University Press, 1972), 733–734.

5. In the minutes of the Massachusetts' branch of the American Home Missionary Society (AHMS), the superintendent registered surprise at the diligence of Swedish preachers, who kept careful records of numbers of people reached and converted. The earnest Swedish workers impressed the society's leaders so much that they increased funding for Scandinavian work at the expense of other immigrant groups. By 1880, when the AHMS supported Swedish Mission Covenant preachers, more than half of their funding went to Swedes. See Maria Erling, "Crafting an Urban Piety: Religion among Swedish Immigrants in New England" (Th.D. diss., Harvard Divinity School, 1996).

6. Anecdote included in William A. Passavant's talk at the dedication of Augustana College and Seminary building on October 14, 1875, as reported in *Augustana* (October 21, 1875).

7. L. P. Esbjörn to T. N. Hasselquist, April 2, 1853, printed in *Tidskrift för Svensk Evangelisk Luthersk Kyrkohistoria i Amerika* (Rock Island, Ill.: Augustana Book Concern, 1899), 254. Translation by author.

8. Herman Amberg Preus, *Vivacious Daughter: Seven Lectures on the Church in America*, trans. Todd Nichol (Northfield, Minn.: Norwegian American Historical Society, 1990).

9. Emmet Eklund, *Peter Fjellstedt: Missionary Mentor to Three Continents* (Rock Island, Ill.: Augustana Historical Society, 1983) discusses the career of this educator and ministerial recruiter. See letter from P. Fjellstedt to T. N. Hasselquist, Göteborg, May 5, 1870, in Gunnar Westin, *Emigranterna och kyrkan: brev från och till svenskar i amerika 1849–1892* (Stockholm: Svenska kyrkans diakonistyrelsens bokförlag, 1932), 262.

10. Conrad Bergendoff, *The Augustana Ministerium: A Study of the Careers of the 2,504 Pastors of the Augustana Evangelical Lutheran Synod/Church, 1850–1962* (Rock Island, Ill.: Augustana Historical Society, 1980), passim.

11. See lecture 6 in Preus, *Vivacious Daughter.*

12. Quoted in *Korsbaneret* (Chicago: Föreningen Ungdomens Vänner, 1881), 94.

13. Ibid., 114.

14. Esbjörn to Hasselquist, March, 1854, printed in *Tidskrift för Svensk Evangelisk Luthersk Kyrkohistoria i Amerika*, 265. Translation by Maria Erling.

15. L. P. Esbjörn to Erland Carlsson, October 5, 1854, in *Tidskrift för Svensk Evangelisk Luthersk Kyrkohistoria i Amerika*, 270.

16. *Hemlandet* (January 3, 1854).

17. Ibid.

18. Eric Norelius, *Hasselquist Lefnadsteckning* (Rock Island, Ill.: Augustana Book Concern, n.d.), 67. Hasselquist's "afskedsord" in the December 18, 1858, issue of *Hemlandet* included these figures. At that point he turned over the editorship to Eric Norelius.

19. *Hemlandet* (January 3, 1854).

20. Norelius's history of the Swedish-American congregations includes references to individuals who had lived in a series of these settlements.

21. *Hemlandet* (January 17, 1855). The extra detail given in the letter, that the slaves had given the travelers a blessing before departing, ought to be noted. Swedish people believed that the blessing of a poor man was especially lucky.

22. Ibid.

23. The Sioux Indian uprising occurred in Minnesota in the spring of 1862, after the Sioux Indians had waited in vain for a promised government food shipment. The violence forced many settlers to abandon their farms and seek shelter in the towns. Many farms were attacked and both women and children brutally killed. The panic that ensued created a mob reaction. After their arrest and trial, thirty-eight Sioux were hung in Mankato, the largest mass execution in American history.

24. In 1853 they disavowed their 1851 constitution and turned in a strictly confessional direction, toward the conservative Missouri Synod. See Preus, *Vivacious Daughter*, passim.

25. Quoted in George Stephenson, *The Founding of the Augustana Synod, 1850–1960* (Rock Island, Ill.: Augustana Book Concern, 1927), 40.

26. Esbjörn advised the young Norelius to attend the German Lutheran seminary in Ohio instead of the General Synod's Gettysburg Seminary, probably because it was closer to Illinois. George Stephenson covers the divergent motives among Swedish preachers in George Stephenson, *The Founding of the Augustana Synod, 1850–1860* (Rock Island, Ill.: Augustana Book Concern, 1927), passim.

27. Stephenson, *The Founding of the Augustana Synod, 1850–1860*, 60–61.

28. Earlier histories of the Augustana Synod go into this episode in some detail. See chapters 3 and 4 in Arden, *Augustana Heritage*.

29. These continued a relationship with the General Synod via a new Ansgarii Synod, a group that emphasized a revival and mission orientation. Later some of the leaders and congregations joined the Evangelical Mission Covenant in the 1880s.

30. Todd W. Nichol, *All These Lutherans: Three Paths toward a New Lutheran Church* (Minneapolis: Augsburg Publishing House, 1986), 47.

31. Stephenson, *The Founding of the Augustana Synod, 1850–1860*, 125–129. Letters between Hasselquist and the Revs. Simeon Harkey and William Reynolds indicated that Americans had little warning of Esbjörn's unhappiness. He was uncommunicative, and they fully expected to get a fair hearing from the Scandinavian representatives at a meeting. This open meeting did not happen.

32. George Stephenson explores the tension between Hasselquist and Esbjörn in Stephenson, *The Founding of the Augustana Synod*; O. Fritiof Ander, *Life of Hasselquist* (Rock Island, Ill.: Augustana Historical Society Publications, 1931) corrects earlier impressions of harmony between the two men in Eric Norelius's biography of Hasselquist; Esbjörn's letters to Norelius are printed in Eric Norelius, ed., *Tidskrift för Ev. Luth. Kyrkohistoria i N. Amerika och för Teologiska och kyrkliga frågor* (Rock Island, Ill.: Lutheran Augustana Book Concern, 1899), 323–335.

33. L. P. Esbjörn to Eric Norelius, January 30, 1862, and May 27, 1862, in *Tidskrift* (1899): 327–329, trans. Maria Erling, italics in printed text.

34.Various models for this proposed farming community relied on purchase of railroad land that would be sold at a slight profit, benefiting the school. Hasselquist advertised his proposal in his newspaper and received scorn for being a land speculator. See Eric Norelius, *Hasselquist Lefnadsteckning* (Rock Island, Ill.: Augustana Lutheran Book Concern, n.d.), 90–100.

35. L. P. Esbjörn to P. Wieselgren, May 27, 1862, in Gunnar Westin, *Emigranterna och Kyrkan* (Stockholm: Svenska Diakonistyrelses Bokförlag, 1932), 107.

36. *Protokoll hållet vid Skandinaviska Ev. Lutherska Augustana Synodens* 4:de årsmötet i Chicago, Illinois, Juni 23–29, 1863, 17.

37. Norelius, *Hasselquist Lefnadsteckning,* 100. Hasselquist's biographer, Eric Norelius, was also his rival in school and newspaper matters, so his account covers a period of time when Hasselquist's decisions were much resented by Norelius and his Minnesota cohorts.

38. Karl A. Olsson, *By One Spirit* (Chicago: Covenant, 1962), tells the Mission Covenant side of this conflict. See especially chapters 1 and 2 in part 2 beginning on page 179.

39.T. N. Hasselquist to P. Wieselgren, Paxton, Illinois, August 12, 1868, in Westin, *Emigranterna och Kyrkan*, 197.

40.Anna Olsson to friends in Värmland, Sweden, Lindsborg, Kansas, summer 1868, included in typescript translation of letters of Olof Olsson in the papers of Karl Mattson, private collection.

41. Ibid.

42. Ibid.

Doctrinal Controversy: Augustana and the Mission Friends

1. Karl A. Olsson discusses the controversy in *By One Spirit* (Chicago: Covenant, 1962), 110–114. Olof Olsson published *Reformation, socinianism och Waldenströmianism. Föredrag wid Augustana College och Seminary i America 1878* (Rock Island, Ill.: Ungdomens Vännen, 1880).

2. E. Clifford Nelson, *The Lutherans in North America* (Philadelphia: Fortress Press, 1976), 267–272, 313–328.

3. J. A. Krantz wrote the necrology for P. Sjöblom in *Tidskrift for Theologiska Frågor* (Rock Island, Ill.: Augustana Book Concern, 1910) with two pages on the aged pastor's reputation for narrow minded argument. Stephenson wrote that Lindahl and Sjöblom in the Olsson case "entirely neglected the amenities due the broken and beloved leader." George Stephenson, *The Religious Aspects of Swedish Immigration* (Minneapolis: University of Minnesota Press, 1932), 347.

4. Olof Olsson to C. A. Swensson, Leipzig, August 29, 1889, Augustana College Special Collections.

5. Carl Swensson to Olof Olsson, Lindsborg, May 23, 1891, Augustana College Archives.

Chapter 3: Mission Impulses

1. Carl Frederick Johansson, *Lefnadsteckning* parts written 1902 and 1917, unpublished ms., 1.

2. Ibid., 3.

3.The Hermannsberg Mission Society was founded by Louis Harms who was popular with mission societies in Sweden because he promoted lay missionary work. Missionaries lived in self-supporting colonies, working as craftsmen, farmers, and laborers, while preaching the gospel to the native people. Harms' mission theory conflicted with the Leipzig Society's founder, Theodore Graul, who insisted on theological and academic preparation for missionaries. See chapter 15 in Bengt Sundkler, *Svenska Missionssällskapet 1835–1876* (Uppsala, Sweden: Almqvist och Wiksell, 1937) and chapter 13 in Oscar Rundblom, *Svenska förbindelser med Leipzigmissionen åren 1853–1876* (Lund, Sweden: Gleerups, 1948). Both books have brief English summaries.

4. The Evangelical Fatherland Foundation (EFS) organized revivals and missions both at home and abroad. Carl Olof Rosenius, the famous leader of the EFS in the 1860s, published a newspaper, *Pietisten.*

5. Johansson, *Levnadsteckning*, 3.

6. Olof Olsson to T. N. Hasselquist, February 18, 1868. Westin, *Emigranterna och Kyrkan*.

7. P. A. Ahlberg to T. N. Hasselquist, February 25, 1868. Westin, *Emigranterna och Kyrkan*.

8. *Protokoll bok för Augustana-synodens Missions-Komite*, 15, Yale University Divinity School Library Special Collections, trans. Maria Erling, emphasis added.

9. G. Everett Arden, *Augustana Heritage: The History of the Augustana Lutheran Church* (Rock Island, Ill.: Augustana Book Concern, 1963), 132.

10. *Protokoll bok för Augustana-synodens Missions-Komite*, 31–33.

11. Arden, *Augustana Heritage*, 141. Arden argues that the presence of the Norwegians in the first decades of the synod's life contributed a flexibility and theological sensitivity to the synod.

12. Maria Erling, "Crafting an Urban Piety: Religion among Swedish Immigrants in New England" (Th.D. diss., Harvard Divinity School, 1996), ch. 3.

13. The Norwegian Synod pastor Herman Amberg Preus reported on the theological carelessness of Erland Carlsson and praised the virile theology of Missouri Synod pastors. See Herman Amberg Preus, *Vivacious Daughter: Seven Lectures on the Religious Situation of Norwegians in America*, trans. Todd Nichol (Northfield, Minn.: Norwegian American Historical Society, 1990), 158.

14. Disputes within the revival circles in Sweden related to Lutheran orthodoxy are discussed by Karl A. Olsson, *By One Spirit* (Chicago: Covenant, 1962), 149–165.

15. *Protokoll bok för Augustana-synodens Missions-Komite*, 143, 145.

16. Johannes Teleen, "Indian Mission," *Jubel-Album tillegnat Augustana Synoden*, ed. C. A. Swensson and L. G. Abrahamson (Rock Island, Ill.: Augustana Book Concern, 1883), 197–198.

17. Ibid., 196.

Chapter 4: Creating a Swedish-American Lutheran Identity

1. Conrad Bergendoff, *The Augustana Ministerium: A Study of the Careers of the 2,504 Pastors of the Augustana Evangelical Lutheran Synod/Church, 1850–1962* (Rock Island, Ill.: Augustana Historical Society, 1980).

2. Adolf Hult, "Ungdomsföreningarna," *Minneskrift med anledning af Augustanasynoden's femtioåriga tillvaro* (Rock Island, Ill.: Augustana Book Concern, 1910), 395.

3. Carlsson wrote more about the revival in the next volume, 1882, and in that context commented on the way that the revival spirit soon petered out, like spring turning to summer. See also Emory Lindquist's discussion of this period in his biography of Erland Carlsson, in *Shepherd of an Immigrant People* (Rock Island, Ill.: Augustana Historical Society, 1978), 55ff.

4. Conrad Bergendoff, *Augustana—A Profession of Faith* (Rock Island, Ill.: Augustana College Library, 1969), 55. The class included Constantine M. Esbjörn, Joshua Hasselquist, Charles J Petri, Johan H. Randahl, Carl Aaron Swensson, and Matthias Wahlstrom.

5. Daniel Nystrom, *A Ministry of Printing: History of the Publication House of Augustana Lutheran Church* (Rock Island, Ill.: Augustana, 1962), 21. The first book published, *Vid Korset*, contained sixteen devotional readings for Lent written by Olof Olsson. A bestseller, it was translated in 1942 as *Salvation in Christ*.

6. Adolf Hult, "Ungdomsföreningarna," 400.

7. T. N. Hasselquist, *Levnadstekning* (Rock Island, Ill.: Augustana Book Concern, n.d.), 188.

8. The many negotiations that must have occurred in relation to printing these volumes are indicated in the migrating printing venues of the first five years. The 1881 edition was printed again by Enander and Bohman, but in 1882, *Korsbaneret* was printed in Moline by the Westrand and Thulin printery. In 1883, it was done by Thulin and Anderson in Moline, and in 1885 a new firm, Augustana Book Concern printery, issued the serial.

9. C. A. Swensson and Olof Olsson, eds., *Korsbaneret 1880* (Chicago: Enander & Bohman, 1880), 95.

10. Eventually it provided an ongoing record of the life of every deceased minister, as well as prominent lay people. Finally, in the 1940s only the very old people in the synod could appreciate or read the little annual. But when it began, it was a fresh look at a growing church for newly won young people. Portraits of newly built parsonages and church buildings gave readers an idea of the accomplishments of other congregations.

11. Doniver Lund, *Centennial History: Gustavus Adolphus College* (St. Peter, Minn.: Gustavus Adolphus College Press, 1963), 51. Wahlström came to Gustavus indirectly. He graduated from the seminary in 1879 and agreed to do mission work with the Indians. Norelius and Wahlstrom began corresponding when Wahlstrom left for mission work in Colorado. His stay there was brief; his friend and classmate C. A. Swensson wrote that he couldn't reveal the reasons for his abrupt end of missionary work, but could note that his health was not good. A year later Norelius prevailed upon him to join the Gustavus faculty and serve as president.

12. Peter Froeberg to Sven Froeberg, Rock Island, Ill., May 4, 1902, trans. Maria Erling, Froeberg Collection, Grand Rapids, Mich. Peter later became president of Upsala College; Sven taught biology at Gustavus for many years.

13. Quoted in Martin Carlson, *Forward by Faith: A History of the Augustana Luther League* (Rock Island, Ill.: Augustana Book Concern, 1947), 21.

14. Lindahl's editorial in *Augustana* 44, no. 6 (February 9, 1899): 88.

Chapter 5: Education for a New American Generation

1. Sermon preached at the final commencement at the Fryxell Girl's School in Rostad, Sweden, by Frederik Thelander, June 6, 1877, *Carlsson Correspondence*, Swenson Center, Augustana College.

2. Patricia R. Hill, *The World Their Household: The American Woman's Foreign Mission Movement and Cultural Transformation, 1870–1920* (Ann Arbor: University of Michigan Press, 1988). Hill's study does not cover Lutheran efforts, as sources are seldom in English. Augustana women's organizing reflected what happened in other denominations some twenty years later.

3. *Autobiographical memories of Augusta Stenholm Flodman*, file drawer folder L144, Archives of Luther College (Wahoo) at Midland College, Fremont, Neb.

4. Ibid.

5. Stephenson wrote a five-part series on the synod's educational history for the *Lutheran Companion* in 1931, when he was a board member and involved in a behind-the-scenes campaign to improve the quality of faculty at the seminary. Stephenson taught at the University of Minnesota and had just published his history, *The Religious Aspects of Swedish Immigration*, with the University of Minnesota Press in 1930.

6. Doniver Lund, *Gustavus Adolphus College: A Centennial History, 1862–1962* (St. Peter, Minn.: Gustavus Adolphus College Press, 1963), 11ff.

7. Conrad Bergendoff, *The Augustana Ministerium A Study of the Careers of the 2,504 Pastors of the Augustana Evangelical Lutheran Synod/Church, 1850–1962* (Rock Island, Ill.: Augustana Historical Society, 1980), 16.

8. Ibid., 12. Letter from Andrew Jackson to Eric Norelius, August 20, 1862.

9. Folk Schools in Elkhorn, Iowa, and Tyler, Minnesota, provided a literary and religious education for Danish settlers in the classic Folk High School ideal. Swedish immigrants also experimented with the idea, based on the use of the name for the congregational schools in Chicago and the Minnesota settlements.

10. By 1893, Martin Luther College in Chicago; Hope College in Moorhead, Minnesota; and Upsala College in New Jersey were in the works. Later efforts included Coeur d'Alene College in Idaho, Northwestern College in Fergus Falls, Minnesota, and Minnesota College in Minneapolis, Minnesota.

11. Carl Swensson and Lars Gustaf Abrahamson, *Jubel-Album tillegnat Augustana-Synoden* (Chicago: National, 1893), 144.

12. Emory Lindquist, *Bethany in Kansas: The History of a College* (Lindsborg, Kan.: Bethany College, 1975), 2.

13. Ibid., 14. Letter from T. N. Hasselquist to C. A. Swensson, October 20, 1885.

14. Swensson and Abrahamson, *Jubel-Album tillegnat Augustana Synoden*, 147.

15. C. A. Swensson, *I Sverige, minnen och bilder från mina fäders land* (Omaha, Neb. and Stockholm: Swedish American Book Company, 1891), 35.

16. Ibid.

17. Ibid., 36.

18. George Stephenson, *The Religious Aspects of Swedish Immigration* (Minneapolis: University of Minnesota Press, 1932), 338.

19. Ibid., 345. According to the estimate of John Jesperson, the business manager at Augustana College, the accumulated debt of the synod's institutions in the early 1890s reached over $120,000 and was growing at a rate of $25,000 a year.

20. Erland Carlsson, "Presidential Report to the Synod," 1888.

21. Oscar Fritiof Ander, *T. N. Hasselquist: The Career and Influence of a Swedish-American Clergyman, Journalist and Educator* (Rock Island, Ill.: Augustana Historical Society, 1931), 151.

22. S. P. A. Lindall, "Presidential Report to the Synod," 1890.

23. Ibid.

24. *Autobiographical memories of Augusta Stenholm Flodman.*

25. Ibid.

26. *Svenska Journalen* 10, no. 45 (Nov. 5, 1896). Clippings from this newspaper are in the archives of Luther College, Wahoo, Nebraska, and at Midland College, Fremont, Nebraska.

27. *Svenska Journalen* 10, no. 53 (Dec. 31, 1896).

28. Ibid.

29. Ibid.

30. *Autobiographical memories of Augusta Stenholm Flodman.*

31. Ibid.

Music for the Journey

1. *Hemlandssånger* 443, *Hymnal* 1901, 338, *Hymnal* 1925, 526.

2. Olof Olsson to Carl A. Swensson, August 18, 1891, Olsson collection, Augustana College Archives, Rock Island, Ill. Olsson used the word *picnic* without translating it. Translation by M. Erling.

3. Olof Olsson to Carl A. Swensson, January 1892, Olson Collection.

Chapter 6: Becoming an American Church

1. Milton Gordon, *Assimilation in American Life: The Role of Race, Religion, and National Origins* (New York: Oxford University Press, 1964), 28–29.

2. Robert C. Ostergren, *A Community Transplanted: The Trans-Atlantic Experience of a Swedish Immigrant Settlement in the Upper Middle West, 1835–1915* (Madison: University of Wisconsin Press, 1988), 282–283.

3. Marcus L. Hansen, *The Problem of the Third Generation Immigrant* (Rock Island, Ill.: Augustana Historical Society, 1938).

4. Conrad Bergendoff, "The Role of Augustana in the Transplanting of a Culture Across the Atlantic," in J. Iverne Dowie and J. Thomas Tredway, eds., *The Immigration of Ideas: Studies in the North Atlantic Community* (Rock Island, Ill.: Augustana Historical Society, 1968), 82–83.

5. C. A. Lindvall, "Svenska språket i Amerika," *Yearbook of the Swedish Historical Society of America* 5 (1914–1915), 17, quoted in Nils Hasselmo, "The Language Question," *Perspectives on Swedish Immigration* (Chicago: Swedish Pioneer Historical Society, 1978), 227.

6. George M. Stephenson, *The Religious Aspects of Swedish Immigration* (Minneapolis: University of Minnesota Press, 1932), 455, 476.

7. Blanck, *Becoming Swedish-American*, 75–80.

8. The *Augustana Journal* (first called the *Alumnus*) was the direct predecessor of what would become the English-language synodical publication, the *Lutheran Companion*. There had been an earlier, short-lived periodical called the *Augustana Observer* published by three pastors on the East Coast beginning in 1882 that did not survive for more than about two years.

9. A. W. Williamson, "Our English Work," *Augustana Journal* 3, no. 5 (March 1895): 103.

10. Olaf Olsson, "Shall We Be Americanized within Our Synod, or Shall We Americanize Our Synod Out of Existence?" *Augustana Journal* 6, no. 24 (December 15, 1896): 2.

11. Mark A. Granquist, "American Hymns and Swedish Immigrants," *Lutheran Quarterly* 20, no. 4 (Winter 2006): 409–428.

12. Blanck, *Becoming Swedish-American*, 140–153.

13. Daniel Nystrom, *A Ministry of Printing: History of the Publication House of the Augustana Lutheran Church, 1889–1962* (Rock Island, Ill.: Augustana, 1962), 72.

14. Sture Lindmark, *Swedish America 1914–1932: Studies in Ethnicity with Emphasis on Illinois and Minnesota*, Studia Historica Upsaliensia, vol. 37 (Stockholm: Läromedelsförlagen, 1971), 211, and Hasselmo, "The Language Question," 229–232.

15. Conrad Bergendoff, "The Augustana Pastor: Sage of a Thousand Immigrants from Sweden," *Swedish Pioneer Historical Quarterly* 31, no. 1 (January 1980): 40.

16. Stephenson, *The Religious Aspects of Swedish Immigration*, 459, 473.

17. Emeroy Johnson, *God Gave the Growth: The Story of the Lutheran Minnesota Conference, 1878–1958* (Minneapolis: T. S. Denison, 1958), 219–221.

18. Ira O. Nothstein, "The Language Transition in the Augustana Synod," *Augustana Quarterly* 24 (1945): 327–331.

19. Ostergren, *A Community Transplanted*, 277–278.

20. The quote is from Bergins' daughter, quoted in Wayne Wheeler, "An Analysis of Social Change in a Swedish-Immigrant Community: The Case of Lindsborg, Kansas," *Immigrant Communities and Ethnic Minorities in the United States and Canada*, no. 9 (New York: AMS, 1986), 262.

21. C. M. Esbjörn, in a 1910 Jubilee address, quoted in Nothstein, "The Language Transition in the Augustana Synod," 222, note 10.

22. J. Tellen, "Is It of Importance That the Augustana Synod Shall Continue to Live in America? Shall It Continue a Swedish or Bi-Lingual Body?" *Augustana Journal* 12, no. 22 (November 15, 1904): 3.

23. "The Language Question," *Lutheran Companion* 19, no. 28 (July 15, 1911): 1.

24. Karl Olsson, *By One Spirit* (Chicago: Covenant, 1962), 506.

25. This history is repeated a number of places, especially in Johnson, *God Gave the Growth*, 209–227, and Stephenson, *The Religious Aspects of Swedish Immigration*, 458–476.

26. *Referat*, Minnesota Conference (1894) 14, quoted in G. Everett Arden, *Augustana Heritage: The History of the Augustana Lutheran Church* (Rock Island, Ill.: Augustana Book Concern, 1963), 241–242.

27. G. A. Brandelle to G. Keller Ruprecht, January 1, 1923, *G. A. Brandelle Presidential Papers*, Archives of the Evangelical Lutheran Church in America, Elk Grove Village, Illinois.

28. M. W. Montgomery, *The Wind from the Holy Spirit in Sweden and Norway* (New York: American Home Missionary Society, 1885), 6–7.

29. George Trabert, *English Lutheranism in the Northwest* (Philadelphia: General Council Publication House, 1914), 68–69.

30. See Mark A. Granquist, "As Others Saw Them: Swedes and American Religion in the Twin Cities," in Philip J. Anderson and Dag Blanck, eds., *Swedes in the Twin Cities: Immigrant Life and Minnesota's Urban Frontier* (St Paul: Minnesota Historical Society Press, 2001), 270–285.

31. Nothstein, "The Language Transition in the Augustana Synod," 334.

32. A. D. Mattson, *The Polity of the Augustana Lutheran Church*, rev. ed. (Rock Island, Ill.: Augustana Book Concern, 1952), 119.

33. See Blanck, *Becoming Swedish-American*, 17–29, and Lindmark, *Swedish America 1914– 1932*, 191–218.

34. For a full discussion of these influences, see Granquist, "American Hymns and Swedish Immigrants," 409–428.

35. These figures are from information in the standard reference for Swedish hymnody, Oscar Lövgren, *Psalm-och Sånglexicon* (Stockholm: Gummessons Bokförlag, 1964).

36. For this new "Awakened" hymnody, see J. Irving Erickson, *Twice-Born Hymns* (Chicago: Covenant, 1976), and C. Howard Smith, *Scandinavian Hymnody from the Reformation to the Present*, ATLA monograph series, no. 23 (Metuchen N.J.: Scarecrow, 1987).

37. Oscar N. Olson, *The Augustana Lutheran Church in America 1860–1910: The Formative Period* (Davenport, Iowa: Arcade Office and Letter Service, 1956), 73. Letter from T. N. Hasselquist to J. Ausland, July 17, 1874.

38. In "Pulpit and Altar," Emmer Engberg, et al., eds., *Centennial Essays* (Rock Island, Ill.: Augustana, 1960), 191, Clifford A. Nelson suggests, "It became rather normal that 'Psalmboken' was used at Sunday morning services and *Hemlandssånger* was used at Vespers and other services." In "Sweden," *Hymnal Companion to the Lutheran Book of Worship* (Philadelphia: Fortress Press, 1981), 46, historian Joel Lundeen said of *Hemlandssånger*, "This collection was expressly *not* intended for use at Sunday morning worship." This, however, seems more like a desire to maintain the intended pattern than to describe the actual practice in synodical congregations.

39. Olson, *The Augustana Lutheran Church in America 1860–1910*, 74.

40. Granquist, "American Hymns," 432.

41. Henry Carl Whyman, "The Conflict and Adjustment of Two Religious Cultures—the Swedish and the American (as found in the Swede's Relation to American Methodism)" (Ph.D. diss., New York University, 1937), 203.

42. One wonders how widespread its use was, because there were so few congregations using English at the time.

43. Arden, *Augustana Heritage*, 229.

44. Bergendoff, "The Augustana Pastor," 40.

45. Brandelle (1861–1936), Bengston (1862–1937), Hult (1869–1943), Evald (1857–1946), and Wendell (1866–1950).

46. Bersell (1892–1967), Miller (1890–1975), Bergendoff (1895–1997), and Ryden (1886– 1981).

47. Data derived from Conrad Bergendoff, *The Augustana Ministerium A Study of the Careers of the 2,504 Pastors of the Augustana Evangelical Lutheran Synod/Church, 1850–1962* (Rock Island, Ill.: Augustana Historical Society, 1980).

48. Mark A. Granquist, "In a Region of their Own: Scholarly Refugees from American Lutheranism," *Essays and Reports of the Lutheran Historical Conference*, vol. 21 (2006).

49. "Prophetic?" *Lutheran Companion* 22, no. 12 (March 22, 1913): 1.

Chapter 7: A New Century Brings Change

1. The biographies of P. A Cederstam and Carl Peter Rydholm that follow are in the 1903 edition of *Korsbaneret*, 129–150.

2. Ibid., 145. This biography was written by a younger historian, Nils Forsander, who also followed Norelius's formula.

3. *Minnes-Skrift Svenska Ev-Luth Immanuels Kyrkan i Chicago 1853–1903*: 29, 122, 127.

4. "Profile of Emmy Evald," *Minnes-Skrift Svenska Ev-Luth Immanuels Kyrkan i Chicago 1853– 1903*: 52.

5. Charlotte Odman, "A Great Leader Gone: Mrs. Emmy Evald, Lover of Missions, Dies," *Lutheran Companion* 45, no. 1 (January 1, 1947): 5.

6. Ibid.

7. C. A. Swensson and L. G. Abrahamson, *Jubel Album Tillegnadt Augustana-Synoden* (Chicago: National, 1893), 499.

8. Patricia R. Hill, *The World Their Household: The American Woman's Foreign Mission Movement and Cultural Transformation, 1870–1920* (Ann Arbor: University of Michigan Press, 1988), 4.

9. Hill, *The World Their Household*, passim.

10. Emmy Evald, "Among Ourselves," *Mission Tidning* (May 1919): 18.

11. *Jubelminnen från Luth. Minnesota Konferensens Halfsekelfest, 7–11, Oktober, 1908* (Rock Island, Ill.: Augustana Book Concern, 1908), 92–93.

12. Ibid.

13. Ibid.

14. George Drach, ed., *Our Church Abroad* (Philadelphia: United Lutheran Publishing House, 1926), 137.

15. Mrs. Peter (Mathilda) Peterson, *These Fifty Years, 1892–1942* (Chicago: Woman's Missionary Society of Augustana Synod, 1942), 31.

16. J. N. Brandelle to C. J. Bengston, Chicago, July 18, 1903, *Bengston Correspondence*, Archives of the Evangelical Lutheran Church in America, Elk Grove Village, Illinois. Brandelle used the Swedish word *from, frommare, frommaste* for the title.

17. Jules Mauritzson to C. J. Bengston, 1903, *Bengston Correspondence*, Archives of the Evangelical Lutheran Church in America, Elk Grove Village, Illinois.

18. Conrad Bergendoff, *The Augustana Ministerium A Study of the Careers of the 2,504 Pastors of the Augustana Evangelical Lutheran Synod/Church, 1850–1962* (Rock Island, Ill.: Augustana Historical Society, 1980). A review of the Augustana ministerium reveals that it wasn't until 1914 that the majority of new ordinands were born in America and not until 1934 that the entire new class of pastors were born in America.

19. Eric Norelius, *De Svenska Lutherska Forsamlingarnas och Svenskarnes Historia i Amerika*, vol. 2 (Rock Island, Ill.: Augustana Book Concern, 1916), 220–222.

20. Oscar Benson, "The Social Thrust of the Augustana Lutheran Church," *Augustana Seminary Review* 12, no. 2 (Spring 1960): 21; and Burnice Fjellman, "Women in the Church," *Centennial Essays* (Rock Island, Ill.: Augustana Book Concern, 1960), ch. 13. It would take another generation—until 1930—before women had a voice in the official affairs of the church.

21. Jules Mauritzson to C. J. Bengston, Feb. 5, 1911, *Bengston Correspondence*, Archives of the Evangelical Lutheran Church in America, Elk Grove Village, Illinois. Extensive quotes from this letter follow in the next two paragraphs.

22. *Augustana* 56, no. 3 (June 29, 1911).

23. G. Everett Arden, *Augustana Heritage: The History of the Augustana Lutheran Church* (Rock Island, Ill.: Augustana Book Concern, 1963), 235.

Chapter 8: An American Church in a Changing America

1. G. A. Brandelle, "Presidential Report," *Minutes of the Augustana Synod, 1923*, 15.

2. G. A. Brandelle, "The Significance of the Augustana Synod to the Swedish Lutherans in America," *Augustana Synod, 1869–1910* (Rock Island, Ill.: Augustana Book Concern, 1910), 232. Quoted in Emmer E. Engberg, "Augustana and Code Morality," in Emmer Engberg, et al., eds., *Centennial Essays* (Rock Island, Ill.: Augustana, 1960), 123–4.

3. Mark A. Granquist, "The Augustana Synod and the Episcopal Church," *Lutheran Quarterly* 14, no. 2 (Summer 2000): 178–179, especially.

4. "Sacrifices to Drink," *Lutheran Companion* 103, no. 32 (August 7, 1957): 5.

5. *Referat*, 1880, 82. Quoted in A. D. Mattson, *The Polity of the Augustana Lutheran Church*, rev. ed. (Rock Island, Ill.: Augustana Book Concern, 1952), 434.

6. See D. Verner Swanson, *Index: Minutes of the Augustana Lutheran Church, 1860–1962* (Rock Island, Ill.: Augustana Book Concern, 1962), especially under "liquor" and "temperance."

7. *Minutes*, 1938, 224.

8. "Want Rum in Christmas," *Lutheran Companion* 103, no. 50 (December 11, 1957): 5.

9. Oscar A. Benson to Mrs. Axel Olund, May 11, 1954, *Oscar A. Benson Presidential Papers*, Archives of the Evangelical Lutheran Church in America, Elk Grove Village, Illinois.

10. G. A. Brandelle to Albin Lindgren, December 15, 1933, *G. A. Brandelle Presidential Papers*, Archives of the Evangelical Lutheran Church in America, Elk Grove Village, Illinois.

11. "The Motion Picture Curse," *Lutheran Companion* 21, no. 32 (August 9, 1913): 2; "The Moving Picture Theater and the Children," *Lutheran Companion* 4, no. 125 (June 24, 1933): 773; and an editorial, *Lutheran Companion* 35, no. 13 (March 26, 1927): 291.

12. "Moving Pictures," *Bible Banner* 3, no. 3 (March 1927): 13.

13. "Editorial," *Lutheran Companion* 35, no. 28 (July 9, 1927): 659.

14. "Through Eye and Ear," *Lutheran Companion* 55, no. 9 (February 26, 1947): 5; and "Motion Picture Council Indicts Movie Industry," *Lutheran Companion* 55, no. 45 (November 5, 1947): 3.

15. Leanus I. Johnson, "The Dance," *Lutheran Companion* 19, no. 43 (October 28, 1911): 7.

16. Adolf Hult, "The Dancing Church," *Bible Banner* 5, no. 3 (March 1929): 12.

17. "'It's Not Hurting Me!' A Letter from a College Girl," *Lutheran Companion* 45, no. 47 (November 18, 1937): 1489.

18. "The Popular Amusement Devil," *Lutheran Companion* 20, no. 10 (March 9, 1912): 6.

19. *Lutheran Companion* 35, no. 48 (November 11, 1927): 3.

20. Adolf Hult, "Do Christians Need the Card Table?" *Bible Banner* 3, no. 8 (August 1927): 7.

21. "Gamblers Adopt Repeal Strategy," *Lutheran Companion* 45, no. 39 (September 23, 1937): 3.

22. Quoted in Jeanne Johnson, *The Lighted Spire: The Story of the First 100 Years of the Cambridge Lutheran Church* (Cambridge, Minn.: Cambridge Lutheran Church, 1964), 120–121.

23. Quoted in Engberg, "Augustana and Code Morality," 136. Engberg does not identify the source of the quote, or the official involved.

24. "Motion Picture Council Indicts Movie Industry," *Lutheran Companion* 55, no. 45 (November 5, 1947): 3.

25. C. A. Strandberg, "The Menace of Smoking," *Lutheran Companion* 98, no. 46 (November 1, 1957): 10.

26. Engberg, "Augustana and Code Morality," 123.

27. Gustavus Adolphus College, *Catalogue, 1930–1931* (St. Peter, Minn.: Gustavus Adolphus College, 1930), 19–20.

28. "The Radio," *Bible Banner* 11, no. 2 (February 1935): 3.

29. Pearl Rosser, "What Do You Want on Radio?" *Lutheran Companion* 55, no. 8 (February 19, 1947): 8.

30. Doniver Lund, *Gustavus Adolphus College: A Centennial History, 1862–1962* (St Peter, Minn.: Gustavus Adolphus College Press, 1962), 138.

31. Ibid.

32. Conrad Bergendoff, *Augustana—A Profession of Faith: A History of Augustana College, 1860–1935* (Rock Island, Ill.: Augustana College Library, 1969), 171.

33. *Minutes*, 1950, 316–323.

34. On this period of time, see O. Fritiof Ander, "An Immigrant Community During the Progressive Era," in J. Iverne Dowie and Ernest Espelie, eds., *The Swedish Immigrant Community in Transition* (Rock Island, Ill.: Augustana Historical Society, 1963), 147–166.

35. "A Noble (?) Discontentment," *Young Lutheran's Companion* 18, no. 35 (August 27, 1910): 1.

36. "Editorial," *Young Lutheran's Companion* 15, no. 36 (September 7, 1907): 1.

37. "The Good and Bad of the Bill," *Lutheran Companion* 21, no. 28 (August 12, 1913), 2.

38. See, for example, "Child Labor Legislation," *Lutheran Companion* 22, no. 10 (March 6, 1915): 1; "A Minimum Wage," *Lutheran Companion* 21, no. 2 (May 24, 1913): 1; and J. H. F., "Conservation," *Young Lutheran's Companion* 18, no. 45 (November 5, 1910): 4.

39. "A Minimum Wage," *Lutheran Companion* 21, no. 2 (May 24, 1913): 1.

40. "Another Wrong to be Righted," *Lutheran Companion* 21, no. 4 (January 25, 1913): 1.

41. "Socialism," *Young Lutheran's Companion* 17, no. 25 (June 19, 1909): 1.

42. C. J. Södergren, "He Made Them Male and Female," *Young Lutheran's Companion* 15, no. 13 (March 30, 1907); "$3 a week," *Young Lutheran's Companion* 18, no. 3 (January 15, 1910): 3; "The Suffrage Amendment," *Lutheran Companion* 23, no. 5 (January 30, 1915): 8; and I. O. Nothstein, "Women's Suffrage," *Lutheran Companion* 22, no. 22 (May 30, 1914): 6.

43. Samuel M. Miller, "A Statement Concerning the Use of Women Workers on Home Mission Fields," *Bible Banner* 2, no. 5 (May 1926): 15–16.

44. Alfred Appell, "The Tyranny of Labor Organizations, *Augustana Journal* 2, no. 12 (October 1894): 281.

45. Hans Norman, "Swedes in North America," in Harold Runblom and Hans Norman, eds., *From Sweden to America: A History of the Migration* (Minneapolis: University of Minnesota Press, 1976), 260–76.

46. *Augustana Journal* 11, no. 12 (June 15, 1903): 1.

47. *Augustana Journal* 10, no. 8 (April 15, 1902): 6.

48. "Industrial Conditions," *Lutheran Companion* 20, no. 41 (October 12, 1912): 1; "Civil War in Colorado," *Lutheran Companion* 22, no. 19 (May 9, 1914): 2.

49. "Industrial Unrest Disturbs Nation," *Lutheran Companion* 45, no. 11 (March 11, 1937): 324.

50. "Labor Discord Grows Serious," *Lutheran Companion* 45, no. 17 (April 22, 1937): 514; Arnold Nelson, "Defends 'Sit Down' Strikes," *Lutheran Companion* 45, no. 30 (July 22, 1937): 932.

51. *Minutes*, 1937, 263–265.

52. See Gregory Lee Jackson, *Prophetic Voice for the Kingdom: The Impact of Alvin Daniel Mattson Upon the Social Consciousness of the Augustana Synod* (Rock Island, Ill.: Augustana Historical Society, 1986), 78–82.

53. A. D. Mattson, "Holds Labor not to Blame," *Lutheran Companion* 103, no. 32 (August 7, 1957): 8.

54. Malvin H. Lundeen to A. D. Mattson, November 14, 1960, *Malvin Lundeen Presidential Papers*, Archives of the Evangelical Lutheran Church in America, Elk Grove Village, Illinois.

55. For the general economic situation of the Swedish-American community, see Sture Lindmark, *Swedish America 1914–1932: Studies in Ethnicity with Emphasis on Illinois and Minnesota*, Studia Historica Upsaliensia, vol. 37 (Uppsala, Sweden: Läromedelsförlagen, 1971), especially 162–190.

56. E. O. Valberg to G. A. Brandelle, September 11, 1933, *G. A. Brandelle Presidential Papers*.

57. "Resolution from the Meeting of the Augustana Theological Faculty on December 15, 1932," and "G. A. Brandelle to Missionaries of the Board of Missions of the Augustana Synod," February 19, 1933, both in *G. A. Brandelle Presidential Papers*, ELCA Archives.

58. "When Emergencies Arise," *Lutheran Companion* 41, no. 21 (May 27, 1933): 662.

59. P. O. Bersell, "This is No Time to Quit," *Lutheran Companion* 41, no. 11 (March 18, 1933): 336.

60. G. Everett Arden, *Augustana Heritage: The History of the Augustana Lutheran Church* (Rock Island, Ill.: Augustana Book Concern, 1963), 329. It would appear that Bersell himself may have been setting the stage for the presidential election at the synodical convention in 1935, where he defeated Brandelle for the position. Brandelle complained bitterly to friends after the election that Bersell had engineered a political "campaign" against him.

61. "A sincere friend" to G. A. Brandelle, March 8, 1934, *G. A. Brandelle Presidential Papers.*

62. Theodore E. Matson, "The New Year Challenges the Christian Church," *Lutheran Companion* 41, no. 3 (January 21, 1933): 78.

63. "National Recovery," *Lutheran Companion* 41, no. 46 (November 18, 1933): 1443.

64. "President Urges Social Justice," *Lutheran Companion* 45, no. 6 (February 4, 1937): 163.

65. "Sundry Observations," *Augustana Journal* 9, no. 11 (June 1, 1901): 1; and *Lutheran Companion* 35, no. 18 (April 30, 1927): 411.

66. "The Leo M. Frank Case," *Lutheran Companion* 23, no. 35 (August 28, 1915): 8.

67. G. A. Brandelle to Zenah M. Corbe, April 6, 1932, *G. A. Brandelle Presidential Papers.*

68. "A Christian Remedy For Race Problems," *Lutheran Companion* 51, no. 28 (July 14, 1943): 857.

69. Frederick Nordquist, "Information Regarding Jewish Missions and the Position of the Augustana Synod Toward the Missionary Project," *Lutheran Companion* 41, no. 24 (June 17, 1933): 749.

70. "The Jew," *Lutheran Companion* 20, no. 15 (April 13, 1913): 1.

71. "Charles W. Erickson, "The Sign of the Budding Fig Tree," *Lutheran Companion* 41, no. 14 (April 8, 1933): 432.

72. S. M. Hill, "The Public School Question," *Alumnus* 1, nos. 10 and 11 (June/July 1893): 226.

73. *Young Lutheran's Companion* 16, no. 19 (May 9, 1908): 1.

74. George M. Stephenson, "The Roman Catholic Church and American Schools," *Lutheran Companion* 19, no. 52 (December 30, 1911): 6.

75. "Rome's Idea of Toleration," *Lutheran Companion* 45, no. 19 (May 6, 1937): 578.

76. "The Immigration Problem," *Lutheran Companion* 22, no. 22 (May 30, 1914): 6. For a general discussion of this topic, see Lindmark, 137–161.

77. "Restricted Immigration," *Lutheran Companion* 23, no. 2 (January 9, 1915): 8; *Augustana* 67, no. 11 (March 16, 1922): 168, quoted in Lindmark, 151; *Lutheran Companion* 37, no. 43 (October 26, 1929): 1349.

78. *Minutes*, 1926, 163–164.

79. Engberg, "Augustana and Code Morality," 122.

80. Augustana Evangelical Lutheran Church, Commission on Morals and Social Problems of the Church, *Social pronouncements of the Augustana Lutheran Church and its Conferences, 1937–1956* (Rock Island, Ill.: Augustana Book Concern, 1956), 3. This is a good source for understanding the social attitude of the synod at this time.

81. A. D. Mattson, "Social Problems of Our Day," *Lutheran Companion* 45, no. 1 (January 2, 1937): 14.

82. Paul H. Andreen, "The Pastor Faces Problems," *Lutheran Companion* 45, no. 44 (October 28, 1937): 1384.

83. *Lutheran Companion* 35, no. 7 (February 12, 1927): 1.

84. Roswell V. Peterson, "Relocating Our Urban Churches," *Lutheran Companion* 55, no. 11 (March 12, 1947): 21; Henry Hokenson, "America's Other Half . . . Who Are They?" *Lutheran Companion* 51, no. 35 (September 1, 1943): 968.

85. Earl G. Gustafson, "Another California Parsonage," *Lutheran Companion* 98, no. 6 (February 11, 1953): 2.

86. Paul R. Olson, "Protests Action on Negroes," *Lutheran Companion* 55, no. 3 (January 15, 1947): 2; Emil Chinlund, "The Race Problem," *Lutheran Companion* 55, no. 18 (April 30, 1947): 2.

87. "Pastor's Home Bombed," *Lutheran Companion* 103, no. 6 (February 6, 1957): 5; "A Disgrace to the Nation," *Lutheran Companion* 103, no. 41 (October 9, 1957): 7.

88. "Strange Maneuvers by Roman Church," *Lutheran Companion* 51, no. 18 (May 5, 1943): 2; "Rome's Infiltration of Public Schools," *Lutheran Companion* 98, no. 24 (June 17, 1953): 7; and "Bigotry in Chicago," *Lutheran Companion* 103, no. 2 (January 9, 1957): 7. On the reaction to

the endorsement of Kennedy, see E. E. Ryden to Malvin Lundeen, November 23, 1960, *Malvin Lundeen Presidential Papers*, Archives of the Evangelical Lutheran Church in America, Elk Grove Village, Illinois.

89. "United Nations Votes for a New Jewish State," *Lutheran Companion* 55, no. 51 (December 17, 1947): 3; "Into Troubled Waters . . . Where Jew and Arab Clash," *Lutheran Companion* 55, no. 12 (March 19, 1947): 8; and "Is Palestine Becoming a World Storm Center?" *Lutheran Companion* 98, no. 9 (March 4, 1953): 7.

Chapter 9: Growth and Expansion of the Synod

1. Norway and Ireland saw the immigration of 25 percent of their population during this time. For the Swedish background to this immigration, see Florence E. Jansen, *The Background of Swedish Immigration, 1840–1930* (Chicago: University of Chicago Press, 1930).

2. The reasons for immigration are as varied as the individuals involved, but for the most part the strongest reasons for going to North America were economic.

3. Sten Carlsson, "Chronology and Composition of Swedish Emigration to America," in Harald Rundblom and Hans Norma, eds., *From Sweden to America: A History of the Migration* (Minneapolis: University of Minnesota Press, 1976), 115–130.

4. On the development of the ethnic concept of "Swedish America," see Dag Blanck, *Becoming Swedish-American: The Construction of an Ethnic Identity in the Augustana Synod, 1860–1917*, Studia Historica Upsaliensia, vol. 182 (Uppsala, Sweden: Acta Universitatis Upsaliensis, 1997), especially 17–57; and Sture Lindmark, *Swedish America 1914–1932: Studies in Ethnicity with Emphasis on Illinois and Minnesota*, Studia Historica Upsaliensia, vol. 37 (Uppsala, Sweden: Läromedelsförlagen, 1971).

5. For a detailed look at the range of Swedish immigrant settlement in the United States, see Helge Nelson, *The Swedes and the Swedish Settlements in North America*, vol. 2, Atlas (Lund: C. W. K. Gleerup, 1943).

6. H. Arnold Barton, "Stage Migration and Ethnic Maintenance," *Swedish Pioneer Historical Quarterly* 30, no. 4 (October 1979): 231–232.

7. Mark A. Granquist, "A Minority within a Minority: Scandinavian Lutherans in the Southeast," in Raymond A. Bost, ed., *Lutheranism . . . with a Southern Accent*, Essays and Reports, vol. 16 (St. Louis: Lutheran Historical Conference, 1998), 231–244.

8. From the Fourteenth, Fifteenth, and Sixteenth United States Census, averaged for figures of foreign-born and children of foreign-born. See Lindmark, *Swedish America 1914–1932*, 30.

9. On the early efforts in Home Missions, see Peter Peterson, "Our Missions at Home," in *After Seventy-Five Years, 1860–1935: A Jubilee Publication* (Rock Island, Ill.: Augustana Book Concern, 1935), 189–98; and Oscar N. Olson, *The Augustana Lutheran Church in America, 1860–1910: The Formative Period* (Davenport, Iowa: Arcade Office and Letter Service, 1956), 15–30.

10. Peterson, "Our Missions at Home," 195.

11. For the relation of the Augustana Synod to the General Conference, see Hugo Söderström, *Confession and Cooperation: The Policy of the Augustana Synod in Confessional Matters and the Synod's Relation's with other Churches up to the Beginning of the Twentieth Century*, Bibliotheca Historica-Ecclesiastica Lundensis, vol. 4 (Lund: C. W. K. Gleerup Bokförlag, 1973), especially 138–158.

12. G. Everett Arden, *Augustana Heritage: The History of the Augustana Lutheran Church* (Rock Island, Ill.: Augustana Book Concern, 1963), 333–337.

13. But the synod saw a net increase of only 80 congregations over this period, due to the loss or dissolution of other congregations.

14. "Report of the Director of Evangelism," *Minutes of the Augustana Lutheran Church*, 1962, 197–199.

15. Mark A. Granquist, "The Swedish Ethnic Denominations in the United States: Their Development and Relations, 1880–1920" (Ph.D. diss. University of Chicago, 1992).

16. This is the estimate of Conrad Bergendoff, "Augustana in America and Sweden," *Swedish Pioneer Historical Quarterly* 24 (October 1973): 238.

17. For these figures, see Granquist, "The Swedish Ethnic Denominations in the United States," 31–35.

18. "Mississippi" in this sense referring to the upper Mississippi River valley; it consisted chiefly of congregations in Illinois and Iowa. In 1870 this conference was renamed the Illinois Conference.

19. The Illinois Conference was renamed the Central Conference in 1958, and the Kansas Conference was renamed the West Central Conference in 1959.

20. "Summary Statistics, Augustana Lutheran Church," *Minutes of the Augustana Lutheran Church*, 1950 and 1960.

21. Finance Committee of the Evangelical Lutheran Augustana Synod, *Faith in Action: The Building of the Church*, vol. 2 (Minneapolis: Finance Committee of the Evangelical Lutheran Augustana Synod, 1938), 63.

22. A. D. Mattson, *A Study of the Town and Country Churches of the Lutheran Augustana Synod* (Rock Island, Ill.: Augustana Book Concern, 1945), 20.

23. Emeroy Johnson, *God Gave the Growth: The Story of the Lutheran Minnesota Conference, 1878–1958* (Minneapolis: T. S. Denison and Company, 1959), 206–207.

24. See William A. Flachmeier, *The Lutherans of Texas in Confluence: With Emphasis on the Decade 1951–1961* (Austin, Tex.: Southeastern District of the American Lutheran Church, 1972), 75–84, and Oscar N. Olson, ed., *A Century of Life and Growth: Augustana, 1848–1948* (Rock Island, Ill.: Augustana Book Concern, 1948), 68.

25. On this area, see Mark A. Granquist, "A Minority within a Minority: Scandinavian Lutherans in the Southeast," in Bost, *Lutheranism . . . with a Southern Accent*, 231–244.

26. Verner A. Granquist to C. A. Lund, July 2, 1929, *G. A. Brandelle Presidential Papers*, Archives of the Evangelical Lutheran Church in America, Elk Grove Village, Illinois.

27. For the beginnings of Augustana along the Pacific coast, see Oscar N. Olson, *The Augustana Lutheran Church in America, 1860–1910: The Formative Period* (Davenport, Iowa: Arcade Office and Letter Service, 1956), 29–30, and Olson, *A Century of Life and Growth*, 69–70.

28. Daniel M. Pearson, *The Americanization of Carl Aaron Swensson* (Rock Island, Ill.: Augustana Historical Society, 1977), 147–148.

29. Phillip Nordquist, "Lutheran Educational Institutions on the West Coast," in *Lutherans on the Pacific Rim*, Essays and Reports of the Lutheran Historical Conference, no. 12 (St. Louis: Lutheran Historical Conference, 1988), 122–146.

30. Ibid., 130–131. See also, Richard Solberg, *Lutheran Higher Education in North America* (Minneapolis: Augsburg Publishing House, 1985), 245–247.

31. Solberg, *Lutheran Higher Education in North America*, 312.

32. On Augustana in Canada, see Johnson, *God Gave the Growth: The Story of the Lutheran Minnesota Conference, 1878–1958*, 20–34; Olson, *A Century of Life and Growth*, 74–75; Valdimar J. Eylands, *Lutherans in Canada* (Winnipeg: Icelandic Evangelical Lutheran Synod in North America, 1945), 288–298; and Ferdy E. Baglo, *Augustana Lutherans in Canada* (n.p.: Canada Conference of the Augustana Lutheran Church, 1962).

33. Johnson, *God Gave the Growth*, 25.

34. Carl R. Cronmiller, *A History of the Lutheran Church in Canada* (n.p.: Evangelical Lutheran Synod of Canada, 1961), 246–247.

35. Ibid., 28.

36. Eylands, *Lutheran in Canada*, 296.

37. Olson, *A Century of Life and Growth*, 75.

38. Norman Threinen, *Fifty Years of Lutheran Convergence: The Canadian Case Study*, Lutheran Historical Conference Publication, no. 3 (n.p.: Lutheran Historical Conference, 1983), 114–115.

Chapter 10: Growing the Structures of Ministry

1. On education in the synod, see Emmet Eklund, "Faith and Education" in Emmer Engberg, et al., eds., *Centennial Essays* (Rock Island, Ill.: Augustana, 1960), 70–88. On the development of the academies and colleges, see Richard W. Solberg, *Lutheran Higher Education in North America* (Minneapolis: Augsburg Publishing House, 1985), especially 177–204.

2. See Conrad Bergendoff, *Augustana—A Profession of Faith: A History of Augustana College, 1860–1935*, Augustana Library Publications, vol. 33 (Rock Island, Ill.: Augustana College Library, 1969).

3. George Stephenson, *The Religious Aspects of Swedish Immigration* (Minneapolis: University of Minnesota Press, 1932), 335.

4. For the academies, see Paul M. Lindberg, "The Academies of the Augustana Lutheran Church," in J. Iverne Dowie and Ernest M. Espelie, eds., *The Swedish Immigrant Community in Transition* (Rock Island, Ill.: Augustana Historical Society, 1963), 93–106.

5. On the LBI movement, see Ray F. Kibler III, *Lutheran Bible Institute: The Original Vision* (n.p.: Lutheran Bible Institute of California, 2000), and G. Everett Arden, *Augustana Heritage: The History of the Augustana Lutheran Church* (Rock Island, Ill.: Augustana Book Concern, 1963), 311–139.

6. Robert W. Holmen, "The Ministry of Mercy" in Emmer Engberg, et al., eds., *Centennial Essays*, 227–246, and E. G. Chinlund, "The Ministry of Mercy," *After Seventy-Five Years* (Rock Island, Ill.: Augustana Book Concern, 1935), 159–172.

7. Arden, *Augustana Heritage*, 118–119; notes 16 and 17 have a full listing of the institutions of mercy founded within the Augustana Synod.

8. Robert W. Holmen, "Facts, Figures, and a Warning," *Lutheran Companion* 103, no. 5 (January 30, 1957): 5.

9. For the details of the constitutional history of the Augustana Synod, see A. D. Mattson, *Polity of the Augustana Lutheran Church*, rev. ed. (Rock Island, Ill.: Augustana Book Concern, 1952).

10. Mattson, *Polity of the Augustana Lutheran Church*, 169.

11. Mark A. Granquist, "The Augustana Synod and the Episcopal Church," *Lutheran Quarterly* 14, no. 2 (Summer 2000): 173–192.

12. For a long discussion of the changes made during the administration of Bersell, see G. Everett Arden, *Augustana Heritage: The History of the Augustana Lutheran Church* (Rock Island, Ill.: Augustana Book Concern, 1963), 328–358.

13. Ibid., 330.

14. See Mattson, *Polity of the Augustana Lutheran Church*, 169–268.

15. "Summary Statistics, Augustana Lutheran Church," *Minutes of the Augustana Lutheran Church*, 1950 and 1960.

16. See Daniel Nystrom, *A Ministry of Printing: History of the Publication House of the Augustana Lutheran Church, 1889–1960* (Rock Island, Ill.: Augustana, 1962).

17. Conrad Bergendoff, *The Augustana Ministerium: A Study of the Careers of the 2,504 Pastors of the Augustana Evangelical Lutheran Synod/Church, 1850–1962*, vol. 28 (Rock Island, Ill.: Augustana Historical Society, 1980).

18. Mattson, *Polity of the Augustana Lutheran Church*, 63–89.

19. "A Suggested Standard of Church Efficiency," *Lutheran Companion* 35, no. 3 (January 15, 1927): 60.

20. Alfred Bergin, "Phatteicher and the Spot," *Lutheran Companion* 41, no. 21 (May 27, 1931): 657.

21. C. E. Cesander, "Are We Centralizing in Our Church Work or Disintegrating?" *Lutheran Companion* 35, no. 4 (January 22, 1927): 82.

22. Finance Committee of the Evangelical Lutheran Augustana Synod, *Faith in Action: The Building of the Church*, vol. 2 (Minneapolis: Finance Committee of the Evangelical Lutheran Augustana Synod, 1938), 70.

23. Paul H. Andreen, "Startling Times, But What of It?" *Lutheran Companion* 41, no. 10 (March 11, 1933): 305.

24. Herbert S. Magney, "Is There Danger of a Surplus of Ministerial Candidates?" *Lutheran Companion* 41, no. 34 (August 26, 1933): 1072.

25. Walter A. Lundeen, "Augustana's Acre," *Lutheran Companion* 45, no. 32 (August 5, 1937): 1001.

26. "Synod Approves Centralization," *Lutheran Companion* 45, no. 27 (July 1, 1937): 837.

27. Conrad Bergendoff, "How Strong is the Augustana Synod?" *Lutheran Companion* 51, no. 3 (January 20, 1943): 72.

28. Roy H. Stetler, "Chat . . ." *Lutheran Companion* 103, no. 5 (January 30, 1957): 5.

29. Thomas W. Wersell, "A 'Grass-Roots' Church," *Lutheran Companion* 103, no. 13 (March 27, 1957): 7.

30. Evald B. Lawson, "The Ministry," in Emmer Engberg, ed., *Centennial Essays: Augustana Lutheran Church 1860–1960* (Rock Island, Ill.: Augustana, 1960), 163–164.

Chapter 11: Go to Tanganyika

1. Edman graduated from medical school after seminary and worked both as a pastor and physician in India. Oscar Larson, *Augustana in India*, unpublished ms. (n.d.—1954, unpaginated), 5. Conrad Bergendoff, *The Augustana Ministerium: A Study of the Careers of the 2,504 Pastors of the Augustana Evangelical Lutheran Synod/Church, 1850–1962* (Rock Island, Ill.: Augustana Historical Association, 1980), 37.

2. Quoted in Paul Gullander, *Tre År i Afrika samt minnen från Sverige och det Heliga Landet*, 2nd ed. (Rock Island, Ill.: Privately published, 1903), 235.

3. Ibid., 209.

4. Other books about travel were written by Olof Olsson, who published a record of his European trip, *To Rome and Home Again*, in 1890, and C. A. Swensson, who published *To Sweden*, and *Again in Sweden*, in quick succession after trips in 1888 and 1897. Peter August Mattson, *Minnen och Bilder från Bibelns Länder* (Rock Island, Ill.: Augustana Book Concern, 1911), 304.

5. Sydney Ahlstrom, *A Religious History of the American People* (New Haven, Conn.: Yale University Press, 1972), 864.

6. Ibid., 865. The motto for the Student Volunteer Movement for Mission was coined by John R. Mott, national college secretary of the YMCA.

7. More on Franson's career is in Karl Olsson, *By One Spirit* (Chicago: Covenant, 1962), 434–437. The Moody Bible Institute was very near the Swedish neighborhoods on the North Side of Chicago, near Immanuel Lutheran Church.

8. A. P. Matson, *Missionsbilder från Kina* (Minneapolis: Missionförbundets bokförlag, 1906), 63.

9. Ibid., 254.

10. Swan Hjalmar Swanson, *Foundation for Tomorrow: A Century of Progress in Augustana World Missions* (Rock Island, Ill.: Augustana Book Concern, 1962), 74.

11. *Korsbaneret*, 1931, 193.

12. Swanson, *Foundation for Tomorrow*, and George Hall, *The Missionary Spirit in the Augustana Church* (Rock Island, Ill.: Augustana Historical Society, 1984), 23.

13. Swanson, *Foundation for Tomorrow*, 77.

14. Larson, *Augustana in India*, 7.

15. Ibid., 13.

16. James Reed, *The Missionary Mind and American East Asia Policy, 1911–1915*, Harvard East Asian Monographs (Cambridge, Mass.: Harvard University Press, 1983), 18.

17. The quotations in this paragraph come from Vikner's letter to readers of *Lutheran Companion* 27, no. 12 (March 22, 1919): 143.

18. John Benson's history gave Swedish readers material similar to the well-supplied English readers of the synod. *Tjugu* [sic] *År i Kina 1905–1925*, Augustana Synodens Hednamissionsstyrlse, n.d., 9.

19. Ibid., 88.

20. Interview with George Lindbeck, April 2005, New Orleans, La.

21. *Lutheran Companion* 55, no. 29 (July 9, 1932): 887.

22. *Lutheran Companion* 24, no. 22 (May 28, 1926) and *Mission Tidings* 20, no. 1 (June 1926) provide overviews of the conflict.

23. This school was started by the General Council to provide a Lutheran seminary education for English-speaking students. Augustana pastors in Chicago engaged in English language work argued that Augustana students ought to be able to study in that city, but the synod insisted that candidates had to attend the seminary in Rock Island.

24. Ralph Hult to O. J. Johnson, Hartford, Conn., February 20, 1919, *Personal Papers of Ralph Hult*, Archives of the Evangelical Lutheran Church in America, Elk Grove Village, Illinois.

25. The 1932 Layman's Report on Mission, was written by Ernest Hocking after touring the world mission stations on behalf of the Presbyterian, Congregationalist, and YMCA boards. Lutheran mission stations were not visited; Lutherans, however, registered strong reactions against the Hocking report as another example of liberalism gone awry.

26. Ralph Hult to Fred Wyman, November 13, 1919, *Personal papers of Ralph Hult*.

27. The following citations come from Ralph Hult to C. A. Blomgren, April 1, 1922. *Personal papers of Ralph Hult*.

28. William Hutchison, *Errand to the World: The Protestant Missionary Movement* (Cambridge: Cambridge University Press, 1988), ch. 4.

29. Bengt Sundkler, *Svenska Missionssällskapet 1835–1876* (Uppsala, Sweden: Alqvist och Wiksell, 1937), 261–270. The Leipzig Society held a conservative view of the caste system, deciding not to challenge it and holding to more strictly "confessional" views. The neo-confessional movement in Prussia and in America grew partly out of debates over the application of "Lutheran" vs. "Reformed" (that is, more activist) oriented methods. The Leipzig Mission disciplined Swedish missionaries who worshiped with Anglican Church mission society missionaries and then refused to recognize caste among converts. Confessional scruples were the ostensible reason. The Leipzig society in Tanganyika held conservative positions in relation to women's and indigenous leadership. (Augustana leader Olof Olsson was trained at Leipzig.)

30. Gustav Bernander, *Lutheran Wartime Assistance to Tanzanian Churches, 1940–1945* (Uppsala, Sweden: Gleerup, 1968), passim. Tanzania became the name of the country after it was united with Zanzibar at the time of independence. There were also other mission societies besides the Leipzig work that Augustana tended—two Berlin societies and Bethel; some cooperated with the Moravian mission.

31. Ray Cunningham to Oscar Larson, quoted in *Augustana in India*, 30.

32. Eleanor Danielson Anderson wrote an account of the event from the perspective of the children called, *Miracle at Sea: The Sinking of the Zamzam and Our Family's Rescue* (Bolivar, Mo.: Quiet Waters Publications, 2001).

Assimilation: "Condensed in the last hours of a long day"

1. Henry Pratt Fairchild, *The Melting Pot Mistake* (Boston: Little Brown, 1926), 1.

2. Through secular newspapers, such as *Scandinavia* in Worcester, Massachusetts, *Svea* in New York, *Svenska Tribunen* in Chicago, and *Minnesota Posten* in Minneapolis, readers saw how the Augustana churches and other immigrant churches shaped a Swedish-American nationalist identity. For more on this interesting ethnic question, see Dag Blanck, *Becoming Swedish-American: The*

Construction of an Ethnic Identity in the Augustana Synod, 1860–1917, Studia Historica Upsalensia, vol. 182 (Uppsala, Sweden: Acta Universitatis Upsalensis, 1997).

3. S. G. Öhman, "Our Swedish Heritage," *Korsbaneret* (1924): 116–117.

4. President Brandelle's Report to the Synod, 1927 convention, 21.

Chapter 12: Reconnecting with the Church of Sweden

1. Carl Swensson, *Åter i Sverige* (Chicago: Swedish Book Company, 1897), 322.

2. S. G. Youngert, "Augustana-synoden och Moderkyrkan i Sverige," *Minneskrift med anledningen af augustana-synodens femtioåriga tillvaro*, ed. L. A. Johnston (Rock Island, Ill.: Augustana Book Concern, 1910), 411–425.

3. T. N. Hasselquist, Erland Carlsson, Olof Olsson, and P. A. Mattson also went on long tours in Sweden. Mattson published his account in 1910.

4. Mrs. Peter (Mathilda) Peterson, *These Fifty Years: Women's Missionary Society of Augustana Synod, 1892–42* (Chicago: Woman's Missionary Society of Augustana Synod, 1942), 52. Alma went on to become the editor of *Mission Tidings*, the newspaper for the society for thirty-three years.

5. This topic is covered in chapters 5 and 6. Recognition of the college and Swensson's leadership was widespread among American Lutherans. Already in 1890, when the college was not even a decade old, a biographer pointed to its phenomenal success as an "illustration of the progress and process of western development." J. C. Jensson, *American Lutheran Biographies* (Milwaukee, Wis.: Houtkamp, 1890), 795; Daniel Pearson, *The Americanization of Carl Aaron Swensson* (Rock Island, Ill.: Augustana Historical Society, 1977) applied Milton Gordon's model of acculturation to Swensson.

6. Conrad Bergendoff noted that at the time of von Schéele's visits, when he represented the aristocratic type then typical of Church of Sweden bishops, Augustana was very happy to see a visiting bishop, but also happy to see him go. The synod had *made up its mind* [emphasis added] not to have a bishop. After Söderblom's visit, Bergendoff felt it had made a great difference, for "he was so democratic with little or no pomp about him." Interview with author on July 5, 1995.

7. The section on Lindsborg is entitled "En svensk-amerikansk mogenhetsförklaring" (a Swedish-American declaration of independence/maturity) in von Schéele, *Hemlandstoner* (Stockholm: Hemlandstoner, 1895), 78–81.

8. Söderblom, speaking for the theological faculty, weighed in on von Schéele's side, emphasizing that such a meeting should also include Augustana representatives. Bengt Sundkler, *Nathan Söderblom, His Life and Work* (Uppsala, Sweden: Lutterworth, 1968), 94–95.

9. See *Bengston Correspondence*, Archives of the Evangelical Lutheran Church in America, Elk Grove Village, Illinois.

10. The orthodoxy of von Schéele was confirmed for confessional purists when his dogmatics were reportedly used at Missouri's Seminary in St. Louis. The brief obituary on von Schéele was written by L. G. Abrahamson in the synod's devotional annual *Korsbaneret* (1921): 244.

11. S. G. Öhman to C. J. Bengston, July 1908, *Bengston Correspondence*.

12. Abrahamson's speech is printed in a pamphlet "Uppsala 6–8 November 1914, Tal och Predikningar," (Uppsala, Sweden: Svenska Kyrkans Diakonistyrelse, 1914), 10–25.

13. Glenn Stone interview with Conrad Bergendoff, June 22–23, 1977, Archives of Cooperative Lutheranism, Archives of the Evangelical Lutheran Church in America, Elk Grove Village, Illinois. The St. Louis-based German Lutherans had questioned Augustana's orthodox Lutheran reputation as early as 1867, when Herman Amberg Preus detailed the inter-Lutheran disagreements in his seven lectures for audiences at the university in Oslo. See Herman Amberg Preus, *Vivacious Daughter: Seven Lectures on the Religious Situation of Norwegians in America*, trans. Todd Nichol (Northfield, Minn.: Norwegian American Historical Society, 1990). See also letters from Adolf Hult in *Norelius Correspondence*, Swenson Center, Augustana College, Rock Island, Illinois.

14. L. G. Abrahamson, *"Att finna honom i hans ensamhet var att finna honom i bönumgänge med sin Gud,"* *Hågkomster och livsintryck till minnet av Nathan Söderblom, femtonde samlingen*, ed. Sven Thulin (Uppsala, Sweden: Svenska Kyrkans Diakonistyrelse, 1934), 254–266.

15. Ibid.

16. Abrahamson returned to this theme several times in his writings. See also "The Heart and Soul of Augustana," *Diamond Jubilee* (Rock Island, Ill.: Augustana Book Concern, 1935).

17. Söderblom had been invited to participate in the Federal Council's celebration of the Reformation. See Söderblom's introduction to *Från Uppsala till Rock Island* (Stockholm: Svenska kyrkans diakonistyrelsens bokförlag, 1925). Bishop Lindahl had agreed to represent the Church of Sweden at Augustana's festival during the synod meeting in June. The course of his changing plans was followed in the synod's paper, *Augustana*, during the spring of 1917.

18. Söderblom delivered sections of his book, *Gudstrons uppkomst* in his lectures. The appendix in Nathan Söderblom, *Från Uppsala till Rock Island* contains a bibliography for the lectures and sermons that he gave on his tour.

19. Bergendoff interview, June 1977, and Sundkler, *Nathan Söderblom*, 301–302.

20. Anna Söderblom, *En Amerikabok* (Stockholm: Svenska kyrkans diakonistyrelsens bokförlag, 1925), 8.

21. Ibid. Anna was aware of the literary and social precedent set by her famous countrywoman Fredrika Bremer, and she paid close attention to home life in America and to the special role that women played in the development and refining of church and family life.

22. Nathan Söderblom, *Från Uppsala till Rock Island*, 303–338.

23. Ibid., 337–339.

24. Anna Söderblom, *En Amerikabok*, 84–88.

Chapter 13: Meeting the Challenges of a New Century

1. G. A. Brandelle, *Augustana Journal* 5, no. 22 (November 15, 1897): 4.

2. "To an Anxious Friend," *Lutheran Companion* 21, no. 36 (September 6, 1913): 2.

3. I. O. Nothstein, "Evolution," *Lutheran Companion* 22, no. 48 (November 28, 1914): 4.

4. C. J. Södergren, "Evolution," *Lutheran Companion* 22, no. 52 (December 26, 1914): 1–2. This issue was his last as editor, so perhaps he felt emboldened to set off a final shot.

5. "Resolution," *Minutes of the Minnesota Conference of the Augustana Synod*, 1923. Quoted in *Bible Banner* 4, no. 3 (May 1923): 7.

6. Samuel Miller, "The Evolution Controversy," *Bible Banner* 4, no. 3 (May 1923): 7–8.

7. Emil Johnson, "A Brief Inquiry into the Theory of Evolution," *Augustana Quarterly* 4, no. 2 (June 1927): 159.

8. C. Emil Bergquist, "Types of Piety in the Augustana Synod—The Fundamentalist," *Augustana Quarterly* 8, no. 2 (April 1929): 125–134.

9. See Conrad Bergendoff, *Augustana—A Profession of Faith: A History of Augustana College, 1860–1935* (Rock Island, Ill.: Augustana College Library, 1969); and Doniver Lund, *Gustavus Adolphus College: A Centennial History, 1862–1962* (St. Peter, Minn.: Gustavus Adolphus College, 1962). Geology was taught at the schools before the official development of a department of geology. Bethany College in Lindsborg, Kansas, also had early instruction in geology and the start of a museum of natural history after C. A. Swensson recruited a teacher to do geological surveys in the area.

10. *Joshua Edquist Papers*, folder #6, Archives of Gustavus Adolphus College, St. Peter, Minn.

11. A. S. Segerhammar, "Are Modern Pursuits of Knowledge Dangerous to Loyal Lutheranism? The Affirmative," *Augustana Quarterly* 7, no. 4 (December 1928): 317.

12. Otto Bostrom, "Are Modern Pursuits of Knowledge Dangerous to Loyal Lutheranism? The Negative," *Augustana Quarterly* 7, no. 4 (December 1928): 322–23.

13. J. A. Elson, "What Should Be the Objectives of Science Teaching in Lutheran Colleges?" *Augustana Quarterly* 38, no. 2 (July 1939): 113.

14. Luther Anderson, "New Contacts Between Science and Religion," *Lutheran Companion* 41, no. 21 (May 27, 1933): 653.

15. H. Bradford Thompson, "Miracles and Modern Science," *Lutheran Companion* 103, no. 17 (April 24, 1957): 12.

16. C. J. Bengston, "Baron von Munchhausen Speaks," *Lutheran Companion* 41, no. 6 (February 11, 1933): 2.

17. E. E. Ryden, "Psychologist Calls Faith Basic Need," *Lutheran Companion* 98, no. 38 (September 23, 1953): 7.

18. Axel E. Berg, "Science and Theology," *Augustana Quarterly* 20, no. 4 (December 1941): 340–341.

19. Karl E. Mattson, "The Ethical Problem in the Modern Scientific World," *Augustana Quarterly* 14, no. 3 (September 1935): 266–70.

20. G. A. Brandelle, *Augustana Journal* 8, no. 10 (May 15, 1900): 6.

21. O. V. Holmgrain, *Young Lutheran's Companion* 15, no. 9 (March 2, 1907): 1.

22. G. A. Brandelle to F. G. Knight, April 24, 1929, *G. A. Brandelle Presidential Papers*, Archives of the Evangelical Lutheran Church in America, Elk Grove Village, Illinois.

23. Adolf Hult, "Outmoded Old Testament Criticism," *Bible Banner* 2, no. 2 (February 1926): 4.

24. O. N. Olson, *Lutheran Companion* 35, no. 24 (June 11, 1927): 3.

25. Emeroy Johnson, "Luther League Topic: How Do We Know That the Bible Is the Word of God?" *Lutheran Companion* 41, no. 3 (January 21, 1933): 83.

26. Samuel M. Miller, "At the Dean's Desk," *Bible Banner* 12, no. 5 (May 1936): 13.

27. Victor Tengwald, "The Verbal Inspiration of the Bible," *Augustana Quarterly* 19, no. 2 (June 1940): 125–126.

28. See essay by C. A. Wendell in *What Is Lutheranism?* Vergilius Ferm, ed. (New York: MacMillan, 1930), 235.

29. George F. Hall, "Luther's Standards of Canonicity," *Augustana Quarterly* 15, no. 4 (December 1936): 299–300.

30. A. D. Mattson, *Christian Ethics* (Rock Island, Ill.: Augustana Book Concern, 1938), 98.

31. Hjalmar Johnson, "Some Thoughts on Inspiration," *Journal of the American Lutheran Conference* 4, no. 2 (May 1939): 30.

32. For a complete view of this, see Sture Lindmark, *Swedish America, 1914–1932: Studies in Ethnicity with Emphasis on Illinois and Minnesota*, Studia Historico Upsaliensia, vol. 37 (Stockholm: Läromedelsförlagen, 1971), especially 64–136.

33. C. A. Larson, "Which Would You Chose?" *Lutheran Companion* 22, no. 49 (December 5): 1914.

34. *Augustana* (January 15, 1914), quoted in Finis Herbert Capps, *From Isolationism to Involvement: The Swedish Immigrant Press in America, 1914–1945* (Chicago: Swedish Pioneer Historical Society, 1966), 33.

35. "The British Empire and the Kingdom of God," *Lutheran Companion* 23, no. 19 (May 8, 1915): 1.

36. "On the War," *Lutheran Companion* 22, no. 37 (September 12, 1914): 1.

37. George M. Stephenson, "The Dawn of the Campaign," *Lutheran Companion* 25, no. 17 (April 28, 1917): 200. Stephenson had a doctoral degree from the University of Chicago, and he taught for many years in the history department at the University of Minnesota.

38. "Editorial," *Lutheran Companion* 25, no. 38 (September 22, 1917): 461.

39. Carl J. Bengston, "The Relation of Lutherans to Their Government," *Lutheran Companion* 25, no. 31 (August 4, 1917): 378.

40. "The Prospects for Permanent World Peace," *Lutheran Companion* 35, no. 27 (July 2, 1927): 645.

41. C. L. Esbjörn to G. A. Brandelle, June 5, 1933, *G. A. Brandelle Papers*.

42. *Minutes*, 1937, 241 and *Minutes*, 1939, 266.

43. "Tricking America into Conflict," *Lutheran Companion* 45, no. 8 (February 18, 1937): 228.

44. For this group, see Steven Schroeder, *A Community and a Perspective: Lutheran Peace Fellowship and the Edge of the Church, 1941–1991* (Lantham, Md.: University Press of America, 1993), especially 15–26. Schroeder counts the ALFOR as a forerunner of the Lutheran Peace Fellowship.

45. Edgar Carlson, "If War Comes . . . ," *Lutheran Companion* 46, no. 44 (November 3, 1938): 1388–1389.

46. A. T. Lundholm, "Vår lutherska kyrka här landet i krigstid," *Augustana* 84, no. 46 (November 14, 1939): 728. See Capps, *From Isolationism to Involvement: The Swedish Immigrant Press in America, 1914–1945* (Chicago: Swedish Pioneer Historical Society, 1966), 163–200 for a complete review of this struggle.

47. Carl Lund-Quist to P. O. Bersell, February 21, 1939; Carl Lund-Quist to Dr. Otto Willimut, German-American Bund, February 17, 1939; and P. O. Bersell to Carl Lund-Quist, February 23, 1939; in *P. O. Bersell Presidential Papers*, Archives of the Evangelical Lutheran Church in America, Elk Grove Village, Illinois.

48. *Minutes*, 1940, 197.

49. Samuel Miller, "At the Dean's Desk," *Bible Banner* 17, no. 2 (February 1941): 13.

50. "Shall We Pray for Victory?" *Bible Banner* 18, no. 2 (February 1942): 3; *Minutes*, 1942, 232.

51. G. Everett Arden, *The School of the Prophets: The Background and History of Augustana Theological Seminary, 1860–1960* (Rock Island, Ill.: Augustana Theological Seminary, 1960), 238; Lund, *Gustavus Adolphus College,* 161–64.

52. Paul A. Andreen, "When the Tides of War Sweep in . . . A Visit to the Pacific Coast," *Lutheran Companion* 51, no. 5 (February 3, 1943): 138; Albert Larson, "A Plea for Japs and Negroes … These Minorities," *Lutheran Companion* 51, no. 6 (February 10, 1943): 177.

53. P. O. Bersell to Mrs. Eban Lindgren, June 23, 1944, *P. O. Bersell Presidential Papers*.

54. "After the War—Then What?" *Lutheran Companion* 51, no. 8 (February 24, 1943): 236.

55. Miller, "At the Dean's Desk," 13.

56. Swan Hjalmar Swanson, *Foundation for Tomorrow: A Century of Progress in Augustana World Missions* (Minneapolis: Board of Foreign Missions, Augustana Lutheran Church, 1960), 136.

57. Conrad Peterson, "What About Communism?" *Lutheran Companion* 55, no. 24 (June 11, 1947): 18; Kirby Page, "God or Stalin?" *Lutheran Companion* 98, no. 10 (March 11, 1953): 15; and "Communism in Decline," *Lutheran Companion* 103, no. 18 (May 1, 1957): 7.

58. "President Again Urges Conscription of Youth," *Lutheran Companion* 55, no. 4 (January 22, 1947): 3; Emmer Engberg, "Exposes Pentagon Methods," *Lutheran Companion* 98, no. 52 (December 30, 1953): 11; and "Our Military Burden," *Lutheran Companion* 103, no. 15 (April 10, 1957): 7.

59. "Dims Disarmament Hopes," *Lutheran Companion* 103, no. 33 (August 14, 1957): 5.

60. Thomas Basich, "Witch-Hunting in the Church: Proposed Probe Resembles Hitler Purge," *Lutheran Companion* 98, no. 28 (July 15, 1953): 11.

61. Ralph Hjelm to Oscar Benson, November 28, 1953, and Oscar Benson to Ralph Hjelm, December 8, 1953, *Oscar Benson Presidential Papers*, Archives of the Evangelical Lutheran Church in America, Elk Grove Village, Illinois.

Chapter 14: Changes at the College and Seminary

1. This story is covered extensively by George Marsden in *Fundamentalism and American Culture: The Shaping of Twentieth-Century Evangelicalism 1870–1925* (Oxford: Oxford University

Press), passim. A Lutheran example is missing in his account, which focuses on the English roots of the Fundamentalist movement in a decidedly Reformed theological context. Lutheran conservatives had theological barriers to participation in the classic Fundamentalist movement but they were influenced by it.

2. Claus Wendell to Fritiof Fryxell, April 20, 1939, *Fryxell Correspondence*. Augustana Special Collections, Rock Island, Ill.

3. This periodization is from Conrad Bergendoff, "Theology in the Augustana Church," in *Papers given at Gustavus Adolphus College, St. Peter, Minnesota, April 30, 1985 on the occasion of observing the 125th Anniversary of the Augustana Synod* (photocopied), 35.

4. Samuel Miller, "Comments," *Bible Banner* 4, no. 6 (November 1923): 4.

5. Ole Kristian Hallesby was a Norwegian theologian and a leader in conservative Lutheranism during the first half of the twentieth century. He taught at the Free theological faculty in Oslo from 1909 to 1951. In the United States, he was well known more for his devotional works. Hallesby's *Prayer* (Minneapolis: Augsburg Fortress, 1994) is still in print.

6. Adolf Hult, "Söderblom as a Temptation to the Augustana Synod," *Bible Banner* 5, no. 1 (January 1924): 6.

7. Oral History interview with Conrad Bergendoff by Byron Swanson, June 23–24, 1966 and December 7, 1966, typescript manuscript in the Jesuit-Krauss-McCormick Library, Lutheran School of Theology at Chicago, Chicago, Illinois, 27.

8. Adolf Hult, "Can Christians Be Modern?" *Lutheran Companion* 35, no. 10 (March 5, 1927): 227.

9. Adolf Hult, "What Is Our Lutheran Creed?" *Lutheran Companion* 35, no. 22: (May 28, 1927): 514.

10. O. N. Olson, *Lutheran Companion* 35, no. 9 (February 26, 1927): 201.

11. Conrad Bergendoff, *I Believe in the Church: Confessions and Convictions* (Rock Island, Ill.: Augustana Book Concern, 1937), 87.

12. Bengt Sundkler, *Nathan Söderblom: His Life and Work* (Lund, Sweden: Gleerups, 1968), 30.

13. Pastor Carl E. Bergquist wrote about the Chicago effort in *Lutheran Companion* March 15, 1919, issue. By then he had moved to Minneapolis and taken the call to Messiah Lutheran Church after Samuel Miller left to become dean of the Twin Cities school. For more on the developments of LBI's relationship with the synod, see G. Everett Arden, *Augustana Heritage: The History of the Augustana Lutheran Church* (Rock Island, Ill.: Augustana Book Concern, 1963), 313 f.

14. Adolf Hult to P. O Bersell, December 5, 1937, *P. O. Bersell Presidential Papers*, Archives of the Evangelical Lutheran Church in America, Elk Grove Village, Illinois.

15. "An Epoch-making Church Convention," *Lutheran Companion* 38, no. 45 (November 8, 1930): 1419.

16. Ernest Findlay Scott, "The Limitations of the Historical Method," *Studies in Early Christianity*, ed. Shirley Jackson Case (New York, London: Century, 1928), 3.

17. Conrad Bergendoff, *The Augustana Ministerium: A Study of the Careers of the 2,504 Pastors of the Augustana Evangelical Lutheran Synod/Church 1850–1962* (Rock Island, Ill.: Augustana Historical Society, 1980). Vergilius Ferm was a synod pastor ordained in 1919 who was teaching at the college of Wooster in 1930. His father, Augustana pastor Otto Ferm, initiated the pension fund in the synod.

18. Virgilius Ferm, ed., *What Is Lutheranism?* (New York: MacMillan, 1930), 296–297.

19. Ibid., 242.

20. Samuel Miller, "What Is Lutheranism?" *Bible Banner* 6, no. 10 (October 1930): 13.

21. Adolph Hult, "Lutheranism and the Word of God," *Bible Banner* 6, no. 8 (August 1930): 10.

22. George Stephenson to Vergilius Ferm, October 16, 1930, *Stephenson Papers*, University of Minnesota, Minneapolis.

23. Ibid.

24. George Stephenson to Conrad Bergendoff, August 7, 1930, *Bergendoff Papers*, Special Collections, Augustana College Archives, Rock Island, Ill.

25. Ibid.

26. Conrad Bergendoff to Charles Jacobs, March 26, 1930, June 17, 1930, and August 16, 1930, *Bergendoff Papers*.

27. Samuel Miller to Conrad Bergendoff, October 28, 1920, *Bergendoff Papers*.

28. Conrad Bergendoff to Charles Jacobs, June 17, 1930, *Bergendoff Papers*.

29. George Stephenson, "The Educational Problem of the Augustana Synod," *Lutheran Companion* 39, no. 7 (February 14, 1931): 208.

30. George Stephenson, *Religious Aspects of Swedish Immigration* (Minneapolis: University of Minnesota Press, 1932), 342.

31. John P. Milton had a master's degree in theology and subsequently taught at Luther Seminary in St. Paul, Minnesota. A. T. Lundholm had served as the conference president in Iowa, and Oscar Olson had studied briefly at Yale before attending Philadelphia Seminary and finishing at Augustana Seminary in 1903. Before coming onto the faculty he worked for the *Lutheran Companion*. Olson had not continued his scholarly research when they had appointed him in 1927, and the board of directors gave him a semester of leave to do research in the areas he would soon be teaching: English exegesis of the Bible, ethics, and sociology.

32. Arden, *Augustana Heritage*, 284–285.

33. Stephenson is referring to C.A Blomgren, professor of Old Testament from 1904 to 1926, who had received a Ph.D. from Yale in 1893, and who also did post graduate work at the University of Pennsylvania.

34. Vergilius Ferm to George Stephenson, October 17, 1930, *Stephenson Papers*.

35. Arden, *Augustana Heritage*, 284.

36. George Stephenson to Vergilius Ferm, December 17, 1930, *Stephenson Papers*.

37. Ibid.

38. Ibid.

39. Ibid.

40. George Stephenson to Vergilius Ferm, February 27, 1930, *Stephenson Papers*.

41. George Stephenson to Vergilius Ferm, January 8, 1932, *Stephenson Papers*.

42. Ibid.

43. Vergilius Ferm to George Stephenson, January 15, 1932, *Stephenson Papers*.

Chapter 15: New Voices within the Synod

1. Carol K. Coburn, *Life at Four Corners: Religion, Gender, and Education in a German-Lutheran Community, 1868–1945*. (Lawrence, Kan.: University Press of Kansas, 1992), 121.

2. *Referat*, 1872, 24; 1901, 97; and 1894, 27.

3. C. A. Rosander, "Synodical and Conference Reflections," *Lutheran Companion* 41, no. 32 (August 12, 1933): 1008.

4. "Editorial," *Lutheran Companion* 15, no. 26 (June 29, 1907): 1. *Referat*, 1907, 141.

5. *Referat*, 1910, 208, and Bernice Fjellman, "Women in the Church," in Emmer Engberg, et al., eds., *Centennial Essays: Augustana Lutheran Church 1860–1960* (Rock Island, Ill.: Augustana, 1960), 220.

6. *Referat*, 1915, 176; 1921, 171–72; *Minutes*, 1926, 168; and 1927, 191.

7. Fjellman, "Women in the Church," 219–220.

8. *Minutes*, 1951, 353; Fjellman, "Women in the Church," 221.

9. Oscar A. Benson to Howard B. Pettersen, September 21, 1953, *Oscar A. Benson Presidential Papers*, Archives of the Evangelical Lutheran Church in America, Elk Grove Village, Illinois.

10. Conrad Bergendoff, "'No Male or Female:' Biblical Basis for Women's Work in Church," *Lutheran Companion* 97, no. 42 (October 15, 1952): 10.

11. E. E. Ryden, "Women as Pastors," *Lutheran Companion* 104, no. 43 (October 22, 1958): 5.

12. *Minutes*, 1957, 414.

13. Swan Hjalmar Swanson, *Foundation for Tomorrow: A Century of Progress in Augustana World Missions* (Minneapolis: Board of World Missions, Augustana Lutheran Church, 1960), 328–348.

14. G. Everett Arden, *Augustana Heritage: The History of the Augustana Lutheran Church* (Rock Island, Ill.: Augustana Book Concern, 1963), 217. The figures are from Emil G. Chinlund, "The Ministry of Mercy," in *After Seventy-Five Years, 1860–1935: Seventy-fifth Anniversary of the Augustana Synod and Augustana College and Theological Seminary* (Rock Island, Ill.: Augustana Book Concern, 1935), 168.

15. *Minutes*, 1954, 207; 1958, 279–99; and 1961, 263–67.

16. Bertha Lunde, "A Christian Calling: Nursing . . ." *Lutheran Companion* 97, no. 43 (October 22, 1952): 12.

17. Mrs. Peter (Mathilda) Peterson, *These Fifty Years: Women's Missionary Society of Augustana Synod, 1892–1942* (Chicago: Woman's Missionary Society of Augustana Synod, 1942), 52.

18. Dag Blanck, *Becoming Swedish-American: The Construction of an Ethnic Identity in the Augustana Synod, 1860–1917*, Studia Historica Upsalensia, vol. 182 (Uppsala, Sweden: Acta Universitatis Upsalensis, 1997), 72.

19. Titus A. Conrad, "The Augustana Pension Aid Fund," in *After Seventy-Five Years*, 177.

20. John C. Christianson, "The Augustana Brotherhood," in *After Seventy-Five Years*, 244–254.

21. This was a bit controversial, as some more conservative elements within the synod thought that the Boy Scouts were "unionistic" in their religious practices.

22. Martin E. Carlson, "Stewardship," in Emmer Engberg, et al., eds., *Centennial Essays: Augustana Lutheran Church 1860–1960* (Rock Island, Ill.: Augustana, 1960), 258.

23. Arden, *Augustana Heritage*, 207–208.

24. Victor E. Beck, "Our Luther League," in *After Seventy-Five Years*, 255–67.

25. *Referat*, 1905, 23; 1906, 148; 1907, 151–53; and 1908, 159–61.

26. Nettie M. Yarp, "Are our Young People's Societies of any Benefit to our Church?" *Young Lutheran's Companion* 18, no. 51 (December 17, 1910): 16.

27. *Referat*, 1910, 200–02, and 1911, 158–60.

28. "On the Report of the Synodical Y.P.S. Committee," *Young Lutheran's Companion* 15, no. 20 (July 16, 1907): 6.

29. *Referat*, 1916, 30.

30. See "Life on Campus of a Swedish-American Educational Institution," in Stephenson, *Religious Aspects of Swedish Immigration*, 372–383.

31. Bergendoff, *Augustana—A Profession of Faith: A History of Augustana College, 1860–1935*, 170. The LSA had been formed in 1922 in Toledo, Ohio.

32. Doniver Lund, *Gustavus Adolphus: A Centennial History, 1862–1962* (St. Peter, Minn.: Gustavus Adolphus College Press, 1963), 97–98.

33. "Clearing Up," *Lutheran Companion* 21, no. 8 (February 8, 1913): 1.

34. Stephenson, *Religious Aspects of Swedish Immigration*, 376.

35. Bergendoff, *Augustana—A Profession of Faith*, 165.

36. *Referat*, 1905, 125.

37. "Inter-collegiate athletic contests," *Young Lutheran's Companion* 18(28), July 9, 1910, 1. Why the YMCA is included on this list of otherwise disreputable organizations is unclear!

38. Bergendoff, *Augustana—A Profession of Faith*, 171.

39. Blanck, *Becoming Swedish-American*, 215.

40. "Too Much Johnson," *Lutheran Companion* 19, no. 3 (January 21, 1911): 2.

41. Gustav Andreen to G. A. Brandelle, February 15, 1923. *G. A. Brandelle Presidential Papers*, Archives of the Evangelical Lutheran Church in America, Elk Grove Village, Illinois.

The Far Reaches of Art

1. Sandzen to Fryxell, *Fryxell Correspondence*, Augustana Special Collections, Rock Island, Ill.
2. Ibid.
3. Ibid.
4. Ibid.

Chapter 16: Augustana's Youthful Edge

1. Martin Carlson, *Forward in Faith: A History of the Augustana Luther League* (Minneapolis: Augustana Synod Luther League, 1947), 54–55. Sig Engstrom reported on Bergstrand's work to the synodical Luther League council. The structure was reorganized in 1945, as the Board of Youth Activities. The board monitored youth activities that were provided for young people from confirmation until the age of thirty.
2. Ibid.
3. Emmy Evald and *Women's Missionary Society Papers*, Archives of the Evangelical Lutheran Church in America, Elk Grove Village, Illinois.
4. Ibid.
5. *Minutes*, Augustana Synod (North High, Omaha, Nebraska, 1927).
6. *Minutes*, Augustana Synod (Des Moines, Iowa, June 8–13, 1928).
7. Joshua Oden quoted by Martin Carlson, *Forward in Faith: A History of the Augustana Luther League* (Minneapolis: Augustana Synod Luther League, 1947), 77.
8. Luther League notes, P. N. Sjogren, *Lutheran Companion* 42, no. 27 (July 7, 1934): 1.
9. The citations for the Bible conference material come from *Lutheran Companion* 42, no. 27 (July 7, 1934): 860, and *Lutheran Companion* 42, no. 28 (July 14, 1934): 884.
10. Virginia Brereton, *Training God's Army: The American Bible School, 1880–1940* (Indianapolis: Indiana University Press, 1990), 7, 118, 134.
11. Carlson, *Forward in Faith,* 80–81.
12. Wilton E. Bergstrand, "The Master's Magnificent Minority," *A Talk at the Caravan Celebration*, August 1995, *Bergstrand Papers*, Archives of the Evangelical Lutheran Church in America, Elk Grove Village, Illinois.
13. Youth Issue, *Lutheran Companion* 48, no. 42.
14. Steven Schroeder, *Lutheran Peace Fellowship and the Edge of the Church, 1941–1991* (Ann Arbor: University Press of America, 1993).
15. "Youth Conference Views," *Lutheran Companion* 38, no. 42 (October 16, 1940).
16. Bergstrand, "The Master's Magnificent Minority," 16.
17. World Council of Churches Youth Department, Oslo Conference, 1946, page 3 of report to Scandinavians, *Bergstrand Papers.*
18. "Leadership Schools for Youth 1955–56," (Minneapolis: Board of Youth Activities, Augustana Evangelical Lutheran Church), 1, *Bergstrand Papers.*
19. Sharon Anderson Teleen correspondence about Luther League dates from 1961 to 1964 when she went to Augustana College. There seems to be no indication in her letters that the Augustana Church was merging with others to form the LCA. The programs she was involved in continue uninterrupted. Private collection.
20. Wilton Bergstrand to Martin Carlson, October 21, 1960, copy to Malvin Lundeen, *Bergstrand Papers.*
21. Wilton Bergstrand, "What's the Score re: The Youth Work in the L.C.A?" unpublished 5 page brief, n.d. but sometime in 1961, *Bergstrand Papers*, 3. Dr. Franklin Clark Fry was president of the United Lutheran Church in America (ULCA), the largest of the church bodies that merged to form the LCA. Fry was also elected the first LCA president.
22. Ibid., 4.

Chapter 17: Augustana's Ecumenical Vision

1. For general background on the trends within American Lutheranism, see E. Clifford Nelson, *Lutheranism in North America, 1914–1970* (Minneapolis: Augsburg Publishing House, 1972). On the specific Augustana history see G. Everett Arden, *Augustana Heritage: The History of the Augustana Lutheran Church* (Rock Island, Ill.: Augustana Book Concern, 1963), and for the earlier period, Oscar N. Olson, *The Augustana Lutheran Church in America, 1860–1910* (Davenport, Iowa: Arcade Office and Letter Service, 1956). On the experience of Augustana in relations with other Christians, see Conrad Bergendoff, "Ecumenical Experiences," in Emmer Engberg, ed., *Centennial Essays: Augustana Lutheran Church, 1860–1960* (Rock Island, Ill.: Augustana, 1960), 89–106.

2. Hugo Söderström, *Confession and Cooperation: The Policy of the Augustana Synod in Confessional Matters and the Synod's Relation with Other Churches up to the Beginning of the Twentieth Century*, Bibliotheca Historico-Ecclesiastica Lundensis, vol. 4 (Lund, Sweden: C. W. K. Gleerup Bokförlag, 1973), 10.

3. For the tangled ethnic and theological relations between these groups, see Mark A. Granquist, "The Swedish Ethnic Denominations in the United States: Their Development and Relations, 1880–1920" (Ph.D. diss., University of Chicago, 1992).

4. There were cooperative efforts among the Swedish ethnic denominations during the late 1920s, including the formation of a "Committee on Conference" to discuss common work. Though President Brandelle was involved in this, it seems that he was less interested in working with these groups than with other American Lutherans, and the effort soon came to nothing.

5. For the history of this relationship, see Mark A. Granquist, "Swedish-American Episcopalians and Lutheran-Episcopal Relations in North America, 1850–1935," *Anglican and Episcopal History* 74, no. 1 (March 2005): 23–44.

6. G. A. Brandelle to Thomas Burgess, December 5, 1921, *G. A. Brandelle Presidential Papers*, Archives of the Evangelical Lutheran Church in America, Elk Grove Village, Illinois. Burgess was the Secretary of the Foreign-Born Americans Division of the Protestant Episcopal Church.

7. On these negotiations, see Mark A. Granquist, "The Augustana Synod and the Episcopal Church," *Lutheran Quarterly* 14, no. 2 (Summer 2000): 173–92.

8. A record of the 1935 discussions exists in a typed verbatim transcript of almost the whole discussion, which is very illuminating. See "Records of a Conference between the Commission of Comity of the Evangelical Lutheran Augustana Synod and the Sub-Committee of the Joint Commission for Conference on Church Unity of the Protestant Episcopal Church, held at Evanston, Illinois, December 3–4, 1935," typescript copy (Evanston: Seabury-Western Theological Seminary, 1936). Copy at the ELCA Archives.

9. Ibid., 34.

10. Adolf Hult to P. O. Bersell, April 21, 1938, *P. O. Bersell Presidential Papers*, Archives of the Evangelical Lutheran Church in America, Elk Grove Village, Illinois.

11. *Minutes of the Augustana Synod*, 1950, 369.

12. G. A. Brandelle to F. H. Knubel, April 15, 1925, *G. A. Brandelle Presidential Papers*.

13. C. J. Bengston, "Nicaea and Stockholm," *Lutheran Companion* 33, no. 39 (September 26, 1925), 616.

14. S. J. Sebelius, "Confessional Lutherans and the Stockholm Conference," *Lutheran Companion* 33, no. 32 (August 8, 1925): 507.

15. "Report of the Delegation to Oxford and Edinburgh, 1937," Augustana Synod papers, Archives of the ELCA, 24.

16. P. O. Bersell to Conrad Bergendoff, January 26, 1942, *P. O. Bersell Presidential Papers*.

17. For details on this involvement, see Dorris A. Flesner, *American Lutherans Help Shape World Council: The Role of the Lutheran Churches of America in the Formation of the World Council of Churches*, Lutheran Historical Conference Publication, no. 2 (Dubuque, Iowa: Brown, 1981).

18. P. O. Bersell, "Impressions from Amsterdam . . . World Council of Churches," *Lutheran Companion* 56, no. 42 (October 20, 1948): 7.

19. "Ecumenical Experiences," in *Centennial Essays*, 105.

Chapter 18: The Social Purpose of Theology

1. Confessionalism refers to the way in which churches subscribe to and base their teachings upon the historic sixteenth-century Reformation confessional documents, primarily the Augsburg Confession, Smalcald Articles, and Small Catechism, but also additional formulations created during controversy with the Reformed, such as the Formula of Concord. These confessions are gathered into a Book of Concord. American Lutheran history records a process by which subscription to the Book of Concord became a mechanism through which various church traditions would recognize each other. This process is not yet complete.

2. The members of the American Lutheran Conference were Augustana, the American Lutheran Church (formed in 1930 with the merger of three German Midwestern church bodies), the Norwegian Lutheran Church in America, the Lutheran Free Church (also Norwegian), and the United Danish Evangelical Lutheran Church. The conference was formed on the basis of the Minneapolis Theses (named after the city in which the meeting was held), which included a strongly anti-ecumenical provision called the Galesburg Rule: "Lutheran pulpits for Lutherans only; Lutheran altars for Lutheran communicants only." Despite initial willingness to merge with the other churches in the American Lutheran Conference, Augustana later withdrew, citing that it was unwilling to enter a union where ecumenical relations were not important issues. The remaining four churches merged to form the American Lutheran Church (ALC).

3. The complex history of the process of drafting multiple *Theses* as a basis for unity, and the continuing distrust between Midwestern and Eastern Lutheranism that made this a futile effort, is traced in E. Clifford Nelson, *The Lutherans in North America* (Philadelphia: Fortress Press, 1980), chs. 19, 21.

4. Hjalmar Johnson, "Some Thoughts on Inspiration," *Journal of the American Lutheran Conference* vol. 4 (May 1939):11–32, cited in G. Everett Arden, *Augustana Heritage: The History of the Augustana Lutheran Church* (Rock Island, Ill.: Augustana Book Concern, 1963), 295.

5. A. D. Mattson to P. O. Bersell, January 20, 1945, *P. O. Bersell Presidential Papers*, Archives of the Evangelical Lutheran Church in America, Elk Grove Village, Illinois.

6. Conrad Bergendoff to P. O. Bersell, January 6, 1945, *P. O. Bersell Presidential Papers*.

7. Two seminary graduates from the 1946 class, Charles Curtis and S. Bernhard Erling, were singled out at their ordination exam before the ministerium, and seemed to be challenged with questions that really were directed at the faculty and their modern methods. Both students went on to further graduate study and scholarship in Swedish theology—Erling on Anders Nygren and his motif research and Curtis on the ecumenical work of Nathan Söderblom—as well as pastoral leadership after a few years. The ordination exam before the ministerium was changed after 1946 to a more private examination by committee.

8. Conrad Bergendoff, *The Augustana Ministerium: A Study of the Careers of the 2,504 Pastors of the Augustana Evangelical Lutheran Synod/Church, 1850–1962* (Rock Island, Ill.: Augustana Historical Society, 1980). During the 1940s S. B. Erling, Charles Curtis, George Lindbeck, Emmet Eklund, Carl Fjellman, Reuben Joseph Swanson, Sydney Ahlstrom, Paul Holmer, Gene Lund, Ralph Hjelm, George Olson, Louis Almen, Lyman Lundeen, Joel Lundeen, Clair Johnson, and Robert Esjbornson, went on to graduate work at these university divinity schools, while another group completed doctoral work to assist them in missionary work at the Hartford Kennedy School of Missions.

9. P. O. Bersell to Vergilius Ferm, September and October, 1946, *P. O. Bersell Presidential Papers*.

10. Ibid.

11. A. D. Mattson, *Christian Social Consciousness: An Introduction to Christian Sociology* (Rock Island, Ill.: Augustana Book Concern, 1953), 136.

12. Ibid., 252.

13. P. O. Bersell to Karl Mattson, July 16, 1951, *P. O. Bersell Presidential Papers.*

14. Karl Mattson to P. O. Bersell, October 5, 1951, *P. O. Bersell Presidential Papers.*

15. Ibid.

16. Interview by author with Kenneth Senft, in Gettysburg, November 2000.

17. "Lutheran World Federation," *Lutheran Companion* 55, no. 35 (August 27, 1947), 5.

18. Ibid.

19. Ibid.

20. Ibid.

21. Carlfelt competed against Samuel Miller for the position. On Carlfelt and his tenure at the seminary, see S. Bernhard Erling, "Augustana's Theological Tradition: Hasselquist, Olsson, Lindberg, Bergendoff, Carlfelt," in Arland Hultgren and Vance Eckstrom, eds., *The Heritage of Augustana* (Chicago: Augustana Heritage Association, 1999), 95.

22. Anton Fridrichsen's 1925 Strasbourg dissertation was eventually translated by Roy Harrisville and John Hanson as *The Problem of Miracle in Primitive Christianity* (Minneapolis: Augsburg Publishing House, 1972). This biblical scholar riveted the Swedish theological students during the 1930s and 1940s, and some American students as well.

23. Gustaf Wingren to Carl Rasmussen, February 6, 1947, *Rasmussen Papers*, Lutheran Theological Seminary at Gettysburg Special Collections, Gettysburg, Penn.

24. Hartmut Lehmann, *Martin Luther in the American Imagination: American Studies*, A Monograph Series, vol. 63 (Munich: Wilhelm Fink Verlag:, 1988), passim. This statement will surprise modern readers who can hardly imagine Lutheranism without Luther, but any survey of American Lutheranism before 1917, either in English or in any of the immigrant languages, will find scant reference to the founder.

25. These and the following reflections on Fry and other Americans were published in *Franklin Clark Fry: A Palette for a Portrait*, ed. Roberg H. Fisher, supplementary Number of the *Lutheran Quarterly* vol. 24 (1972): 227–8; 231–2.

Chapter 19: The Road to Lutheran Merger

1. G. Everett Arden, "Enroute to Unity," in Herbert T. Neve and Benjamin A. Johnson, eds., *The Maturing of American Lutheranism* (Minneapolis: Augsburg Publishing House, 1968), 229.

2. For a full account of this, see Oscar N. Olson, *The Augustana Lutheran Church in America* (Rock Island, Ill.: Augustana Book Concern, 1950), especially 42–45. As most of this conflict was on the territory of the Minnesota Conference, see also Emeroy Johnson, *God Gave the Growth: The Story of the Lutheran Minnesota Conference 1878–1958* (Minneapolis: T. S. Denison, 1958), especially 209–227.

3. C. J. Södergren, "Our Relation to the General Council," *Lutheran Companion* 22, no. 50 (December 12, 1914): 1.

4. N. Oscar Montan, "Whither Are We Drifting?" *Lutheran Companion* 26, no. 9 (May 2, 1918): 107.

5. Adolf Hult, "Eastern and Western Lutheranism," *Lutheran Companion* 26, no. 50 (December 14, 1918): 38.

6. Alfred Bergin, "The United Lutheran Church and the Augustana Synod," *Lutheran Companion* 26, no. 10 (March 9, 1918): 122.

7. G. A. Brandelle, "Presidential Report to the Synod, 1918," *Augustana Synod Referat*, 1918, 24.

8. Adolf Hult, "Augustana's Idealism in Her 'Federation' Action," *Lutheran Companion* 26, no. 35 (August 31, 1918): 443.

9. *Augustana Synod Referat*, 1918, 146.

10. C. J. Södergren to G. A. Brandelle, March 3, 1919, *G. A. Brandelle Presidential Papers*, Archives of the Evangelical Lutheran Church in America, Elk Grove Village, Illinois.

11. See E. Clifford Nelson, *The Lutherans in North America, 1914–1970* (Philadelphia: Fortress Press, 1980), especially 18–27.

12. For a detailed study of the events leading up to 1930, see Fred Meuser, *The Formation of the American Lutheran Church* (Columbus, Ohio: Wartburg, 1958), 238–247.

13. *Minutes of the Augustana Synod*, 1930, 233.

14. Adolf Hult, "A Notable Lecture on American Lutheran Church Unity," *Lutheran Companion* 35, no. 16 (April 16, 1927): 370.

15. "The American Lutheran Conference," *Lutheran Companion* 38, no. 42 (October 18, 1930): 1316.

16. P. A. Mattson to G. A. Brandelle, December 27, 1929, *G. A. Brandelle Presidential Papers.*

17. G. A. Brandelle to P. A. Mattson, December 31, 1929, *G. A. Brandelle Presidential Papers.*

18. G. Everett Arden, *Augustana Heritage: The History of the Augustana Lutheran Church* (Rock Island, Ill.: Augustana Book Concern, 1963), 280.

19. "Proceeding of the American Lutheran Conference, 1942," *Journal of Theology of the American Lutheran Conference*, 8 (January 1943): 84.

20. Nelson, *The Lutherans in North America, 1914–1970*, 500. Nelson adds, parenthetically, "the sociological factor of Norwegian-Swedish tension is not to be underestimated in inter-Lutheran relations."

21. E. E. Ryden, "American Lutherans Close Ranks: Missouri Synod, However, Remains Aloof," *Lutheran Companion* 50, no. 22 (May 28, 1942): 675.

22. *Minutes of the Augustana Synod*, 1948, 406.

23. "Free" in this sense means a meeting where no delegates officially representing their own Lutheran denominations, but where issues and ideas could be freely expressed.

24. E. E. Ryden, "Conference in Definite Lutheran Unity Move," *Lutheran Companion* 56, no. 48 (December 1, 1948): 4.

25. E. E. Ryden, "Editorial," *Lutheran Companion* 57, no. 3 (January 19, 1949): 3.

26. Arden, *Augustana Heritage*, 391. G. Everett Arden has an extended discussion of the ins and outs of the merger debates during these three years in his chapter entitled "Destiny Fulfilled" where he quotes Bergendoff's speech at the Des Moines meeting in June 1952.

27. "Augustana and Union: Would We Gain or Lose?" *Lutheran Companion* 97, no. 4 (January 23, 1952): 10.

28. "Lutheran Unity Issue Confronting Church," *Lutheran Companion* 97, no. 13 (March 26, 1952): 7.

29. "Lutheran Unity is Desirable On a National Lutheran Council Basis," *Lutheran Companion* 91, no. 15 (April 9, 1952): 11.

30. "What Should Augustana Do with Church Union?" *Lutheran Companion* 97, no. 21 (May 21, 1952): 7.

31. "Augustana Quits Merger Negotiations," *Lutheran Companion* 97, no. 48 (November 26, 1952): 7.

32. The American Lutheran Church (ALC) was formed in 1960 by the merger of the Evangelical Lutheran Church (ELC-Norwegian), United Evangelical Lutheran Church (UELC-Danish), and the American Lutheran Church. The Lutheran Free Church twice defeated proposals to join the union, finally entering the ALC in 1963. Lutheran Free congregations not wishing to join the ALC withdrew and formed the Association of Free Lutheran Congregations.

33. Jack Schreiber, "Why Not With ULCA?" *Lutheran Companion* 100, no. 3 (January 19, 1955): 14.

34. "What Kind of Unity?" *Lutheran Companion* 100, no. 3 (January 19, 1955): 7.

35. Lloyd Malmstrom, "Confirm our Friendship," *Lutheran Companion* 100, no. 11 (March 16, 1955): 3.

36. "A Merger Invitation," *Lutheran Companion* 100, no. 15 (April 13, 1955): 10.

37. For a detailed look at the merger negotiations of the 1950s, see Nelson, *Lutheranism in North America, 1914–1970*.

38. Joint Commission on Lutheran Unity, *Statement of Agreement on Unity, 1958* (Philadelphia: n.p., n.d), 4.

39. Glenn Stone interview with Conrad Bergendoff, June 22–23, 1977, Archives of Cooperative Lutheranism, Lutheran Council in the USA. Archives of the Evangelical Lutheran Church in America, Elk Grove Village, Illinois, 60.

40. W. Kent Gilbert, *Commitment to Unity: A History of the Lutheran Church in America* (Philadelphia: Fortress Press), 1988, 102.

41. For an "insiders look" at the theoretical and practical issues involved in the JCLU negotiations, see Johannes Knudsen, *The Formation of the Lutheran Church in America* (Philadelphia: Fortress Press, 1978).

42. "Appendix G," *Minutes of the Joint Commission on Lutheran Unity*, September 18, 1957.

43. E. E. Ryden, "Is the Cause Hopeless?" *Lutheran Companion* 104, no. 18 (April 30, 1958): 5.

44. "Where Does ULCA Stand?" *Lutheran Companion* 104, no. 46 (November 12, 1958): 9.

45. Martin T. Ringstrom, "Pleased Over Progress," *Lutheran Companion* 104, no. 52 (December 24, 1958): 9.

Chapter 20: Augustana's Legacy

1. On the history of the LCA, see W. Kent Gilbert, *Commitment to Unity: A History of the Lutheran Church in America* (Philadelphia: Fortress Press, 1988). This is a good history, but Gilbert does not deal with the question of the lingering power differentials or the continuation of the separate pre-merger traditions in the LCA.

2. From an interview with Richard Pearson by the author in June 1992 in Cheshire, Conn.

3. See Harold Skillrud, *LSTC: Decade of Decision (A History of the Merger of the Lutheran School of Theology at Chicago)* (Chicago: Lutheran School of Theology at Chicago, 1969). The four seminaries that merged with Augustana to form LSTC included Central Lutheran Seminary, Midland, Neb.; Suomi Theological Seminary, Hancock, Mich.; Grand View Theological Seminary, Des Moines, Iowa; and Chicago Lutheran Seminary, Maywood, Ill.

4. Although he had begun his graduate study at Union, and even returned in 1954 to do more work, he never completed the doctoral degree.

5. Gunnar Hillerdal to Karl E. Mattson, December 16 1958, *Mattson Papers*, Private Collection.

6. Wilton Bergstrand, "Notes to the Youth Activities Board, Augustana Lutheran Church," November 1961, in *Wilton Bergstrand Papers*, ELCA Archives, Elk Grove Village, Ill.

7. Richard Koenig, "The New Lutheran Church: The Gift of Augustana," *The Christian Century* 104, no. 19 (June 9, 1987): 555.

8. For more on this, see "Doctrinal Controversy: Augustana and the Mission Friends" on page 43.

APPENDIX

Table 1. *The Growth of Swedish-America*[1]

	Immigrants	Second generation	Total
1900	582,000	542,000	1,124,000
1910	665,000	752,000	1,417,000
1920	625,000	888,000	1,513,000
1930	595,000	967,000	1,562,000
1940	445,000	856,000	1,301,000

Table 2. *Regional Distribution of Swedish-America*[2]

	Midwest	West	Northeast	South
1890	560,000	76,000	127,000	12,000
1910	857,000	194,000	287,000	25,000
1930	893,000	285,000	346,000	37,000
1950	507,000	255,000	223,000	57,000

Table 3. *Major Urban Centers of Swedish-America, 1930 (foreign-born)*[3]

Chicago	140,000	Worcester, Mass.	16,000
Minneapolis/St. Paul	95,000	San Francisco	14,000
New York	67,000	Detroit	11,000
Los Angeles	23,000	Portland	11,000
Seattle	21,000	Boston	10,000
Duluth, Minn.	16,000	Rockford, Ill.	10,000

Table 4. Growth of the Augustana Synod by Decades[4]

Year	Pastors	Congregations	Members
1860	32	60	900
1870	54	137	3,000
1880	146	332	71,000
1890	325	637	145,000
1900	458	921	201,009
1910	625	1,145	261,000
1920	754	1,250	292,000
1930	865	1,227	320,000
1940	911	1,184	349,000
1950	988	1,173	459,000
1960	1,311	1,255	618,000

Table 5. Growth in Conferences in the Augustana Synod[5]

Year formed	Conference name	Total number
1853	Mississippi (in 1870, Illinois)	1
1858	Minnesota	2
1868	Iowa	3
1870	Kansas, New York	5
1886	Nebraska	6
1893	Columbia, California (Pacific in 1888)	8
1910	Superior	9
1912	New England, Red River	11
1913	Canada	12
1923	Texas	13

Table 6. Membership in Conference by Decade (in thousands)[6]

	1880	1890	1900	1910	1920	1930	1940	1950	1960
Illinois (1853)	24	42	33	60	60	69	76	95	123
Minnesota (1858)	26	49	69	80	80	87	100	133	180
Iowa (1868)	9	14	16	18	19	23	23	27	30
Kansas (1870)	9	11	13	16	18	15	15	19	25
New York (1870)	5	10	22	53	31	29	31	40	53
Nebraska (1886)		7	9	11	13	14	13	16	19
Columbia (1893)			2	6	7	9	10	23	38

Membership in Conference by Decade (in thousands)[6]							
California (1893)	1	3	4	6	8	16	37
Superior (1910)		12	13	11	14	18	20
New England (1912)			27	34	34	39	48
Red River (1912)			12	14	16	24	28
Canada (1913)			4	3	4	5	9
Texas (1923)				3	4	5	7

Table 7. *Rural and Urban Congregational Comparison, 1960*

Conferences	Rural	Urban	Percentage urban
East (New York and New England)	24	188	88%
West (Columbia and California)	16	129	89%
Upper Midwest (Minnesota, Red River, and Superior)	358	125	21%
Remaining Conferences	175	253	59%

Table 8. *Schools Founded in the Augustana Synod*[7]

1860	Augustana College and Seminary, Rock Island, Illinois
1862	Gustavus Adolphus College, St. Peter, Minnesota
1881	Bethany College, Lindsborg, Kansas
1883	Luther College, Wahoo, Nebraska (merged into Midland College, 1962)
1888	Hope Academy, Moorhead, Minnesota (closed 1896)
1889	Emmanuel College, Minneapolis, Minnesota (closed 1894)
1893	Upsala College, East Orange, New Jersey (closed 1995)
1893	Martin Luther College, Chicago, Illinois (closed 1895)
1900	Northwestern College, Fergus Falls, Minnesota (closed 1932)
1904	Minnesota College, Minneapolis (closed 1930)
1904	Trinity College, Round Rock, Texas (merged into Texas Lutheran, 1929)
1907	Coeur d'Alene College, Coeur d'Alene, Idaho (closed during World War 1)
1908	North Star College, Warren, Minnesota (closed 1936)

Table 9. *Presidents of the Augustana Synod*[8]

Tufve Nilsson Hasselquist	1860–1870	Per Johan Sward	1891–1899
Jonas Swensson	1870–1873	Lawrence A. Johnston	1911–1918
Eric Norelius	1874–1881, 1899–1911	Gustav A. Brandelle	1918–1935
Erland Carlson	1881–1888	Petrus O. Bersell	1935–1951
Sven P. A. Lindahl	1888–1891	Oscar A. Benson	1951–1959
		Malvin H. Lundeen	1959–1962

Table 10. *Translation of Letter from Bishop U. L. Ullman*

During the course of many years I have, with much sympathy, followed the development of the so-called Swedish Augustana Lutheran Church in the United States. Because of the knowledge of it that I have secured, I am willing to respond to the request to certify that, so far as I have been able to determine, that this synod, with its teaching based on the unaltered Augsburg Confession of 1530, which name it bears, has done a great service to the evangelical Lutheran church and the preservation of the confession among the immigrant Swedish population. Therefore I testify, that so far as my knowledge of the churchly situation in North American stretches, that I do not recognize any other Swedish Lutheran church body than that represented by the Augustana Synod.

Strängnäs Bishop Residence, January 18, 1892

Signature, Bishop U. L. Ullman

Seal

Sources

1. Department of Commerce, Fifteenth Census of the United States, 1930, Population, vol. 2, 269, and Sixteenth Census of the United States, 1940, Population, Country of Birth of the Foreign-born Population, 225.

2. Lars Ljungmark, Swedish Exodus (Carbondale, Ill.: Southern Illinois University Press, 1979), 89.

3. Department of Commerce, *Fifteenth Census of the United States, 1930, Population*, Vol. II, 314–37.

4. "Augustana Church Statistics, Every Five Years, 1860–1940, Every Year Since 1940," Minutes of the Augustana Synod, 1961, 770.

5. For a helpful summary of the Conferences of the Augustana Synod, see Robert C. Wiederaenders and Walter G. Tillmanns, *The Synods of American Lutheranism* (St. Louis: Lutheran Historical Conference, 1968), 67–69.

6. Statistics taken from the Minutes of the Augustana Synod, 1881–1961.

7. See Stephenson, *The Religious Aspects of Swedish Immigration* (Minneapolis: University of Minnesota Press, 1932), 341–345, and Solberg, *Lutheran Higher Education in North America* (Minneapolis: Augsburg Publishing House, 1985), 368, n. 44.

8. From 1860 to 1894, presidents were elected annually; from 1894 to 1922 they served a two-year term; and from 1922 to 1962 they served four-year terms.

SUGGESTED READING

There is an extensive historical record for the Augustana Synod, and many more publications than could be listed here. The primary repositories of Augustana materials can be found at the following institutions and libraries: the Archives of the Evangelical Lutheran Church in America, Elk Grove Village, Illinois, the Lutheran School of Theology at Chicago, Chicago, Illinois, the Swenson Center at Augustana College, Rock Island, Illinois, Gustavus Adolphus College, St. Peter, Minnesota, and Bethany College, Lindsborg, Kansas.

Printed Historical Materials

Virginia Follstad. *The Augustana Evangelical Lutheran Church in Print: A Selective Union List with Annotations of Serial Publications.* ATLA Bibliography Series, no. 53. Lanham, Md.: Scarecrow Press, 2007. 351 pages. (A treasure trove of information.)

Ira O. Nothstein. "The Evangelical Lutheran Augustana Synod: Its History, Doctrines, and Activities: A Bibliography." *Augustana Quarterly* 22 (July 1943): 227–43; 23 (January 1944): 36–50; 23 (March 1944): 158–70; and 23 (October 1944): 368–72.

D. Verner Swanson. *Index: Minutes of the Augustana Synod, 1860–1962.* Rock Island, Ill.: Augustana Book Concern, 1962. 28 pages.

There is a cardfile index to the *Lutheran Companion* at the Archives of the Evangelical Lutheran Church in America, Elk Grove Village, Illinois.

Primary Documents (collected)

O. Fritiof Ander and Oscar L. Nordstrom, eds. *The American Origin of the Augustana Synod, from Contemporary Lutheran Periodicals, 1851–1860.* Augustana Historical Society Publications, vol. 10. Rock Island, Ill.: Augustana Historical Society, 1942. 192 pages.

Augustana Evangelical Lutheran Church, Commission on Morals and Social Problems, *Social Pronouncements of the Augustana Lutheran Church and its Conferences, 1937–56.* Rock Island, Ill.: Augustana Book Concern, 1956. 32 pages.

Ira O. Nothstein, ed. *Selected Documents Dealing with the Organization of the First Congregations and Conferences of the Augustana Synod and their Growth Until 1860.* 2 vols. Augustana Historical Society Publications, vol. 10 and 11. Rock Island, Ill.: Augustana Historical Society, 1944. 195 and 163 pages.

Daniel Nystrom, ed. *A Family of God: Echoes from the Saga of the Augustana Lutheran Church.* Rock Island, Ill.: Augustana, 1962. 262 pages. (More popular, but helpful.)

———. *Samling af Augustana-Synodens, dess konferenser och inrattningars oktrojer, stadgar och ordningsregler.* Rock Island, Ill.: Augustana Book Concern, 1918. 407 pages. (A compilation of official documents from the synod and its organizations; about half of the materials are in English.)

Histories

G. Everett Arden. *Augustana Heritage: A History of the Augustana Lutheran Church.* Rock Island, Ill.: Augustana, 1963. 424 pages. (The standard and official history.)

Eric Norelius. *De Svenska Lutherska Formsamlingarnas och Svensksarnes Historia i Amerika,* 2 vols. Rock Island, Ill.: Lutheran Augustana Book Concern, 1890 and 1916. Selected chapters of the first volume are translated by Conrad Bergendoff in *The Pioneer Swedish Settlements and Swedish Lutheran Churches in America, 1845–1860.* Rock Island, Ill.: Augustana Historical Society, 1984. 419 pages.

Oscar N. Olson. *The Augustana Lutheran Church in America: Pioneer Period, 1846–1860.* Rock Island, Ill.: Augustana Book Concern, 1950. 397 pages.

Oscar N. Olson. *The Augustana Lutheran Church in America, 1860–1910.* Davenport, Iowa: Arcade Office and Letter Service, 1956. 131 pages. (Valuable, especially for its sources.)

———. *The Augustana Synod: A Brief Review of its History, 1860–1910.* Rock Island, Ill.: Augustana Book Concern, 1910. 267 pages. (The first history in English.)

Additional Historical Works

Dag Blanck. *Becoming Swedish-American: The Construction of an Ethnic Identity in the Augustana Synod, 1860–1917.* Acta Universitatis Upsalensis 182. Upsala: University Library, 1997. 240 pages.

A. D. Mattson. *The Polity of the Augustana Synod,* rev. ed. Rock Island, Ill.: Augustana Book Concern, 1952. 459 pages. (Very helpful on the institutional growth of the Synod.)

Karl Olsson. *By One Spirit,* Chicago: Covenant Press, 1962. 811 pages. (Very good on the religious awakening in Sweden, and the early relations between Augustana and the Covenant.)

Hugo Soderstrom. *Confession and Cooperation: The Policy of the Augustana Synod in Confessional Matters and the Synod's Relations with other Churches up to the Beginning of the Twentieth Century.* Bibliotheca Historico-Ecclesiastica Lundensis, IX. Lund, Sweden: C. W. K. Gleerup Bokförlag, 1973. 200 pages. (A very valuable Swedish study in English.)

George M. Stephenson. *The Founding of the Augustana Synod, 1850–1860.* Rock Island, Ill.: Augustana Book Concern, 1927. 160 pages.

George M. Stephenson. *The Religious Aspects of Swedish Immigration.* Minneapolis: University of Minnesota Press, 1932. 542 pages. (Good, but a strong slant to the book.)

Collected Historical Essays and Anniversary Collections

Emmer Engberg, et al., eds. *Centennial Essays: Augustana Lutheran Church 1860–1960.* Rock Island, Ill.: Augustana, 1960. 268 pages.

Hartland Gifford and Arland Hultgren, eds. *The Heritage of Augustana: Essays on the Life and Legacy of the Augustana Lutheran Church.* Minneapolis: Kirk House Publishers, 2004. 297 pages.

Arland Hultgren and Vance Eckstrom, eds. *The Augustana Heritage: Recollections, Perspectives, and Prospects.* Chicago: Augustana Heritage Association, 1999. 301 pages.

Oscar N. Olson, ed. *A Century of Life and Growth, Augustana 1848–1948.* Rock Island, Ill.: Augustana Book Concern, 1948. 158 pages.

After Seventy-five Years, 1860–1935: A Jubilee Publication. Rock Island, Ill.: Augustana Book Concern, 1935. 288 pages.

Conference Histories

(California) *History of the California Conference of the Augustana Lutheran Church in North America 1893–1953.* n.p.: n.p., 1953. 63 pages.

(Canada) Ferdy E. Baglo. *Augustana Lutherans in Canada.* n.p.: Canada Conference of the Augustana Lutheran Church, 1962. 96 pages.

(Columbia) Carl J. Renhard and Carl H. Sandgren. *Fifty Years of the Columbia Conference*. n.p.: Columbia Conference, 1943. 180 pages.

(Columbia) Philip Nordquist, et al., eds. *New Partners, Old Roots: A History of Merging Lutheran Churches in the Pacific Northwest*. Tacoma: J & D Printing, 1986. 316 pages.

(Florida District) Willard D. Allbeck, et al. *History of the Florida Synod of the Lutheran Church in America*. n.p.: Florida Synod of the LCA, 1978. 228 pages + indexes.

(Illinois) *Illinois Conference, 1853–1928, Jubilee Album . . .* Rock Island, Ill.: Augustana Book Concern, 1928. 191 pages.

(Illinois) G. Everett Arden. *History of the Illinois Conference of the Augustana Evangelical Lutheran Church, 1853–1953*. Rock Island, Ill.: Augustana Book Concern, 1953. 48 pages.

(Iowa) Reuben C. Anderson, ed. *Forward in Faith: the Seventy-fifth Anniversary of the Iowa Conference of the Evangelical Lutheran Augustana Synod*. n.p.: n.p., 1943.

(Kansas-West Central) Wymore Goldberg. *Ninetieth Anniversary of the West Central Conference, Augustana Lutheran Church, 1870–1960*. n.p: n.p., 1960.

(Kansas) Emroy Lindquist. *Smoky Valley People: A History of Lindsborg, Kansas*. Lindsborg: Bethany College, 1953. 269 pages.

(Minnesota) Emeroy Johnson, *A Church is Planted: The Story of the Lutheran Minnesota Conference, 1851–1876*. Minneapolis: Lutheran Minnesota Conference, 1948. 386 pages.

(Minnesota) Emeroy Johnson. *God Gave the Growth: The Story of the Lutheran Minnesota Conference, 18756–1958*. Minneapolis: T. S. Denison, 1958. 266 pages.

(Nebraska) Charles Frederick Sandahl. *The Nebraska Conference of the Augustana Synod*. Rock Island, Ill.: Augustana Book Concern, 1931. 445 pages.

(Nebraska) James Iverne Dowie. *Prairie Grass Dividing*. Rock Island, Ill.: Augustana Historical Society, 1959, 262 pages.

(New England) Luther E. Lindberg. *Fifty Years in New England: A History of the New England Conference, 1912–1962*. n.p.: New England Conference, 1962. 314 pages.

(Red River) J. Eldor Larson. *History of the Red River Conference of the Augustana Lutheran Church*. Blair, Neb.: Red River Valley Conference, 1953. 173 pages.

(Texas) M. L. Lundquist. *One Family of God: A Brief History of the Texas Conference*. Rock Island, Ill.: Augustana Book Concern, 1962. 24 pages.

Organizations and Auxiliaries

(Book Concern) Daniel Nystrom. *A Ministry of Printing: History of the Publication House of the Augustana Lutheran Church, 1889–1962*. Rock Island, Ill.: Augustana, 1962. 112 pages.

(Foreign Missions) Swan Hjalmar Swanson. *Foundation for Tomorrow: A Century of Progress in Augustana World Missions*. Minneapolis: Board of Foreign Missions, Augustana Lutheran Church, 1960. 370 pages.

(Foreign Missions) George Hall. *The Missionary Spirit in the Augustana Church*. Rock Island, Ill.: Augustana Historical Society, 1984. 166 pages.

(Luther League) Martin E. Carlson. *Youth March: A History of the Augustana Synod Luther League*. Minneapolis: Augustana Synod Luther League, 1947. 95 pages.

(Woman's Missionary Society) Mrs. Peter (Mathilda) Peterson. *These Fifty Years, 1892–1942*. Chicago: Woman's Missionary Society of the Augustana Synod, 1942, 172 pages.

Educational Institutions

Conrad Bergendoff. *Augustana . . . A Profession of Faith: A History of Augustana College, 1860–1935*. Rock Island, Ill.: Augustana College Library, 1969. 220 pages.

G. Everett Arden. *The School of the Prophets: The Background and History of the Augustana Theological Seminary, 1860–1960*. Rock Island, Ill.: Augustana Theological Seminary, 1960. 280 pages.

Doniver Lund. *Gustavus Adolphus College: A Centennial History, 1862–1962.* St Peter, Minn.: Gustavus Adolphus College Press, 1962. 216 pages.

Emory Lindquist. *Bethany in Kansas: the History of a College.* Lindsborg: Bethany College, 1975. 309 pages.

Ray F. Kibler III. *Lutheran Bible Institute: The Original Vision.* n.p.: Lutheran Bible Institute of California, 2000. 55 pages.

Biography

Brief biographies, in the form of obituaries, can be found in the pages of the annual publications *Korsbaneret* (1880–1950—indexes in 1929 and 1950), *My Church* (1915–1946—indexes in 1928 and annually thereafter), and *Augustana Annual* (1948–62).

Conrad Bergendoff. *The Augustana Ministerium: A Study of the Careers of the 2,504 Pastors of the Augustana Evangelical Lutheran Synod/Church, 1850–1962.* Rock Island, Ill.: Augustana Historical Society, 1980. 246 pages. (Brief entries on every Augustana pastor. Invaluable.)

S. J. Sebelius. *Master Builders of Augustana: Biographical Sketches, Reminiscent and Appreciative, of Great Teachers at Augustana College.* Rock Island, Ill.: Augustana Book Concern, 1949. 104 pages.

(O. C. T. Andrén) Oscar Olson. *Olof Christian Telemark Andrén: Ambassador of Good Will.* Rock Island, Ill.: Augustana Historical Society, 1954. 103 pages.

(Gustav Andreen) Esther Andreen Albrecht. *Gustavus Andreen and the Growth of Augustana College and Theological Seminary.* (M.A. Thesis, University of Illinois), Urbana, Ill.: n.p., 1943. 96 pages.

(Conrad Bergendoff) Raymond Jarvi, ed. "Aspects of Augustana and Swedish America: Essays in Honor of Dr. Conrad Bergendoff's 100th year." *Swedish-American Historical Quarterly* 46 (July 1995) 328 pages.

(P. O. Bersell and C. A. Wendell) G. L. Bongfeldt. *Pen Portraits of P. O. Bersell and C. A. Wendell.* Rock Island, Ill.: Augustana Book Concern, 1950. 115 pages.

(Erland Carlson) Emroy Lindquist. *Shepherd of an Immigrant People: The Story of Erland Carlson.* Rock Island, Ill.: Augustana Historical Society, 1978. 236 pages.

(L. P. Esbjörn) Sam Rönnegård. *Prairie Shepherd: Lars Paul Esbjörn and the Beginnings of the Augustana Lutheran Church.* Rock Island, Ill.: Augustana Book Concern, 1952. 308 pages.

(T. N. Hasselquist) Oscar Fritiof Ander. *T. N. Hasselquist: The Career and Influence of a Swedish-American Clergyman, Journalist and Educator.* Rock Island, Ill.: Augustana Historical Society, 1931. 260 pages.

(L. A. Johnston and P. J. Sward) Oscar Olson *Swärd—Johnston: Biographical Sketches of Augustana Leaders.* Rock Island, Ill.: Augustana Historical Society, 1955. 80 pages.

(A. D. Mattson) Gregory Lee Jackson. *Prophetic Voice for the Kingdom: The Impact of Alvin Daniel Mattson Upon the Social Consciousness of the Augustana Synod.* Rock Island, Ill.: Augustana Historical Society, 1986. 239 pages.

(Eric Norelius) *The Journals of Eric Norelius: A Swedish Missionary on the American Frontier.* edited and translated by G. Everett Arden. Philadelphia: Fortress Press, 1967. 207 pages.

(Eric Norelius) Emeroy Johnson. *The Early Life of Eric Norelius, 1833–1862.* Rock Island, Ill.: Augustana Book Concern, 1934. 320 pages.

(Eric Norelius) Emeroy Johnson. *Eric Norelius: Pioneer Midwest Pastor and Churchman.* Rock Island, Ill.: Augustana Book Concern, 1954. 255 pages.

(Olof Olsson) Ernest William Olson. *Olaf Olsson: The Man, His Work, and His Thought.* Rock Island, Ill.: Augustana Book Concern, 1941. 352 pages.

(Olof Olsson) Emroy Lindquist. *Vision for A Valley: Olof Olsson and the early history of Lindsborg.* Rock Island, Ill.: Augustana Historical Society, 1970. 138 pages.

(C. A. Swensson) Daniel M. Pearson, *The Americanization of Carl Aaron Swensson,* Rock Island, Ill.: Augustana Historical Society, 1977, 169 pages.

(Jonas Swensson) Emmet Eklund, *His Name was Jonas: A Biography of Jonas Swensson,* Rock Island, Ill.: Augustana Historical Society, 1988, 176 pages.

INDEX

Please note: this index follows the Swedish custom of alphabetization. Vowels with accent markings go at the end of the alphabet, following the letter "Z".

Abrahamson, Lars G., 114, 123f, 201, 205–12, 244
Academic standards, 173, 244–252, 266, 307
African Americans (Negroes), attitudes toward, 30f, 50, 139, 143, 232
Ahlberg, P. A., 19, 25f, 50, 164
Ahnfelt, Oscar, 106
American Home Missionary Society, 22, 104
American Lutheran Church (1930), 240, 317, 327f, 331, 343, 375n2, 377n32
American Lutheran Conference, 43, 167, 214, 227, 240, 302, 304, 322–31, 343, 375n2, 377n15
Anderson, Dennis, 339
Anderson, George, 194
Andover, Illinois, 12, 15f, 29, 39, 64, 68f, 71, 165, 263
Andreen, Gustaf, 70, 111, 173, 229, 249, 268, 372n41
Andreen, Paul, 142, 360n82, 364n23, 369n52
Andrén, Olof Christian Telemak, 41
Anjou, John, 40
Arden, G. Everett, 108, 124, 170, 248, 258, 313, 318, 325, 335, 349n3, 352n11
Art, 270f
Atonement controversy, 40, 43f, 54f, 92, 291
Augustana Book Concern, 100f, 117, 171f, 201
Augustana Brotherhood, 198, 261–262
Augustana College, 44, 65, 69, 73f, 81–89, 92, 97f, 102,

108, 111, 131, 138, 162f, 168, 174, 182, 189, 220, 227, 245–9, 257, 261, 266f, 270, 275f, 303, 339
Augustana Heritage Association, 344
Augustana Tract Society, 68
Aulén, Gustaf, 312f, 347n8, 348n22
Awakening movement, 7, 12, 17, 52, 62, 91, 105,126, 208, 236

Beckman, Peter, 35
Bengston, Carl J., 108, 110, 122f, 139, 141, 222, 228, 297, 324, 357n16
Benson, Oscar Algot, 128, 168, 171, 257, 327, 341, 371n9
Bergendoff, Conrad, 98, 109f, 175, 238, 242, 244f, 250, 257, 266f, 298f, 301, 304f, 311, 326, 328, 332f, 340, 366n6, 366n13
Bergin, Alfred, 102, 130, 243
Bergstrand, Lorraine, 273
Bergstrand, Wilton, 273, 280f, 285f, 342, 373n1, 378n6
Bersell, Petrus Olof, 109f, 137f, 149f, 168f, 175, 231f, 240, 273, 280, 296f, 301f, 307f, 326f, 356n46
Bethany College, 44f, 65, 69, 80, 82f, 116, 155, 186, 202f, 230, 270, 279
Bethel Ship, 8, 23
Bethphage Mission, 167, 261
Bible Camps, 239, 274, 277f, 287, 343
Bishop's Cross, 214
Bishop Hill, 8, 9
Brandelle, Gustav Albert, 103, 108, 110, 122, 124f, 135f, 168f, 179, 192, 198, 213f
Bring, Ragnar, 312, 341
Brodeen, Eugene, 339
Burke, Lloyd, 339

"Caravaning," 287, 289
Carlfelt, Carl Gustaf, 311, 376n21
Carlson, August, 180
Carlson, Edgar, 230, 281, 283, 369n45
Carlson, Martin E., 338
Carlson, Peter, 35–7, 154
Carlson, Walter, 339
Carlsson, Erland, 35–43, 49, 57, 63, 69, 72–78, 85, 108, 114, 203, 207, 259, 352n13
Cassell, Peter, 14, 20, 31
Cederstram, Pehr Anderson, 35, 113
Chautauqua Institution, 287, 345
Chicago, Immanuel Lutheran Church, 17, 26f, 35f, 63f, 75, 80, 114–120
Chilstrom, Herbert, 339, 344
China Mission, 184–189
Church of Sweden, 11, 18f, 21, 27, 37, 39f, 43, 54, 62, 73, 91, 126, 180, 184, 194, 199f, 291, 294, 311f, 341, 344
Colleges, list of, 381
Communism, attitudes toward, 233f
Conferences: Canada, 156–7; Central, 79, 151; California and Columbia, 154; Illinois, 111, 150, 212; Iowa, 77f, 137, 49, 169, 273; Kansas, 80, 83, 88, 124, 153, 264; Minnesota, 52, 79, 80, 103, 105, 119, 124, 137, 149f, 170, 181f, 219f, 258, 325; Nebraska, 51, 61, 78f, 85, 87f, 147, 167, 187, 190, 258, 261, 305, 338; New England, 150f, 278, 330, 338f, 352; Red River, 338; Superior, 131; Texas, 152f, 279
Conservatism, 85, 102, 205, 240

Constitutions, 32f, 39f, 44, 51–54, 56, 65, 67, 72, 86, 105, 121, 123, 148, 168f, 171, 184, 250, 265, 305, 306, 308, 314f, 322, 333

Dancing, card playing, drinking, 17, 125, 127–30
Dahlberg, J. A., 117
Danielson, Elmer, 144, 195
Danielson, Lillian, 194
Danish Lutherans, 2, 44
Deaconess, 64, 80, 116, 134, 167, 191, 256, 258f

Ecumenical participation, 168f, 201, 232, 235, 238f, 241, 244f, 252, 286, 290f, 344
Edlund, John A., 196f
Edquist, Joshua, 87, 220
Edwins, August William, 184
Eielsen, Elling, 32
Engberg and Holmberg Company, 67f, 100, 171
English language congregations, early, 101
Episcopal Church, 22, 92, 104, 107, 126, 152, 169f, 200, 204, 293f, 344
Erlander, John, 35
Esbjörn, Constantine, 73
Esbjörn, Lars Paul, 2, 9–14, 17, 20–6, 28f, 32–8, 68, 87, 99, 207
Evald, Carl, 64, 115, 121f, 197
Evald, Emmy Carlsson, 89, 108, 110, 115–121, 189f, 202, 212, 259, 263, 275f, 342
Evangelical National Foundation (Evangeliska Fosterlandsstiftelse), 25
Evolution, 87, 217–24, 227, 235, 270

Ferm, Vergilius, 110, 242–4, 247–51, 305–8
Fjellstedt, Peter, 119, 26, 34, 49, 61
Flodman, Augusta Stenholm, 77–78, 87–90
Folk School, 80, 353n9
Foreign missions, 10, 13, 50, 116, 148, 168f, 170, 175, 179, 182f, 190, 232, 257,

258, 260, 277, 292, 297, 317, 319, 321, 325, 347n8
Founders of the Augustana Synod (1860), 35
Friberg, C. P., 184, 188, 194
Froeberg, Peter, 70, 117
Fry, Franklin Clark, 289f, 314f, 342
Fryxell, Cecilia, 75f
Fryxell, Fritiof, 87, 221, 236, 270
Fundamentalism, 220, 226

Galesburg Rule, 375n2
General Council, 46, 96, 102f, 106, 118, 121, 148f, 168, 179f, 183, 292f, 318, 320–4, 333
General Synod, 1f, 24, 32f, 118, 121, 179, 242, 292f, 296, 317, 319, 349n1, 350n26, 350n29
German Lutherans, 27, 366n13
Gullander, Paul, 180
Gustavus Adolphus College, 58, 64, 69, 76, 84–88, 108, 130f, 162f, 181, 190f, 196, 220–2, 230, 232, 235, 266, 279, 281–3, 287, 303, 339

Hallquist, Magda, 258
Hammarberg, Melvin, 339
Hasselquist, Tufve Nilsson, 13, 17, 20, 21–42, 46, 49f, 54–6, 61, 63, 67, 71, 78, 81f, 85, 99, 106, 108, 113, 122, 207, 347n10
Hedeen, N. Everett, 339
Hedstrom, Jonas and Olof, 8f, 12, 15, 23f
Hemlandet, Det Gamla och Nya, 29–31, 50, 67
Hill, Samuel, 88f
Hillerdal, Gunnar, 341
Holden Village, 343
Home missions, 103, 138, 142, 148–58, 167, 169, 170, 174, 175, 183, 260f, 291, 292, 297, 319
Hospitals, 83, 114, 121, 165f, 175, 184, 186, 189, 194, 232, 259f, 342
Hult, Adolf, 62, 108, 110, 129, 164, 207, 225, 232f, 236–8, 240, 243, 249, 251, 265, 297, 303, 321, 324

Hult, Ralph, 179, 190–5
Hultkrans, Johan G., 184
Hymnals, 91f, 100, 103, 108f, 111f, 235, 277, 325f
Håkanson, Magnus Frederik, 35

Immanuel Deaconess Institute, 167, 258
Immigrant letters, 15
India, 121, 167, 179f, 182f, 185f, 188f, 191–4, 232, 258, 260
Indian encounters, 31, 56–8, 80, 113, 194, 199, 350n23, 353n11
Iramba Mission, 193, 195, 277

Jackson, Andrew, 80
Jacobs, Charles, 245, 246, 322
Johansson, Carl Frederick, 47–56, 196
Johansson, Martin, 199, 201
Johnson, Oscar John, 190f
Johnston, Lawrence Albert, 124, 134, 168
Joint Commission on Lutheran Unity (JCLU), 317, 332, 374n8
Joint Union Committee (JUC), 328
Jubilee celebration, 108, 109, 116, 168, 203, 204

Kendall, Leonard, 339
Knubel, Frederick, 297, 322
Koenig, Richard, 343f
Korsbaneret ("The Banner of the Cross"), 49, 68f, 72, 113f, 117, 196, 241, 352n8
Krantz, J. A., 123

Labor unions, 135f
Language transition, 98f, 168, 197, 228, 241, 266, 277f
Larson, Oscar and Lilie, 185f
Lawson, Evald B., 176f
Laymen in the Augustana Synod, 261f
Lennertson, Otto, 169
Life and Work, Conference on, 297f
Lilje, Hans, Bishop, 315
Lind, Jenny, 11
Lindahl, Joshua, 84
Lindahl, Sven Petter August, 44–6, 64, 73, 86, 122, 206, 351n3

Lindberg, Conrad E., 53–5, 173, 180, 236, 244f
Lindbeck, John, 187
Lindell, Johan J., 187
Lindell, Jonathan and Paul, 281
Lindquist, Emeroy, 230
Lindsborg, Kansas, 41, 43f, 65, 69f, 81–4, 116, 203, 270f
Lindwall, Raynold, 339
Literary Societies, 60, 68f, 72, 266
"Lodge Issue," 132, 302, 333f
Lohr, Harold, 339
Lund University, 19
Lundeen, Malvin, 136f, 168, 171, 338, 360n88
Lundensian Theology, 312f
Lundholm, Algot Theodore, 230
Lund-Quist, Carl, 231, 296
Luther College, Wahoo, Nebraska, 78, 80, 87–90, 339
Luther League, 263–6, 274f, 279–290, 342f
Lutheran Bible Institutes, 150, 163f, 219f, 239f, 274, 281, 340
Lutheran Brotherhood, 229, 262, 318
Lutheran Church Missouri Synod, 22, 169, 302, 327
Lutheran School of Theology in Chicago, 340
Lutheran World Action, 295f
Lutheran World Conventions, 295
Lutheran World Federation, 296, 307–11
Lutheranism, 2, 22f, 39, 44, 55, 81, 91, 173, 227, 235, 242, 281, 297, 301, 303f, 314
Läsare (Readers), 9

Major Urban Centers of Swedish-America, 379
Matson, Theodore, 138, 339
Mattson, Alvin Daniel, 105, 136f, 142, 151f, 227, 230f, 242, 251, 304, 306, 334
Mattson, Karl, 223, 307f, 340f
Mattson, Peter August, 181, 184, 191, 325
Mauritzson, Jules A., 123f
McCarthy Hearings, 234

Messiah, Oratorio (Handel), 44, 271
Methodists, Swedish-American, 8, 11
Midland Lutheran College, 339
Militarism (see Pacifism)
Miller, Samuel, 109, 174, 219f, 226, 237, 239, 243, 246, 303–5
Milton, John Peterson, 247–9
Ministries of Mercy, Augustana Synod, 165–7
Minneapolis Theses, 322
Mission Covenant, 81
Mission Friends, 53–6
Mission School, Sweden (Alberg), 19, 25f
Missionaries, 179–95
Missionary Training Institute, Sweden (Fjellstadt), 19, 25f
Missions-Tidning ("Mission Tidings"), 119, 172
Mississippi Conference, Synod of Northern Illinois, 34
Modernism (theological), 236f
Montgomery, M. W., 104
Morality Code, 125–32
Mormons, 23
Motion pictures, 128f
My Church, 172

National Council of Churches, 296
National Lutheran Commission for Soldiers' and Sailors' Welfare, 318
National Lutheran Council, 302, 321–3
Navy V-12 training program at Gustavus, 232
Nazi sympathizers, 231
Nelson, Clifford Ansgar, 310, 356n38
New England, 44, 53f, 84, 117, 135, 196
New Sweden, Iowa, 14
New York City, 8, 29, 53, 203, 318
Newspapers, as unifying, 29–31
Nilsson, Charlotte, 186
Norelius, Eric, 25f, 33, 41, 57, 67f, 78f, 103, 108, 113, 123f, 168f, 204, 289, 350n26, 353n11

Northern Illinois, Synod (General Synod), 32–5
Nothstein, Ira O., 219
Norwegian-American Lutherans, 11, 21f, 32
Norwegians, split from Augustana (1870), 52f, 96
Nursing schools, 259
Nystul, Ingeborg, Sister, 258
Nygren, Anders, 307–13, 341

Olander, Karl, 339
Olive Leaf, 100
Olson, Hakon, 35
Olson, Oscar N., 225f, 238
Olson, Otto, 339
Olsson, Anna, 40, 44
Olsson, Karl, 102
Olsson, Olof, 8, 40f, 43–6, 49, 56f, 65, 69–71, 73, 91–3, 100, 108, 197, 241, 248, 271, 308, 352n5
Orphanages, 165
"Orphaned Missions," 193, 321
Ostergren, Robert, 97
"Overture for Lutheran Unity," 331

Pacific Coast, 154–6
Pacific Lutheran University, 155
Pacifism, 227–32, 284
Palestine, 181
Passavant, William Alfred, 23
Patterns of Settlement, 8–12
Paxton, Illinois, 38f
Pearson, Richard, 339
Pherson, John, 35
Peters, Gustav, 35
Peterson, Conrad, 233
Peterson, Mathilda (Mrs. Peter), 212
Pietism, 18, 126
Prayer budgeting, 281
Presidents of the Augustana Synod, 381
Preus, Herman Amborg, 24, 32
Progressive Era, 132–4
Princell, Johan Gustaf, 54f
Prärieblomman, 172
Psalmbok, 91–3, 106f
"Pure Congregations," 40

Radio broadcasting, 130f
Rasmussen, Carl, 313

Racial issues, 139, 142
Reformation, 400th Anniversary celebration, 317f
Regional Distribution of Swedish-America, 379
Revival movements, 13, 17f, 39, 105f
Reynolds, William, 35
Republican party, 30, 85, 138
Riley, William Bell, 219
Roman Catholicism, 140f, 143f
Rosenius, Carl Olof, 45
Routte, Jesse, 139
Rural and Urban congregations, shift, 151f, 381
Ryden, Ernest Edwin, 109f, 138f, 143, 222f, 230, 283, 326, 331
Rydholm, Carl Peter, 113–114

San Francisco, California, 154
Sanctification, 18
Sandell, Lina, 107
Sandzen, Birger, 270f
Schmucker, Samuel Simon, 33
Scholarship, 226, 237, 311, 328, 341
Schools of the Augustana Synod, 381
Sebelius, Sven Johan, 278, 298
Segerhammer, Aron S., 221
Segerhammer, Carl, 156, 339
Service Book and Hymnal (1958), 326
Sioux Uprising (1862), 31
Sjoberg, Donald, 339
Sjogren, Peter N., 277
Sjöblom, Peter, 44–6
Slavery, Swedish-American attitudes toward, 30f
Social Responsibility, 283
Socialism, 133
South Africa, 180, 194
Southeastern United States, 153f
Stage Migration, 147
Stephenson, George, 79, 110, 162, 241–5, 247–51
Stub, Hans Gustaf, 322
Student Organizations at Augustana Colleges, 266f
Sudan, 190–2
Sugar Grove, Pennsylvania, 15f, 25
Sundin, Martin, 39

Sundkler, Bengt, 194
Suomi Synod, 332
Surnames, reform of, 268
Svenska Posten, 28
Swanson, Hjalmar, 170
Swanson, Rueben, 338
Sward, Per Johan, 381
Sweden, Church of, 199–215
Swedish-American Episcopalians, 293f
Swedish-American ethnic denominations, 22f, 293–5
Swedish immigration to North America, 145–8
Swedish language, 73
Swedish Mission Society, 11, 194
Swensson, Alma Lind, 116f, 202f
Swensson, Carl Aaron, 65, 68f, 81–4, 199–204
Swensson, Charlotte, 186
Swensson, Jonas, 62, 64, 68f
Synod of the Northwest, 149, 184
Söderblom, Anna, 209–13
Söderblom, Nathan, Bishop, 176, 205–7, 209–13, 237f
Södergren, Carl Johan, 236

Tanganyika (Tanzania), 192–5
Teleen, Johan, 57f, 101, 154, 180
Teleen, Sharon (Anderson), 287f
Temperance, 12, 127f
Tengwald, Victor, 226
Texas, 152f
Texas Lutheran College, 339
Theater, 128
Theological Education in the Augustana Synod, 172f
Thompson, H. Bradford, 222
Trabert, George, 103f
Travelogues, 201f

Udden, J. A., 84
Udden, Svante, 156
Ullman, U. L., Bishop, 200, 382
Ungdomsvännen ("Friends of Youth"), 65–68
United Evangelical Lutheran Church, 328
United Lutheran Church in America, 96, 246f, 288f, 321–3, 337f

United Testimony, 328–30
Unonius, Gustaf, 22, 26f
Upsala College, 108, 163, 176, 266, 279, 339
Uppsala University, 19
"Urbanus" (Carl Evald), 121f

Vasa, Minnesota, 15f
Vikner, David, 187

Von Schéele, Knut Henning Gezelius, Bishop, 203–5

Wahlstadt, Annette, 258
Wahlstrom, Eric, 227, 284
Wahlstrom, Matthias, 58, 69f
Waldenström, Paul Peter, 37f, 43–5, 96
Weenas, August, 38, 52
Weidner, S. Revere, 46
Wendell, Claus August, 108–10, 219f, 226, 236, 243
What is Lutheranism?, 242f
Wieselgren, Peter, 37
Williamson, W. A., 100
Wimmer, Harold, 339
Wingård, Fr. Conrad, Bishop, 9–10
Women: in the Augustana Synod, 256–61; dormitory controversy, 189, 275f; education, 75–8, 80; Women's Missionary Society, 115–9, 149, 257–61; right to vote, 133f, 257
World Council of Churches, 296–300
World Mission Prayer League, 281
World War I, 99–100, 227–9
World War II, 230–3

Young People's Societies, 71–4
Youngert, Sven Gustaf, 124, 247, 259
Youth and missions activities, 181–3
Youth Conferences and Leadership Schools, 279

Zamzam, 194f
Zion Society for Israel, 139

Öhman, S. G., 197